Family
Fun &
Games

Family Fun & Games

The Diagram Group

Sterling Publishing Co., Inc.   New York

**Library of Congress Cataloging-in-Publication Data
Available**

10   9   8   7   6   5   4   3   2   1

First paperback edition published in 1994 by
Sterling Publishing Company, Inc.
387 Park Avenue South, New York, N.Y. 10016
© 1992 by Diagram Visual Information Ltd
195 Kentish Town Road, London NW5 8SY
Distributed in Canada by Sterling Publishing
% Canadian Manda Group, P.O. Box 920, Station U
Toronto, Ontario, Canada M8Z 5P9

Sterling   ISBN 0-8069-8776-6   Trade
                    0-8069-8777-4   Paper

Foreword

This illustrated reference book brings together more than 650 games, card games, and variations that can be relied upon to provide many hours of entertainment for family and friends.

Some of the games are old favorites, others are examples of interesting and challenging games from foreign countries and from ancient times. There are games to suit players of all ages and abilities – from simple party games for young children to the complexities of Chess and Go. Board games, dice games, party games and races, games using pencil and paper, dominoes, coins, marbles, jackstraws – or no equipment at all – are among those included in this fascinating compendium.

The order in which the games appear is basically alphabetical. Alphabetical ordering, however, has not been applied to variants of games; these are included under the same main heading as the parent game (although they are listed separately in the index).

Detailed rules of play are given step-by-step for each game. The clear, concise language of the instructions is complemented by explanatory diagrams. The number of players and the equipment needed for each game are also listed, with suggestions for improvised equipment for the less familiar games.

Card games are placed into one of four categories: general games, children's games, gambling games, and solitaire games. Obviously these divisions are somewhat arbitrary: some general games may be played for money; some children's games are popular with adults; some gambling games require high levels of card-playing skill; and some solitaire games require two players.

The order in which card games appear within each of their four sections is basically alphabetical. In the gambling card games section, for example, the games run literally from a to z, from Ace-deuce-jack to Ziginette. Alphabetical ordering, however, has not been applied to variants of games; these are included under the same main heading as the parent game (although they are also listed separately in the index). Thus Gin Rummy, for example, appears under the main heading for Rummy, not between Forty-five and Grand. Similarly, although the names are quite different, Black Maria appears under the heading for Hearts.

Useful information on selecting a game is to be found in the "Finding a game" section of the book. This includes cross-referenced lists of games using different kinds of equipment and for different numbers of players, as well as a comprehensive index. It is therefore easy to find the correct rules for a familiar game or to attempt an unfamiliar game for the first time. Obviously an important consideration when choosing a card game is the number of players. This book uses a system of symbols to indicate players for each game: solid player symbols appear on their own where a game requires a specific number of players; solid and outline symbols are used together to indicate a range of possibilities (with solid symbols showing the minimum number needed).

Contents

Section 1
Games

16 Alleyway
18 Ashte kashte
20 Backgammon
30 Ball games
34 Checkers/Draughts
48 Chess
64 Chinese checkers
68 Chinese rebels
70 Coin throwing games
74 Conkers
76 Conquest
78 Darts
86 Dice games: family
98 Dice games: gambling
120 Dominoes
140 Dominoes: Chinese
146 Fighting serpents
148 Fivestones
154 Fox and geese
156 Game of goose
158 Go
168 Halma
172 Hex
174 Horseshoe
176 Hyena chase
178 Jacks
180 Lasca
184 Ludo
186 Mah jongg
200 Mancala games
202 Marbles
210 Nine men's morris

214 Nyout
216 Pachisi
220 Party games: blindfold
226 Party games: contests
234 Party games: goal scoring
238 Party games: musical
242 Party games: observation
250 Party games: parcel
254 Party games: trickery
258 Party races: individuals
260 Party races: pairs
264 Party races: teams
276 Pencil and paper games
298 Queen's guard
302 Reversi
304 Ring target games
308 Ringo
312 Salta
314 Sap tim pun
316 Shogi
328 Shove soccer
330 Shove ha'penny
332 Shovelboard
334 Snakes and ladders
336 Solitaire board games
344 Spellicans
346 Squails
348 Tiddlywinks
352 Word games: acting
358 Word games: guessing
368 Word games: vocabulary

Section 2
General card games

378 General rules
384 All fives
386 Auction pitch
388 Bezique
394 Boston
396 Bridge
408 Calabrasella
410 Canasta
414 Casino
418 Cribbage
422 Ecarté
424 Euchre
426 Five hundred
428 Forty-five
432 Grand
436 Hearts
440 Imperial

442 Kalabriasz
446 Knaves
448 Loo
450 Michigan
452 Napoleon
454 Oh hell
456 Pinochle
462 Piquet
468 Pope Joan
472 Preference
474 Rummy
478 Seven up
480 Skat
486 Solo whist
488 Spoil five
490 Vint
492 Whist

Section 3
Children's card games

498 Introduction
500 Beggar my neighbor
502 Card dominoes
504 Cheat
506 Concentration
508 Donkey
510 Give away
512 Go boom
514 Go fish
516 Knockout whist
518 Linger longer
520 Menagerie

522 My ship sails
524 Old maid
526 Play or pay
528 Racing demon
530 Rolling stone
532 Sequence
534 Slapjack
536 Snap
538 Snip-snap-snorem
540 Spit
542 Stealing bundles
544 War

Section 4
Gambling card games

548 Introduction
550 Ace-deuce-jack
552 Baccarat/Chemin de fer
562 Bango
564 Banker and broker
566 Blackjack
582 Blücher
584 Brag
588 Card craps
594 Card put-and-take
596 Chinese fan-tan
598 Faro
604 Hoggenheimer
606 Horse race
608 Injun

610 Kentucky derby
614 Lansquenet
616 Monte bank
624 Poker
648 Polish red dog
650 Red and black
652 Red dog
656 Skinball
660 Slippery Sam
662 Stuss
664 Thirty-five
666 Thirty-one
668 Trente et quarante
672 Yablon
674 Ziginette

Section 5
Solitaire card games

680 Procedure and terms
684 Accordion
686 Beleaguered castle
688 Bisley
690 Braid
692 Bristol
694 Calculation
696 Canfield
698 Clock
700 Crazy quilt
702 Eight away
704 Florentine
706 Flower garden
708 Friday the thirteenth
710 Frog
712 King Albert

714 Klondike
716 La belle Lucie
718 Leapfrog
720 Maze
722 Miss Milligan
724 Monte Carlo
726 Napoleon at St. Helena
728 Poker solitaire
730 Puss in the corner
732 Pyramid
734 Royal cotillion
736 Russian bank
740 Scorpion
742 Spider
744 Spite and malice
746 Windmill

Section 6
Finding a game

750 What type of game?
762 How many players?
766 How many for cards?
776 Card game variations
     and alternative names

778 Index

Section 1
Games

Alleyway

Alleyway is a family game popular in Eastern Europe. It is great fun to play, because although its rules are simple, winning is tantalizingly difficult! There can be any number of players.

Equipment A semi-circle is drawn on a piece of paper or cardboard, and marked with 25 numbered spaces as shown. The thirteenth space or "alleyway" is left open.

Each player has a counter of a different color. One die is used.

Play Each player throws the die and sets his counter on the space with the corresponding number. Players then take turns to throw the die and move their counters the number of spaces indicated by the die.

If at any time a player's counter lands on a space that is already occupied by an opponent's counter, the opponent's counter must be moved back a certain number of spaces, as follows:

a) If the opponent's counter was on any of the spaces from 1–12 or in the alleyway, it must go back to the beginning.

b) Once past the alleyway, however, a counter need only be moved back two spaces – and should that space also be occupied, that counter also must move back the appropriate number of spaces.

c) If the opponent's counter is on space 14 or 15 and has to retreat two spaces (ie to the alleyway or space 12), it has to go right back to the start. If it encounters an "enemy" counter in the alleyway or on space 12, that piece, too, has to go back to the start.

End play If a player's counter lands on space 25, it has to retreat to space 14 (**d**). Thus the winner is the first player whose throw gets him beyond space 25.

Layout

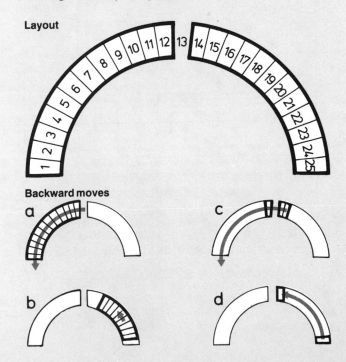

Backward moves

a

b

c

d

©DIAGRAM

Ashte kashte

Pieces

This ancient board game is of Eastern origin and has similarities with Ludo (p. 184) and Pachisi (p. 216). It is a race game for two, three, or four players.

Board This usually has 49 squares, in seven rows of seven. The square at the center of the board (the finish) and the middle square along each side row (starting and resting squares) are colored differently from all the other squares.

Pieces Each player has four shells, stones, counters, or other objects that must be clearly distinguishable from those used by the other players.

Board

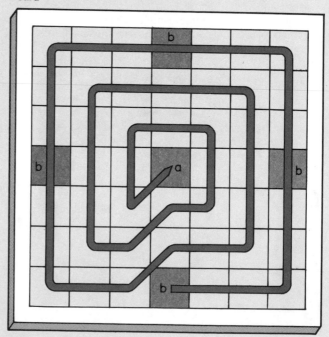

a) Finish
b) Starting and resting squares

Route for one player

Dice Four cowrie shells are used to indicate the number of squares to be moved, as follows:

a) all four shells with openings uppermost, four squares;
b) three shells with openings uppermost, three squares;
c) two shells with openings uppermost, two squares;
d) one shell with opening uppermost, one square;
e) all four shells with openings face down, eight squares.

Dice

Objective Each player aims to be first to move all his pieces from his starting square to the finish. The route for one player is shown on the illustration below left; other players follow a similar route but with a different starting point.

Play Each player selects a different starting square and places his pieces outside the board beside it. Players then take turns to throw the cowrie shells and move one of their pieces the appropriate number of squares onto their starting square and on around the race route.

After their first throw players can choose to bring a new piece into play or may move a piece that is already on the board. Splitting throws between pieces is not allowed (eg a four cannot be used to move one piece three squares and another piece one square).

Taking If a player's piece is on any square but a resting square and another player's move causes one of his pieces to end up on the same square, the first player's piece must be taken off the board to begin again. Pieces on any resting square, not only on a player's own starting square, are safe from taking.

Double pieces If a player moves one of his pieces so that it ends up on the same square as another of his pieces, these two pieces become a "double piece" and are moved together on subsequent throws. A double piece can be taken only by another double piece. No single piece – even one belonging to the same player – can ever overtake a double piece.

End of play The finish can be reached only by throwing the exact number needed to land on the center square. If a player throws a higher number than he needs to finish he must either move one of his other pieces or wait for another turn. A piece that lands exactly on the finish square is immediately removed from the board.

The winner is the first player to move all his pieces from start to finish. The game may be carried on to determine the finishing order of the other players.

Backgammon

Backgammon is an ancient board game developed in the Orient and now played all over the world. It is an excellent game in which the opportunities for strategic play add to the excitement of a race around the board. The fine calculation of odds involved in skilled play has a strong attraction for the player who is prepared to gamble.

Players Only two players compete, but others may participate in the betting when games are played for money.
Pieces Each player has 15 pieces, similar to those used in Draughts. One player has dark pieces (Black) and the other light pieces (White). The pieces are variously known as "counters," "stones" or "men." In the modern game "men" is the commonly accepted term.
Dice Each player has two dice and a cup in which to shake them.

Doubling cube In a game where players agree to bet on the outcome (there is no need to play for anything more than fun), a doubling cube is used. This is a large die on which the faces are numbered 2, 4, 8, 16, 32, 64. (Its significance is explained in the section on gambling, p. 27.)

Board and notation

White

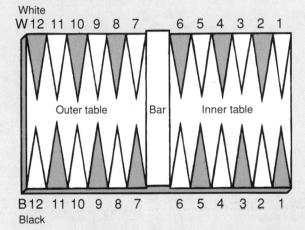

Black

Board Backgammon is played on a rectangular board divided into two halves by a "bar." One half of the board is called the "inner table" or "home table," and the other the "outer table." Along each side of the board are marked 12 triangles, alternately light and dark colored (this coloring has no special significance). Each triangle is called a "point." For the purpose of notation, points are numbered 1–12 as shown in the diagram on this page. (No numbers actually appear on the board.) Points 1 (the first points in the inner table) are called "ace points"; points 7 (the first points on the outer table) are called "bar points." No other points are specially designated.

The board is placed between the two players (called Black and White) so that Black has his inner table to his right. The points on Black's side of the table are known as Black points; those on White's side as White points. In simple notation, points are indicated by their number and the initial B or W.

Objective According to the numbers thrown on the dice, each player moves his men toward his own inner table.

Once all a player's men are located in his own inner table he attempts to remove them – by a process called "bearing off." The first player to bear off all 15 of his pieces wins the game. Although the basic objective of the game is simple, the rules and strategies governing a player's moves are much more complex.

©DIAGRAM

Start of play Players draw for color and then place their men in their prescribed starting positions. White places two men on B1; five men on W6; three men on W8; and five men on B12. Black places two men on W1; five men on B6; three men on B8; and five men on W12.

Having placed their men on their starting positions, each player throws a single die to determine the order of play. The player throwing the higher number has first move. If both players throw the same number they must throw again.

For his first move the opening player moves according to the numbers on both his own and his opponent's dice. Thereafter, play alternates and each player moves according to the numbers on both his own dice.

Play A player throws both his dice to determine how many points he can move. For a valid throw the dice must be: thrown from the cup;

thrown in the player's own half of the board;

thrown so that one face of each die rests wholly on the board; thrown only when an opponent has completed his turn.

The player then moves according to the numbers thrown on the dice.

The direction of play for each player is always from his opponent's inner table, through his opponent's outer table, through his own outer table, and into his own inner table. Thus White always moves his men clockwise and Black moves counterclockwise.

Start of play

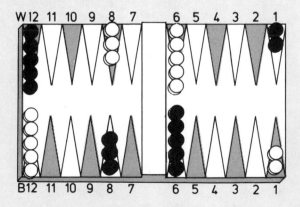

Moving men

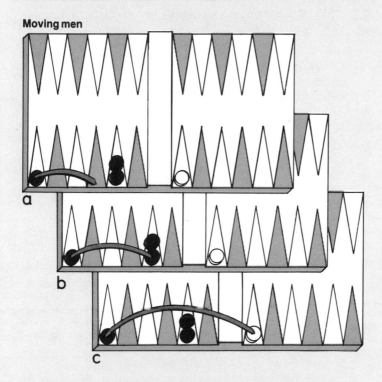

Moving men A player attempts to move the number of points shown on each of his die. He may not merely add them together and move the combined total. The position of the men on the board may affect a player's choice of moves or may even prevent him from moving at all.

Provided that none of his men is off the board, a player may move to any point that is:

a) clear of any other men;

b) occupied by one or more of his own men; or

c) occupied by only one of his opponent's men.

When there is only one man on a point, this man is called a "blot."

A player who moves a man to a point on which he already has one man is said to "make" that point, as his opponent cannot then land on it.

(Also see sections on play after a mixed throw and play after a double, p. 24.)

Play after a mixed throw If the numbers on the two dice are different, the player may make one of four possible moves. For example, a player throwing a 2 and a 6 may move:

a) one man two points, then the same man six points further;

b) one man six points, then the same man two points further;

c) one man two points, and another man six points;

d) one man six points, and another man two points.

At first glance alternatives a) and b) appear to be the same. This is not in fact the case, since the order in which the numbers are taken can affect whether or not a man may be moved (see the section on moving men).

If he can use only the number shown on one of his dice, the other number is disregarded. If he has a choice of two numbers, he must use the higher one.

Play after a double If a player throws a double, then the number shown on both dice is played four times (or as many times as possible up to four). Thus if a player throws two 2s he may move:

a) one man four times two points;

b) one man twice two points and another man twice two points;

c) one man twice two points and another two men two points each;

d) four men two points each.

As before, the number shown on the dice is the limit of a move. A player moving one man four times two points must land on open points at the end of each two point move.

Play after a mixed throw

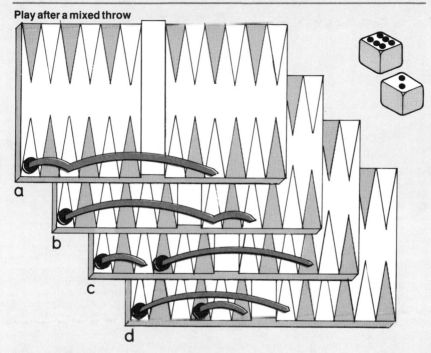

Play after a double

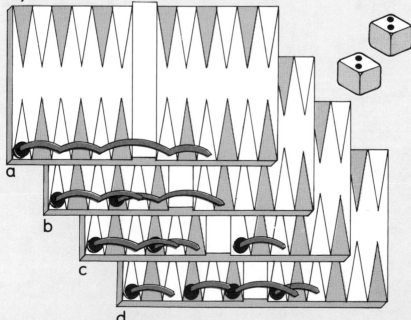

©DIAGRAM

Hitting a man If a player moves a man onto a point on which his opponent has only one man (**a**) he is said to "hit" that man. The hit man is removed from play and placed on the bar (**b**). A player who has any hit men on the bar must re-enter them before he can move any of his men on the board.

Re-entering men To re-enter a hit man, a player must throw the number of an open point on his opponent's home table. He may then use the number on his second die to re-enter another man, or, if all his men are on the board, to move any of his men the number of points shown on that die.

Bearing off men Once a player has succeeded in moving all his men into his own inner table, he bears them off by removing them from those points corresponding to the numbers thrown. For example, if White throws a 4 and a 2 when he has men on both W4 and W2 he may bear off a man from each of these points.

If he throws a 4 and a 2 when he has a man on W4 but not on W2, he may bear off a man from W4 and must then move another man two points down from his highest occupied point. If he wishes, a player may always move men down the board from his highest point rather than bearing off from the points corresponding to the numbers on the dice.

If both numbers thrown are higher than the player's highest point, the player bears off from his highest point.

If a player's man is hit after he has started bearing off, that man must re-enter and be moved around again to the inner table before bearing off is resumed.

Bearing off continues until one player succeeds in bearing off all his men.

Hitting a man

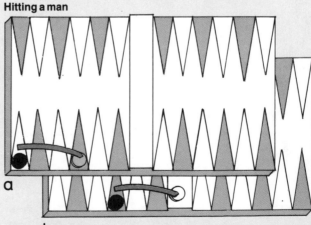

a

b

Fouls and penalties In addition to the rules on throwing the dice, players must observe the following:

a) a player may not change his move after taking his hand from a moved piece;

b) if a player makes an incorrect move, his opponent may insist that the error be corrected provided that he has not made his own following move;

c) a game must be restarted if the board or pieces are found to be incorrectly set up during play.

Scoring The game is won by the player who first bears off all his men. The number of units scored depends on the progress of the loser:

a) if the loser has borne off at least one man and has no men left in the winner's inner table, the winner scores one unit;

b) if the loser has not borne off any men, the winner has made a "gammon" and scores two units;

c) if the loser has not borne off any men and also has a man on the bar or in the winner's inner table, the winner has made a "backgammon" and scores three units.

Gambling Backgammon is often played for an agreed base stake for each game. This stake may be doubled and redoubled during play (in addition to the double payment for a gammon and treble for a backgammon). A doubling cube is often used to show the number of times that the stake has been doubled. (At the start of play it should be placed with the number 64 face uppermost.)

Unless players previously agree otherwise, stakes are automatically doubled if the dice match at the first throw of a game. In this case both players then throw again. The number of automatic doubles is usually limited by agreement to one or two per game. There is no limit to the number of voluntary doubles.

Either player has the right to offer the first voluntary double – after which the right alternates between players. A player who wishes to double the stake must offer to do so before throwing the dice when it is his turn to play. His opponent then has the choice of accepting the doubled stake or of forfeiting the game and the stake.

DUTCH BACKGAMMON
This is the same as the basic game except that:
a) all the men are placed on the bar for the start of play and players must enter all 15 before moving any man around the board;
b) a player may not hit a blot until he has advanced at least one of his own men to his own inner table.

Dutch backgammon: start

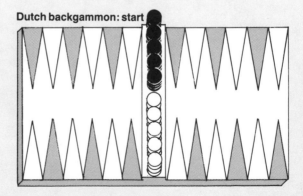

ACEY DEUCY

This is an elaboration of Dutch backgammon and is popular in the US Navy. It differs from the basic game in the following ways:

a) men are entered from the bar as in Dutch backgammon;

b) if a player throws a 1 and a 2 (ace-deuce), he moves his men for this throw and then moves his men as if he had thrown any double that he chooses;

c) the stake is usually automatically doubled when an ace-deuce is thrown;

d) some players give each man an agreed unit value and the winner collects as many units as the opponent has left on the board.

GIOUL

This popular Middle Eastern form of Backgammon is played in the same way as the basic game except that:

a) each player positions all his men on his opponent's number 1 point for the start;

b) a blot is not hit but is blocked and cannot be moved while an opposing man is on the same point;

c) when a player throws a double, he attempts to move for the double thrown and then for each subsequent double in turn up to double 6. (For example if he throws double 4 he goes on to move for double 5 and double 6);

d) if a player is unable to use any of his moves from a double, all these moves may be taken by his opponent.

PLAKATO

This form of Backgammon is widely played in Greek cafes. It is the same as the basic game described here except that:

a) each player positions all his men on his opponent's number 1 point for the start of play;

b) a blot is not hit but is blocked and cannot be moved as long as an opposing man is on the same point;

c) a player must move all his men all 24 points instead of bearing them off when they reach his inner table.

Plakato: start

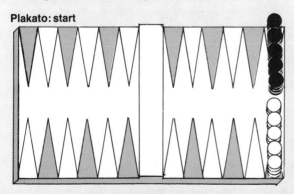

Ball games

Although ball games are usually associated with outdoor play, there are many enjoyable games that can be played indoors. A table tennis ball is recommended for minimum damage!

Cup and ball

CUP AND BALL

Cup and ball is a game for one person that was first played several hundred years ago. It was especially popular among children in the late nineteenth century and can still be bought today. The cup and ball are made of wood and joined by a length of string. Sometimes the cup is replaced by a wooden spike and the ball has a hole bored through its center.
The player holds the cup around its base and stretches out his arm so that the ball hangs toward the ground. He then swings his arm and tries to catch the ball in the cup – with a little practice this can be done almost every time. The version with a spike is more difficult to accomplish, as the ball has to be impaled on the spike.

JAM JARS

This is a game needing only a few table tennis balls and some jam jars for equipment. Five or six jam jars are placed close together on the floor or on a table.
Players stand a few feet away and take it in turns to throw a set number of table tennis balls (usually two or three) in an attempt to get them into the jars. As table tennis balls are extremely bouncy, this task is more difficult than it might at first seem!
The player who manages to get the most balls into the jam jars after each round of play is the winner. (Any number of rounds may be played.)

IN THE BOWL

In the bowl is a game very like Jam jars. A deep bowl or bucket is placed on the floor.
Each player in turn tries to throw a table tennis ball so that it lands (and remains!) in the bowl. If the player is successful he may throw again. At the end of a set time, the player with the most successful throws wins the game.

CONTAINERS

This game is played in the same way as In the bowl, except that players try to get a ball into one of several containers – each with a points value depending on its size. The player with most points wins the game.

BLOW FOOTBALL

Blow football is a game played at a table by two players or by two teams of two or three. Each person blows through a drinking straw at a table tennis ball, and tries to get the ball into the opposing goal. The player or team that scores the most goals after a given time wins the game.

Equipment Blow football is best played at a long table, although it can also be played on the floor. A goal must be marked at each end of the table – using pencils or other suitable objects.

It is a good idea to make a wall around the edges of the table to help keep the ball in play. (Strips of wood or cardboard can be used.)

Each player is given a drinking straw, and the only other equipment needed is a table tennis ball.

Play The table tennis ball is placed in the middle of the table. At a given signal, the players start to blow through their straws in an attempt to get the ball into the opponents' goal – while at the same time defending their own goal from attack.

Whenever a goal is scored (ie the ball passes between the "goalposts"), the ball is repositioned at the center of the table and the game is restarted.

If the ball is blown off the table, the opposing side places the ball on the table at the spot where it came off and then takes a "free" blow before the other side may continue blowing.

Blow football

THROUGH THE TUNNEL

Through the tunnel is similar to Archboard – a game played with marbles (see p. 208). Playing procedure is exactly the same as for Archboard, but table tennis balls are used instead of marbles, and the arches through which they are rolled are correspondingly bigger.

HOLEY BOARD GAME

This is a target game in which players score points by throwing a table tennis ball through a "holey board."

The holey board can be made quite easily out of stiff carboard. A random number of holes is cut out, each one a different size. (The smallest hole should be just big enough for a table tennis ball to pass through it.) A scoring value is written above each hole – the bigger the hole, the lower the value.

The board is held or propped up in an upright position – books can be used to keep it in place. Players stand as far away from the board as possible and take turns to throw the ball.

Each time a player gets the ball through a hole, he scores the number of points written above the hole. (The smaller the hole, the more difficult it is to get the ball through it!) The player with the highest score after a set number of throws is the winner.

Once players have become quite skilled, they can try throwing the ball so that it bounces on the floor before going through a hole.

Holey board game

©DIAGRAM

Checkers/Draughts

Known as Checkers in the United States and Draughts in
Britain, this is a popular board game for two players. Played in
southern Europe in medieval times, it appears to have been
derived from much older games played in the Middle East.
Each player attempts to "take" (capture and remove) his
opponent's pieces or to confine them so that they cannot be
moved.

Board The game is played on a board made of wood, plastic, or
cardboard and 14½–16in square.
It is divided into 64 squares, eight along each side. The squares
are alternately a light and a dark color (usually black and
white, or sometimes black and red or red and white). Play is
confined to squares of only one color – usually the darker
color.

Start of play

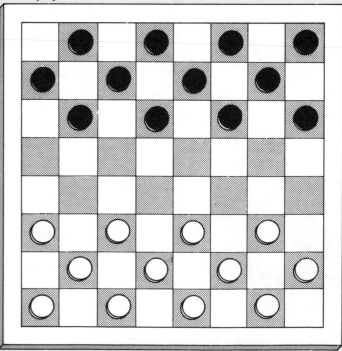

Pieces Each player has a set of 12 pieces – wooden or plastic disks 1¼–1½in in diameter and about ⅜in thick. One set is usually white, and the other red or black.

Objective A player aims to "take" all his opponent's pieces or to position his own pieces so that his opponent is unable to make any move.

Start of play The players sit facing each other, and the board is positioned so that the players have a playing square at the left of their first row. Lots are drawn to decide who will have the darker pieces for the first game. Each player has the darker pieces for alternate games.

For the start of play each player positions his pieces on the playing squares in the three rows of the board nearest to him. The player with the darker pieces always makes the first move in a game.

Moving A player may make only one move at a turn. As play is confined to squares of only one color, all moves are diagonal. Individual pieces or "men" may only be moved forward (**a**); double pieces or "kings" may be moved either forward or backward (**b**).

A piece may only be moved into a square that is vacant.

Moving

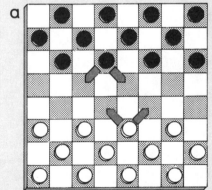

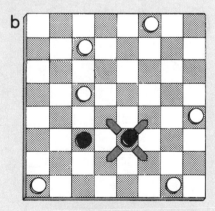

Touch and move Except when he has given notice of his intention to arrange pieces properly in their squares, a player whose turn it is must when possible make his move with the first piece that he touches.

If he first touches an unplayable piece, he is cautioned for a first offense and forfeits the game for a second offense.

Time limit for moves If a player fails to make a move within five minutes, an appointed timekeeper shall call "time." The player must then move within one minute, or forfeit the game through improper delay. (At master level in some tournaments, players must make a prescribed number of moves within set time limits.)

A non-taking move Except when "taking" an opponent's piece, a player may only move a piece into a touching playing square.

A taking move One of the game's objectives is to "take" (capture and remove) the opposing pieces.

A piece may be taken if it is in a playing square touching the taker's square when there is a vacant square directly beyond it (**1**). Several pieces can be taken in one move provided that each one has a vacant square beyond it (**2**).

Whenever possible, a player must make a taking move rather than a non-taking move (even if this means that his own piece will in turn be taken). If a player has a choice of taking moves he may take a smaller instead of a larger number of pieces (**3a**), but if he begins the move enabling him to take the larger number he must continue until he has taken all the pieces possible (**3b**).

Taking moves

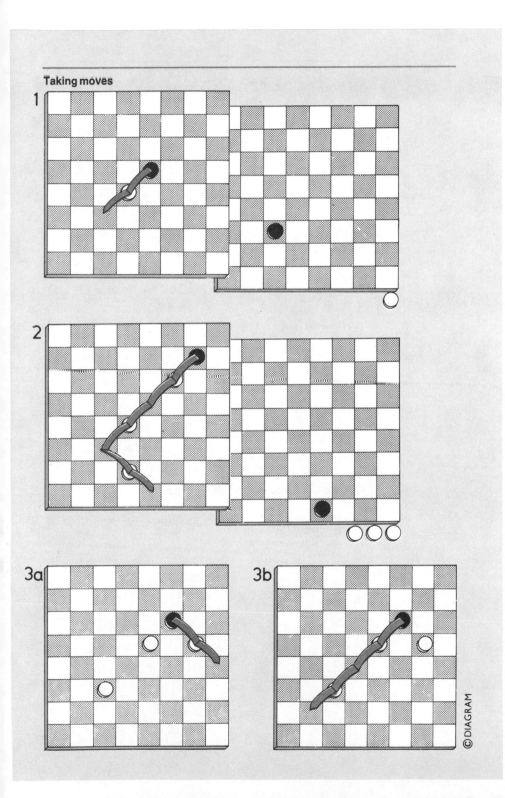

©DIAGRAM

Failure to take If a player fails to take a piece when he is able (**1a**), modern tournament play rules state that his opponent should point this out and so force him to take back the wrongly moved piece and make the taking move instead (**1b**).

This ruling has replaced the old "huff or blow" rule, by which a player who failed to make a possible taking move forfeited the piece moved in error.

King

Crowning When a man reaches the farthest row on the board (known as the "king row" or "crownhead"), it becomes a "king" and is "crowned" by having another piece of its own color placed on it (**2**). A player's turn always ends when a man is crowned.

A tied game occurs when neither player can remove all his opponent's pieces or prevent him making a move (**3a, 3b**). If one player appears to be in a stronger position, he may be required to force a win within 40 of his own moves or else place himself at a decided advantage over his opponent. If he fails, the game is counted as tied.

TOURNAMENT CHECKERS
To reduce the number of tied and repeated games at expert level, a system of restricted openings is applied at major championships and tournaments in the United States and elsewhere.

The first three moves of each game are determined by cards bearing the various openings and subsequent moves. The cards are shuffled and cut, and the top card is turned face up. Opposing players then play two games with the prescribed opening, each player making the first move in one of the games.

LOSING/GIVEAWAY CHECKERS
This is played under the same rules as standard British or American checkers. The tactics, however, are very different, as the objective is to be the first player to lose all his pieces.

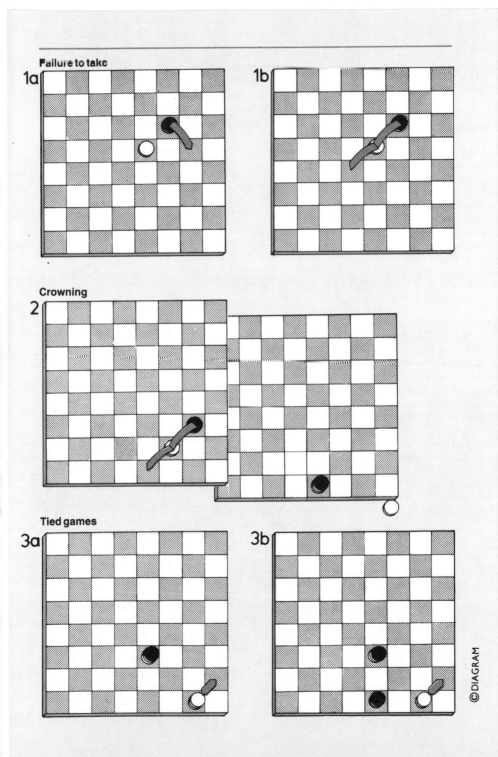

Failure to take

1a

1b

Crowning

2

Tied games

3a

3b

©DIAGRAM

DIAGONAL CHECKERS

This is an interesting variant of the standard game. It can be played with 12 pieces per player, in which case starting position (**a**) is used, or with nine pieces each if starting position (**b**) is used. Men are crowned when they cross the board to reach the opponent's corner squares (marked K in the diagrams).

Otherwise, rules are the same as for standard checkers.

ITALIAN CHECKERS

This is played in the same way as standard British or American checkers except that:

a) the board is positioned with a non-playing square at the left of each player's first row;

b) a player must make a taking move whenever possible – or forfeit the game;

c) a man cannot take a king;

d) if a player has a choice of captures he must take the greater number of pieces;

e) if a player with a king to move has a choice of capturing equal numbers of pieces, he must take the most valuable pieces (ie kings rather than men).

SPANISH CHECKERS

This is played in the same way as Italian checkers, except that kings are moved differently. A player may use a king to take a piece anywhere on a diagonal, provided that there are no pieces between and there is an empty square beyond it. (This is sometimes called the "long move.") The jump need not end in the square immediately behind the taken piece, but may continue any distance along the diagonal if there are no intervening pieces (**a**).

A king must make all its jumps before any taken pieces are removed, and these pieces may not be jumped a second time in the same move (**b**).

Diagonal checkers: alternative starts

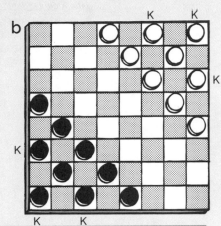

Italian checkers: start

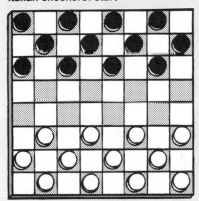

Spanish checkers: taking with a king

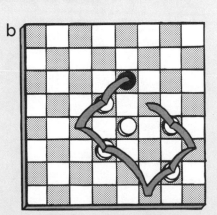

©DIAGRAM

GERMAN CHECKERS

This is played in the same way as Spanish checkers except that:
a) men can make taking moves either forward or backward;
b) a man is only crowned if its move ends on the far row – if it is in a position to make further jumps away from that line it must always take them.

RUSSIAN CHECKERS

This is played like German checkers except that:
a) a player with a choice of captures need not take the larger number of pieces;
b) a man is made into a king as soon as it reaches the far row and then jumps as a king for the rest of the move.

CONTINENTAL CHECKERS

Also called Polish checkers, this is played on a board with 100 squares, 10 along each side. Each player has 20 pieces – positioned on the first four rows for the start of play. The game is played under the same rules as German checkers.

German checkers: moving

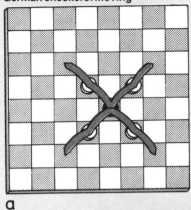

a

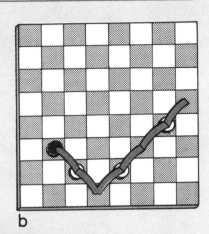

b

Russian checkers: moving

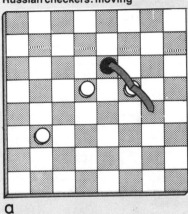

a

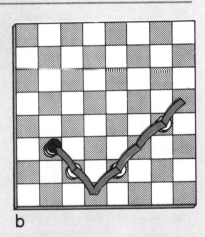

b

Continental checkers: start

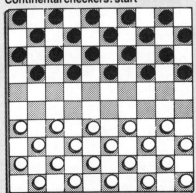

CANADIAN CHECKERS

This is another variant of German checkers. It is played on a board with 144 squares, 12 by 12. Each player has 30 pieces – positioned on the first five rows for the start of play.

TURKISH CHECKERS

This may be played on a standard checker board, but the traditional Turkish board has squares all the same color. Each player has 16 pieces – positioned on each player's second and third rows for the start of play.

Men move as in British or American checkers, but directly forward or sideways and not diagonally (**a**). Kings move any number of squares directly forward, sideways, or backward. Multiple captures by kings are made as shown (**b**) – as for Spanish checkers except that moves are not diagonal and pieces are removed as soon as they are jumped (instead of staying on the board to prevent further jumps).

A player must make a capture whenever possible, and must always take the greater number of pieces when he has a choice of captures.

Turkish checkers may be won in the usual ways, and also by a player with a king when his opponent has only a single man remaining on the board.

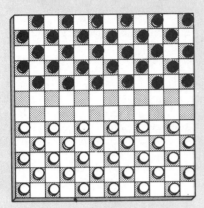

Turkish checkers: start

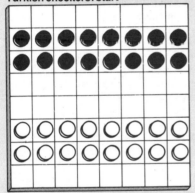

Turkish checkers: moving

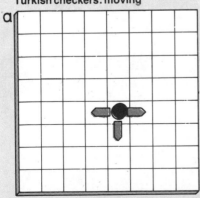

a

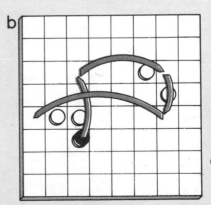

b

©DIAGRAM

CHECKERS GO-MOKU

This is an adaptation of the Japanese game described on page 166. Play is on all the squares of a standard checker board, and the two players have 12 checkers each.

The board is empty at the start of a game, and the players take it in turns to place one checker on any square. After all the checkers have been placed, a player uses his turn to move one checker into any vacant, adjoining square.

If, at any stage of the game, a player succeeds in placing five checkers in a row (horizontally, vertically, or diagonally), he is entitled to remove any one of his opponent's checkers from the board.

The game is won when a player has removed all his opponent's checkers.

CHECKERS FOX AND GEESE

Two versions of Fox and geese (p. 154) are often played on a checker board and are particularly popular with children. In both checkers versions, one player has one dark checker (the "fox") and his opponent has several white checkers (the "geese").

Play is only on the black squares of the board. A player moves only one checker at a turn. The fox wins the game if it can break through the line of geese. The geese win if they can trap the fox so that it cannot move.

FOUR GEESE VERSION

At the start of play, the player with the geese positions them on the four playing squares of his first row; the player with the fox positions it wherever he chooses.

The geese move diagonally forward one square at a time like the men in British or American checkers. The fox moves diagonally forward or backward; it is not permitted to jump over the geese, so there is no taking in this version.

TWELVE GEESE VERSION

This version is sometimes played with a "wolf" and "goats." At the start of play the geese are positioned on the first three rows, as for British or American checkers; the fox is positioned on one of the corner playing squares on the opposite side of the board. The geese move like the men and the fox like a king in British or American checkers. (Jumping and taking geese is permitted in this version.)

Checkers go-moku: won game

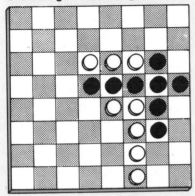

Checkers fox and geese: alternative starts

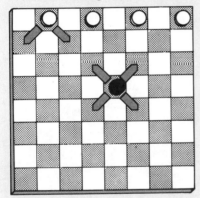

Four geese version

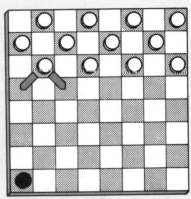

Twelve geese version

Chess

Originating in the East over a thousand years ago, Chess has developed into one of the most popular of all games. Despite being highly complex and sophisticated, it can also be enjoyed at a simpler level by inexperienced players. It is a game of strategy for two people, with each piece – from the king to the pawn – representing units in an army.

The board is a large square divided into eight rows of eight squares each. The squares are alternately dark and light colored (usually black and white).
The board is placed between the facing players so that each has a white square at the near righthand corner.
The rows of squares running vertically between facing players are called "files"; those running at right angles to the files are called "ranks." Rows of squares of the same color that touch only at their corners are called "diagonals."

Start of play

Pieces At the start of a game 32 pieces are positioned on the board. 16 of these pieces are dark in color, 16 light. They are called black and white respectively and make up the two sides. A player's side is made up of six different kinds of pieces. These are – in descending order of importance: king, queen, rook (castle), bishop, knight, pawn. Each player has one king and one queen; two rooks, bishops, and knights; and eight pawns.

Objective The objective of each player is to capture his opponent's king. Unlike the other pieces, the king cannot be removed from the board; it is held to be captured when it has been "checkmated" (see section on check and checkmate, p. 58).

The player forcing checkmate wins the game – even if the pieces he has left on the board are outnumbered by the opponent's pieces.

A player seeing the imminent checkmate of his king or recognizing a losing situation will often resign. The player forcing the resignation wins the game.

Moves Each kind of piece can move a certain distance in one or more directions. Moves are limited by conditions **on the board** at the time of play.

A piece may move to any square within its range, provided that:

a) the square is unoccupied by a piece of its own color;

b) if the square is occupied by an opponent's piece, that piece is first "captured" and removed from the board;

c) it does not, with the exception of the knight's move, cross a square that is occupied by a piece of either color.

Names of rows

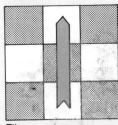
File

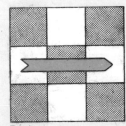
Rank

Diagonal

©DIAGRAM

The king is the most important piece on the board, and its capture by checkmate ends the game. It is represented diagrammatically by a crown.

The king can move one square in any direction, provided that this square is not one where it can be taken. Opposing kings can never stand on touching squares.

Castling The only time that a king may move more than one square is in the "castling" move involving the rook. A player can make a castling move only once in a game.

The move is made to produce a defensive position around the king and to allow a rook to come into play. It comprises:

1) moving the king two squares to left or right from its original position and toward one of the rooks; then

2) transferring that rook to the square over which the king has just passed.

Castling is permitted only if:

a) neither the king nor the rook involved has moved from its original position;

b) no piece of either color is between the king and the rook involved in the castling move;

c) the square that the king must cross is not under attack by an opponent's piece.

The queen, represented diagrammatically by a coronet, is the most powerful attacking piece. It can move to any square on the rank, file, or either of the two diagonals on which it is placed.

King's moves

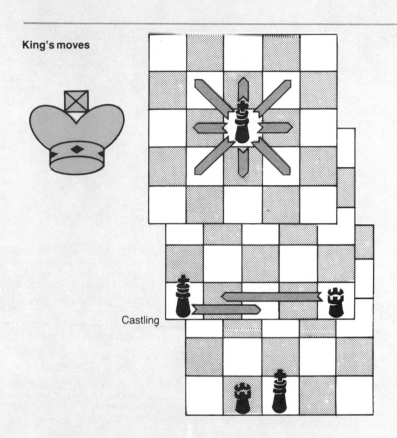

Castling

Queen's moves

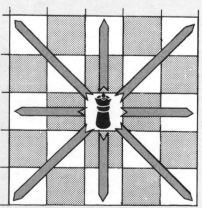

©DIAGRAM

The rook, sometimes called the castle, is represented diagrammatically by a tower. It can move to any square on the rank or file on which it is placed. In addition, either one of the rooks in each side may be involved with the king in the castling move (p.50).

The bishop, represented diagrammatically by a miter, can move to any square on the diagonal on which it is placed. Thus each player has one bishop that can move on a black diagonal and one on a white diagonal.

The knight is represented diagrammatically by a horse's head. In a single move it travels two squares in any direction along a rank or file, then one square at right angles to that rank or file. Thus whenever a knight moves from a black square it must land on a white square – and vice versa.
In moving, a knight may cross a square occupied by any other piece; it is the only piece allowed to do this.

Rook's moves

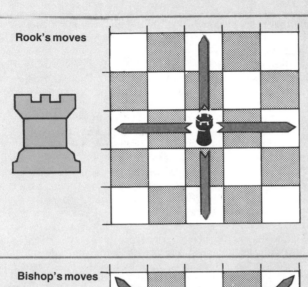

Bishop's moves

Knight's moves

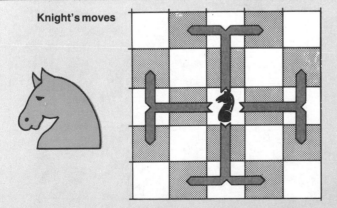

The pawn, represented diagrammatically by a small ball on a collared stem, has the most restricted movements of any piece: it can only move forward.

In its opening move, a pawn may be moved forward either one or two squares on the file that it occupies. Thereafter, a pawn can only move forward one square at a time, except when capturing.

Unlike other pieces, a pawn does not capture in the same way that it moves. Instead of capturing in a forward direction, it does so diagonally – taking a piece that occupies either of the two squares diagonally next to it.

In addition, a pawn may capture an opposing pawn *"en passant"* (in passing). If the opposing pawn moves forward two squares in its opening move, the square it crosses is open to attack as though the pawn had only advanced one square. Thus the capturing pawn may make its usual taking move (ie one square diagonally forward) onto the square just crossed by the opposing pawn – the opposing pawn is then considered "captured" and is removed from the board. (The *en passant* capture must be made immediately the opposing pawn has moved forward two squares.)

Pawn promotion Whenever a pawn reaches the end of the file on which it is moving (ie it reaches the far side of the board) it must – in the same move – be exchanged for a queen, rook, bishop, or knight.

The choice of piece is made by the player promoting the pawn, and is made without taking into account the number and kind of pieces on the board. Theoretically, therefore, a player could have up to nine queens on the board.

The effect of the promoted piece on play is immediate.

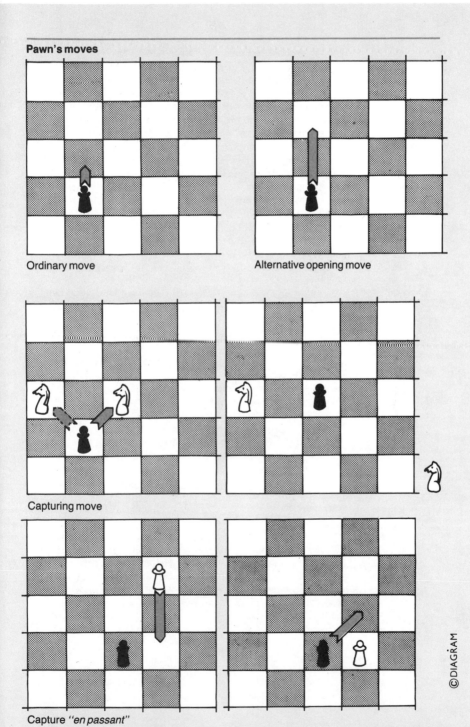

Pawn's moves

Ordinary move

Alternative opening move

Capturing move

Capture "en passant"

Starting procedure Players draw for sides, and position their pieces on the board. The player drawing white makes the first move, and thereafter the players move alternately.

Play The position of the pieces at the start of play is such that each player can move only a knight or a pawn. After the first move by each player, more pieces can come into play.

In moving their pieces, players are governed not only by the movements laid down for each piece but also by rules that affect how pieces can be handled.

If a player touches a piece that can legitimately be moved, then he must move that piece – unless he has previously warned his opponent that he is adjusting the piece on its square. The usual warning used is *"J'adoube"* (I adjust). Similarly, if a player touches an enemy piece that can be taken, the touched piece must be captured unless the player has given a prior warning.

Capturing move

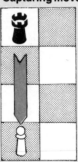

A move is completed when:

a) a player's hand has left a piece after it has been moved to a vacant square;

b) a player, having captured a piece and placed his attacking piece on the captured square, removes his hand from the piece;

c) in castling, a player's hand has left the rook (once the king has been moved, the castling move must always be completed);

d) in pawn promotion, a player's hand has left the piece that replaces the pawn.

Phases of play Chess players commonly divide a game into three phases: opening game, middle game, and end game. These phases are not clear-cut divisions – they simply reflect the strategies and tactics employed.

1) In the opening game, both players position their pieces into what each considers to be an advantageous situation. Castling moves are usually made during this phase.

2) In the middle game, players attempt to capture enemy pieces, thereby reducing the opponent's attacking ability. However, as the main objective is to checkmate the opponent's king, moves or captures should not be made unless they weaken the opponent's defense of his king. The player should also beware of making moves that jeopardize his own position.

3) In the end game, players attempt to checkmate the opponent's king. If, during this phase, a player has few attacking pieces, he will attempt – where possible – to promote a pawn to a more powerful piece.

©DIAGRAM

Check and checkmate Whenever a king is attacked by an opposing piece, the king is said to be "in check." The check must be met on the following move by either:
a) moving the king one square in any direction onto a square that is not attacked;
b) capturing the piece that is checking the king; or
c) interposing a piece between the king and the attacking piece (if the king is checked by an opponent's knight, it is not possible to intercept the check in this way). A piece that intercepts a check can – in the same move – give check to the opposing king.

Meeting check

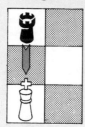 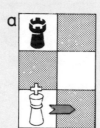 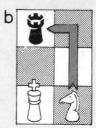 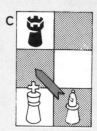

Check

If the check cannot be met then the king is deemed "in checkmate" or simply "mate." When a checking or checkmating move is made, it is customary for the player making such a move to declare "Check" or "Checkmate" as appropriate.
Winning A player wins if he:
a) checkmates his opponent's king; or
b) forces his opponent to resign.
Checkmate may be made, or a player may resign, at any time during the course of the game.

Examples of checkmate

Drawn game Many games of chess do not end in a victory for either player. A game is drawn in any of the following cases.
a) When the player whose turn it is to move can make no legal move (a situation known as "stalemate").
b) When neither player has sufficient pieces to force checkmate.
c) When a player can check the opponent's king indefinitely but cannot checkmate it (a situation called "perpetual check").
d) When no capture or pawn move has been made by either side during 50 successive moves of each player.
e) When the same position recurs three times, always when it is the same player's turn to move. The right to claim a draw then belongs either to the player who is in a position to play a move leading to such repetition (provided that he declares his intention of making this move), or to the player who must reply to a move by which the repeated position is made.
f) When both players agree to call the game drawn.
Illegal positioning If an illegal move is made during the course of a game, the pieces are set up as they were just before the illegal move. If this is impossible, the game is annulled.
If pieces are accidentally displaced and cannot be correctly repositioned or if the initial position of the pieces was incorrect, the game is also annulled.
If the chessboard is found to have been incorrectly placed, the pieces on the board are transferred to a correctly placed board in the same positioning as when the error was discovered and play then continues.
Competition chess is strictly controlled. It differs from the informal game in the following ways.
a) Each player must write down every move made.
b) Each player must make a certain number of moves in a given time (time is kept by a special control clock).
c) If a game is adjourned, the player whose turn it is must write down his move and place it in a sealed envelope, together with his and his opponent's scoresheets. The sealed move is made on the resumption of play.
d) It is forbidden to distract or worry an opponent; ask or receive advice from a third party; use any written or printed notes; or to analyze the game on another chessboard.
e) A designated person must direct the competition. The competition director must ensure that the rules of play are strictly observed – he may impose penalties on any player who infringes these rules.
(These notes on competition chess are an outline only. The official international governing body – the Fédération Internationale des Echecs (FIDE) – lays down the full rules and interprets any problems arising in the game. Its decision is binding on all affiliated federations.)

Chess notation is the method by which moves in a game are recorded. Two of the systems officially recognized are: the descriptive system and the algebraic system.

Descriptive system

Each piece is represented by its initial letter, but the knight may be represented by either Kt or N.

With the exceptions of the pawns and the king and queen, pieces are further distinguished by the side of the board on which they stand:

pieces to the right of the king take the prefix K;

pieces to the left of the queen take the prefix Q.

Thus the rook to the left of the queen is a queen's rook and is represented as QR.

Each file is represented by the initials of the pieces that occupy the squares at either end. The eight files (from left to right for white, and inversely for black) are represented as follows:

QR, QKt, QB, Q, K, KB, KKt, KR.

Each rank is numbered from 1 to 8; both players count from their own ends of the board. Consequently each square has two names: one name as seen from white's side, and one from black's. For example, QKt3 (white) equals QKt6 (black).

A move is described by the initial letter of the piece moved and the square to which it moved. For example, the king's knight move to the third square of the king's rook file is represented by KKt–KR3.

If two pieces of the same kind can move to the same square, both the square from which the piece moved and the square it arrived at are given. For example, KKt (KB4)–KR3 means that the knight on the fourth square of the king's bishop file made the move, although another knight on the board could have reached the same square in the same move.

Other explanatory abbreviations are:

O–O or Castles K denotes a castling move involving KR;

O–O–O or Castles Q denotes a castling move involving QR;

x denotes captures;

ch or + denotes check;

! denotes well played;

? denotes a bad move.

QR1	QKt1	QB1	Q1	K1	KB1	KKt1	KR1
Q 2	QKt2	QB2	Q2	K2	KB2	KKt2	KR2
Q 3	QKt3	QB3	Q3	K3	KB3	KKt3	KR3
QR4	QKt4	QB4	Q4	K4	KB4	KKt4	KR4
QR5	QKt5	QB5	Q5	K5	KB5	KKt5	KR5
Q 6	QKt6	QB6	Q6	K6	KB6	KKt6	KR6
Q 7	QKt7	QB7	Q7	K7	KB7	KKt7	KR7
QR8	QKt8	QB8	Q8	K8	KB8	KKt8	KR8

Descriptive system: black

Q 8	QKt8	QB8	Q8	K8	KB8	KKt8	KR8
Q 7	QKt7	QB7	Q7	K7	KB7	KKt7	KR7
Q 6	QKt6	QB6	Q6	K6	KB6	KKt6	KR6
Q 5	QKt5	QB5	Q5	K5	KB5	KKt5	KR5
Q 4	QKt4	QB4	Q4	K4	KB4	KKt4	KR4
Q 3	QKt3	QB3	Q3	K3	KB3	KKt3	KR3
Q 2	QKt2	QB2	Q2	K2	KB2	KKt2	KR2
Q 1	QKt1	QB1	Q1	K1	KB1	KKt1	KR1

Descriptive system: white

a8	**b8**	**c8**	**d8**	**e8**	**f8**	**g8**	**h8**	**Algebraic system of notation**
a7	**b7**	**c7**	**d7**	**e7**	**f7**	**g7**	**h7**	Black
a6	**b6**	**c6**	**d6**	**e6**	**f6**	**g6**	**h6**	
a5	**b5**	**c5**	**d5**	**e5**	**f5**	**g5**	**h5**	
a4	**b4**	**c4**	**d4**	**e4**	**f4**	**g4**	**h4**	
a3	**b3**	**c3**	**d3**	**e3**	**f3**	**g3**	**h3**	
a2	**b2**	**c2**	**d2**	**e2**	**f2**	**g2**	**h2**	White
a1	**b1**	**c1**	**d1**	**e1**	**f1**	**g1**	**h1**	

Algebraic system

Each piece, with the exception of the pawns, is represented by its initial letter (and the knight by Kt or N). The pawns are not specially indicated.

The eight files (reading from left to right for white) are represented by the letters from a to h.

The eight ranks (counting from white's first rank) are numbered from 1 to 8. Initially, the white pieces stand on ranks 1 and 2, and the black pieces on ranks 7 and 8.

Thus each square is represented by the combination of a letter and a number.

A move is described by the initial letter of the piece moved and the square from which it moved, plus the square at which it arrived. For example, a bishop moving from square f1 to square d3 is represented by Bf1 – d3 or in a shortened form Bd3.

If two pieces of the same kind can move to the same square, both the square from which the piece moved and the square it arrived at are given. For example, two knights stand on the squares f3 and g4; if the knight on f3 makes the move to h2, the move is written Ktf3–h2 or in the shortened form by Ktf–h2.

The other abbreviations used in the algebraic system are the same as those for the descriptive system, with the following additions:

: or x denotes captures;

‡ denotes checkmate.

Chinese checkers

Chinese checkers is a modern game derived from Halma
(p. 168). It can be played by two to six persons, playing
individually or with partners.

The board is made of metal, plastic, wood, or heavy card. The
playing area is a six-pointed star, with holes or indentations to
hold the pieces. Each of the star's points is a different color.
The pieces There are six sets of 15 pieces. Each set is the same
color as one of the star's points. The most common types of
pieces are plastic pegs or marbles.

Start of play

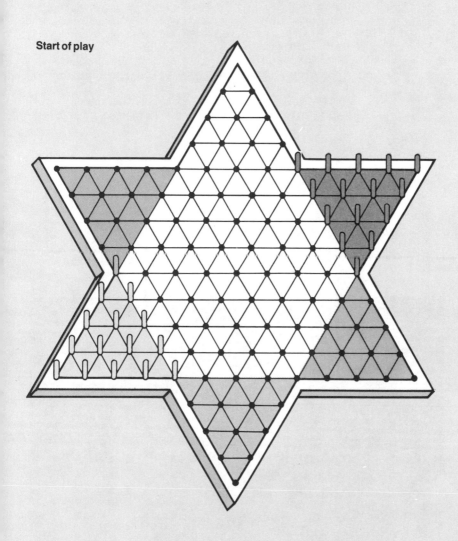

Objective Players attempt to move their pieces into the opposite point. The game is won by the first player or pair to do so.

Start of play For a game between two players, each positions 15 pieces of appropriate colors in opposite points of the star. When there are more than two players, each one positions 10 pieces in any point; partners usually take opposite points.

Turns Each player moves one piece in turn.

Moves may be made along any of the lines, ie in six directions. Moves may be "steps" or "hops." A player may hop over his own or another player's pieces and may make several hops in one move. Steps and hops may not be combined in a single move. There is no compulsion to make a hop. All hopped pieces are left on the board.

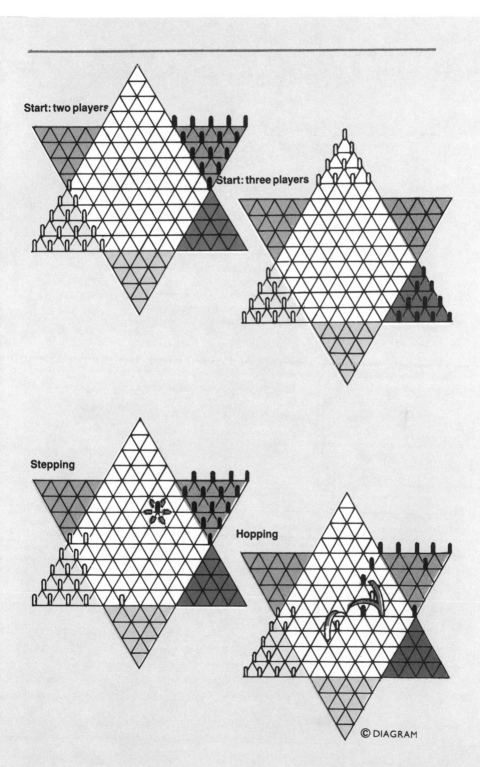

Start: two players

Start: three players

Stepping

Hopping

© DIAGRAM

Chinese rebels

Similar to Fox and geese (p. 154), this game is thought to have
originated in China. One player (the "general") attempts to
evade the rebelling soldiers that have surrounded him.
Although the general is heavily outnumbered, he has the
advantage of being able to "kill" the soldiers and remove them
from the board.

The playing area may be drawn on a sheet of paper. It consists
of a rectangle enclosing 39 small circles. One circle is
distinctively marked and represents the "camp."
Pieces Counters or other small objects may be used. One piece
represents the general and must be different in appearance
from the 20 pieces representing the soldiers.
Start of play The soldiers are positioned around the general, as
shown.

Play The players decide which of them is to play the general
and which the soldiers.

The general has the opening move, and thereafter the players
take alternate turns. In a turn, a piece may be moved one circle
forward, backward, or sideways onto an adjoining vacant
circle (**a**). Diagonal moves are not permitted.

The general is allowed to "kill" a soldier by jumping over him
from an adjoining circle to an empty circle beyond (**b**). That
soldier is then removed from the board. (The general's
opening move is always a taking move.)

Result If the general kills so many soldiers that not enough
remain to trap him, or if he manages to return to camp, he wins
the game.

The soldiers win if they manage to immobilize the general by
surrounding him or crowding him into a corner.

Alternative result Once players are familiar with playing
tactics, they will find that the general invariably loses the game.
For this reason, two or more games can be played in
succession, with players changing roles after each game.

The person playing the soldiers must note how many moves it
takes him to trap the general.

At the end of a set number of games, the players compare
results, and the winner is the player who trapped the general in
fewest moves.

Start of play

Moving

Trapped
general

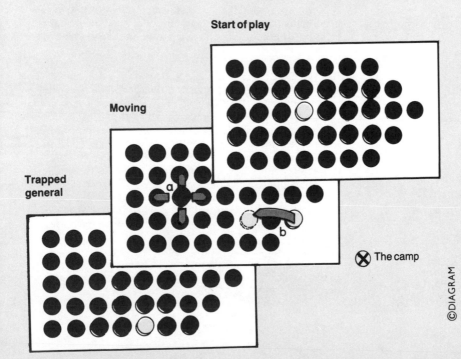

The camp

©DIAGRAM

Coin throwing games

Money has been changing hands in games of chance and skill since time immemorial. In another, much smaller group of games it is the coins themselves that play the principal role.

COVER IT
Cover it is a game for two or more players. The first player throws a coin against a wall and leaves it where it comes to rest on the ground.

Then each player in turn throws a coin against the wall. If his coin is touching another coin when it comes to rest, he picks up both coins. If it is not touching another coin, he leaves his coin on the ground.

HITTING THE MUMMY
This is a variation of Cover it in which the first coin thrown is designated the "mummy" and players aim only to cover this one coin.

A player whose coin is not touching the mummy after being thrown against the wall must leave his coin where it lies.

A player whose coin is touching the mummy is entitled to pick up all coins on the ground except the mummy. If he mistakenly picks up the mummy, he must pay one coin to each of the other players.

BROTHER JONATHAN
This coin throwing game originated in North America in the eighteenth century. It is a game for two or more players, playing for themselves or in teams.

The board may be marked on the ground, or drawn on a large sheet of paper laid on the floor. It is a rectangle divided into sections, with a scoring value marked in each one. Note that the larger sections bear the lower scores whereas the smaller sections contain higher numbers.

Play Each player takes it in turn to pitch a coin from a previously designated spot onto the board. If a coin touches any of the dividing lines it does not count toward the player's score.

The winner may be decided in one of two ways:
a) the first player or team to score an agreed total; or
b) the player or team with the highest score after an agreed number of throws.

WALL JONATHAN
This game is played in the same way as Brother Jonathan
except that players must throw their coins against a wall in such
a way that they rebound onto the board.

CRACK LOO
In this game, players score points by throwing coins onto
numbered cracks on a wood floor (or onto lines drawn on a
large sheet of paper). Otherwise play is the same as for Brother
Jonathan.

Catch

©DIAGRAM

PENNIES ON THE PLATE

A metal plate or lid is placed on the ground. At his turn a player throws an agreed number of coins at the plate. The coins must be thrown one at a time from an agreed distance of several feet.

The player who gets the most coins to stay on the plate wins the game. (It is usually quite easy to hit the plate, but much more difficult to ensure that a coin falls in such a way that it does not immediately bounce or roll off it.)

HOLE IN ONE

For this game players need a coin and a plastic tumbler or similar receptacle. The tumbler is placed on its side on the floor and the players take it in turn to try rolling a coin into it. The winner is the player who gets the coin into the tumbler most times out of an agreed number of shots.

ROLL A GOAL

This game is played in the same way as Hole in one, except that players attempt to roll a coin between two "goalposts" made from folded paper, books, or other objects.

COIN ARCHBOARD

This is a coin version of Marbles archboard (p. 208). Players attempt to roll coins through arches in a board and, when successful, score the number of points indicated above the arch.

PENNY ROLL

This game is popular at fairgrounds in many parts of the world. It can easily be played at home with improvised equipment. Players roll coins down a metal and wood chute onto a board divided into numbered squares. If a player's coin stops completely within a square he receives a sum of money in accordance with that square's number.

CATCH

The skills of juggling and coordination play an important part in the game of Catch.

For the first round, each player:

a) balances one coin on his elbow;

b) drops his hand and tries to catch his coin as it falls.

For the second round, players balance and attempt to catch two coins together, and the number of coins is then increased by one for each further round.

Any player who fails to catch the required number of coins for a round is eliminated from any further rounds, and the winner is the last player left in the game.

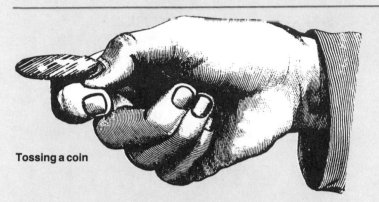

Tossing a coin

TOSSING A COIN

Tossing a coin is a widely known method of deciding the order of play for many games between two players or teams.
The coin is tossed by a player or non-player, who:
a) flicks the coin into the air by releasing his thumb from between his clenched fingers;
b) catches the coin in his other hand;
c) quickly turns this hand over to lay the coin on the back of his tossing hand.
If a non-player makes the toss, he asks one of the players to "call." If a player makes the toss, his opponent should call.
A player calls either "heads" or "tails" in an attempt to forecast which side of the coin will be face up after the toss. He should make his call while the coin is in the air.
A player who "wins the toss" (ie makes a correct forecast) generally has the right to choose the order of play for the game.

HEADS OR TAILS

Heads or tails is an adaptation of Tossing a coin to make a game for any number of players.
Each player tosses a coin in turn, and all players, including the thrower, guess whether it will fall with the head or tail up.
The winner is either:
a) the first player to make an agreed number of correct guesses; or
b) the player with the most correct guesses after an agreed number of throws.

SPINNING A COIN

Spinning a coin

This game is played in the same way as Heads or tails, except that the coins are spun instead of tossed.
(Probably the easiest method of spinning a coin is to hold it on its edge on a smooth, hard surface and then spin it between the thumb of one hand and the forefinger of the other, as shown.)

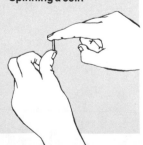

Conkers

Conkers is a popular game with British children. Two players each have a "conker" threaded on a knotted string. Players take alternate hits at their opponent's conker and the game is won when one player destroys the other's conker.

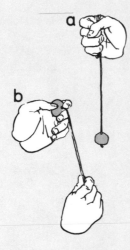

The conkers The game is usually played with nuts from the horsechestnut tree, but is sometimes played with hazelnuts (often called "cobnuts").

When preparing their conkers, players make a hole through the center with a sharp instrument such as a meat skewer or a pair of geometry dividers.

Many players then harden their conkers by soaking them in vinegar or salt and water and/or baking them for about half an hour. Excellent conkers are obtained by storing them in the dark for a year.

When the conker is ready, a strong piece of string or a bootlace is threaded through the hole and knotted at one end. The string should be long enough for about 9in to hang down after it is wrapped once or twice around the hand.

The game Players take alternate hits at their opponent's conker.

The player whose conker is to be hit first, holds his conker as shown (**a**) – with the string wrapped around his hand. He must adjust the height of his hand to suit his opponent, and must then keep his conker perfectly still for the hit.

The striker takes his conker in one hand and holds the opposite end of his string in the other hand (**b**). For the strike, he first draws the conker back and then releases it in a fast swinging motion in the direction of his opponent's conker (**c**).

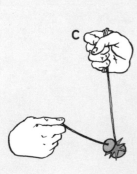

If the striker misses his opponent's conker he is allowed a maximum of two further attempts to make a hit. If the players' strings tangle, the first player to call "strings" can claim an extra shot.

Play continues until one of the conkers is destroyed – ie until no part of it remains on the string.

Scoring Conkers are usually described according to the number of victories won with them – eg "oner," "fiver," "seventy-fiver."

A conker adds one to its title each time it destroys a conker that has never won a game. A conker that defeats a conker with previous wins claims one for defeating it plus all the defeated conker's wins – so a "fiver" that defeats another "fiver" becomes an "elevener."

© DIAGRAM

CONQUERORS

This is a similar game to Conkers and seems to have been very popular in the eighteenth and nineteenth centuries. Two players press empty snail shells tip to tip until one of them breaks. Scoring is the same as for Conkers.

SOLDIERS

This game is now usually played with lollipop or ice cream sticks. One player holds his stick with both hands, one at each end. The other holds his stick in one hand and gives his opponent's stick a sharp blow.

Turns at striking alternate as in Conkers, and the game continues until one of the sticks breaks. Scoring is as for Conkers.

Soldiers

Conquest

Conquest is an interesting game that can be played with checkers pieces on an improvised board.

Board The game is played on a checkered board with 81 squares (nine squares by nine).
The central nine squares, called the "fortress," are enclosed within a thick or colored line.
Pieces There are two sets of pieces, one for each player. Each set is of a different color and comprises eight ordinary pieces and one specially marked king.

Start of play

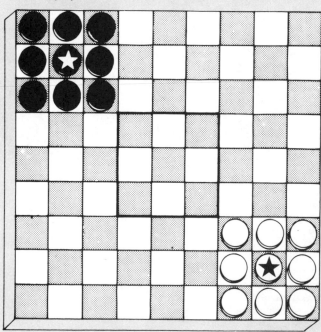

Objective Players attempt to capture the central fortress according to one of the four possible plans of occupation (see illustration). The plan for a particular game must always be agreed before play starts.

Start of play Players position their pieces as illustrated: in diagonally opposite corners of the board and with the kings surrounded by the ordinary pieces.

Turns alternate, and each player makes only one move at a turn.

Moving The only permitted move for any piece is one square diagonally forward or backward (so that each piece stays on squares of the same color throughout the game).

Exiling If a player traps an opponent's piece between two of his own pieces in a diagonal line (so that all three pieces are on the same color square), the player may "exile" the trapped piece to any other square of the same color.

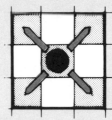

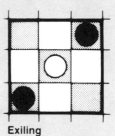

Moving

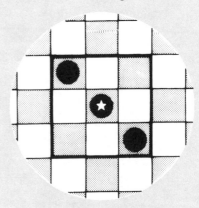

Exiling

Plans of occupation

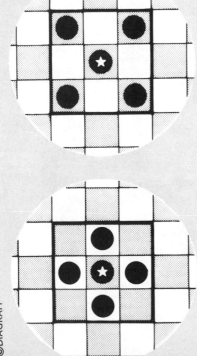

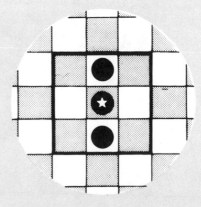

Darts

A traditional English "pub" game, Darts now has enthusiasts in many different countries. Players throw darts at a circular target divided into different scoring areas. Games are played by individuals, pairs, or teams. In the standard game, players aim to reduce a starting score exactly to zero. Other games provide a great variety of objectives designed to test the players' skill.

Standard dartboard Most dartboards are made of cork, bristle, or elm, with the divisions and sector numbers marked by wires.

The standard tournament board is 18in in diameter and has twenty sectors, an outer "doubles" ring, an inner "trebles" ring, and an inner and outer "bull" in the center. Adjacent sectors are differentiated by color.

Standard board

Darts Each player has a set of three darts. Designs vary, but most darts are about 6in long. All darts have:
a sharp point, usually made of steel;
a barrel, made of metal (usually brass), or plastic weighted with metal, or wood;
a tail, "flighted" with feathers, plastic, or paper.

The scoreboard is a slate or blackboard, usually positioned to one side of the dartboard. Each side's score is recorded in chalk.

Playing area The dartboard is hung on a wall, with the center 5ft 8in from the ground. Toe lines may be marked on a mat or on the floor, at distances of 8ft, 8ft 6in, and 9ft from the dartboard.

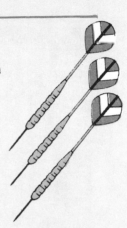

Playing area

8ft
8ft 6in
9ft

©DIAGRAM

STANDARD TOURNAMENT DARTS

Players Games are played by individuals, pairs, or teams of any fixed number of players.

Starting Each player, or one member of each pair or team, must get a dart in the doubles ring to begin scoring. The starting double is scored, as are darts thrown after but not before it in the same turn.

Turns In singles games, opponents take turns to throw three darts each. In pairs and team games, one player from each side throws three darts in turn, with members of each side playing in the order established at the start of the game.

The first turn goes to the player, pair, or team that wins the toss of a coin or gets a dart nearest the bull in a preliminary throw.

Scored throws A throw is invalid if the player is not behind the toe-line when throwing.

Only those darts sticking in the board at the end of a player's turn are scored. Thus darts are not scored if they rebound, stick in another dart, fall from the board, or are knocked out before the player ends his turn.

Re-throws are not permitted. (Also note starting and finishing procedures.)

Scoring Scored throws are deducted from a starting total – usually 301, 501, or 1001.

Darts in the inner bull score 50, and in the outer bull 25. Darts in a sector score according to the sector number – unless they are within the outer (doubles) ring (**a**), when they score double the sector number, or the inner (trebles) ring (**b**), when they score three times the sector number.

Finishing The game ends with a double bringing the score exactly to zero. If the scores in a player's turn take him past zero, or to one, he goes back to the score before that turn and forfeits any darts remaining in that turn.

Scoring

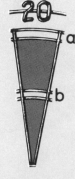

AROUND THE CLOCK

This is a singles game for any number of players. Each player throws three darts in a turn.

After a starting double, each player must throw one dart into each of the sectors, in order, from 1 to 20. Darts in the doubles or trebles rings of the correct sector are usually allowed. The winner is the first player to finish.

As a variation, players may be awarded an extra turn for scoring with the last dart of a turn.

SHANGHAI

Shanghai is another "around the clock" game for any number of players with three darts each.

In his first turn, each player throws all his darts at sector number 1. Singles, doubles, and trebles all score their value. In his second turn, each player throws all his darts at sector number 2 (even if he made no score in his first turn).

Play proceeds in this manner right "around the clock," and the winner is usually the player with the highest total score.

In a popular variation of this game, a player may win by going "Shanghai," ie by scoring in one turn a single, double, and treble of the required number.

CLOSING

This is a game for two players, each with three darts. Each player aims to make as high a score as possible while seeking to prevent his opponent from making a high score.

As soon as one of the players has scored three times from any one sector, that sector is "closed" and no further score may be made from it by either player.

Doubles and trebles score their value, and count as two and three scores respectively. The winner is the player with the highest score when the last sector is closed.

**Closing:
sample scoreboard**

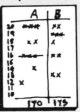

SCRAM

Scram is a game for two players throwing three darts in each turn.

The player with the first turn is the "stopper," and any sector he hits with a dart is closed to his opponent.

The second player is known as the "scorer," and he aims to score as many points as possible before all the sectors are closed.

When all the sectors are closed, the two players change roles. The winner is the player who scores most when playing scorer.

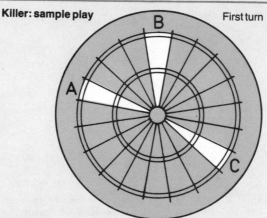

Killer: sample play   First turn

KILLER

Killer is probably best with four to eight players, but can be played by either more or less.

In his first turn, each player throws one dart with the hand that he normally does not use for throwing darts. This throw decides a player's own sector for the rest of the game. Unless a very large number of people are playing, it is usual for a player to throw again if a sector has already been given to another player.

In every other turn, each player throws three darts with his usual hand. The game has several versions, but in all cases the winner is the player left in the game when all other players have lost all their "lives."

First version In one version of the game, all players begin with no lives and a player's first objective is to acquire three lives by throwing three darts into his own sector (two lives for a double and three for a treble).

Once a player has three lives he becomes a "killer" and starts throwing darts at other player's sectors. (In the example illustrated, players B and C become killers after their second turns and player A after the first throw of his third turn.)

If a killer throws a dart into the sector of a player with three or two lives, that player loses one life (or two for a double or three for a treble).

If a killer throws a dart into the sector of a player with one or no lives, that player is out (player B after C's third turn in the example illustrated).

A killer who loses a life loses his right to kill until he makes up his lost life by throwing another dart into his own sector.

Second version All players start with an agreed number of lives – usually three or five. To start killing, a player has to throw a double of his own number. Kills are made by throwing doubles and trebles of other players' numbers – one kill for a double and two kills for a treble. Lost lives cannot be won back again.

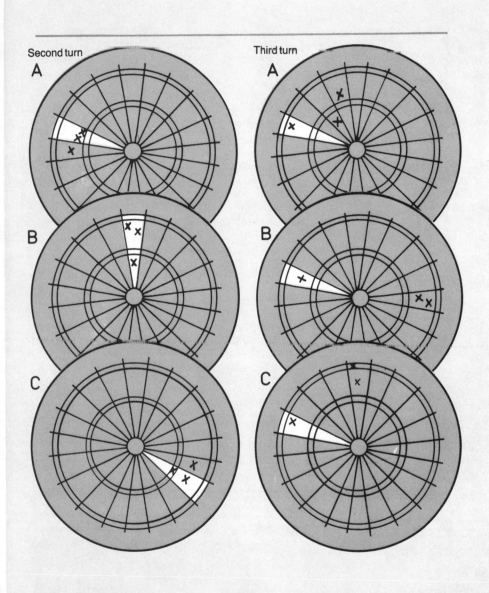

**Halve it:
sample
scoreboard**

	A	B
20	1	20
19	19	39
18	37	75
DOUBLE	18	105
17	8	122
16	2	61
15	14	80
TREBLE	9	90
14	4	45
13	30	71
12	15	48
DOUBLE	7	49
TREBLE	3	24
11	25	60
10	35	30
BULL	17	40

HALVE IT

Halve it is a game for any number of players, each throwing
three darts in a turn.

Before play begins, players select a series of objectives and
chalk them up on the scoreboard. A typical series would be:
20, 19, 18, any double, 17, 16, 15, any treble, 14, 13, 12,
double, treble, 11, 10, bull.

In his first turn, each player aims for 20 and scores for each dart
in that sector (doubles and trebles count their value).

Players then take turns to make their way through the list of
objectives, scoring for each dart in the correct sector or halving
their total score (rounding down) whenever none of their darts
scores. There are no minus scores, and a player whose score is
reduced to zero stays at zero until he throws a dart that scores.

FIVES

Fives can be played by two players or sides using a standard
dartboard. The winner is the first player to reach an agreed
number of points, usually 50.

Each player throws three darts in a turn. He scores only if the
sum of his three darts can be divided by five – in which case he
scores the result of this division.

A player who throws a dart out of the scoring area when he has
a total divisible by five, scores no points for that turn.

DARTS FOOTBALL

This is a game for two players, each throwing three darts in a turn.

A dart in the inner bull "gains control of the ball." This player can then start scoring "goals" – one for each double.

He continues scoring until his opponent "takes the ball away" by scoring an inner bull. The first player to score ten goals wins the game.

DARTS CRICKET

Darts cricket is a game for two teams of equal size.

The team that wins the toss of a coin decides whether to "bat" or to "bowl." Turns alternate between teams, and each player throws one dart in a turn.

When "batting," a team aims to score as many "runs" as possible; when "bowling," to "take wickets" by scoring inner bulls.

The teams change roles after five wickets are taken. The team with the highest batting score wins the game.

DARTS BASEBALL

This is a game for two players, each representing a baseball team.

There are nine innings, and each player has a turn at "bat" in each inning. A player's turn consists of three throws.

In the first inning players throw darts at sector 1, in the second inning at sector 2, through to sector 9 in the ninth inning. Extra innings are played if there is a tie.

A single "run" is scored by getting a dart into the correct sector for the inning (with two runs for a double and three for a treble). Getting a bull at any stage of the game is a "grand slam home run" and scores four runs.

DARTS SHOVE HA'PENNY

This game for two players or pairs is based on the rules of the board game described on p. 330. Each player throws three darts in a turn, and the objective is to score three times in each of the sectors numbered 1 through 9. The scores may be made in any order, and doubles count as two scores and trebles as three.

If a player scores more than three times in any one sector, the extra scores are given to the opposition. The score that wins the game, however, must always be actually thrown by the winner. The game is won by the first side to finish.

Dice games: family

Plan of die faces

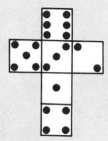

Dice games were played in ancient times and remain universally popular. Here we look first at family games – ways of passing a happy hour with little or no gambling involved. (A selection of private gambling games begins on p. 98.)

Dice A standard modern die is a regular cube, with the six sides numbered with dots from 1 through 6. Any two opposing sides add up to 7.

Odds With one true die, each face has an equal chance of landing face up. With two dice thrown together, some scores are more likely than others because there are more ways in which they can be made.

Possible throws with two dice

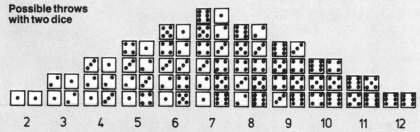

| 2 | 3 | 4 | 5 | 6 | 7 | 8 | 9 | 10 | 11 | 12 |

FIFTY

This game, for two or more players, is one of the simplest dice games. It requires two dice, and the winner is the first player to score 50 points.

Each player in turn rolls the two dice, but scores only when identical numbers are thrown (two 1s, two 2s, and so on). All these doubles, except two 6s and two 3s score five points. A double 6 scores 25 points; and a double 3 wipes out the player's total score and he has to start again.

ROUND THE CLOCK

This is a game for three or four players, using two dice.

Objective Players try to throw 1 through 12 in correct sequence. The winner is the first to complete the sequence.

Play Players throw both dice once on each turn.

From 1 through 6, a player can score with either one of the two dice or with both of them – eg a throw of 3 and 1 can be counted as 3, 1, or 4. It is also possible at this stage to score twice on one throw – eg if a player needs 2 and throws a 2 and a 3 he can count both of these numbers.

From 7 through 12, however, a player will obviously always need the combined spot values of both dice to score.

SHUT THE BOX

This is a game for two or more players.

Equipment:

1) two dice;
2) a board or sheet of paper with nine boxes numbered 1 to 9;
3) nine counters used to cover the boxes in play.

(In some parts of the world, specially made trays with sliding covers for the numbers are available.)

Objective Players aim to cover as many of the numbers as possible, in accordance with the throws of the dice. The winner is the player with the lowest penalty score from uncovered boxes.

Play The player taking first turn throws the two dice and then decides which boxes he will cover. He may cover any two boxes that have the same total as his throw – eg a throw of 10 would allow him to cover 6 and 4, 7 and 3, 8 and 2, or 9 and 1.

The same player then throws the two dice again and tries to cover another two boxes. He is not allowed to use combinations involving numbers that he has already covered. After covering boxes 9, 8, and 7 a player may throw only one die on a turn, but he must still cover two boxes at a time.

A player's turn continues until he is unable to make use of a combination from his latest throw. All the uncovered numbers are then added up and become his penalty score.

Play then passes to the next player.

Shut the box: sample play

6+4=10 thrown
8+2=10 covered

©DIAGRAM

DROP DEAD

This is an exciting game for any number of players.

Equipment:

1) five dice;

2) a sheet of paper on which to record players' scores.

Objective Players aim to make the highest total score.

Play At his turn each player begins by rolling the five dice. Each time he makes a throw that does not contain a 2 or a 5, he scores the total spot value of that throw and is entitled to another throw with all five dice.

Whenever a player makes a throw containing a 2 or a 5, he scores nothing for that throw and any die or dice that showed a 2 or a 5 must be excluded from any further throws that he makes. A player's turn continues until his last remaining die shows a 2 or a 5 – at which point he "drops dead" and play passes to the next player.

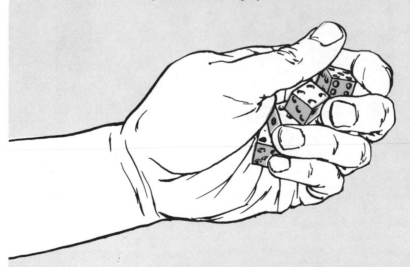

CHICAGO

Chicago, also called Rotation, is a game for any number of players. Two dice are used. The game is based on the 11 possible combinations of the two dice – 2, 3, 4, 5, 6, 7, 8, 9, 10, 11, and 12 – and so consists of 11 rounds.

The objective is to score each of these combinations in turn. The player with the highest score is the winner.

Play Each player in turn rolls the dice once in each round. During the first round, he will try to make a total of 2, during the second, a total of 3, and so on up to 12.

Each time he is successful, that number of points is added to his score. For example, if he is shooting for 5 and throws a total of 5, he gains five points. If he fails to make the desired number, he scores nothing on that throw.

PIG

This simple game, for any number of players, requires only one die. The winner is the first player to reach a previously agreed high score (usually 100).

Order of play is determined by a preliminary round. Each player throws the die once and the player with the lowest score becomes first shooter. The next-lowest scoring player shoots second, and so on. The order of play is important because the first and last shooters have natural advantages (see below).

Play begins with the first shooter. Like the other players, he may roll the die as many times as he wishes. He totals his score throw by throw until he elects to end his turn. He passes the die to the next player, memorizing his score so far.

But if he throws a 1, he loses the entire score he has made on that turn, and the die passes to the next player. Play passes from player to player until someone reaches the agreed total. Given a little luck, the first shooter is the player most likely to win. But his advantage can be counteracted by allowing other players to continue until they have had the same number of turns. The player with the highest score is then the winner.

The last shooter still has the advantage of knowing the scores made by all his opponents. Provided he does not roll a 1, he can continue throwing until he has beaten all those scores.

The fairest way of playing the game is to organize it as a series, with each player in turn becoming first shooter.

GOING TO BOSTON

Also known as Newmarket or Yankee grab, this game is ideal for three or four players, although more can play.

Equipment: three dice.

Play Each player in turn rolls the three dice together. After the first roll, he leaves the die showing the highest number on the table, then rolls the other two again. Of these, the die with the highest number is also left on the table and the remaining die is rolled again. This completes the player's throw and the total of his three dice is his score.

When all players have thrown, the player with the highest score wins the round. Ties are settled by further rolling.

A game usually consists of an agreed number of rounds: the player who wins the most rounds is the winner.

Alternatively, each player can contribute counters to a pool that is won at the end of each game.

MULTIPLICATION

This game is played like Going to Boston, but with one important difference. When each player has completed his turn, his score is the sum of the spot values of the first two dice rolled, multiplied by that of the third. For example, if his first throw is 5, his second throw 4, and his final throw 6, his score will be 54: $(5+4)\times6$.

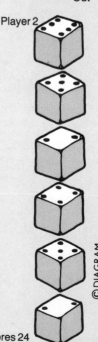

Pig: sample play

Player 1

Out

Player 2

Stops, scores 24

©DIAGRAM

Beetle: scoring

BEETLE

This is a lively game for two or more players – more than six tend to slow down the game.

Equipment:
1) one die, either an ordinary one or a special "beetle die" marked B (body), H (head), L (legs), E (eyes), F (feelers), and T (tail);
2) a simple drawing of a beetle as a guide, showing its various parts and (when an ordinary die is used) their corresponding numbers;
3) a pencil and a piece of paper for each player.

Objective Each player, by throwing the die, tries to complete his drawing of the beetle. The first to do so scores 13 points and is the winner. The 13 points represent one for each part of the beetle (body, head, tail, two feelers, two eyes, and six legs).

Play Each player throws the die once only in each round. Each player must begin by throwing a B (or a 1); this permits him to draw the body.

When this has been drawn, he can throw for other parts of the beetle that can be joined to the body.

An H or a 2 must be thrown to link the head to the body before the feelers (F or 5) and eyes (E or 4) can be added. Each eye or feeler requires its own throw.

A throw of L or 3 permits the player to add three legs to one side of the body. A further throw of L or 3 is necessary for the other three legs.

Sometimes it is agreed that a player may continue to throw in his turn for as long as he throws parts of the body he can use.

Continuing play When a series of games is played, each player counts one point for every part of the beetle he has been able to draw and cumulative scores are carried from round to round. The winner is the player with the highest score at the end of the series, or the first to reach a previously agreed total score.

HEARTS

Hearts, or Hearts due, is a game for two or more players.

Equipment Six dice are used. Special dice marked with the letters H, E, A, R, T, S instead of numbers are sometimes used, but the game is now more commonly played with ordinary dice.

The objective is simply to score more than your opponents over an agreed series of rounds, or a single round, or to be the first to reach an agreed total.

Play begins after a preliminary round has decided the first shooter (usually the player with the highest score).

Each player in turn rolls the six dice once and calculates his score according to the following ratings:

1 (H) = 5 points;
1, 2 (HE) = 10 points;
1, 2, 3 (HEA) = 15 points;
1, 2, 3, 4 (HEAR) = 20 points;

1, 2, 3, 4, 5 (HEART)=25 points,
1, 2, 3, 4, 5, 6 (HEARTS)=35 points.
If a double (two dice of the same spot value) or a treble appears
in the throw, only one of the letters or numbers counts. But if
three 1s (or Hs) appear, the player's whole score is wiped out
and he has to start again.

CENTENNIAL
Also known as Martinetti or Ohio, this is a game for two to
eight players.
Equipment:
1) three dice;
2) a long board or piece of paper marked with a row of boxes
numbered 1 to 12;
3) a distinctive counter or other object for each player.
Objective Each player tries to be the first to move his counter,
in accordance with throws of the dice, from 1 to 12 and back.
Play begins after a preliminary round has determined who will
take the first turn. Each player on a turn throws all three dice at
once. Turns pass clockwise around the table.
In order to place his counter in the first box, a player must
throw a 1. He can try then for a 2, a 3, and so on, box by box up
to 12 and back again. He can make any number with one or
more dice. For example, a 3 can be scored with one 3, a 1 and a
2, or with three 1s. It is possible to move through more than
one box on a single throw. For example, a throw of 1, 2, 3
would not only take him through the first three boxes, but on
through the fourth (1+3=4), to the fifth (2+3=5) and finally
the sixth (1+2+3=6).
Other players' throws must be watched constantly. If a player
throws a number he needs but overlooks and does not use, that
number may be claimed by any other player. He must do this as
soon as the dice are passed, however, and must be able to use it
at once.

EVEREST
This game is like Centennial but has a different layout and
scoring system.
Equipment Each player has a sheet of paper showing two
columns, each divided into 12 boxes. In one column the boxes
are numbered from 1 to 12 in ascending order. In the other they
are numbered from 1 to 12 in descending order.
Objective Each player tries to be the first to score all 24
numbers. The numbers do not have to be scored consecutively
as in Centennial, but as desired and in either column.
Scoring Each die in a throw can be counted only once.

Centennial: scoring

Everest: scoring

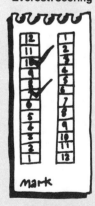

©DIAGRAM

Dice baseball: sample play

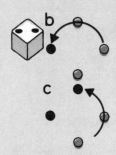

Moves ↺

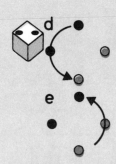

DICE BASEBALL

As a dice game for two players, baseball can be played in several different ways. A popular version using one die is described here.

Equipment:

1) one die;

2) at least three counters for each player to represent his men;

3) a sheet of paper with a simple diagram of a baseball diamond drawn on it;

4) another piece of paper for recording scores.

The objective is to score the highest total number of runs in the nine innings per player that constitute the game. If the two players have equal scores after the usual nine innings, an extra-inning game is played. (Note that in baseball, each player's turn at bat is called a "half-inning.")

Order of play The players throw the die to decide who shall "bat" first (ie shoot the die first). Each player in turn then throws a half-inning. A half-inning is ended when a player has thrown three "outs" (see below).

Making runs At the start of the game, or whenever all bases are empty, a throw of 1, 2 or 3 permits the player to put a man (counter) on whichever of those three bases he has thrown – 1 in the example illustrated (**a**).

If the player throws 1, 2, or 3 again, this permits him to move the man around the diamond by the number of bases thrown, and to place another man on the base that bears the number thrown. For example, if he has a man on 1, and throws a 2, the man advances to base 3 (**b**) and a new man is entered on base 2 (**c**).

Each time a man reaches the home (fourth) base or "home plate," a run is scored. A single throw may give a score of more than one run if it takes more than one man to home base.

For example, if a player with men on bases 2 and 3 throws a 2, both men advance to home base and two runs are scored (**d**). At the same time a new man is entered on base 2 (**e**).

A throw of 4 counts as a home run and advances all men on the bases to home base. The score is thus the home run plus one run for each man brought home.

Outs Throws of 5 or 6 are "outs."

A throw of 5 is as though there had been a hit and a throw-in, so that men on the bases may also be out, as follows:

if the shooter has only one man on the bases, he is out;

if he has men on all bases, the man on base 1 is out;

if he has men on bases 1 and 2, the man on base 2 is out;

if he has men on bases 1 and 3, the man on base 1 is out;

if he has men on bases 2 and 3, both are safe.

Men on the bases who are not out remain where they are.

A throw of 6 is also an out, but it is as if the batter were out without striking the ball; men on bases are safe, and remain where they are.

Note that three outs end a half-inning. The other player then throws his half-inning to complete the inning.

DICE BASKETBALL

As a dice game, basketball is usually played by two players, but more can take part, each player representing a team. As in the real game, the winner is the team (ie player) making the highest score in the game or series of games.

Equipment Basketball may be played with only two dice or with as many as 10. Many players use eight dice as there are then enough to ensure a rapid game and realistic scores.

Play A game consists of four quarters. In each quarter each player in turn rolls the eight dice once, their total being his score for that quarter.

If the game is played with only two dice, each player rolls the dice four times to determine his score for that quarter.

The player with the highest score for the four quarters wins the game. If the game, or agreed series of games, ends in a tie, this is resolved by playing extra quarters until the outright winner is established.

CHEERIO

This game can be played by any number of players up to a maximum of 12. The greater the number of players, the slower the pace of the game.

Equipment:
1) five dice;
2) a dice cup;
3) a sheet of paper showing the various combinations and with a scoring column for each player.

Objective Each player tries to score the maximum possible for each of the 11 scoring combinations (see below). The player with the highest total score wins the game.

Games are often played as a series, the player who wins the most games in the series being the overall winner.

Alternatively, the scores in each game can be carried forward to the next game until a player has reached a previously agreed cumulative total. If two or more players exceed the total, the player with the highest score wins.

Ties are settled by an extra game.

Play Each player in turn rolls all five dice. Having rolled the dice once, he may pick up all or any of them and roll once more in an attempt to improve his score.

He does not have to try for combinations in any particular order, and he does not have to declare his combination until he has finished rolling. This gives him considerable freedom of choice. For example, if he has rolled 6, 6, 2, 3, 3 he might call sixes (score 12). But if he wanted to keep sixes for a later turn, when he might roll more than two of them, he could call a different combination even if this would give him a lower score or even no score for the throw.

A player is not permitted to call the same combination more than once in a game.

Combinations

Ones Scores one point for each die showing one spot (maximum score five points).

Twos Scores two points for each two-spot die (maximum 10).

Threes Scores three points for each three-spot die (maximum 15).

Fours Scores four points for each four-spot die (maximum 20).

Fives Scores five points for each five-spot die (maximum 25).

Sixes Scores six points for each six-spot die (maximum 30).

Little straight A show of 1, 2, 3, 4, 5 scores 20 points.

Big straight A show of 2, 3, 4, 5, 6 scores 25 points.

Full house Three of a kind plus two of a kind scores according to the numbers shown on the dice (6, 6, 6, 5, 5 scores the maximum 28 points).

Big hand The total spot value of the dice (6, 6, 6, 6, 6 scores the maximum 30 points).

Cheerio Five of a kind in any value, 1 through 6. Always scores 50 points.

Cheerio combinations

Ones (score 3)

Twos (score 4)

Threes (score 9)

Fours (score 12)

Fives (score 15)

Sixes (score 18)

Little straight (score 20)

Big straight (score 25)

Full house (score 16)

Big hand (score 28)

Cheerio (score 50)

Cheerio score sheet

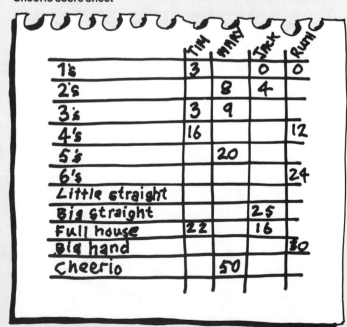

	TIM	MARY	JACK	RUTH
1's	3		0	0
2's		8	4	
3's	3	9		
4's	16			12
5's		20		
6's				24
Little straight				
Big straight			25	
Full house	22		16	
Big hand				30
Cheerio		50		

GENERAL

This game has many similarities with Cheerio (p. 94). It is a major gambling game in Puerto Rico, but can also be played without stakes for amusement only.

Equipment:

1) five dice;

2) a score sheet showing combinations and players' names.

Players Any number may play, either singly or in partnership.

Objective Each player or partnership aims to win by scoring a "big general" (see five of a kind) or by scoring most points for the 10 General combinations. As in Cheerio, each combination may be scored only once in a game.

Order of play is determined by a preliminary round in which each player rolls the dice once. The player with the lowest spot score shoots first, the player with the next lowest score second, and so on.

Play A game normally consists of 10 turns ("frames") per player, but ends immediately if any player rolls a big general. Each player may roll the dice once, twice, or three times during each frame.

If, on his first throw, he fails to make a combination that he wishes to score, he may pick up all or any of the dice for a second roll. But the value of any combination he now rolls is diminished, and a big general now becomes a small general. After his second roll he may again, if he wishes, pick up all or any of the dice for a third roll. After the third roll, he must state which combination he is scoring.

Play then passes to the next player.

If the game runs its full course of ten frames, the player with the highest score wins.

Aces wild "Aces" (1s) may be counted as 2 or as 6 if one or both of these are needed to complete a straight – but not as any other number or for any other purpose.

Combinations

Numbers 1 through 6 Score their spot values.

Straight Either 1, 2, 3, 4, 5 or 2, 3, 4, 5, 6 scores 25 points if made on the first throw, but only 20 points if made on the second or third throw. Only one straight is scored.

Full house Scores 35 points on first throw, but only 30 points on the second or third throw.

Four of a kind Scores 45 points on first throw, but only 40 points on the second or third throw.

Five of a kind If made on the first throw, it ranks as the "big general" and immediately wins the game. Made on the second or third throw it is a "small general" and scores 60 points.

Payment When General is played as a gambling game, the winner receives from each of the other players the difference between his own and that player's point score. The monetary value per point is settled before the game.

DOUBLE CAMEROON

This game is similar to General but has important differences.
It is played with ten dice.
After a player has rolled them for the third time in each turn,
he divides them into two groups of five, and then allots the
score of each group to one of the ten combinations in the game.
So in the course of a game, each player has five turns.

Combinations

Numbers 1 through 6 Score their spot values.

Full house Scores its spot value.

Little Cameroon (1, 2, 3, 4, 5) scores 21 points.

Big Cameroon (2, 3, 4, 5, 6) scores 30 points.

Five of a kind Scores 50 points.

(Unlike in General, a score does not decrease if the
combination is made on a second or third throw.)

©DIAGRAM

Dice games: gambling

Poker die faces

These dice games can be played for amusement using counters or matchsticks as stakes, but they are generally better known as private gambling games played for money.

POKER DICE
This game, for two or more players, is usually played for a "pot" (pool) to which each player contributes at the start of each round.
Equipment Five dice are used, and these are normally special poker dice marked with a, k, q, j, 10, 9. The game may also be played with standard dice, with 1 ranking highest, then 6, 5, 4, 3, 2; or alternatively with 6 ranking highest, followed by 5, 4, 3, 2, and with aces wild.
Objective Players aim to make the best possible poker "hand" in not more than two rolls of the dice (or three rolls of the dice in an older form of the game).
Rank of hands is as follows:
1) five of a kind (highest rank);
2) four of kind;
3) straight (an unbroken sequence, either a, k, q, j, 10 or k, q, j, 10, 9);
4) full house (three of a kind and one pair);
5) three of a kind;
6) two pairs;
7) one pair;
8) no pair (the lowest rank – five unmatched values not in sequence).
Hands of the same rank need not tie. They compare as follows.
1) Five of a kind: five aces rank higher than five kings, and so on.
2) Four of a kind: as for five of a kind.
3) Straight: a, k, q, j, 10 beats k, q, j, 10, 9.
4) Full house: the threes decide, with a, a, a, j, j ranking higher than k, k, k, q, q, and so on.
5) Three of a kind: three aces rank higher than three kings, and so on.
6) Two pairs: the highest pair wins.
7) One pair: the higher pair wins.
8) No pair: the highest die wins.
The odd dice in any combination are used by some players as tiebreakers. For example, a, a, q, q, j (two pairs) would rank above a, a, q, q, 9. It is more common, however, for the odd dice to be disregarded, and if two or more players make equal-ranking hands they must roll again.

Order of play is decided by a preliminary round in which each player throws a single die. The highest scorer throws first in the first round. The second highest scorer sits to his left, and so on. Play goes clockwise and each round is commenced by a different player in turn.

Play Each player rolls in turn. He may accept the hand produced by his first throw, or, if he wishes, he may pick up one or more of the dice and roll them again in an attempt to improve his hand. (Some players choose to limit to three the number of dice that may be picked up.) The outcome of his second throw completes his hand and the dice are passed to the next player.

The highest hand in the round wins. If there are only two players, the best two out of three rounds, or the best three out of five, win.

Aces wild Poker dice may be played with aces "wild," ie they may rank normally or count as any other value the player wishes. For example, a throw of q, q, q, q, a could rank as five queens; a throw of a, a, a, a, j could rank as five jacks; or a throw of k, q, j, a, 9 could rank as a straight.

Rank

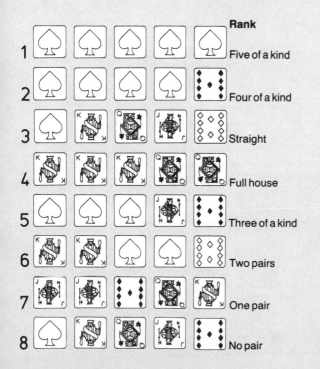

1 Five of a kind
2 Four of a kind
3 Straight
4 Full house
5 Three of a kind
6 Two pairs
7 One pair
8 No pair

INDIAN DICE

Indian dice, a popular game in the United States, is very
similar to Poker dice (p. 98). It is played with five ordinary
dice, with 6 ranking highest and 1s ("aces") wild. Any number
of players may take part.

Objective Players aim to make the highest poker hand. The
hands rank as in Poker dice except that straights do not count.

Play begins after a preliminary round to decide the order of
play. The highest scorer becomes first shooter, the second
highest scorer sits to his left, and so on.

The player who shoots first may have up to three throws to
establish his hand. He may "stand" on his first throw, or pick
up all or any of the dice for a second throw. He may then stand
on that throw or pick up all or any of the dice again for a third
and final throw.

No subsequent player in the round or "leg" may make more
throws than the first player.

A game usually consists of two legs, with the winners of each
leg playing off if stakes are involved.

If there are only two players, the victor is the one who wins two
out of three legs.

Rank

Five of a kind

Four of a kind

Full house

Three of a kind

Two pairs

Pair

No pair

©DIAGRAM

LIAR DICE

The essence of this game, for three or more players, is deception!

Equipment The game may be played with five ordinary dice, 1s (aces) ranking high, or with poker dice. Each player also needs three betting chips (or counters).

Rank of hands is as in Poker dice (p. 98). Hands of the same rank are also compared as in Poker dice, but in Liar dice the odd dice are always used as tiebreakers if necessary.

Order of play is established by a preliminary round in which each player throws a single die. The highest scorer becomes first shooter. The second highest scorer sits to his left, and so on.

Start of play rotates one player to the left after each game.

Play Each player puts three betting chips in front of him. The first shooter then throws all the dice, keeping them covered so that the other players cannot see them.

He declares his throw in detail, eg "full house, queens on nines" (q, q, q, 9, 9). This call may be true or false and it is for the player to his left to accept or challenge the call. The declaring player may call below the actual value of his throw if he wishes.

If the player to his left thinks the caller is lying and challenges him, all the dice are exposed. If the caller has in fact lied, he must pay one chip into the pot; but if the value of the throw is equal to or higher than the call, it is the challenger who pays into the pot. In either case, it now becomes the challenger's turn to throw.

If the player to the left of the caller accepts the call, he takes over the dice (still unexposed). He may now throw all, any, or none of them, but must say truthfully how many he throws. Keeping the dice covered, he then makes his call, which must be higher than the call he accepted – but it need not be a higher rank of hand; it can be a higher hand of the same rank. His call may be accepted or challenged by the player to his left, and so play continues round the table.

When a player has lost all three of his chips, he is out of the game. Play continues until all but one of the players has been knocked out. The survivor is the winner and collects the pot.

CROWN AND ANCHOR

This is a fast game in which any number of players play against a banker.

Equipment Three special dice are used, each marked with a crown, anchor, heart, spade, diamond, and club.

These symbols also appear on the layout, which is marked on a cloth or board set in front of the banker.

Play Each player puts a wager on one or more of the symbols on the layout. The banker then throws the three dice from a cup and pays out on the result of the throw.

The usual odds are evens on singles, 2 to 1 on pairs, and 3 to 1 on three of a kind. The advantage always lies with the banker.

Crown and anchor

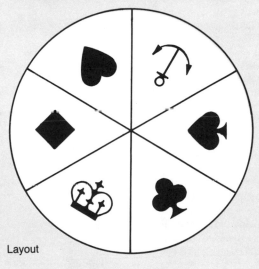

Layout

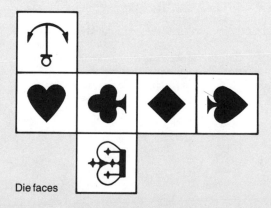

Die faces

TWENTY-ONE

Twenty-one

21 points scored

This game is based on the card game Blackjack. Any number of players may take part.

Equipment: one die, and a supply of chips or counters for each player.

Objective Players try to score 21 points.

Play Each player puts one chip into the pool or kitty.

Then each player in turn rolls the dice as many times as he likes in an attempt to make a total of 21 or a number near but below it. If, for example, a player's first four throws are 4, 6, 2, 6 (totaling 18), it would probably be safer to "stick" on this number than risk a fifth throw that might take his total over 21. If his total does exceed 21, he "goes bust" and is eliminated from that round.

Players often agree on a minimum number, eg 16, at which sticking is permissible.

When all the players have thrown, the player with 21, or the number nearest to it, takes the pool, and a new round commences. If two or more players have the same score, the pool may either be shared or decided by a play-off.

Start of play rotates one player to the left with each round.

PAR

Par

24 points scored

Par can be played with any number of players, but is best played with six or seven.

Equipment:
1) five dice;
2) chips or counters representing the betting unit.

Objective Each player tries to achieve a total score of 24 or more by throwing the dice.

Order of play is established by a preliminary round in which the highest scoring player becomes the first shooter. The second highest scorer throws next, and so on.

Play The first shooter rolls all five dice. He may "stand" on that throw if it makes 24 or more, or he may make up to four more throws in an attempt to improve his score, throwing first four, then three, then two, and then one of the dice.

If he makes 24, he neither gains nor loses. If he fails to make 24, he pays each other player the difference between his score and 24.

If he makes more than 24, the difference between his score and 24 becomes his "point." For example, if he has thrown 26, he has a point of 2. He then throws all five dice again (but once only), and for every 2 that appears he collects two chips from each of the other players. (If 6 was his point, he would collect six chips for every 6 that appeared.)

THIRTY-SIX

This is a game for any number of players, using only one die.
Order of play is determined by a preliminary round in which
each player throws a single die. The lowest scorer becomes first
shooter, the next-lowest second shooter, and so on.
Each player puts an agreed stake in the pot.

Objective Players aim to score a total of 36 points. Any player
scoring more than 36, however, is eliminated from the game.
The winner is the player with the score nearest 36 points and he
takes the pot.

Play Each player in turn rolls the dice once, totaling his score
round by round. As he nears 36 he may choose to stand on his
score in the hope that no other player will score nearer 36.
In the event of a tie, the pot is divided.

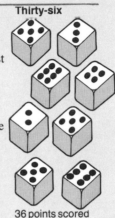

Thirty-six

36 points scored

HELP YOUR NEIGHBOR

Help your neighbor, for two to six players, is usually played for
small stakes or just for fun with counters.

Equipment:
1) three dice and a dice cup;
2) betting chips or counters for each player.

Objective Each player tries to be the first to get rid of all his
counters. The winner takes the pot formed during the course
of play.

Order of play is determined by a preliminary round in which
each player throws a single die. This throw also decides which
number(s) each player takes. The highest scoring player in the
preliminary round becomes the first shooter and takes the
number 1. The second-highest scorer becomes the second
shooter and, taking the number 2, sits to the left of player
number 1, and so on.

If there are only two players, the higher scoring player takes
numbers 1, 2, and 3, and the other the remainder. With three
players, the numbers are paired off: 1 and 2, 3 and 4, 5 and 6.
With four players, numbers 5 and 6 are "dead," with five
players, 6 is dead.

Play begins with each player placing ten counters in front of
him, and then proceeds in a clockwise direction from the first
shooter.

Each player in turn throws all three dice once. Any player
whose number comes up in that throw has to put one counter
into the pot for each of his own numbers thrown.

For example, if the first shooter throws 4, 6, 6, the player who
has number 4 puts one counter into the pot; and the player with
number 6 puts two counters into the pot.

When the pot has been taken by the winning player (the first to
lose all his ten counters), the next game is started by the player
to the left of the first shooter in the previous game, and he now
takes the number 1.

©DIAGRAM

BUCK DICE

This is a game for any number of players, using three dice.
Preliminaries Order of play is established by a round in which each player throws a single die. The highest scorer becomes first shooter. The lowest scorer then throws one die to determine a point number for the first game.
Objective Players aim to score a "buck" or "game" (exactly 15 points). On achieving this score the player withdraws from the game, which continues until one player is left: the loser.
Play Each player in turn takes the three dice, and each goes on throwing for as long as he throws the point number on one or more of the dice. As soon as he makes a throw that does not contain the point number, play passes to the next player.
Each player keeps count, aloud, of the number of times he has thrown the point number. Each occasion counts one point.
If, when he is nearing 15 points, a player makes a throw that carries his score beyond 15, the throw does not count and he must roll again.
Some throws rate special values. Three point numbers in one throw ("big buck" or "general") count 15 points. A player making this throw withdraws immediately from the game irrespective of any score he has made previously.
Three of a kind that are not point numbers count as a "little buck" and score five points.
Variation Some players follow the rule that when a player has scored 13 points, he rolls with only two dice; and when 14 is reached, with only one die.
Continuing play Start of play rotates one player to the left after each game. The right to determine the point number also rotates in this way, so that it is always with the player to the starter's right.

HOOLIGAN

Hooligan is played with five dice and a throwing cup. Any number of players may take part. Hooligan is a point-scoring game; the winner is the player making the highest total score.
Preliminaries Aside from a preliminary round to determine the order of play, a scoresheet must be prepared. This sheet should have a column divided into seven sections marked 1, 2, 3, 4, 5, 6, and H (hooligan), against which the score of each player can be recorded.
The game consists of seven rounds, each player throwing in turn. A turn ("frame") consists of three throws.
After his first throw, each player declares which of the numbers on the scoresheet (including H) he is shooting for (ie his point number). He must shoot for H on his final turn, if he has not previously done so. "Hooligan" is a straight, either 1, 2, 3, 4, 5 or 2, 3, 4, 5, 6, and counts 20 points.
If he wishes, a player need not declare a point number after his first throw. In this case he picks up all five dice, shoots again, and then declares his point number; but this counts as his

second throw, so he has only one throw left in this frame.
If he declares his point number after his first throw, he puts
aside all dice bearing that number, then throws a second time
with the remaining dice. Once more, any dice bearing the point
number are put aside. He then makes his third and final throw
with the remaining dice.

Scoring A player's score is determined by mutiplying his point
number by the number of times that he has made that number.
For example, if he were throwing for 4s and made three of
them, his score would be 12.

If a player throws the maximum of five point numbers in his
first or second throw, he counts this score and plays the
remaining throw(s) of the frame with five dice, setting aside
any dice bearing the point number after the first throw if two
throws are involved. The point numbers made on these throws
are added to the five made on the first throw.

A player has only one turn to shoot for each point number. He
must choose a different point number for each frame.

Sometimes games of Hooligan are operated by a banker.
Players play against the bank, and must pay to enter the game.
The odds and rules of such games vary from place to place.

Hooligan score card

Point number	K	J	P	T
1	2	4	1	
2			6	4
3	12	9	3	9
4	12			16
5		10	25	15
6	6	24	18	24
H	20	20		

ACES

This is a game for any number of players. It is usually played for a pot and the winner is the player throwing the last ace (1) with the last die.

Equipment Each player requires five dice and a throwing cup.

Order of play is determined by a preliminary round in which each player tries to throw the highest poker hand (see p. 98). Numbers rank: 1 (high), 6, 5, 4, 3, 2 (low).

The player with the highest ranking hand becomes first shooter. The other players then sit in clockwise order in accordance with the hands they have thrown. Ties are resolved by further throws.

Play The first shooter throws his dice and transfers to the center of the table any 1s that come up. Any 2s in his throw are passed to the player to his left, and any 5s to the player to his right.

He continues throwing until he fails to make any of these numbers on a throw, or until he has disposed of all his dice. Although he may have no dice left, he is still in the game, since he may later receive dice from the players to his left and right.

Play continues in a clockwise direction around the table until all the dice except one have been transferred to the center.

The winner (or loser) is the player who throws the last ace with that die.

SHIP, CAPTAIN, MATE, AND CREW

This game may be played by any number of people. Five dice are used.

Objective Players try to throw 6 (the ship), 5 (the captain), and 4 (the mate) in that order and within three throws.

Order of play is established by a preliminary round, in which each player throws a single die. The highest scorer becomes first shooter. Play then moves in a clockwise direction around the table.

Start of play rotates one player to the left after each game.

Play The players each put an agreed stake into the pot.

Each player in turn is allowed not more than three throws of the dice.

If he makes a 6 and 5 on his first throw, he can set those dice aside. In his second throw he then rolls the other three dice hoping to make a 4. If, however, he makes a 6 and 4 on his first throw, only the 6 can be set aside, and the remaining four dice must be rolled again for a 5 and a 4. (Similar rules for setting dice aside apply to second-round throws.)

If the player makes 6, 5, and 4 in his three throws, the remaining two dice (the crew) are totaled as his score. But if he makes 6, 5, and 4 in his first or second throw, he may, if he wishes, use the remaining throws to try to improve the total of the crew dice.

The pot goes to the player with the highest score in the round. A tie nullifies all scores and a further round has to be played.

ENGLISH HAZARD

This is a centuries old game played with two dice and a
throwing cup. Any number may play.

Play begins when a first shooter, called the "caster," puts his
stake in a circle marked on the center of the table. Any other
player wishing to wager also puts his stake in the center and the
caster accepts his challenge by knocking the table with the
throwing cup.

When all betting has finished, the caster throws the dice to
establish a "main point," a total of either 5, 6, 7, 8, or 9. If he
throws any other total it is "no main" and he must continue
throwing until a main point comes up.

Having established a main point, he throws the dice again to
establish a "chance point" (a total of either 4, 5, 6, 7, 8, 9, or 10
– but not the same number as the main point number).

When he throws to establish the chance point, the caster
immediately loses the bet if he throws an "out." An out is any
throw of 2 or 3 (called a "crab"); or a throw of 12 if the main
point is 5, 6, 8, or 9.

The caster wins, however, if he throws a "nick." He makes a
nick if he throws an 11 when the main point is a 7, or if he
throws a 12 when the main point is a 6 or an 8. If he throws the
main point itself, this also counts as a nick and he wins
immediately.

If he establishes a chance point, he then continues throwing. If
he throws the chance point again, he wins the bet. But if he
throws the main point again, he loses.

Special combinations Highest first
2, 1, 1*
2, 2, 1
4, 2, 1
6, 6, 6
5, 5, 5
4, 4, 4
3, 3, 3
2, 2, 2
1, 1, 1*
3, 3, 6
3, 3, 5
3, 3, 4
3, 3, 2
3, 3, 1
1, 1, 6
1, 1, 5
1, 1, 4
1, 1, 3
3, 2, 1
4, 3, 2
5, 4, 3
6, 5, 4
*See text

BIDOU

This game can be played by any number of players, but procedures differ according to the number of players. The version for two players is described below. The multihand version is described on p. 112.

Equipment Each player needs three dice and a throwing cup. The game also requires a supply of chips or counters.

Objective Players aim to get rid of their chips by betting on combinations of dice thrown. The last player still holding chips is the loser. If desired, he pays each other player a previously agreed amount.

Bidou combinations There are 22 special combinations, given in ranking order in the table, left. The combination 2,1,1 is sometimes referred to as "bidou" and 2,2,1 as "bidé."

Although 2,1,1 appears first in the table, this combination is beaten by 1,1,1. In all other cases, however, the ranking of 1,1,1 is as given in the table, ie below the other three-of-a-kind combinations.

The remaining 34 possible combinations are ranked according to the spot total, eg 6,3,2(=11) beats 4,3,1(=8). All of these combinations rank below the 22 special combinations.

TWO-HAND BIDOU

Two-hand bidou is played in games made up of three separate rounds. The loser is the player losing at least two of the rounds. (Also see the general rules given above.)

Preliminary round Only nine betting chips are used. They are placed on the table between the two players.

Each player then throws a die once. The player making the higher score becomes "captain" (first shooter) for the first hand.

Play: first round The captain takes his turn first, followed by his opponent. In his turn each player may throw the dice up to three times to achieve the best possible score.

In each throw he must throw all the dice, keeping them concealed beneath his dice cup. He must declare the number of throws he makes.

When both players have thrown, betting on that hand begins.

Opening the betting If both players have made the same number of throws, or if the captain has made fewer throws than his opponent, then the captain bets or passes first.

If the captain has made more throws than his opponent, the latter becomes captain and makes the first bet, or passes.

Betting limits The maximum bet or raise is one chip.

Betting procedure Players use the center chips for betting until these run out. As each player states his bet, he moves the appropriate number of chips away from the center pile and slightly toward him.

When all the center chips have been used up, players may use any chips they have received during the round, moving them slightly toward the center as they use them.

Betting A player need not have a strong hand to make a bet; he may choose to bluff his opponent.

If both players pass, the hand ends. Once one player has bet, the other must call (ie bet an equal amount), raise (ie bet a greater amount), or drop out. If one player raises, the other must call, reraise, or drop out. The betting continues until one player has called or dropped out.

Outcome If one player calls the other, both show their dice. All chips bet are then taken by the loser. The winner becomes the next captain.

If one player drops out, he must take one penalty chip (from the center if possible). All other chips bet are returned to their positions before the hand began. The player who has not dropped out is the next captain.

If both players pass, neither takes any chips, and the captaincy changes for the next hand.

Play: second round Play is exactly as in the first round, except that on any throw a player may put aside any dice whose score he wishes to keep, and throw only the remainder. The dice put aside must remain hidden from the opponent.

Having put aside dice on one throw, a player may still throw all the dice on his third throw of that turn.

Play: third round Play reverts to the rules for the first round.

"Open throw" occurs when one player has eight chips, leaving one chip with his opponent or in the center.

The player with one or no chips is then entitled to not more than three throws of the dice to make the highest possible exposed combination. (Whether he must rethrow all the dice or may select depends on the rules for the round they are playing.)

His opponent then throws in similar fashion and if he loses the throws he takes the single chip and so loses the game. If the single-chip player loses, he takes one chip from his opponent and normal play is resumed.

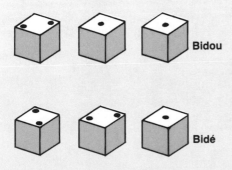

Bidou

Bidé

MULTIHAND BIDOU

When three or more players take part no chips are placed in the center of the table. Instead, each player begins with six chips. (Also see the general rules given on p. 110.)

Captaincy A preliminary round decides who is first captain, as in Two-hand bidou. Play begins with the captain and proceeds in a clockwise direction. The winner of each round becomes captain of the next.

If all players pass, the player to the left of the captain of that round becomes captain of the next.

Play is as in Two-hand bidou. All players must keep their dice hidden from the others until betting has closed.

Opening the betting If all players have made the same number of throws, the same player remains captain. Otherwise, the player making the fewest throws and nearest to the original captain's left becomes captain.

Betting limits The maximum bet is three chips, the maximum raise two chips.

Betting procedure Each player uses his own store of chips, and places his bets in the center of the table to form a common pot.

Betting situations

1) On a showdown between two or more players, the loser collects all chips still in the pot.

2) Players dropping out without betting receive no penalty.

3) For players dropping out after betting at least once, the following rules apply:

the first in a round to do so must take from the pot whichever amount he has put in on that hand, plus the same amount for each player still betting, plus one penalty chip;

each player dropping out thereafter on that round must take one penalty chip.

If the players remaining have bet unequal amounts, whichever number of chips is left in the pot is called or raised by the next player in turn.

4) If all players drop out after a player has raised, any chips left in the pot after penalties have been taken are returned to the raising player.

5) A player who bets his last chips has the right to stay in for the showdown, even if other players take the betting further. If he loses, he receives back his bet and the equivalent amount from each showdown player. Other chips still in the pot are returned to the players who bet them.

6) If there is a tie when a player has bet his last chips, that player takes back his bet, and the other players take back all their chips except one each. The remaining chips are removed from the game. If there is a tie in any other circumstance, each showdown player takes back one chip, and any other chips in the pot are removed from the game.

7) If only one player bets on a round and all the others pass, he can discard one chip even if it is his last.

8) If only two players are left with chips, these two continue until one has lost. Should the two players have more than nine chips between them, each discards one chip whenever he bets and is not called, until the players have a total of nine chips between them. The two then fight out the game as in Two-hand bidou.

9) Any player who passes after betting has begun automatically drops out of that round.

Poor fish is a variation that requires all players to expose their last throws if all have passed. The player with the highest throw is the "poor fish" and receives one chip from each of the other players.

MONTEVIDEO

This game requires three dice, a throwing cup, and chips or counters for each player.

The objective is to win all the chips.

Players Three or more players can take part.

Ante At the start of play each player has six chips. In each round he antes one chip into the pot before throwing the dice.

Betting After the dice have been thrown, betting proceeds as in Bidou.

Play is as in Bidou, with the same combinations, but at showdown, the highest combination wins the pot.

If the game reaches a stage where only two players have any chips, it is speeded up by increasing, round by round, the number of chips each must ante into the pot, to a maximum of six. If there are many players, the same procedure should be followed for the last three players.

Any player may, if he wishes, open the betting by "betting the pot," ie stay in without putting up chips. When this happens, any other player – even if he has already passed – may call the pot. The bet may, of course, be raised in the usual way.

Throws

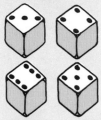

Natural throws

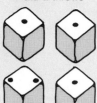

Crap throws

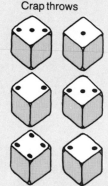

Point throws

CRAPS

Craps developed in the early nineteenth century, when black Americans adapted the game of English hazard (p. 109). Today, the money wagered at Craps in the United States alone makes it the biggest gambling game in history. Its attractions are its speed of action and large element of participation; yet its essence is that of a mathematical game of numbers and odds. Here we describe the private form of the game, in which players arrange bets among themselves.

Basic equipment is:
1) two matched dice;
2) a playing surface, preferably edged by a wall or backboard;
3) betting chips or cash.

Players: any number over two.

General procedure

a) Any player by common agreement may shoot the dice first; thereafter the dice are passed around in a clockwise direction.

b) A new player may join a game at any stage and sit anywhere in the circle of players – provided that the players raise no objection at the time. He takes his turn in the normal way when the dice reach him.

c) A player may leave a game at any time, regardless of his gains or losses.

Throw of the dice The shooter shakes the dice in his closed hand and throws them onto the playing area. If there is a backboard, it is usually ruled that the dice must rebound from it before they come to rest.

The two numbers face uppermost when the dice come to rest, added together, give the result of the throw.

Basic play The first throw in a shooter's turn is called a "come-out" throw as is the first throw after each time the dice win or lose.

If on a come-out throw, the shooter throws a 7 or 11 he has thrown a "natural": the dice "pass" (ie win) immediately. The shooter may keep the dice for another come-out throw.

If on a come-out throw, the shooter throws a 2, 3, or 12, he has thrown a "craps": the dice "miss out" or "crap out" (ie lose) immediately. The shooter may keep the dice for another come-out throw.

If on a come-out throw, the shooter throws a 4, 5, 6, 8, 9, or 10, he has thrown a "point": for the dice to win he must "make the point," ie throw the same number again before he throws a 7 – no other numbers matter.

If the shooter throws the same number again before he throws a 7, the dice pass (win). The shooter may keep the dice for another come-out throw.

If he throws a 7 before he throws the number again, the dice miss out or "seven out" (lose). The shooter must give the dice to the next player in turn.

© DIAGRAM

Giving up the dice If the shooter sevens out, he must give up the dice.

He may also, if he wishes, pass the dice if:

a) he has not thrown the dice in his turn; or

b) he has not thrown a "decision:" ie a natural, a craps, or a pass on a point.

Change of dice If more than one pair of dice is being used, any player may call for the dice in use to be changed at any time. This is called a "box-up." The change is made immediately before the next come-out throw.

Betting and settlement of bets

Center bet On each come-out throw, the shooter places the amount he wishes to bet in the center of the playing area. He announces the amount, saying "I'll shoot . . ."

Any of the other players then "fade" (accept) whatever part of the total they wish, by placing that amount in the center alongside the shooter's bet.

Unless previously agreed otherwise, the fading of center bets is in no set order and by no fixed amount. Players simply place money in the center until all the shooter's bet has been faded, or until no one wishes to place any further amount. (It is sometimes agreed that any player who faded the entire center bet on the preceding come-out, and lost, can claim the right to fade the entire present bet.)

If the center bet is not entirely faded by the players, the shooter may either:

a) withdraw the part not faded; or

b) call off all bets, by saying "No bet."

Players may not fade more than the shooter's center bet; but if the players show eagerness to bet more, the shooter can decide to increase the amount of his bet.

Settlement of center bet If the dice miss out (lose), the players who faded the center bet each receive back their money together with the equivalent amount of the center bet.

If the dice pass (win), all the money in the center is collected by the shooter.

The center bet is therefore an even money (1 to 1) bet. Since the probability of the dice passing is in fact 970 occasions in 1980, the shooter has 1.414% disadvantage on the center bet.

Other bets are known as side bets. Like the center bet, they must be arranged before the dice are thrown, not while they are rolling. Note that the shooter himself may make any of the side bets he wishes, in addition to the center bet.

Right and wrong bettors All these bets require agreement between two players. One is the "wrong" bettor: he "lays" odds that the dice will not pass or will not make the number(s) bet on.

The other is the "right" bettor: he "takes" odds that the dice will pass or will make the number(s) bet on.

The bet and odds may be proposed by either the right or the wrong bettor; in practice, however, more experienced players tend to be "wrong" bettors and propose odds that the less experienced player will "take."

Flat bet This is a normal bet on whether a shooter's come-out throw will pass, and is made as a side bet between two players (of which one may be the shooter). Flat bets occur especially if one player has faded the entire bet.

Point bet If the shooter throws a point on his come-out throw, players may bet on whether he will "make the point." (The center and flat bets still remain to be settled in the same way.)

Come bet This is a bet on whether the dice will pass – but treating the next throw of the dice, after the bet, as the bet's come-out throw (when in fact the shooter is throwing for a point).

For a "come bet," one player lays odds that the dice will not come, while another player takes odds that they will.

The first throw of the dice after the bet is the "come-out" throw for the come bet. If the shooter rolls a 7, he sevens out on his point – but for the come bet the dice "come," because a 7 on a come-out throw is a natural.

Similarly, 11 is a natural for the come bet, and 2, 3, or 12 is craps – the dice "don't come." (But all these leave the center bet undecided, because they are neither the point number nor a 7.)

If the shooter rolls a point number on the come-out throw for the come bet, this number becomes the point for the come bet. The outcome then depends, in the usual way, on whether the point or a 7 appears first.

If the shooter makes the point on his center bet without making the come bet point, the players making the come bet can agree to withdraw the bet or to continue the number sequence into the shooter's next turn.

Hardway bet (or gag bet) This is a bet on whether the shooter will throw a certain number "the hard way" – ie as the sum of a double. Hardway bets can be placed on 4 (2+2), 6 (3+3), 8 (4+4), or 10 (5+5).

The right bettor loses if a 7 is thrown, or if the number bet on is thrown any other way before being thrown as a double.

Off-number bet Two players agree to bet on any number they choose. The right bettor wins if the shooter throws the number before he throws a 7. Bettors may call off this bet before a "decision" is reached.

Proposition bet refers to any other kind of side bet agreed upon – limited only by players' imaginations! Such bets are always offered at odds designed to give the proposing player an advantage. There are two main categories:

a) bets on whether the specified number(s) will appear within a certain number of rolls after the bet: "one-roll bets," two-roll bets," "three-roll bets;" or

b) bets on whether the specified number(s) will appear before other specified number(s) or before a 7.

In each case, the specified number(s) bet on may be:

a) a certain number to be thrown in any way;

b) a certain number to be thrown in a specified way;

c) any one of a group of numbers (eg a group of specified numbers, odd numbers, numbers below 7, etc).

Table 1: True odds for bets on or between single numbers

Number on dice	Ways of making (**a**)	Single roll (**b**)	Before a 7 (**c**)
12	1	35-1	6-1
11	2	17-1	3-1
10	3	11-1	2-1
9	4	8-1	3-2
8	5	31-5	6-5
7	6	5-1	—
6	5	31-5	6-5
5	4	8-1	3-2
4	3	11-1	2-1
3	2	17-1	3-1
2	1	35-1	6-1

Table 2: Hardway bets

Bet	Ways of making (**a**)	Other ways of making (**b**)	Ways of making a 7 (**c**)
4	1 (2+2)	2	6
6	1 (3+3)	4	6
8	1 (4+4)	4	6
10	1 (5+5)	2	6

True odds Table 1 gives the true odds for various bets on or between single numbers, while table 2 gives the true odds for hardway bets.

True odds for other common one-roll bets are:

a) against any specified pair (eg 3+3): 35-1;

b) against any specified combination of two different numbers (eg 6+5): 17-1;

c) against any craps (2, 3, or 12): 8-1.

Notes on table 1

a) Number of different combinations of two die faces that will give the number. Total of all possible combinations is 36.

b) Odds against making a number on a single roll – calculated by comparing the number of ways of making the number (x) with the number of ways of making another number (36−x).

c) Odds against throwing the number before throwing a 7.

d) Odds against making the higher number before the lower number (eg 12 before 4: 3-1). Reverse the odds to give odds against making the lower number before the higher (eg 4 before 12: 1-3).

Notes on table 2

a) Number of ways of making the specified number "the hard way."

b) Number of other ways of making the same total number as the hardway number bet on.

Comparative
odds (**d**)
12
2-1 **11**
3-1 3-2 **10**
4-1 2-1 4-3 **9**
5-1 5-2 5-3 5-4 **8**
6-1 3-1 2-1 3-2 6-5 **7**
5-1 5-2 5-3 5-4 1-1 5-6 **6**
4-1 2-1 4-3 1-1 4-5 2-3 4-5 **5**
3-1 3-2 1-1 3-4 3-5 1-2 3-5 3-4 **4**
2-1 1-1 2-3 1-2 2-5 1-3 2-5 1-2 2-3 **3**
1-1 1-2 1-3 1-4 1-5 1-6 1-5 1-4 1-3 1-2 **2**

Total ways *of losing* (**d**)	*Odds against hardway bet*
8	8-1
10	10-1
10	10-1
8	8-1

c) Number of ways of making a 7.
d) Total number of ways of losing (**b+c**).
Irregularities at private craps include the following. (The shooter must throw again after a void throw.)
1) If the playing area has been specified at the start of the game, the throw is void if either die rolls out of the area.
2) If either die comes to rest under any object on the playing area or tilted on an obstruction, so that it is not clear which of its faces is uppermost, any agreed neutral player or bystander is nominated to decide the question. If he cannot decide, the throw is void.
3) When there is a backboard and neither die hits it, the roll is void. If only one die hits the board the roll counts, but the shooter must be reprimanded. If it occurs again, the other players may designate a player to complete the shooter's turn for him. They may also bar the shooter from shooting for the rest of the game.
4) If either die hits any object or person after hitting the backboard, the roll is counted.
5) A player may not knock either or both dice aside on the roll and call "No dice." If he does this once, the throw counts as it finally shows; if he repeats it, he may be barred from shooting for the rest of the game.

©DIAGRAM

Dominoes

Games with dominoes are played in many countries all over the world. They are now particularly popular in Latin America. It is thought that dominoes may have been brought from China to Europe in the fourteenth century. Certainly domino games were played in Italy in the eighteenth century. In most Western games players add matching dominoes to a pattern or "layout" formed in the center of the table.

Players Some domino games are for two players only. Others are for two or more players, playing singly or as partners. Partnerships may be decided:
a) by mutual agreement;
b) by draw – in which case each player draws one domino and the two players with the heaviest dominoes form one pair. Partners sit opposite each other at the table.
Playing area Dominoes can be played on a table or any other flat surface.
The dominoes are rectangular tiles made of wood, ivory, bone, stone, or plastic. They are sometimes called "bones," "stones," or "pieces." A typical size is 1in by 1⅞in by ⅜in. Each domino's face is divided by a central line and each half is either blank or marked with indented spots (sometimes called "pips"). Dominoes with the same number of spots on either side of the central line are called "doubles" or "doublets." A domino is said to be "heavier" than another if it has more spots, or "lighter" if it has fewer spots. So a double 6 is heavier than 6:5.
The standard Western domino set has 28 tiles (with double 6 the heaviest domino). Larger sets have 55 dominoes (double 9 the heaviest) or 91 dominoes (double 12 the heaviest).
Suits Dominoes belong to different suits according to the number of spots on each of their halves. There is a suit for each number, a blank suit, and a doubles suit.
"Mixed number" dominoes belong to two number suits or to a number suit and the blank suit. Doubles belong to one number suit and to the doubles suit.

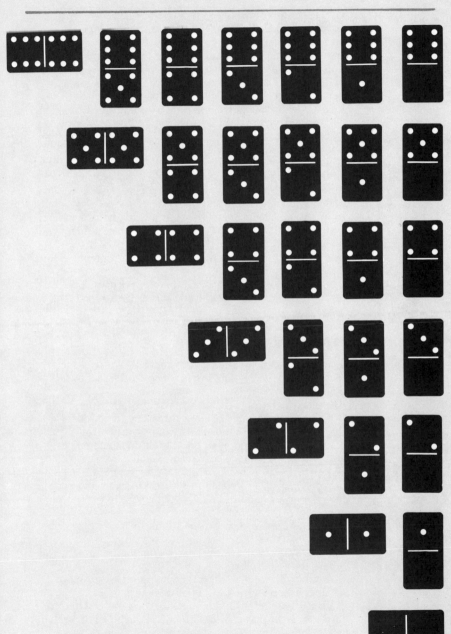

©DIAGRAM

General features of play Western domino games are characterized by the principle of matching and joining dominoes end to end.

In some games, players add dominoes to either end of a line of dominoes. More common are games in which players may build on four ends of a pattern or "layout." In one game, Sebastopol (p. 127), the layout has up to eight ends.

Doubles in most games are placed across the line of dominoes, and in some rules (eg Tiddle-a-wink, p. 125) a player who, for example, plays a double 6 may immediately play another domino with a 6 at one end.

In some games, players use only the dominoes picked up at the start of play, and must miss a turn (called "renouncing," "passing," or "knocking") whenever they are unable to add a matching domino to the pattern. In other games, players must draw a domino from a reserve of downward-facing dominoes (called the "boneyard") whenever they are unable to play a matching domino.

General rules No domino may be withdrawn after it has been added to the layout.

If the wrong domino is accidently placed face up by a player during his turn, it must be played if it matches an end of the layout.

A player is liable to lose the game if:
a) he fails to play within two minutes;
b) he renounces when he is able to play;
c) he plays a domino that does not match (except that the domino is accepted if the error is not noticed before the next domino is played);
d) he makes a false claim that he has played all his dominoes.

Drawing a hand All the dominoes are placed face downward in the center of the table and are then moved around by all the players. Each player now selects the number of dominoes required for the game to be played – usually seven or five.

Except in the few games in which players do not look at their own dominoes (eg Blind Hughie, p. 125) players may keep their dominoes standing on edge on the table, on a rack, or concealed in their hand.

Turns There are several ways of deciding which player is to have the first turn.
a) The player who draws the heaviest domino in a preliminary draw is the first to play.
b) One player draws a domino and his opponent guesses whether its spots add up to an odd or even number.
c) Each player draws his dominoes for the game and the first turn goes to the player with the heaviest double or, if there are no doubles, to the player with the heaviest domino.

In most countries, turns then pass clockwise around the table; in Latin America, the direction of play is counterclockwise.

End of play Games end:
a) when one player has played all his dominoes – after which he calls "domino!" or makes some other recognized signal;
b) when no player can add a matching domino in games with no drawing from the boneyard;
c) in drawing games when no player can add a matching domino and only two dominoes remain in the boneyard.
Result Most games are played to a set number of points.
In some games, the player who first plays all his dominoes claims one point for each spot on his opponents' unplayed dominoes.
If all play is blocked, the player with fewest spots on his unplayed dominoes claims the difference between the number of spots on his own and his opponents' unplayed dominoes.
The hand is replayed if opponents' dominoes have an equal number of spots.
In other games (eg Bergen, p. 130), players score points for adding a domino that makes the two ends of the layout match.

BLOCK DOMINOES

The basic Block dominoes game is usually played by two, three, or four players using a standard set of 28 dominoes. (More players can play with larger sets.) Two players usually play with seven dominoes each, and three or four players with five dominoes each.

The first player begins by laying any of his dominoes face up in the center. Turns then pass around the table – with players adding matching dominoes to either end of the line or missing a turn if none of their dominoes matches.

Spots are counted and points scored after one player has played all his dominoes or the game is blocked so that no one can play (see result, p. 123).

The winner of one hand plays first in the next hand. A game is usually played to 100 or 200 points.

PARTNERSHIP BLOCK DOMINOES

The partnership form of Block dominoes is played by four players with a standard set of 28 dominoes.

Play is the same as for basic Block dominoes except that:

a) players sitting opposite each other form a pair;

b) each player draws seven dominoes at the start of the game;

c) the player with the double 6 starts the first hand by laying it on the table;

d) subsequent hands are started by the winner of the previous hand and this player may play any of his dominoes to start;

e) pairs score jointly – as soon as one player has played all his dominoes, he and his partner score the sum of the spots on each of their opponents' unplayed dominoes.

f) in blocked games, the pair with the lowest total of spots on their unplayed dominoes score the difference between their own and their opponents' total of spots on their unplayed dominoes.

LATIN AMERICAN MATCH DOMINOES

This Latin American form of dominoes is played in the same way as Partnership block dominoes except that:

a) the player with the double 6 always starts;

b) each hand won counts as one game;

c) a match ends when one pair has won 10 hands;

d) a match is scored only if the other pair failed to win five hands – otherwise the match is tied.

DOMINO POOL

The rules of standard Block dominoes apply to Domino pool except that, before each hand, players place equal bets in a pool or pot. The winner of the hand takes all; or if players tie they share the pool between them.

TIDDLE-A-WINK

This is a form of Block dominoes particularly suited to larger groups of people. It is often played with sets of 55 or 91 dominoes.

At the start of each hand the dominoes are shared out equally between the players; any remaining dominoes are left face downward on the table. Play proceeds as for the basic block game except that:

a) the player with the highest double always starts:

b) any player who plays a double may add another domino if he is able;

c) a player who has played all his dominoes calls "tiddle-a-wink."

(Another version of the game is played by six to nine players with three dominoes each from a set of 28 dominoes. In this version, dominoes are added to only one side of the starting double and bets are made as in Domino pool.)

BLIND HUGHIE

Blind Hughie is a Block dominoes game of chance.

If four or five players are playing with 28 dominoes, each draws five dominoes without looking at them; two or three players each draw seven dominoes. Each player lays his dominoes in a line face downward in front of him.

The first player starts play by taking the domino at the left of his line and laying it face up in the center of the table.

Turns then pass around the table. At his turn each player takes the domino at the left of his line and:

a) if it matches an end of the layout, he plays it;

b) if it doesn't match, he lays it face downward at the right of his line.

Play continues until one player finishes his dominoes or until the game is obviously blocked.

DRAW DOMINOES

Draw dominoes is characterized by the drawing of dominoes from the boneyard after the start of play.

Players usually start with seven or five dominoes each. Play is as for basic Block dominoes except that:

a) a player who is unable or unwilling to add a domino to the layout must draw dominoes from the boneyard until he draws one that he is able or willing to play, or until only two dominoes remain in the boneyard;

b) when only two dominoes remain in the boneyard, a player who cannot play a domino must end or miss a turn;

c) a player who draws or looks at an extra domino, or who turns a domino up so that other players see it, must keep that domino.

DOUBLES

This game, also called Maltese cross, is played in the same way as basic Draw dominoes except that:

a) the player with the heaviest double leads;

b) play is on four ends from the starting double;

c) a player may add a mixed number domino only if the double of the number he is matching has already been played (eg in the hand illustrated, a player could add 2:3 to the double 2 but could not play the same domino as 3:2 on the 5:3).

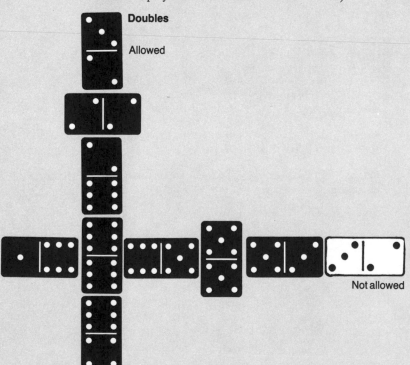

Doubles

Allowed

Not allowed

FORTRESS, SEBASTOPOL, CYPRUS

These are names for two closely related games.

a) The first game, usually called Fortress but sometimes called Sebastopol, is a Block dominoes game for four people with 28 dominoes. Each player draws seven dominoes and the player with the double 6 starts.

Play is on four ends from the double 6, and a domino must be added to each of these ends before play proceeds as for Standard block dominoes.

b) The second game, more usually called Sebastopol but sometimes called Cyprus, is a Draw dominoes game played with a set of 55 dominoes. Four or five players start with nine dominoes each; more players start with seven or five.

Double 9 always starts and if no player has this domino, players should draw one domino in turn until someone draws it. Play is on eight ends from the double 9, and all ends must be opened before a second domino may be added to any end.

Players draw one domino from the boneyard whenever they are unable to add a domino to the layout.

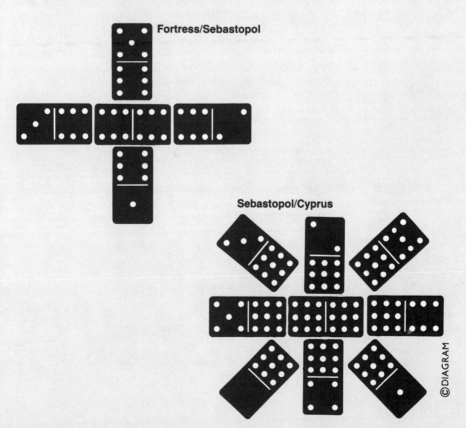

Fortress/Sebastopol

Sebastopol/Cyprus

©DIAGRAM

ALL FIVES

This game, also called Muggins and Fives up, is a form of Draw dominoes that is particularly popular in the United States. It is an interesting game characterized by its scoring system based on multiples of five.

Using a 28-domino set, two, three, or four players start with five dominoes each. The first player may lead with any domino – and scores if its ends add up to five (**a**) or 10. The next player scores if the ends of the layout still add up to five or a multiple of five after he has played (**b**). If he is unable to score, he may play another domino (eg the 1:3, which would make the ends of the layout add up to seven), or may draw one domino from the boneyard.

The first double of the game (**c**) opens up a third end (in this case there would be no score since 6+6+4=16).

The next domino (**d**) opens up the fourth and final end of the layout (and in this case it scores since 6+6+4+4=20). Play continues on four ends of the layout until one player finishes all his dominoes or until the game is blocked.

Scoring In one version of the game, a player scores one point for each spot whenever the layout's ends total five or a multiple of five. The winner of a hand also scores points for the spots on his opponents' remaining dominoes. Game is usually 150 or 200 points.

More usual, however, is the scoring system in which players score one point when the ends total five, two points for 10, three for 15, and so on. The winner of the hand scores a fifth of the face value of his opponents' remaining dominoes. In this version, the game is won by the first player to score exactly 61 points.

If a player fails to claim his points after playing a domino, the first opponent to call "muggins" (or sometimes "fives") claims those points for himself.

The game is sometimes played by partners – in which case the dominoes left in the losing partner's hand are ignored for scoring purposes.

All fives

ALL THREES

All threes, or Threes up, is played in the same way as All fives
but scoring is based on multiples of three.

FIVES AND THREES

This is played in the same way as All fives, but scoring is based
on multiples of both five and three. A player scores one point
for each spot whenever the ends of the layout total five or a
multiple of five, or three or a multiple of three. If a number is a
multiple of both five and three, the player scores two points for
each spot. The winner also scores for each spot on an
opponent's remaining dominoes.

©DIAGRAM

MATADOR

In this unusual draw game, dominoes are played when they make a specified total with a domino on an end of the layout. There are also wild dominoes called "matadors" that can be played at any turn. These are versions of the game for different sizes of domino sets.

When a 28-domino set is used, added dominoes must make a total of seven and the matadors are the 6:1, 5:2, 4:3 (ie those with ends totaling seven), and the 0:0.

For a 55 set the required total is 10 and the matadors are the 9:1, 8:2, 7:3, 6:4, 5:5, and 0:0. (In the game illustrated, play opened with the double 9. This was followed by the 7:3, a matador, and then by three dominoes making totals of 10.) For a 91 set the total is 13 and the matadors are the 12:1, 11:2, 10:3, 9:4, 8:5, 7:6, and 0:0.

Players usually start with seven or five dominoes each, depending on the number of players and the size of set. The player with the heaviest double starts. In this game doubles are not placed crossways and the layout has only two ends.

If a player is unable or unwilling to add a domino, he must draw one domino from the boneyard. When only two dominoes remain in the boneyard, he must play a domino if he is able.

A hand is won by the player who finishes his dominoes or who holds dominoes with the fewest spots if the game is blocked. Points are scored for the spots on an opponent's remaining dominoes, and game is an agreed number of points.

BERGEN

Bergen is a Draw dominoes game in which players score points when there are matching dominoes at the ends of the layout.

Using a set of 28 dominoes, two or three players start with six dominoes each and four players with five dominoes each. The player with the highest double starts. Subsequent play is on two ends only, and a player who is unable or unwilling to add a domino to the layout must draw one domino from the boneyard.

A player scores two points whenever two ends of the layout match (a "double heading") – as, for example the 6:2 and the 3:2 in the illustration (ie before the addition of the double 2). A player scores three points for a "triple heading" – ie when there is a double at one end and a matching domino at the other, as after the addition of the double 2 in the example illustrated.

A player scores two points for winning a hand. If no player finishes his dominoes and the game is blocked, the hand is won by the player holding no doubles, the player with fewest doubles, or the player with fewest spots on his dominoes. Game is usually 10 or 15 points.

Matador

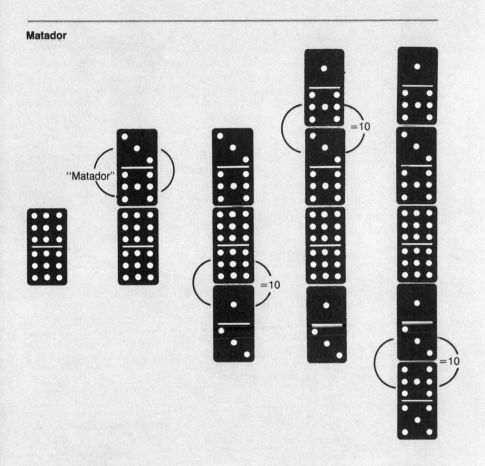

Bergen

©DIAGRAM

Five-spot dominoes

5 points

5 points

5 points

Ten-spot dominoes

10 points

10 points

FORTY-TWO

Forty-two, or Domino rounce, is an adaptation of a card game for play with dominoes. The object is to score points by winning tricks.

The game is usually played by four players with a set of 28 dominoes. Play is usually with partners. Each player draws seven dominoes at the start of a hand.

Bidding is the first stage of play, and tricks are valued as follows:

a) one point for each trick taken;

b) five additional points for a trick containing the 5:0, 4:1, or 3:2 (ie the dominoes with a total of five spots each);

c) 10 additional points for a trick containing the 5:5 or 6:4 (ie ten spots each).

The total tricks value is 42 points (and hence the name of the game).

The player holding the 1:0 domino makes the first bid, and the other players bid in turn. Players may make only one bid and no bid may be for less than 30 points or be lower than a preceding bid. A player may pass if he does not wish to bid.

Taking tricks The player or pair with the highest bid then attempts to take tricks worth the value of their bid (or more). There are eight suits – blanks, the numbers 1 through 6, and doubles. Except when a trump is led, the highest number on a domino determines the suit. The highest bidder plays the first domino and this establishes the trump suit for the hand. If he leads a "mixed number" domino he calls out which number is the trump suit. The other players then play one domino in turn.

Except when a trump or a double is played, a trick goes to the player who played the heaviest domino of the correct suit. A double is the strongest domino of its suit, and can be taken only by a trump. As in card games a higher number in the trump suit takes a lower one.

The player who takes a trick always leads for the next trick. In the examples illustrated:

a) double 3 takes the trick – and scores five extra points because the 3:2 is taken;

b) if 2s are trumps, the 2:1 takes the trick – and scores 10 extra points because the 6:4 is taken.

Scoring If the bidder and his partner take tricks worth as many or more points than the bid, they score the full value of their tricks plus the number of points bid.

If the bidder and his partner fail in their objective, their opponents score the number of points bid plus the value of the tricks that they have taken.

Taking tricks

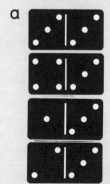 

Value of tricks
(2s trumps)

28 points

14 points

10 points

10 points

DOMINO BINGO

This is another game in which dominoes are used like playing cards and players score points for taking tricks.

It is a game for two players with a set of 28 dominoes. Players make a preliminary draw to determine who will lead for the first trick.

At the start of play, each player draws seven dominoes from the boneyard. The leader then establishes trumps for the hand by turning over a domino in the boneyard. This domino is left exposed and its highest number becomes the trump suit for the hand.

The leader for the first trick then plays one domino and his opponent follows him. There is no need for a player to follow suit, except when the game is "closed" or the boneyard is empty.

Taking a trick The double blank, called "bingo," takes any other domino

If two trumps are played, the higher trump takes the trick.

If one trump is played, the trump takes the trick.

If no trumps are played, the heaviest domino wins the trick.

If no trumps are played and both dominoes have the same total of spots, the leader's domino takes the trick.

As long as any dominoes remain in the boneyard, each player draws a domino after each trick. The winner of a trick always draws first and then leads for the next trick.

When only two dominoes remain in the boneyard, the winner of the preceding trick may take the trump domino or the domino that is face down, and the losing player takes the remaining domino.

Value of tricks There is no score just for taking a trick. The value of a trick depends on the dominoes it contains. Only the following dominoes have any points value (with 2s as trumps in the examples illustrated):

a) the double of trumps is worth 28 points;

b) except when blanks are trumps, "bingo" is worth 14 points;

c) the 6:4 is worth 10 points;

d) the 3:0 is worth 10 points;

e) other doubles are worth their total number of spots;

f) trumps other than the double are worth their total number of spots.

Value of doubles A player can also claim points for having more than one double in his hand at any time when it is his turn to lead. To claim these points he should play one double and expose the others.

For two doubles in his hand he calls "double" and claims 20 points;

for three doubles he calls "triple" and claims 40 points;

for four doubles he calls "double doublet" and claims 50 points;

for five doubles he calls "king" and claims 60 points;

for six doubles he calls "emperor" and claims 70 points;

Value of tricks
(2s trumps)

e

2 points	6 points	8 points	10 points	12 points

f

2 points	3 points	5 points	6 points	7 points	8 points

for all seven doubles he calls "invincible" and claims
210 points;
if "bingo" is among his doubles he claims an extra 10 points.
A player is not entitled to these points if he fails to claim them
when laying down a double; nor do they count if he fails to take
the trick.

Closing If a player with the lead believes that he can bring his
score from tricks and doubles to at least 70 points without
drawing any further dominoes, he can "close" the game by
turning over the trump domino.

After the game is closed neither player may draw any further
dominoes and rules for following suit come into force.

Following suit After the game is closed or the boneyard is
empty, a player is obliged when possible to follow suit.
If a trump is led, he must play another trump.
If a domino that is not a trump is led, he must try and follow its
higher number or, failing that, its lowest number. If he can
follow neither of these, he may play a trump. Only if he has
none of these is he permitted to discard.

Scoring A game is won by the first player to score seven sets or
game points.
Sets are scored as follows:
a) one set for every 70 points from tricks or doubles;
b) one set for being the first player to reach 70 points if the
other player has at least 30 points;
c) two sets for reaching 70 points after the other player has won
a trick but has not scored 30 points;
d) three sets for reaching 70 points before the other player wins
a trick;
e) one set for taking the double of trumps with "bingo."

© DIAGRAM

DOMINO CRIBBAGE

This game is an adaptation of playing card cribbage. The basic domino game is for two players, using a standard set of 28 dominoes. As in the card game, the score is usually kept on a cribbage board.

Objective The game is won by the first player to score 61 points. Scoring takes place during play and also at the end of a hand.

Play Each player draws six dominoes at the start of play. He then discards two of them, face downward, to form the crib (an extra hand scored by the dealer after the other hands have been scored).

The leader then turns over a domino in the boneyard. This domino is the "starter." It is not used during play but is scored with all hands after play.

Turns alternate. The leader's opponent begins by placing any domino from his hand face upward on the table in front of himself and calling out its total number of spots.

The leader then turns over one of his dominoes and calls out the sum total of spots on both dominoes played so far.

Play proceeds in this way, with each player calling the sum total of spots played, until the "go" rule comes into play. If, at his turn, a player is unable to play a domino that will bring the count to 31 or below, he must call "go." The other player must then play as many tiles as he can until he reaches 31 or is unable to play.

Once a count of 31 has been reached, or if no one can play, a new count from 0 is begun. (Pairs etc cannot be carried over into the next count.)

After both players have played all their dominoes, the leader's opponent scores the points in his hand. The leader then scores the points in his hand and then the points in the crib. The lead then passes to the other player and another hand is started.

Scoring during play For turning up a double for starter, one point.

For reaching a count of exactly 15, two points.

For a "pair" (playing a domino with the same total spot count as the last played domino), two points.

For a "triplet" (a third domino with the same total spot count) six points.

For a fourth domino with the same spot count, 12 points.

For a run of three or more dominoes, not necessarily in order (eg dominoes totaling 7, 8, 9), one point for each tile of the run.

For reaching exactly 31, two points.

For being nearest to 31, one point.

For the last tile of the hand, one point.

For reaching 15 with the last tile, three points.

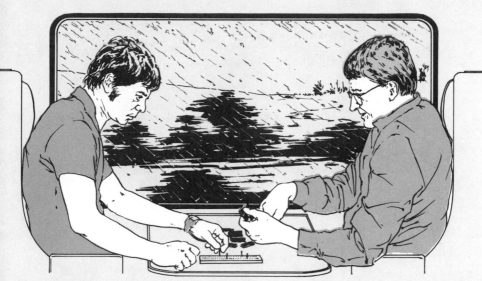

Scoring after play For a combination totaling 15, two points. For a double run of three (a three-tile run with a pair to one of them), eight points. For a double run of four (a run of four with one pair), 10 points. For a triple run (a triplet with two other dominoes in sequence), 15 points. For a quadruple run (two pairs and a domino in sequence with both), 16 points.

Scoring during play

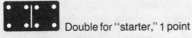 Double for "starter," 1 point

 15, 2 points

 Pair, 2 points

 Run, 3 points

©DIAGRAM

PICTURE DOMINOES

Dominoes with pictures are very popular with young children and can be easily bought or made. A typical set contains 28 brightly colored dominoes with combinations of seven different pictures. They are usually made of wood or heavy card.

All the dominoes are shared out among the players, who should keep the pictures hidden from the other players.

One player starts by placing one domino face upward on the table. Players then take turns at adding a matching domino. If a player doesn't have a matching domino he misses his turn. The winner is the first player to add all his dominoes to the row on the table.

Picture dominoes

Sample play

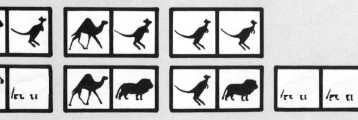

Dominoes: Chinese

Most Chinese domino games are characterized by the collecting of matching pairs. They are played with sets of 32 dominoes divided into two series – the civil and the military. Players can make their own "Chinese set" from two sets of Western dominoes.

The dominoes Chinese dominoes are longer and narrower than Western dominoes – typically 3in by ⅞in by ⅜in.
Spots on Chinese dominoes are colored red or white:
all 4s or 1s are red;
double 6 is red and white;
other dominoes have white spots.
There are no blank dominoes in a Chinese set.
The civil series comprises 22 dominoes, forming 11 identical pairs: all the doubles plus the 6:5, 6:4, 6:1, 5:1, and 3:1.
The military series comprises 10 dominoes. These form five mixed pairs:
the 4:2 and 2:1 (known as the "supreme pair");
the 6:3 and 5:4 (mixed 9s);
the 6:2 and 5:3 (mixed 8s);
the 5:2 and 4:3 (mixed 7s);
the 4:1 and 3:2 (mixed 5s).
The woodpile The dominoes are stacked in a row – called the "woodpile" – at the start of most Chinese domino games.
The banker for the first hand of a game is usually decided by throwing three dice. The total number thrown is counted around the table and the banker is the player sitting where the count stops.
Turns pass around the table in a counterclockwise direction.

Woodpile

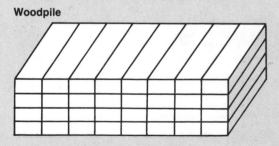

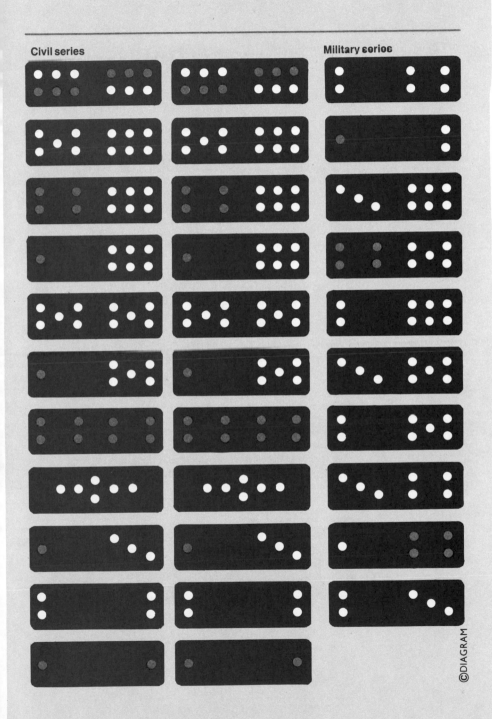

Civil series

Military series

©DIAGRAM

K'AP T'AI SHAP

K'ap t'ai shap (Collecting tens) was a forerunner of Mah jongg (p. 186), and is popular in Chinese gambling houses in the United States.

Objective The game is won by the first player to complete his hand. A complete hand consists of:

a) four pairs, each with a total spot count of 10 or a multiple of 10; and

b) any identical pair.

Start of play A long woodpile five dominoes high is built down the center of the table, using several sets.

Players join the game by placing equal stakes, and dice are thrown to decide who will have the first turn.

The woodpile is then prepared for play by removing the top domino from the third stack from one end and placing it face down at the other end of the woodpile. The top domino is then taken from each alternate stack up to one less than the number of players, and these are also added in order to the far end of the woodpile.

The first player then takes the end two stacks (with 10 dominoes) and the other players in turn each take two stacks (with nine dominoes).

Turns If the first player does not have a winning hand, he starts play by discarding one domino and placing it face up on the table.

Then each player in his turn:

1) may take any discarded domino to complete his hand or to exchange it for one of his own dominoes; and

2) draws one domino from the end of the woodpile, which he may immediately discard or keep in place of another domino from his hand.

Result The game ends when one player completes his hand. This entitles him to the total staked, less the gambling house commission.

Objective

a

b

TIU U

Tiu u, or Fishing, is a game for two or three players with two sets of Chinese dominoes. Players win points for matching dominoes in their hand with dominoes lying face up in the center of the table.

Pairs The 4:2 and 2:1 (the supreme pair) count as one pair. Other pairs are formed whenever two dominoes have the same total number of spots (regardless of whether they are civil or military dominoes).

Start of play At the start of a hand the dominoes are thoroughly mixed and placed face down in a woodpile four dominoes high. Four stacks (16 dominoes) are then taken from one end of the woodpile and placed face up on the table.

Each player then draws his own dominoes. If there are three players, each draws two stacks (eight dominoes); if there are only two players, each draws three stacks (12 dominoes).

Turns In his turn, each player first attempts to match a domino in his hand with a domino exposed on the table. If he succeeds, he places the pair face up in front of him.

Whether he finds a pair or not, he then draws the top domino from the end of the woodpile where the players first drew their hands. If the drawn domino matches a domino exposed in the center of the table, he takes the pair and places it face up in front of him. If it doesn't match, he adds the drawn domino to the dominoes exposed in the center of the table.

Scoring When the woodpile is empty, players score points as follows:

a) the total score for dominoes with less than eight spots (small fish) is obtained by counting one point for each red spot and then rounding up the total to 10 or a multiple of 10.

b) dominoes with eight or more spots (big fish) score two points for every spot – red or white.

The player with the highest score then receives from each opponent the number of points by which their scores differ.

Pairs

Supreme pair

Examples of other pairs

©DIAGRAM

TIEN KOW

Tien kow is a game for four players with one set of Chinese dominoes. The object of the game is to score points by winning tricks made up of single dominoes or pairs.

Start of play The dominoes are thoroughly mixed and stacked in a woodpile. The first banker (selected by dice) then deals each player eight dominoes from the woodpile.

Turns The banker plays the first domino for the first trick and the other players follow in turn. After the first trick, the lead goes to the winner of the preceding trick.

At his lead, a player may play either one domino or one or two pairs.

If he leads one domino, the other players must follow with one domino from the same series (discarding if they have no domino from that series).

If he leads one or two pairs, the other players must do likewise.

Taking tricks If one domino is led, the trick goes to the player who plays the heaviest domino from the correct series.

If one pair is led, the trick is taken by the highest ranking pair.

If two pairs are led, the trick goes to the player who plays the highest pair of all – regardless of what pair is played with it.

Ranking of pairs is as follows:

1) the 4:2 and 2:1 (supreme);
2) double 6s (heaven);
3) double 1s (earth);
4) double 4s (man);
5) pair of 3:1s;
6) double 5s;
7) double 3s;
8) double 2s;
9) pair of 6:5s;
10) pair of 6:4s;
11) pair of 6:1s;
12) pair of 5:1s;
13) 6:3 and 5:4 (mixed 9s);
14) 6:2 and 5:3 (mixed 8s);
15) 5:2 and 4:3 (mixed 7s);
16) 4:1 and 3:2 (mixed 5s);
17) double 6 and either of the mixed 9s;
18) double 1 and a mixed 8;
19) double 4 and a mixed 7;
20) 3:1 and a mixed 5.

Scoring Players settle their scores after each hand. Scoring is as follows:

a) a player with no tricks pays four points to the winner of the last trick (except when the banker for one hand wins the last trick and retains the bank – in which case he pays eight points the first time, 12 points the second, 16 the third, and so on until the bank changes);

b) a player with one, two, or three tricks deducts his number of tricks from four and pays the difference to the winner of the last trick;

c) a player with more than four tricks deducts four from his total and claims the difference from the winner of the last trick;

d) if the banker leads the supreme pair, he claims four points from each player;

e) if a player leads the supreme pair, he claims four points from the banker and two points from each other player;

f) the banker claims eight points from each player if he leads two of the following pairs: the double 6 and a mixed 9; the double 1 and a mixed 8; the double 4 and a mixed 7; the 3:1 and a mixed 5;

g) a player claims eight points from the banker and four points from each other player if he makes the leads given under (f).

Ranking of pairs

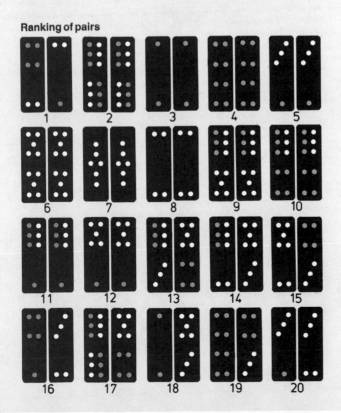

© DIAGRAM

Fighting serpents

Fighting serpents is a board game of North American Indian origin. Although similar in some ways to Fox and geese (p. 154), Fighting serpents is a contest between two forces of equal strength. The player who succeeds in capturing all his opponent's pieces is the winner.

The board has a playing area of three parallel lines, intersected by short lines forming a diamond pattern as shown.
The length of the playing area may vary (the one illustrated here with 49 intersections is of average size) and the ends may be either rounded or straight.
Pieces are placed on all the intersections except three along the middle parallel: the two outermost intersections and the one at the center. Each player has pieces of a different color, positioned at the start of the game as shown. Traditionally, small black and white stones are used, but the game can also be played with counters or other objects.
The objective is to capture all the opponent's pieces, the first player to achieve this being the winner.
Play After the starting order has been determined, the first player moves one of his pieces along a line to any of the three vacant points. Thereafter, turns alternate between players. Capturing is compulsory whenever possible and takes precedence if there is a choice of moves.

Start of play

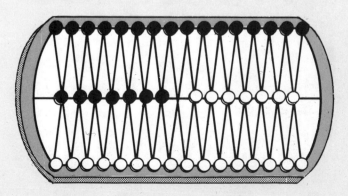

A piece is captured by jumping over it to an empty point beyond (**a**). A taking move is not permitted if it entails a change of direction.

Double or multiple captures in one move are permitted; direction may be changed after each enemy piece has been jumped (**b**).

Whenever a piece is captured it is removed from the board. In a non-taking move, players may move one of their pieces one intersection along a line in any direction (**c**).

The game ends as soon as one player has lost all his pieces.

Moving

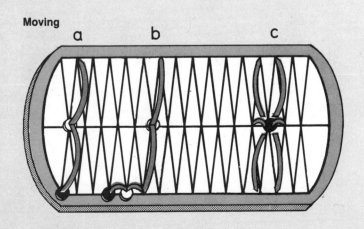

©DIAGRAM

Fivestones

Fivestones, like Jacks (p. 178), is derived from Knucklebones, an ancient form of Dice played with sheep's knucklebones. Today, Fivestones is played in many countries. Players crouch to throw small objects in the air and catch them in various ways in a usually increasingly difficult series of throws.

Equipment Fivestones is played with five small rounded stones or with five small plastic cubes of different colors.
The objective is to complete a series of throws in an agreed sequence.
Players The game can be enjoyed by a player on his own – or two or more players may attempt to be first to complete an agreed sequence of throws.
Turns If there are two or more players, the usual practice is to play in turn. First turn may be decided by a preliminary throw, by the toss of a coin, or by agreement.
A player's turn ends when he fails to accomplish any part of a particular throw, and his next turn begins with another attempt at the failed throw.
Throws There are many hundreds of variations of the game, but those given here are among the most widely known.

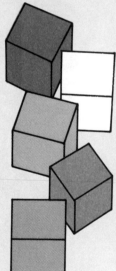

BASIC THROW
For the basic Fivestones throw, sometimes called the "jockey," the player must:
a) put the five stones in the open palm of one hand;
b) toss the stones up in the air;
c) while the stones are in the air, turn his hand over and catch the stones on the back of his hand;
d) toss the stones from the back of his hand;
e) turn his hand over and catch the stones in the palm of his hand.

ONES, TWOS, THREES, FOURS
Ones The player attempts the basic throw. If he catches all the stones, he goes on to twos. If he fails to catch any stones his turn ends.
If he catches one or more stones, he must:
leave any stones on the ground where they lie;
transfer to his other hand all but one of he stones he has caught;
throw the single stone in the air;
pick up one stone from the ground with his throwing hand;
catch the thrown stone with the same hand.
The player must repeat the procedure for picking up individual

stones until all have been retrieved.

Twos The player scatters the stones on the ground, taking care that they do not land too far apart.

He then selects one stone, throws it up in the air, and must pick up two other stones from the ground with his throwing hand before catching the thrown stone with that same hand.

When he has done this, he transfers the two stones to his other hand, tosses up the third stone, and must pick up the remaining two stones from the ground.

Threes is like twos, except that the player must pick up one stone followed by three, or three stones followed by one.

Fours In fours, all four stones are picked up at one time.

Basic throw

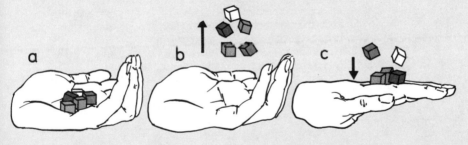

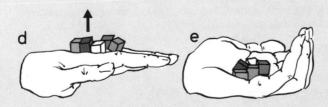

©DIAGRAM

PECKS, BUSHELS, CLAWS

Pecks The player attempts the basic throw. If he succeeds in catching all five stones, he goes on to Bushels. If he fails to catch any stones his turn ends.

If he catches one or more stones, he must:
keep the caught stones in his throwing hand;
push one stone out between his forefinger and thumb and then:
toss the pushed out stone into the air (**1**);
pick up one stone from the ground with his throwing hand (**2**);
catch the thrown stone with his throwing hand (**3**);
repeat this procedure until all stones are picked up.

Bushels The player attempts the basic throw. If he is successful, he goes on to Claws. If he fails to catch any stones his turn ends.

If he catches one or more stones, he must:
throw all the caught stones in the air;
pick up one stone from the ground with his throwing hand;
catch the thrown stones;
repeat this until all stones on the ground are picked up.

Claws The fivestones are tossed from the palm onto the back of the hand – as in the basic throw. If all five are caught, the player attempts to complete the basic throw and if successful may go on to the next throw in the sequence. If none is caught on the back of the hand, the player's turn ends.

If one or more are caught on the back of the hand, the player:
leaves the caught stones on the back of his hand;
picks up the stones on the ground between the outstretched fingers of his throwing hand, with only one stone between any two fingers or between finger and thumb;
tosses the stones from the back of his hand and catches them in his palm;
maneuvers the stones from between his fingers into his palm.

OVER THE LINE

The non-throwing hand is placed with the palm on the ground, and four stones are scattered on the ground to its outer side. The player then throws the fifth stone in the air, and before catching it must transfer one of the other stones to the other side of his non-throwing hand.

This is repeated until all four stones on the ground have been transferred. (It is advisable to place the transferred stones as close together as possible.)

The player then throws up the fifth stone and before catching it must pick up the other four stones in his throwing hand.

OVER THE JUMP

This variation is similar to Over the line, except that the non-throwing hand is placed on edge to make a jump or wall – so making the transference of stones more difficult.

THREADING THE NEEDLE

This also resembles Over the line, but the stones have to be dropped one at a time through a circle formed by the thumb and forefinger of the non-throwing hand held about 8in above the ground.

UNDER THE ARCH

Ones under the arch The player first scatters the stones on the ground and makes an arch near them with the thumb and forefinger of his non-throwing hand.

He then selects one stone and throws it up in the air (**a**). While the stone is in the air, he knocks the other stones through the arch (**b**), and then catches the thrown stone (**c**).

When all four stones have been knocked through the arch, the player throws the fifth stone in the air and before catching it must pick up the other four stones.

Twos under the arch is similar to ones under the arch, except that the stones must be knocked through the arch in two pairs.

Threes under the arch is similar except that the stones are knocked through as a three and a one or a one and a three.

Fours under the arch requires all four stones to be knocked through together.

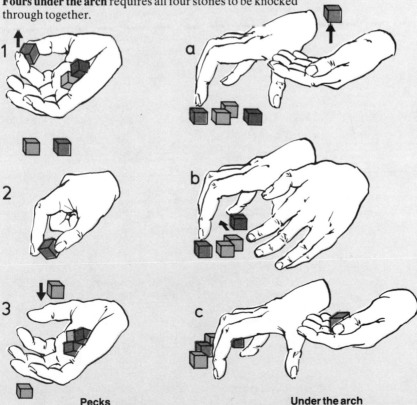

Pecks   Under the arch

©DIAGRAM

HORSE IN THE STABLE

The stones are scattered on the ground and the non-throwing hand is placed near them, with the fingers and thumb spread out, the fingertips touching the ground, and the palm raised. The gaps between the fingers and thumb are the "stables." One stone is then thrown into the air (**a**), and before catching it the player must knock a stone into or toward one of the stables (**b**). No more than one stone may be knocked into any one stable.

The player continues throwing, knocking, and catching in this way until all four stables are filled. He then moves his non-throwing hand away from the four stones, tosses the throwing stone and before catching it must pick up the four stones from the ground.

Horse in the stable

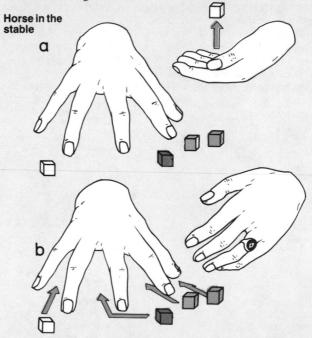

TOAD IN THE HOLE

The stones are first scattered on the ground. A "hole" is then made by laying the thumb of the non-throwing hand straight along the ground and curling the fingers around so that the tip of the forefinger touches the tip of the thumb.

One stone is then thrown into the air, and before catching it the player must pick up one of the other stones, a "toad," and drop it into the hole.

This is repeated until four toads are in the hole. The player then moves his non-throwing hand, tosses up the single stone and before catching it must pick up all four toads.

BACKWARD ONES, TWOS, THREES, FOURS

Backward ones After first scattering four stones on the ground, the player throws the fifth stone in the air and catches it on the back of his throwing hand.

He then tosses the fifth stone into the air from the back of his hand and before catching it in the normal way must pick up one stone from the ground.

The player then throws the two held stones in the same manner and picks up a third stone. The three held stones are used for the next throw, and four stones for the throw to pick up the fifth stone.

Backward twos is similar to Backward ones, except that the player must pick up two stones at his first throw and then the remaining two.

Backward threes is similar except that three and then one or one and then three stones must be picked up.

Backward fours requires the player to pick up all four stones at one time.

TOWERS

These variations can only be played with fivestones that are cubes.

Building a tower. The player first scatters four of his stones. He then throws the other stone and before catching it moves one of the stones on the ground away from the others.

At his second throw he places a second stone on top of the first, at his third throw he places a third stone on top of the other two, and at his fourth throw he completes the tower.

Demolishing a tower is the obvious sequel to Building a tower. At each throw, the player must remove a single stone from the tower.

SNAKE IN THE GRASS

The player sets out four stones in a straight line, with a gap of several inches from one stone to the next.

He then throws the fifth stone in the air, and before catching it, must pick up one of the end stones, use it to trace part of the pattern illustrated, and lay the picked stone down at the point of the pattern reached.

A player is allowed any number of throws to complete his tracing, but his turn ends if he drops the throwing stone, fails to touch the stone he is using for tracing, or touches any other stone.

Building a tower

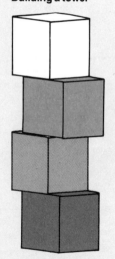

Snake in the grass

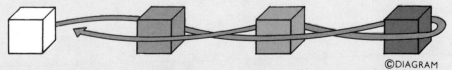

©DIAGRAM

Fox and geese

European Fox and geese games originated in Scandinavia in the Middle Ages. Similar games are played in many other parts of the world. In all of them, two unevenly matched forces compete against each other. The smaller force usually comprises one or two pieces and has considerable freedom of movement; the larger force is made up of numerous pieces but has only restricted maneuverability.

Pieces Any suitable pieces such as checkers, counters, or stones may be used (or marbles or pegs if played on a solitaire board). One of the pieces, representing the fox, must be distinguishable in color from the 15 (or sometimes 17) pieces representing the geese.
Board Fox and geese can be played on several different layouts. The layout in these illustrations probably gives the players the most even chance of winning.
Start of play The two players decide which of them is to play the fox and which the geese; they change over after each game. The pieces are put into position on the board – with the geese at

Start of play

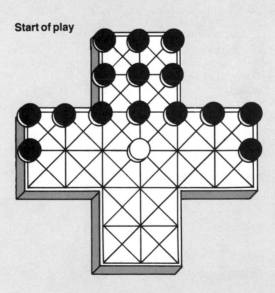

the top of the board (as shown) and the fox usually at the center (although it may be placed on any vacant point that the player chooses).

Moves Players take alternate turns, with the fox starting first. **The fox** may move in any direction along connecting lines, moving one point at each turn (**a**).

It may also "kill" a goose by jumping over it to an adjacent vacant point; the goose is then removed from the board. The fox may make two or more jumps in one move (killing each goose that it jumps over), provided there is an empty point for it to land on next to each goose that it kills (**b**).

The fox is obliged to jump if there is no alternative move, even if it puts itself in a vulnerable position by doing so.

Geese may move along connecting lines in any direction except toward the top of the board (**c**). One goose moves one point in a turn. Geese may not jump over and capture the fox; their aim is to surround the fox so that it cannot move.

Result The fox wins if it:

a) kills so many geese that those remaining are not sufficient in number to trap it; or

b) manages to evade the geese so as to give it a clear path to the top of the board (where the geese cannot chase it).

The geese win if they can immobilize the fox by surrounding it or crowding it into a corner.

Moving

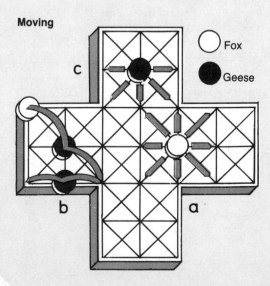

Game of goose

Reputedly invented in sixteenth-century Italy, the Game of goose was a favorite in Europe until the end of the nineteenth century. It was the forerunner of many race board games in which the participants' progress may be either hindered or advanced by landing on certain specially marked squares.

Boards of many different designs were used, but the main feature of all of them was a spiral route divided into 63 numbered spaces – starting at the outside and finishing at the center. The boards were often illustrated by, for example, scenes from history or mythology.

In addition, certain spaces on the route were marked with symbols and printed instructions – sometimes these instructions were shown at the center of the board. One of these symbols, appearing on about every fifth space, was a goose. By landing on a marked space, the player was instructed to either:

have another throw;

forfeit a turn;

advance a certain number of spaces; or

retreat a certain number of spaces.

Sometimes the instructions would be linked with the theme of the illustrations. For example, on a board with a military theme, the instruction might state that because of an injury received in battle, the player must forfeit a turn.

For contemporary play, the circuit may be drawn on paper or other suitable material. Geese should be drawn on about every fifth space, and other symbols or instructions may be marked at random on the circuit. (See also the section on play.)

Other equipment To mark his position on the circuit, each player needs a colored counter or other object different from his opponents'. One die is used.

The objective is to travel around the circuit as quickly as possible, the first player to land on the finish with an exact throw being the winner.

Play Throwing the die in turn, players move their counters the thrown number of spaces. If a player's counter lands on a goose space, the player may throw again. By landing on another of the specially marked spaces, the player is instructed to either:

miss one or more turns;

advance a prescribed number of spaces; or

move back a prescribed number of spaces.

End of play The finish can only be reached by an exact throw. Thus a player throwing more than the number required to reach the finish must go back the number of spaces by which he has exceeded the finish. For example, if his counter is on 62 and the player throws a 3, he must move his counter one space forward to the finish, and then back two spaces to space 61.

©DIAGRAM

Go

Go is thought to be one of the oldest games in existence. It originated in China over 3000 years ago (its Chinese name is Wei-ch'i) and was later adopted by Japan and other oriental countries. It is considered one of the greatest games of strategic skill. Two players compete to secure as much of the playing area as possible.

Board and notation

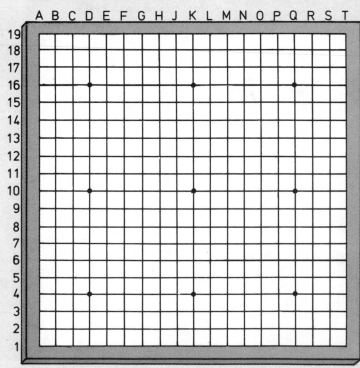

Board The traditional Japanese go table *(go-ban)* is made of wood and is stained yellow. It is about 17½in long, 16in wide, and 4–5in thick, and has four legs roughly 3in high.

The playing area (about 16½ by 15in) is marked out in black lacquer in a grid pattern of 19 parallel lines and 19 lines at right angles to these, forming a total of 361 intersections or points.

The intersections of the fourth, tenth, and sixteenth lines in each direction are marked by dots and are known as handicap points.

The two players kneel opposite each other, at the shorter sides of the table.

Pieces There are two sets of stones: a set of 181 black stones and a set of 180 white stones (361 in all). Each player has one set.

The stones are disk shaped, about ⅞in in diameter, and ⅛–½in thick. The stones may be kept in a lacquered box *(go-tsubo)* or other container.

Stones

©DIAGRAM

Objective By the positioning of his stones on the board, each player aims to surround more unoccupied territory and enemy stones than his opponent.

Order of play Players take alternate turns. The opening move is usually made by the player with the black stones. (Players take it in turn to play black unless there is a known disparity of playing skill – see handicapping section, below.)

A turn consists of placing a stone on an unoccupied point. Except in the "*ko* situation" (see p. 161), a stone may be placed on any vacant point.

Once in position the stone is not moved again during the game unless it is captured, in which case it is removed from the board.

Playing procedure At the beginning of the game the board is empty except for any handicap stones.

Stones must be placed on the points (line intersections) and not on the squares formed by the lines.

Each player places his stones to form connected groups or chains in such a way as to surround as many vacant points and opponent's stones as possible.

Should all the points adjacent to one or more stones be occupied by stones of the other color, the former stone or group of stones is captured and removed from the board. (Adjacent points are those that are linked directly to a point by a line, and not diagonally.) It is possible to win a game without capturing any stones, since the objective is territorial gain.

Handicapping The player taking the first turn is at an advantage. Black (the opening turn) normally alternates between players. If there is a known disparity of playing skill or if one player wins three consecutive games, the weaker player may be allowed to keep the black stones.

If further handicapping is necessary, the weaker player may place two or more of his stones on the dotted handicap points before the game starts (see the table below), and the opening move then goes to the player with the white stones.

Should the stronger player continue to win, the number of handicap stones may be increased.

Table showing positions for handicap stones

Handicap	Positions
2 stones	D4, Q16
3 stones	D4, Q4, Q16
4 stones	D4, D16, Q4, Q16
5 stones	D4, D16, K10, Q4, Q16
6 stones	D4, D10, D16, Q4, Q10, Q16
7 stones	D4, D10, D16, K10, Q4, Q10, Q16
8 stones	D4, D10, D16, K4, K16, Q4, Q10, Q16
9 stones	D4, D10, D16, K4, K10, K16, Q4, Q10, Q16

Ko situations A *ko* (threat) situation is one that can be repeated indefinitely. In *ko* situations the second player may not recapture until he has made at least one move elsewhere on the board. (Forcing play at other parts of the board is therefore important.)

A single *ko* situation may involve many stones. If there are three *ko* situations on a board at any one time, the game is declared drawn.

Seki situations A *seki* (deadlock) situation exists on any part of the board where opposing groups are so placed that neither player can occupy an uncontrolled point without losing his own pieces. *Seki* situations are left untouched until the end of the game, and all free points in them are disregarded in scoring.

Dame points are vacant points between territories that cannot be played onto with benefit by either side. *Dame* points are left untouched until the end of the game, and then disregarded in scoring.

Prohibitions No move may be made that causes repetition of a position formed earlier in the game.

A stone must not remain on the board if it is entirely surrounded by enemy stones. A stone must not be played onto a point that is completely surrounded by stones of another color, unless the move causes the immediate capture of enemy stones.

©DIAGRAM

Explanation of diagrams
1) Capture of single stones.
2) Capture of groups of stones: a white stone played onto the dotted position would capture the black group attacked.
3a, 4a) Black cannot play onto the point marked with a cross, as the stone would be immediately captured (the arrowed point is vacant – white is not completely surrounded).
3b, 4b) Black can play onto the dotted point because the play puts the white stones out of contact with any empty point. The white stones are captured and removed. All black stones remain.
5a, 5b) A *ko* situation. In (**5a**) a black stone placed on the crossed point captures the white stone; in (**5b**) a white stone replaced on the captured point would recapture the black stone.
5c) A *seki* situation. Neither player can place his stone on the point marked with the cross without losing his formation.

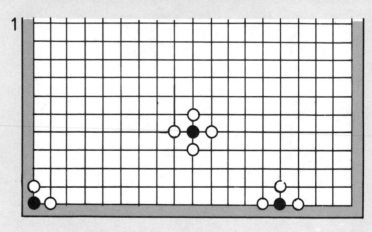

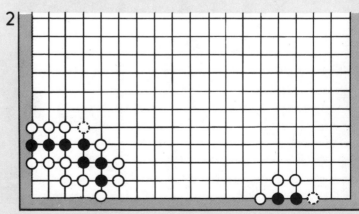

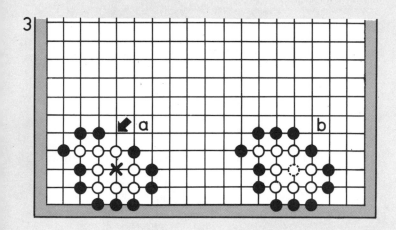

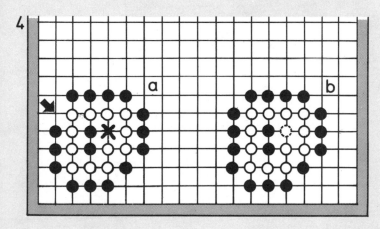

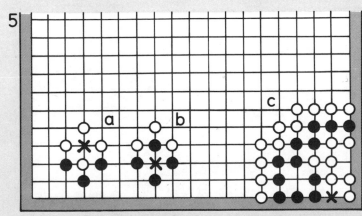

©DIAGRAM

End of play The game ends when both players agree that there are no further advantages to be gained by either side.

If only one player considers the game to be over, his opponent may continue to make moves until he too is satisfied that no points or stones remain to be secured. (The first player may continue play, if he wishes, until both players agree that the game is over. But he may not resume play once he has actually missed a turn.)

Scoring An imaginary board, nine lines by nine lines, has been used to illustrate the basic scoring process. (It should be thought of as a simplified complete board, not as a section of a board.)

1) At the end of play all stones left in enemy territory are ruled captured.

2) These captured stones are removed from the board and added to each player's collection of captured enemy stones.

3) Any vacant points in neutral and *seki* situations have stones placed on them to discount them in the scoring. Either player may use his unused stones for this purpose.

4) In order to facilitate counting, black places all the white stones he has captured on vacant points in white's territory and white places all the captured black stones on vacant points in black's territory.

5) The number of vacant points left in each territory is counted.

Result The winner is the player with the larger number of vacant points left in his territory. He scores the difference between his own and his opponent's count. The game is tied if both players have an equal number of points.

Scoring

(Diagrams show
an imaginary
simplified board)

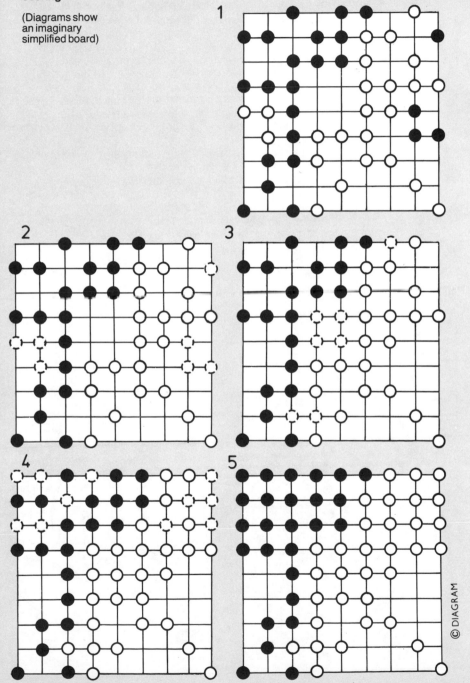

GO-MOKU

This is a straightforward game played on a Go board. It originated in Japan and is sometimes called Go-bang or Spoil five.

Players It is a game for two players.

Board A Go board is used.

Pieces Each player has a set of 100 stones: one set black and the other white.

Objective Players aim to position five stones so that they form a straight line (horizontally, vertically, or diagonally).

Play The board is empty at the start of the game, and black has the opening move.

The players take it in turns to place a stone on any point (line intersection). Once a stone has been placed it may not be moved again until the end of the game.

If all the stones are used up before either player has succeeded in forming a "five," the game may either be declared drawn, or the players may take it in turns to move one stone one point in a horizontal or vertical direction until a "five" is formed.

HASAMI SHOGI

Hasami shogi is an interesting Japanese game that can be
played on a Go board.

Players It is a game for two players.

The board is nine squares by nine. A quarter of a Go board
may be used – but note that play is on the squares not the
points.

Pieces Each player has a set of 18 stones: one uses black stones
and the other white.

The objective is to capture all the opposing stones.

Start of play Each player places his stones on his two home
rows.

Play Players take alternate turns. A player may move only one
stone in a turn.

Moving All moves must be forward, backward, or to the side.
No moves may be diagonal. A stone may:

a) move into an adjacent square;

b) jump over a stone, of either set, into a vacant square
beyond it.

Jumped stones are not removed from the board. Double jumps
are not permitted.

Capture A stone is captured if an opponent's move traps it
between two opposing stones. A stone is not captured if it is
flanked diagonally by opposing stones.

A stone is not captured if it moves into a vacant square
between two enemy stones.

A stone is captured if an enemy move traps it in a corner of the
board.

Hasami shogi
Start

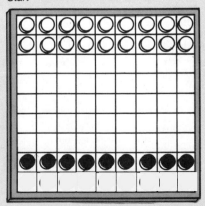

Moving

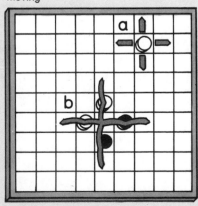

©DIAGRAM

Halma

Halma, which takes its name from a Greek word for jump, was invented in England toward the end of the last century. It is a Checkers type of game for two, three, or four players. There are also Halma solitaire problems to provide an interesting diversion for one player.

Board Halma is played on a board with 256 small squares, 16 along each side.

Heavy lines mark off "yards" in the board's corners. Each corner has a yard with 13 squares, and two diagonally opposite corners have an additional heavy line marking off a yard with 19 squares.

Pieces There are four sets of pieces – each of a different color. Two sets have 19 pieces and the other two only 13.

The pieces may be:

a) small checkers or counters;

b) wooden or plastic cones;

c) wooden or plastic men resembling small chess pawns.

Forms of play The game may be played:

a) by two players;

b) by three or four players, each playing separately;

c) by four players, in partnerships of two.

Partnership halma can be played in two ways:

a) pairs are formed by players with pieces in adjacent yards;

b) pairs are formed by players with pieces in yards that are diagonally opposite.

(The second form provides more scope for partners to help each other.)

Objective Each player attempts to move his pieces from his own yard into the yard diagonally opposite. The game is won by the first player or pair to achieve this objective.

Start of play Starting positions vary with the forms of play:

a) when there are two players, each one takes a set of 19 pieces and positions them in the yards with 19 squares;

b) when there are three or four players, each one takes a set of 13 pieces and positions them in the yards with 13 squares.

Start: two players

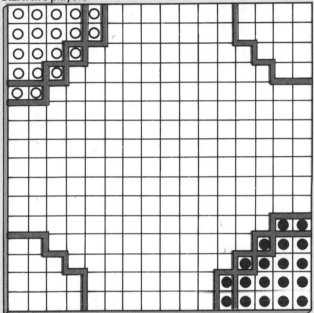

Start: three players

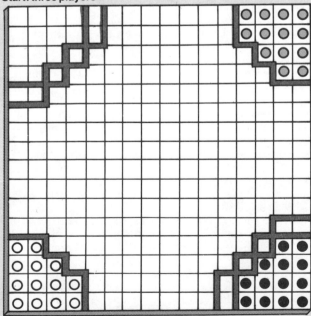

©DIAGRAM

Moving

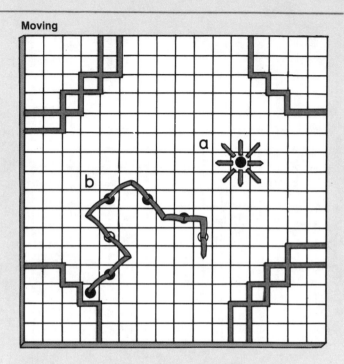

Turns pass clockwise around the table if there are more than two players. A player may move only one piece in a turn.
Moving Pieces may be moved in any direction – straight or diagonally, forward or backward, to one side or the other. Two types of move are permitted:
a) a "step" – by which a player moves a piece into an adjoining square;
b) a "hop" – by which a player moves a piece over a piece in an adjoining square into a vacant square directly behind it.
A player may hop over his own or another player's pieces, and all hopped pieces are left on the board.
A player may make several hops in one move, but may not combine steps and hops in a move. There is no compulsion to make any hop.

HALMA SOLITAIRE
An interesting halma solitaire problem requires the player to place 19 pieces in one of the yards and then in 19 moves position them in a symmetrical figure across the board's diagonal.
This problem can be solved in several hundred ways, and the interest therefore derives from the variety of solutions. A fairly skillful player should be able to find 50 different solutions without too much difficulty.

Halma solitaire: start

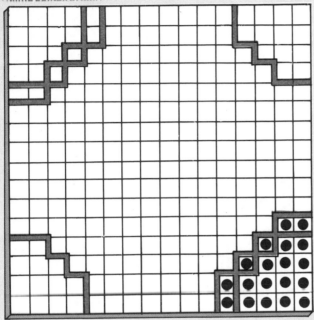

Halma solitaire: objective

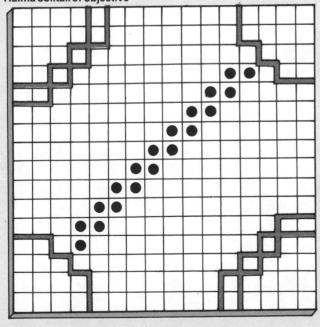

©DIAGRAM

Hex

Hex is a game for two players invented by a Dane, Piet Hein. Hex sets are available in some places, but the game can also be played with improvised equipment. Each player tries to form an unbroken line of pieces between his two sides of the board.

The board has a diamond-shaped playing area made up of adjoining hexagons. Two opposite sides of the board belong to black; the other two to white.

The pieces are all identical in shape, and are in two sets of equal number, one colored black and one white. The highest number of pieces that a player can require for a game is 61; usually he will need far fewer.

Objective The game is won by the first player to place his pieces so that they form a line joining his two sides of the board. The line does not have to be straight, but it must be unbroken. Corner hexagons belong to both players, and either player may use them as hexagons touching his sides of the board.

Play Each player takes one set of pieces. The first player places one of his pieces on the board, on any hexagon he chooses.

Turns then alternate, with each player placing one of his pieces on any unoccupied hexagon.

Pieces may not be moved once they have been placed on the board.

Board

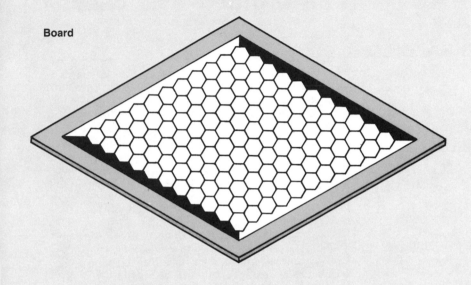

Winning position

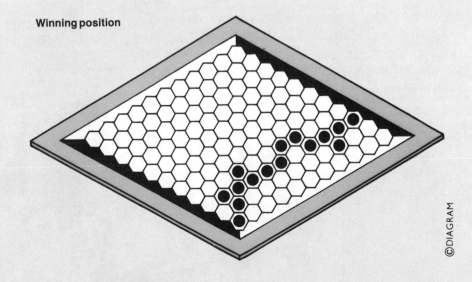

©DIAGRAM

Horseshoe

Horseshoe is a game very like Alleyway (see p. 16), its main difference being that it is played for small stakes. Any number of players may take part.

Equipment The layout is drawn onto paper or cardboard and is in the shape of a horseshoe, divided into 30 numbered spaces as shown.

Instead of using counters, players mark their progress along the horseshoe with a stake – such as a candy, coin, or nut. The only other equipment needed is a die.

Play Each player throws the die and places his stake on the corresponding space. Players then take turns to advance their stakes along the horseshoe in accordance with the throw of the die.

Every time a player's stake lands on an occupied space, the occupier's stake has to retreat to space 1.

End play If a player's throw is higher than the number needed for his stake to reach space 30, he must move his stake around the horseshoe past space 30 and on to space 1 or beyond. For example, if his stake is on space 28 and the player throws a 5, he must move his stake five spaces to space 3. He must then continue round the course from that space.

Winner The first player to get an exact throw onto space 30 wins the game and all the stakes.

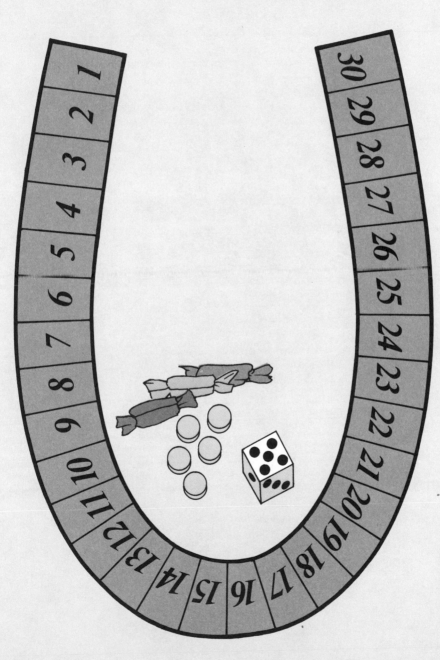

©DIAGRAM

Hyena chase

Hyena chase is a race game from North Africa that provides an amusing alternative to some of the better-known board games.

Board

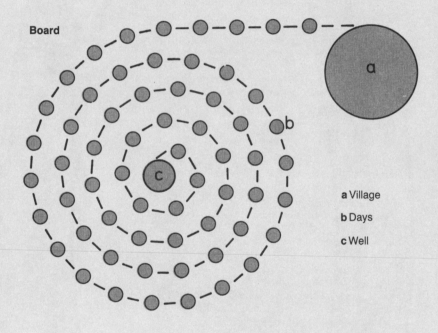

a Village

b Days

c Well

Board Traditionally, the playing area is marked out on the ground, but it may be drawn on paper or other suitable material.

A spiral circle is marked with a random number of small circles along its length, each circle representing a day's journey. Two large circles are drawn:

one (the "village") next to the start of the spiral;

the other (the "well") at the center of the spiral.

Pieces Each player has one counter or other suitable object, different in color or shape from those of his opponents – this counter represents the player's "mother." One other counter is used to represent the hyena; this counter must also be easily distinguishable.

All the counters are placed in the "village" circle before the start of play.

Dice In the traditional game players use pieces of stick, but one ordinary die may be substituted.

Players Two or more can play this game.

Objective Each player tries to be the first to get his mother from the village to the well and back again – entitling him to let loose the hyena on the remaining mothers!

Play Moves are made by each player in turn in accordance with the throw of a die.

Players must throw a 6 to get their mothers from the village onto the first circle.

Whenever a player throws a 6, he is allowed another throw; if he throws two 6s in succession he is permitted a third throw. It is permissible for the mothers of two or more players to occupy the same "day."

The well can only be reached by a direct throw. If, for example, a mother is three days' journey from the well, the player cannot move her if he throws more than a 3 – he must await his next turn.

Return journey Once at the well, the mother "washes her clothes" until the player throws a 6 – allowing her to start on her return journey to the village.

End play The first player to get his mother back to the village (he does not need a direct throw) wins the "hyena" counter. He must throw a 6 to get the hyena from the village onto the first circle; once there the hyena travels along the route to the well at twice the speed of the mothers – moving double the score on the die (ie if the player throws a 5, the hyena moves forward 10 days).

Once at the well (only reached by a direct throw) the player must again throw a 6 before the hyena can return to the village. Any mothers that the hyena passes on its way back to the village are "eaten" and removed from the board.

The winning player is, of course, the player who wins the hyena. But the satisfaction of winning is enhanced by the number of mothers that he can eat during the animal's rampage!

Pieces

Mothers

Hyena

Die

Jacks

Jacks, like Fivestones (p. 148), is a descendant of ancient games played with the knucklebones of sheep. It is a game for one or more players. On these pages we describe only the most basic version of Jacks; for greater variety it is possible to adapt most of the Fivestones games described on pp. 149–153.

Equipment Play is with:
a) Five to 12 small, usually six-legged, metal or plastic objects known as jacks;
b) a small rubber ball.
Objective The aim is to complete an agreed series of throws; only after succeeding with one throw may a player go onto the next throw in the series. If there are two or more players, the winner is the first player to complete the series.
Play In games for two or more, the players may decide to play simultaneously or to take turns.
Turns First turn may be decided by a preliminary throw, by the toss of a coin, or by mutual agreement.
A player's turn ends when he fails to accomplish any part of a particular throw. On his next turn he must begin with another attempt at the failed throw.
Basic game The player scatters the jacks on the ground. He throws the ball in the air, picks up one of the jacks with his throwing hand, and catches the ball with the same hand after it has bounced once on the ground. He transfers the jack he has picked up to his other hand. The player then repeats the procedure for picking up individual jacks until they have all been retrieved.
If the player successfully retrieves all the jacks singly, he scatters them again and picks them up in twos. If he successfully picks up all the jacks in twos, he goes on to retrieve them by threes, fours, etc., up to the maximum number of jacks available. Any jacks remaining after the correct groupings have been retrieved are themselves picked up as a group (eg when playing with 12 jacks and retrieving five at a time, the last two jacks are picked up together).
The player may use any throw to adjust the position of the jacks on the ground without losing his turn, providing that he uses his throwing hand to move the jacks, and catches the ball with the same hand after its first bounce.
Variations A player who successfully completes all the stages of the basic game goes on to more difficult variations. He begins each variation by retrieving the jacks singly, then continues through twos, three, etc., to the maximum number available. The many possible variations include:
retrieving the jacks as they fall, ie the player may not use any throw to adjust the position of the jacks on the ground;
throwing the ball in the air, picking up the appropriate number of jacks with the throwing hand, and catching the ball with the same hand before it has bounced on the ground;
throwing the ball against a wall, picking up the appropriate number of jacks with the throwing hand, and catching the ball with the same hand before (or after) it has bounced on the ground.

Jacks

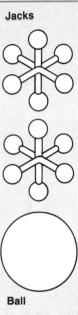

Ball

©DIAGRAM

Lasca

This is an interesting game in the Checkers family. It is characterized by its unusual method of taking, and by the consequent building up of "columns" of pieces.

The board has 49 squares, seven along each side. The squares are alternately light and dark, and play is only on the light squares. (A standard checker board can be used if the squares along two sides are covered, leaving a light square at each corner.)

Pieces Each player has a set of 11 pieces; one set is usually white and the other black or red. Each piece is marked on one side – with a sticker, paint, pen, or pencil.

Objective The game is won when one player makes it impossible for his opponent to make any move.

Start of play Each player positions his pieces, with their unmarked sides face up, on the white squares in the three rows of the board nearest him.

Turns alternate; each player makes only one move in a turn.

Start of play

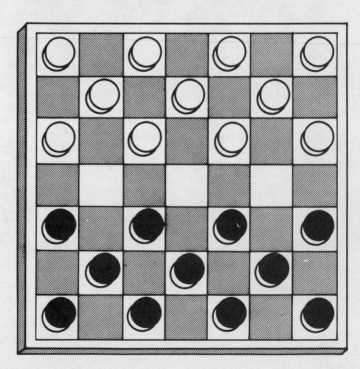

© DIAGRAM

Soldier

Officer

A **"soldier"** is a piece with the unmarked side face up. All pieces are soldiers at the start of play. A soldier moves diagonally forward like a man in British or American checkers. An **"officer"** is a piece with the marked side face up. A soldier becomes an officer after it has crossed to the farthest row of the board (like "crowning" in British or American checkers). A player's turn ends whenever a soldier becomes an officer. An officer moves diagonally backward or forward like a king in British or American checkers.

A **"column"** may be a single piece or a pile of pieces.

A **"guide"** is the top piece of a column. The color of the guide shows to which player that column belongs, and its rank (soldier or officer) determines how the column may be moved.

Taking In Lasca, unlike other Checkers games, a piece is not removed from the board when it is taken. Instead, it is added to the bottom of the column that takes it. If a column contains several pieces, only the guide is taken when another column jumps over it.

In the example illustrated:

1) the black column takes the white guide from the white column;

2) the black column (led by an officer) takes the other white piece and black's turn ends;

3) the other white column (led by a soldier) takes the black guide and white's turn ends (**4**).

If a taken guide was an officer it retains this rank in the other column.

As in British or American checkers a player must take a piece whenever possible, but if he has a choice of captures, he need not take the larger number of pieces.

Taking

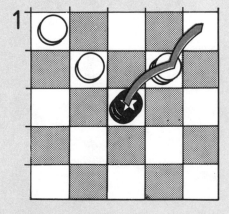

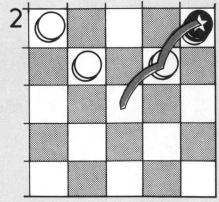

©DIAGRAM

Ludo

Ludo is a popular Western version of the ancient game of Pachisi (see p. 216). It is a game for two, three, or four players.

The board is a square-shaped piece of cardboard, marked out as shown.

The player's "home bases" and starting squares, the central columns of the cross leading to the finish, and the sections of the finish itself are all colored for easy identification – usually red, green, yellow, and blue.

When not traveling around the circuit, the counters are placed on a player's own "home base." There are no resting squares, but once a counter has reached its own colored column leading to the finish, it cannot be followed or taken.

Other equipment Each player has four plastic or cardboard counters – of one of the board's four colors. One die is used; it may be thrown from the hand or from a small plastic dice cup.

Objective Players race each other in trying to be the first to get all four of their counters to the finish.

Board

a Home bases
b Starting squares
c Finish

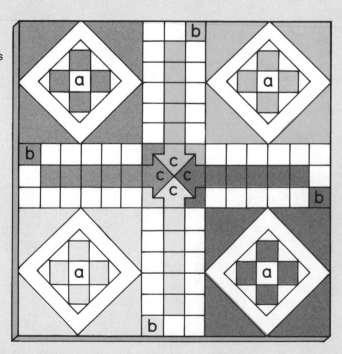

Play Each player chooses a set of counters.

The die is thrown to determine the order of play, the person throwing the highest number starting first.

Players take it in turns to throw the die for a 6 – the number needed to get a counter from its home base onto its starting square.

Whenever a player gets a 6 he is allowed another throw, moving one counter the number of squares indicated by the die.

Counters are moved around the circuit in a clockwise direction, as in Pachisi.

If a player has more than one counter on the circuit and he has a double throw (a 6 followed by another throw), he may move a different counter for each part of the throw.

Should a player throw two 6s in succession, he is allowed a third throw.

Taking If a counter lands on a square already occupied by an opponent's counter, the opponent's counter must be returned to its home base and can only re-enter the circuit on a throw of 6.

End play The finish can only be reached by a direct throw.

For example, if a counter is four squares away from the finish and the player throws more than a 4, he must either await his next throw or move one of his other pieces.

The winner is the first player to get all four of his counters to the finish.

Other equipment

©DIAGRAM

Mah jongg

Mah jongg is a tile game of Chinese origin that reached the West in the 1920s. Its name means "the sparrows." Each of four (or three) players plays for himself. Players collect sets of tiles with the object of completing their hands in a prescribed manner. Scores are settled after each hand, and the winner is the player with the most points when play ends.

The tiles Mah jongg tiles are made of bone, ivory, bamboo, wood, or plastic. Tile designs vary. Sets sold in the West usually have Arabic numerals in one corner of the suit tiles, and letters denoting the four winds.
A standard set has 144 tiles – 136 playing tiles and eight flower or season tiles.

Suit tiles

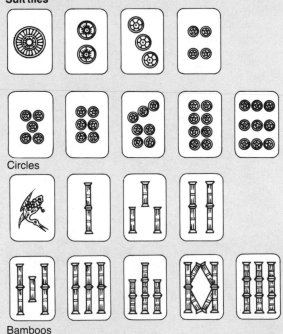

Circles

Bamboos

Suit tiles There are three different suits: circles (or dots), bamboos (or bams), and characters (or craks). Each suit comprises tiles numbered 1 through 9, and there are four of each type of tile. The 1 bamboo usually shows a symbolic bird. All other tiles have symbols for the suits.

Dragon tiles There are three different dragons: white, red, and green (left to right in the illustration). As with the suit tiles, there are four of each type of tile.

Wind tiles East, south, west, and north winds are represented. Again there are four of each type of tile.

Flower and season tiles These are eight individually marked tiles.

Racks Each player is provided with a rack to hold his tiles. The player who is east wind takes the differently colored rack.

Other equipment includes:
a) two dice;
b) scoring counters (small sticks) or a scoring pad;
c) optional wind indicators – either rotating indicators or separate disks.

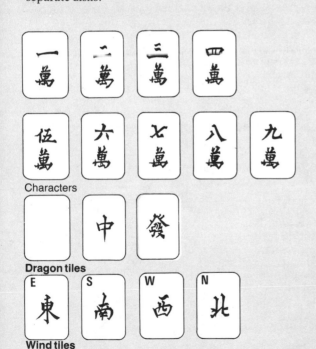

Characters

Dragon tiles

Wind tiles

©DIAGRAM

Flower and season tiles

Seating plan

Players Mah jongg is best played by four players, but can be played by three. Each player plays for himself.

Deciding the winds Each player is designated the name of a wind – east, south, west, and north.

Winds for the first hand are decided after the players are seated, when each player takes a turn to throw two dice. The player with the highest total throw becomes east. The other players' winds are determined by their position at the table relative to east: west sits opposite east, south sits to east's right, and north to east's left (not like a compass).

If the player who is east wind does not win the first hand, the winds pass counterclockwise around the table. Thus east becomes north, south becomes east, west becomes south, and north becomes west. If the player who is east wind wins a hand, the players retain the same winds for the next hand.

Duration A complete game consists of four rounds, but the game is in no way spoiled if players choose to stop earlier. Each round bears the name of a wind: the first is east, the second south, the third west, and the fourth north. As well as indicating the stage of the game, the "wind of the round" has an effect on scoring.

A round consists of however many hands are taken before the fourth player has lost a hand as east wind.

Building the wall All the tiles are placed face down on the table, and are thoroughly shuffled by the players.

Then, without looking at the tiles' faces, each player builds a wall that is 18 tiles long and two tiles high (with the long sides of the tiles touching and the faces down).

Each player then pushes his wall toward the center of the table until the four walls meet to form a hollow square representing a city wall.

Breaching the wall takes place once the wall is built. There are two stages.

1) East throws two dice to determine which side of the wall is to be breached. If he throws two 1s, he must throw again. Otherwise, he takes the total thrown and, starting with the length of his own wall as one, counts out the total counterclockwise around the table. The breach is to be made in the side of the wall where his count ends.

2) The player whose wall is to be breached now throws the two dice and adds his total to the total previously thrown by east. The new total is used to determine exactly where the breach will be made. The player counts clockwise along the top of his tiles, beginning at the right-hand corner. If the total is more than 18 he continues along the next wall. When the count ends, the player takes the two tiles from that stack and places them as shown. These moved tiles are called "loose tiles."

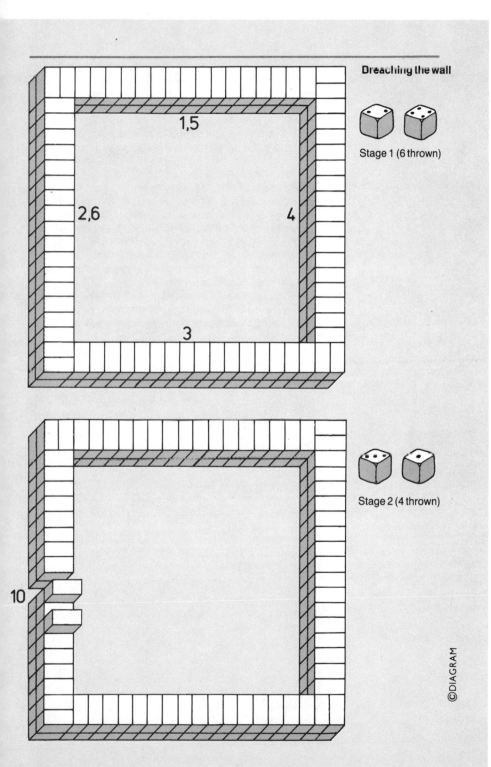

Breaching the wall

Stage 1 (6 thrown)

Stage 2 (4 thrown)

©DIAGRAM

Drawing the hands After the wall is breached east takes the two stacks (four tiles) from the opposite side of the breach to the loose tiles. South then takes the next two stacks, west the next two, and north the next two. The draw continues in this way until each player has 12 tiles.

East, south, west, and north then take one more tile in turn, and finally east takes one extra tile from the top of the next stack.

At the end of the initial draw east has 14 tiles and the other players have 13 tiles each.

Replacing flower and season tiles Any of these tiles drawn in the initial hand or later in the game must be placed face up in front of the player and replaced by a loose tile. Replacement at the start of the game must be in rotation, with east playing first.

For scoring purposes, each wind has its own season and flower. This is usually shown by numbers on Western Mah jongg sets – with east 1, south 2, west 3, and north 4.

Objective Each player aims to complete his hand and go "mah jongg" (sometimes called going "woo"). A complete hand usually consists of four *chows*, *pungs*, or *kongs*, plus an identical pair.

Drawing the hands

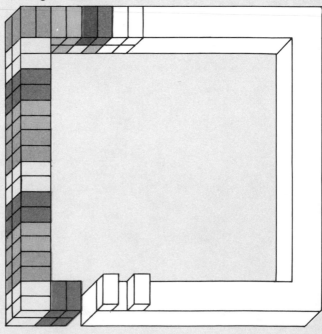

A *chow* is a run of three tiles of the same suit, eg 3, 4, 5 dots (**a**), or 7, 8, 9 craks. Mixed winds or mixed dragons do not count as *chows*.

A *pung* is a set of three identical tiles, eg three green dragons (**b**), three 8 bams, or three south winds.

A *kong* is a set of four identical tiles (**c**).

A pair may be any two identical tiles (**d**).

Special mah jongg hands that do not follow the conventional pattern are accepted by some players as alternative ways of going mah jongg. These special or "limit" hands normally score the maximum permitted for any one hand (see p. 199).

Most commonly accepted of these limit hands are:

1) hand of the thirteen odd majors (a 1 and a 9 of each suit, one of each dragon, one of each wind, and a pair to any of these tiles); and

2) calling nine tiles hand (tiles from the same suit – three 1s, three 9s, one each of tiles 2 through 8, and any one other tile of the same suit).

Parts of a hand

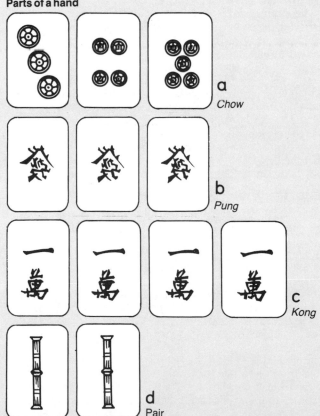

a
Chow

b
Pung

c
Kong

d
Pair

©DIAGRAM

Starting play East starts play by discarding any one of his 14 tiles.

Discarding tiles When a player discards a tile he must always call out its name, eg red dragon, east wind, 6 bams.

Discarded tiles are placed in the center of the table – usually face up in Western countries but face down in China and elsewhere in the East.

Playing order Play passes counterclockwise around the table except when a player interrupts the order to claim a discarded tile.

If more than one player claims a discarded tile, the order of precedence is:

1) a player claiming the tile to go mah jongg;
2) a player claiming the tile to make a *pung* or *kong*;
3) a player claiming the tile to make a *chow*.

If the playing order is interrupted for a claim, intervening players lose their right to any turn they may have missed. Thus if player 1 discards a tile and player 4 claims it, players 2 and 3 lose their turns and player 1 has the next turn unless player 4's discard is claimed by another player.

Playing a turn If no player claims the tile that was last discarded, the player to the right of the last player to discard now takes a tile from the wall. The new tile is taken from the end of the wall without the loose tiles. The player may conceal the tile's face from his opponents.

If he wishes to keep the new tile, he does so and discards another tile from his rack. Otherwise he discards the new tile.

Claiming tiles Only the tile that was last discarded may be claimed. It may be claimed to complete a *chow, pung,* or *kong*, or to go mah jongg.

Claims may be made even after the next player has taken a new tile from the wall – in which case the tile drawn from the wall must be replaced. Claims are not permitted if the next player has already made his discard.

Claiming a chow Only the player sitting to the right of the player who discarded is permitted to claim for a *chow*. The claiming player must already hold in his rack the other two tiles needed for the *chow*.

To claim the discard the player must call *"chow,"* pick up the tile, and then "expose" the complete *chow* by laying it face up in front of him.

The player then ends his turn by discarding a tile from his rack.

Claiming a pung Any player may claim the last discarded tile for a *pung* provided that:

a) he holds in his rack two tiles identical with the tile he is claiming;

b) he has played an intervening turn if he failed to *pung* that same tile on an earlier discard.

To claim the discard he must call *"pung,"* pick up the tile, and "expose" the *pung*. He then ends his turn by discarding a tile from his rack.

Concealed chows or pungs A player who has a *chow* or *pung* in his original hand, or who completes a *chow* or *pung* with a tile drawn from the wall, may keep these tiles "concealed" on his rack. This gives him greater maneuverability, conceals the state of his hand from his opponents, and doubles the value of a *pung*.

© DIAGRAM

Claiming a kong Any player may claim the last discarded tile for a *kong* if he holds in his rack three tiles identical with the tile he is claiming. To claim the discard he must call *"kong,"* pick up the tile, and "expose" the complete *kong*.

The player then draws a loose tile before discarding in the usual way. (A loose tile is always drawn after a *kong* because a complete hand has one extra tile for each *kong* it contains.)

Converting an exposed pung into a kong A player may convert an exposed *pung* into a *kong* if he draws the fourth similar piece from the wall. (This is the only time that an exposed set of tiles may be interfered with.)

Players are not permitted to claim discards to convert exposed *pungs* into *kongs*.

After a player has converted an exposed *pung* into a *kong*, he ends his turn by drawing a loose tile and then discarding in the usual way.

Concealed kong

A concealed kong A kong is "concealed" if:
a) all four tiles are in a player's original hand; or
b) a player with a "concealed" *pung* in his hand draws the fourth similar tile from the wall.

A player with a concealed *kong* may lay it on the table at any time when it is his turn to play.

A concealed *kong* laid on the table is worth double points and is distinguished from an exposed *kong* by turning over the end two tiles. If another player goes mah jongg while a player has a concealed *kong* on his rack, he scores only for a concealed *pung*.

Only after a player has laid a concealed *kong* on the table may he draw the loose tile needed to bring his hand up to the number of tiles required to go mah jongg.

Drawing loose tiles Loose tiles are used to make a player's hand up to the correct number of tiles – after a flower or season tile has been drawn or after a *kong*.

The tile farthest from the breach is used first and then the other loose tile. After both loose tiles have been used they are replaced by the two tiles at that end of the wall – the top tile going farthest from the breach.

Wrong number of tiles A player with the wrong number of tiles in his hand (on his rack and laid out on the table) cannot go mah jongg.

Excluding extra tiles in *kongs*, each player should always have 14 tiles after drawing or 13 tiles after discarding. A player with the wrong number of tiles must draw and discard tiles normally until another player goes mah jongg.

If the player in error had too many tiles, he pays the other players their scores without deducting any score for his own hand. If he had too few tiles, he deducts the score for his own hand before making payment.

Wrong tile drawn If the wall is breached in the wrong place or if tiles are drawn in the wrong order, the tiles should be reshuffled and the wall rebuilt.

Incorrect combinations If a player exposes an incorrect combination of tiles as a *chow, pung,* or *kong,* he must rectify the error before the next player discards or his hand is declared "dead." A player with a dead hand must pay the other players their scores with no allowance for his own hand.

Last 14 tiles A hand is declared "dead" if no player goes mah jongg before play reaches the last 14 tiles in the wall (including the loose tiles). There is no scoring and a new hand is played with the same player as east wind.

Calling A player is "calling" (or "fishing") when he requires only one tile to complete his hand. If two players are calling and both claim the same tile, precedence goes to the player whose turn would have come first.

A standing hand East wind may declare a "standing hand" if he is calling after making his first discard. Any player may declare a standing hand if he is calling after drawing and discarding for the first time in a hand.

A player who has declared a standing hand must not change any of the 13 tiles then in his hand. At each turn, he draws a tile from the wall in the usual way and then discards it if it is not the tile required to go mah jongg.

A player who completes a standing hand receives a bonus of 100 points.

Snatching a kong A player who is calling may complete his hand by "snatching a *kong*" – ie claiming a tile drawn from the wall by another player who uses it to convert an exposed *pung* into a *kong.*

Going mah jongg As soon as a player completes his hand, he stops play by calling "mah jongg." All players then expose their hands for scoring, turning over the middle tile of any *pungs* that were concealed in their hands.

Incorrect mah jongg If a player who has called "mah jongg" completely exposes his hand and then finds he has made an error, he must pay double the points limit to each of the other players. If his hand is only partially exposed when the error is discovered, he may cancel his call and put the tiles back on his rack.

Settling the scores After calculating the value of their individual hands, the players settle with each other in the following way.

If east wind goes mah jongg, he receives double the total value of his score from each of the other players.

If another player goes mah jongg, he receives double the value of his score from east wind, and the value of his score from each of the other players.

Each loser also settles with each of the other losers. When two losers settle (except when one of them is east wind), the player with the lower score pays the difference between his score and the other player's score.

When east wind is a loser, he pays or receives double the difference when settling with another loser.

Scoring Point values vary in different scoring systems, but the system given here shows the typical characteristics. With the exception of certain limit hands (described on p.199), the points value of each player's hand is calculated from the tables.

Using table A: points are scored by all players for *pungs* and *kongs* and for each flower and season tile (no points are scored for *chows*);
the player going mah jongg also scores for some pairs.

Using table B: the player going mah jongg adds any bonus points.

Using table C: players double their points as indicated, and again there are additional doubles for the player going mah jongg.

Table A   **Tile values**

All players	Exposed	Concealed
Any *chow*	0	0
Pung of tiles 2 through 8 of any suit	2	4
Pung of 1 or 9 of any suit	4	8
Pung of winds or dragons	4	8
Kong of tiles 2 through 8 of any suit	8	16
Kong of 1 or 9 of any suit	16	32
Kong of winds or dragons	16	32
Any season or flower	4	
Player going mah jongg		
Pair of any dragon	2	
Pair of player's own wind	2	
Pair of wind of the round	2	

Table B   **Bonus scores**

Player going mah jongg	
For going mah jongg	20
Winning tile drawn from the wall	2
Winning with only possible tile (ie with all other similar tiles exposed)	2
Winning with the last piece from the wall	10
Winning with a loose tile	10
For having no *chows*	10
For having no scoring value except flowers or seasons	10
Completing a standing hand	100

Table C   **Doubling**

	Number of times doubled
All players	
Pung or *kong* of any dragon	1
Pung or *kong* of player's own wind	1
Pung or *kong* of the wind of the round	1
Player's own season or flower	1
Four seasons or four flowers	3
Player going mah jongg	
Hand with no *chows*	1
Hand with no scoring tiles except flowers and seasons	1
Hand all one suit except for winds and/or dragons	1
Hand all 1s and 9s except for winds and/or dragons	1
Snatching a *kong* to go mah jongg	1
Hand all one suit	3
Hand all winds and dragons	3
Original hand (east wind's 14 tiles when play begins)	3

©DIAGRAM

Limit hands Most scoring systems have specified "limit hands," designed to prevent the scoring of an excessive number of points with a single hand.

Limit hands score a fixed number of points – usually 500 – regardless of their actual face value. East wind pays or receives double the limit.

Most limit hands may be obtained only by the player going mah jongg. Typical examples are:

a) hand of all winds and dragons;

b) hand of all 1s and 9s;

c) hand of concealed *pungs* and *kongs*;

d) hand of the thirteen odd majors;

e) calling nine tiles hand;

f) an original hand (east wind's hand when play begins);

g) hand completed with east's first discard;

h) east wind's thirteenth consecutive mah jongg.

Other hands score the limit whether or not completed. If the player with these hands fails to go mah jongg, he scores the limit from the other losers. Examples are:

i) hand with *pungs* or *kongs* of at least three dragons;

j) hand with *pungs* or *kongs* of three winds and a pair of the other wind.

Hand of all winds and dragons

Mancala games

Mancala is the generic name for a group of ancient African and Asian games, in which seeds are moved from cup to cup around a board in an attempt to capture opposing seeds. Names, boards, and rules differ from region to region but the basic principles of play are generally the same. Traditionally played by primitive tribesmen, the strategy of these games is highly complex and demands a fine mathematical calculation of possible moves and their results.

Mancala boards Mancala games are sometimes played in hollows scooped in the ground. They may equally well be played on a layout drawn on paper.
Traditionally, however, play is on a carved wooden board. The finest boards are like pieces of sculpture, intricately carved with patterns of symbolic significance.
Boards can be divided into two basic types according to the number and pattern of their cups. Commonest are two-rank boards. Four-rank boards are largely confined to parts of Southern and East Africa.
Seeds Traditionally Mancala games are played with seeds, beans, or small stones. Counters, marbles, or any small objects may be substituted.
Players Mancala games are for two players.

OWARI
Owari, played in West Africa, is a typical Mancala game and demonstrates the basic principles of Mancala play.
The board has 12 playing cups, in two rows of six, and two scoring cups.
Players face each other across the board and each is allocated the row of cups nearer to him and also one of the scoring cups.
Seeds 48 seeds are required.
Objective Each player attempts to capture as many seeds as possible.
Start of play Four seeds are placed in each of the 12 playing cups. Order of play is usually decided by lot.

Start of play

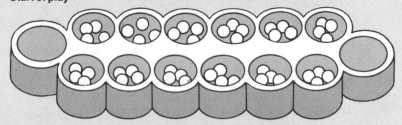

Sowing seeds

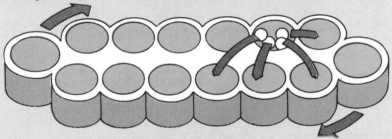

Play Turns alternate. In his turn each player takes all the seeds from a cup on his side of the board and "sows" them one by one in the cups around the board in a clockwise direction – thus if there are four seeds in his cup he sows one of them in each of the next four playing cups.

If there are 12 or more seeds in a cup, then the movement of the seeds from that cup will be more than one circuit of the board. In this case the emptied cup is missed out when sowing.

If all his opponent's cups are empty a player must, if possible, move a seed into his opponent's half of the board.

Capturing A player makes a capture if he sows a seed into one of his opponent's cups so that this cup then contains two or three seeds. This entitles the sower to take all the seeds from this cup and to place them in his scoring cup.

After making any capture, a player is also entitled to capture the seeds in adjacent cups containing two or three seeds.

A player is not, however, allowed to capture all the seeds in his opponent's cups (as this would prevent his opponent moving in his next turn). Instead he must leave intact any one cup that he chooses.

End of game Play ends when a player is unable to make a move or when none of the seeds remaining on the board can be captured.

Result The game is won by the player who captures most seeds.

Marbles

Games with marbles have been popular for thousands of years and are played in countries all over the world. The names and rules of marbles games vary tremendously from place to place, but the basic objective of any marbles game is to test how accurately a player can aim his marbles.

Marbles are small, hard balls made from stone, wood, baked clay, plastic, glass, or steel. They are usually about ½in in diameter. A marble actually being used by a player is sometimes called a "taw."

Shooting In some games players throw or drop their marbles. Usually, however, marbles must be rolled along the ground. Maximum accuracy and distance can be obtained by shooting the marble as illustrated – a method sometimes called "knuckling down." The knuckle of the forefinger is placed on the ground, the marble is balanced on the forefinger, the thumb is put behind the forefinger – and then released to shoot the marble.

Shooting

Claiming marbles is a feature of many marbles games. In some games a player may keep an opponent's marble if his own marble hits it.

Other games are played for points – with the difference in players' scores at the end of the game being settled by the payment of an agreed number of marbles for an agreed number of points.

CAPTURE

This is a simple marbles game for two players. Player A shoots his marble and then player B attempts to hit it with his marble. If player B hits A's marble, he may keep it.

If player B's marble misses A's marble, B's marble stays where it is and A attempts to hit it with a shot from where his marble lay after his first shot. If A hits B's marble he keeps it, otherwise turns alternate until one player takes the other's marble.

Spanning

SPANNERS

Spanners, or Hit and span, is a variation of Capture. As in Capture, a player who hits his opponent's marble may keep it. But in this game, a player may choose to attempt a "span" if his marble is near enough to his opponent's. He does so by placing his thumb on his own marble and a finger on his opponent's marble, and then flicking them together.

In one version of the game a successful span entitles him to take his opponent's marble as if he had hit it with his shot, but an unsuccessful span means that he loses his own marble.

In another version a player gains one point for a successful span – after which both players pick up their marbles and the player who did not win the point shoots first in the next play. (An unsuccessful span is ignored in this version.)

WALL MARBLES

In this variation of Capture several players shoot or throw their marbles against a wall. The first player sends a marble against the wall and leaves it where it stops.

Each of the other players then follows in turn, and:

a) leaves his marble where it stops if it fails to hit another marble as it rebounds from the wall; or

b) claims all the marbles on the ground if his rebounding marble hits any other.

If no player has hit another marble when all the players have had a turn, play continues in the same way but with each player delivering his marble from where it stopped in the first round.

RING TAW

Ring taw is a game for any small number of players.

Two circles are drawn on the ground – an inner circle about 1 ft in diameter and an outer circle about 7 ft in diameter. At the start of the game each player puts one or two marbles in the inner circle.

Each player then shoots in turn from any point outside the outer circle.

If a player knocks one or more marbles from the inner circle, he wins them and is entitled to another shot. This shot is taken from where his "taw" (the marble he last shot with) came to rest.

If a player fails to knock any marble from the inner circle, his turn ends and he must leave his taw where it stopped.

Succeeding players may shoot at any marble within either of the circles – taws as well as the marbles originally placed in the inner circle.

Whenever a taw is hit its owner must pay one marble to the player who hit it.

After his first turn, each player shoots his taw from where it came to rest at the end of his previous turn.

The game ends when all marbles have been cleared from the inner circle.

INCREASE POUND

In this variation of Ring taw the inner circle is known as the "pound" and the outer ring as the "bar." Play is exactly the same as for Ring taw except that:

a) there is no extra shot for hitting a marble out of the pound;

b) a player whose taw stops in the pound must lift his taw and pay a marble into the pound;

c) a player whose taw is struck by the taw of another player must pay that player one marble plus all the marbles that he has won up to this stage of the game.

FORTIFICATIONS

This is another variation of Ring taw, for which players draw four circles one inside the other.

At the start of the game each player places three marbles in the innermost circle or "fort" (**a**); two marbles in the next ring out (**b**); and one in the next (**c**). The outer ring (**d**) is left empty.

Each player plays in turn. With his first shot, made from any point outside the outer circle, each player attempts to knock a target marble from ring (**c**). If he succeeds, he keeps the target marble and leaves his taw in the target marble's place. If he fails, he pays one marble into ring (**c**) and leaves the game.

If a player's taw hits an opponent's taw at any stage of the game, the opponent's taw remains in its new position until its owner uses it for his next turn. When requested, a taw may be temporarily lifted to allow a clear shot at a target marble.

For all turns after the first, each player still in the game plays his taw from where it lies or from any point on the outside circle. As in his first turn, he claims any target marble that he hits and, unless he is entitled to an extra shot, leaves his taw in the target marble's place.

As long as any target marbles remain in ring (c), players must attack that ring and are allowed only one shot in a turn. A miss at this stage of the game, however, does not compel players to drop out.

Once ring (c) is cleared of target marbles, players must attack ring (b). Play then proceeds exactly as for ring (c), except that a player who hits one target marble in ring (b) is allowed a second shot.

Once ring (b) is cleared of target marbles, players may attack ring (a). This time the only difference in procedure is that a player is entitled to a third shot if his first two shots both claim a target marble.

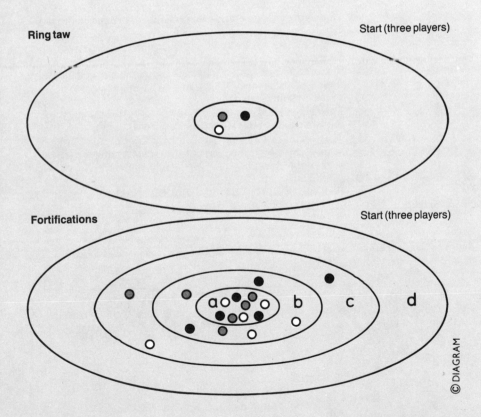

Ring taw

Start (three players)

Fortifications

Start (three players)

a b c d

© DIAGRAM

Die shot

DIE SHOT

In Die shot, or Die marble, players shoot their marbles at a target comprising a die balanced on a marble that has been filed down to make it more stable.

Each player becomes "die-keeper" for one round, while the other players make one shot in each turn. Before making a shot, each player must pay the die-keeper one marble.

If a player knocks the die off the marble, the die-keeper must pay him the number of marbles shown on the uppermost face of the die.

BOUNCE EYE

In this game for two or more players, each player places one or more marbles in a central cluster in a circle about 1 ft in diameter.

The first player then stands over the ring and drops a marble onto the cluster. He may claim any marbles that roll out of the circle, but if no marbles roll out of the circle he must add one marble to the cluster.

Players then drop a marble in turn until all the marbles in the central cluster have been claimed.

SPANGY

Spangy is a game for five players. A square is marked on the floor, and each player places one marble in the square to make the pattern illustrated.

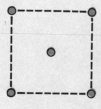

Each player then plays in turn, always shooting his taw from the same point about 10 yd from the square.

A player may claim any marble that he knocks out of the square, and if his taw stops within a "span" of any other marble he may also claim that marble if he makes a successful span (see Spanners, p.203).

Each player picks up his taw at the end of his turn.

Spangy

HUNDREDS

This game for two players is usually played outdoors but can easily be adapted to indoor play. Outdoors, players shoot marbles into a shallow hole; indoors, a drawn circle can be used.

At the start of the game each player shoots one marble toward the ring. If both players' marbles stop in the ring, both players shoot again.

When only one player's marble stops in the ring, he scores 10 points and then continues shooting and scoring until he misses or scores 100 points. If he misses, his opponent shoots and scores until he misses.

The game is won by the first player to reach 100 points.

THREE HOLES

This game can also be played indoors with drawn rings instead of holes. Three rings, about 3in in diameter and 5 ft apart, are marked on the floor.

The game is won by the player who "kills" (puts out) all his opponents or is first to shoot a marble into each ring in the correct order.

Each player plays in turn, and gains an extra shot if his marble stops in the correct ring or hits another player's marble. At the end of his turn a player must leave his marble where it lies.

Only after a player has scored the first ring can he "kill" another player by hitting his marble; he is, however, permitted to hit and move an opponent's marble before this stage.

When a player is "killed" he must pay his hitter the marble that was hit plus any marbles won in the game.

Hundreds

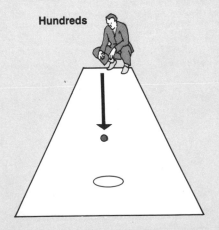

Three holes

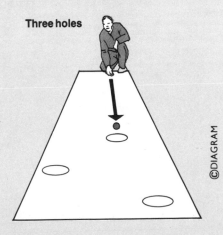

©DIAGRAM

ARCHBOARD

In Archboard, or Bridge board, players attempt to shoot their marbles through arches cut out of a piece of card or board.

Each player is keeper of the arches for one round of the game, while the other players shoot one marble in each turn. Before making a shot, each player pays the keeper one marble.

When his marble passes completely through an arch a player receives from the keeper the number of marbles shown above that arch. (Usually numbers are higher toward the outside of the bridge.)

If a player's marble misses the bridge completely, he must pay another marble to the keeper.

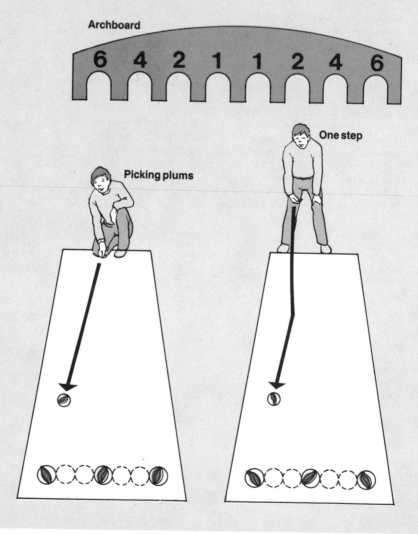

Archboard

One step

Picking plums

PICKING PLUMS

Picking plums is a game for any small number of players. Each player places one or two marbles in a row – with room for two marbles to pass through the gaps.

Each player then shoots in turn and may keep any "plums" knocked from the line. A player is entitled to an extra shot whenever he picks a plum; all shots are made from the original position and not from where the marble lies after the previous shot.

DOBBLERS

This game is played in the same way as Picking plums except that:

a player's taw stays where it lies at the end of a turn;

subsequent turns are played from where the taw lies;

a player whose taw is hit by another player's taw must add one marble to the row.

ONE STEP

One step is another game in which the target is a row of marbles made up by the players. It is played in the same way as Dobblers except that:

a player's first shot is made by taking one step and then throwing his taw from an upright position;

subsequent shots are made from an upright position but with no step forward;

a successful shot entitles a player to an extra shot from where his taw lies.

Nine men's morris

Nine men's morris, also called Mill, Morelles, or Merels, is one of the oldest games played in Europe and was particularly popular during the Middle Ages. It is a game of strategy for two people in which each player attempts to capture or block his opponent's pieces.

Board The game is played on a specially marked-out board, with three squares one inside the other and with points in the centers of the squares' sides connected by ruled lines. Bought boards are now usually made of wood. In the past, boards have been carved out of stone or, often, cut out of turf. A perfectly satisfactory board can be drawn on paper.

Pieces At the start of a game each player has nine "men" (counters, stones, or other appropriate pieces) distinguishable in color from those of his opponent.

Objective By the placing and maneuvering of men on the board, each player attempts to capture all but two of his opponent's pieces or to make it impossible for his opponent to move any piece at his turn.

Board and pieces

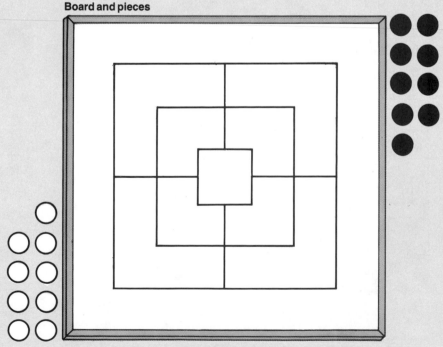

Play There are usually three stages of play:
1) placing the men on the board;
2) moving the pieces around;
3) "hopping" them.
(The third stage is sometimes disallowed, as it gives one player a distinct advantage over his opponent.)

Placing the pieces The players decide which of them is to start. Each one, in turn, then places one man of his own color on the board at any point of intersection not already occupied by another piece.

Players aim to get three of their own men into a straight line along one of the lines of the board, so forming a "mill."

Pounding Once a player has formed a mill he is entitled to "pound" his opponent by removing one enemy piece from the board. A player may not, however, remove an opponent's man that is part of a mill, unless there is no other man available. Once removed from the board, a piece is dead for the rest of the game.

Players continue their turns (nine turns each) until each of their men has been placed onto the board.

Placing the pieces

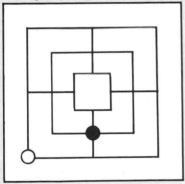

A mill

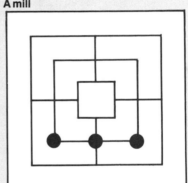

Pounding

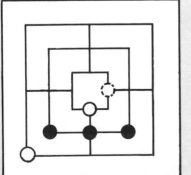

Moving the pieces Still taking alternate turns, players now move their men to try to form new mills and so pound their opponent.

A move consists of moving a man from his existing position on the board to any adjoining vacant point of intersection. (According to some rules players may take pieces by passing over an enemy piece to a vacant spot beyond it, as in Checkers, see p. 36.)

Players may form new mills by opening existing mills. This is achieved by moving a man one place from his position in a mill, and then returning him at the next move to his original position. Mills may be broken and re-made any number of times, and each new mill formation entitles the player to pound his opponent.

Play continues until one of the players is reduced by successive poundings to having only two men on the board; or until one player's pieces have been so blocked by his opponent's men that he is unable to make any move.

Should a player's only remaining pieces form a mill and it is his turn to move, he must do so even if this results in his losing a piece and the game at his opponent's next move.

Hopping is an optional stage of play, and begins when either player has only three men remaining.

The player is now no longer restricted to moving his men along a line to an adjacent point of intersection, but may "hop" to any vacant spot on the board. This freedom of movement gives him a certain advantage over his opponent, and so restores his chance of winning.

Results A player is defeated when either:
he is reduced to having only two pieces; or
his pieces are blocked by enemy men in such a way as to prevent further moves.
(If hopping has been allowed the game ends when one player has only two pieces remaining.)

Moving

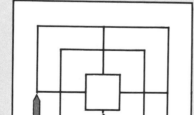

Hopping

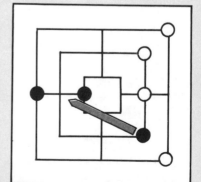

THREE MEN'S MORRIS

Three men's morris is a game for two players, each player having four counters of his own color.
The board is marked out as shown. Players take turns to put one man on a point of intersection, in an attempt to form a mill along one of the lines marked on the board. The first player to achieve this is the winner.

Three men's morris: start

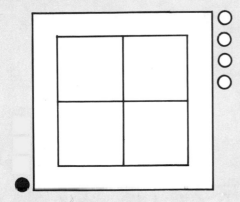

SIX MEN'S MORRIS

This game is played in much the same way as Nine men's morris. Players each have six counters and take turns to place them, one at a time, on the board (which is marked out as shown).
The objective is to form a mill along one of the sides of either of the squares. If a player succeeds in doing this, he may pound his opponent. As in Nine men's morris, once all the men have been played onto the board, the game continues with players moving their men to form new mills. When one player has only two men left, he loses the game.

Six men's morris: start

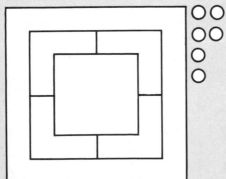

©DIAGRAM

Nyout

Nyout is a Korean race game that was probably played over a thousand years ago. It has retained its popularity over the centuries, now being played chiefly for money.

Board

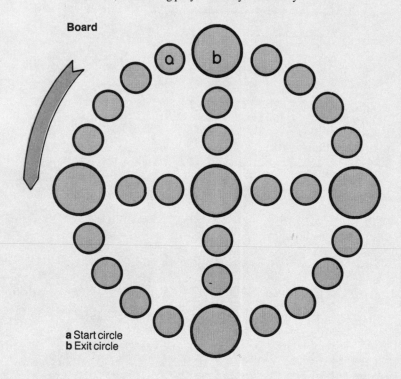

a Start circle
b Exit circle

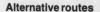

Alternative routes

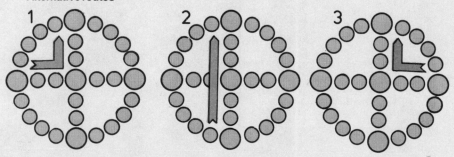

The board is marked out with colored circles; 20 circles form a ring and enclose a cross of nine other circles, as shown. The central circle and the four circles at the cardinal points are larger than the others. (Traditional boards have marks or symbols in place of circles.)

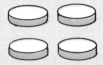

The pieces are traditionally carved from wood or ivory and are known as "horses." Any other counters or pieces may be used, provided that each player's pieces are easily distinguishable from those of his opponents. Each player has an agreed number of horses – usually two, three, or four.

Dice Koreans play with small flat strips of wood that score a maximum of 5, but a standard die may be used – rethrowing if a 6 shows.

Players Any number of players may take part, although the usual number is four – two players sometimes playing in partnership against the other two.

Objective Players race each other to be the first to get their horses around the board.

Play Players throw the die to determine their starting order, the player throwing the highest number starting first.

Each player in turn throws the die, advancing one of his horses the appropriate number of circles, and counting the start circle as 1.

Players may have more than one of their horses in the ring at any time. (In partnership play, a player may move either his own or his partner's horses.)

Horses are moved around the board in a counterclockwise direction, leaving the ring at the "exit" circle.

Alternative routes Whenever a horse lands on one of the large circles, it is allowed to take the alternative route along the horizontal and/or vertical arms of the cross. Routes (**1**) and (**2**) provide a short cut; route (**3**) can be a useful means of evading enemy horses on the circles leading to the exit.

Players need not take the alternative routes if, for strategic purposes, they consider it imprudent to do so.

Taking If a horse lands on a circle occupied by an opponent's horse, the opponent's horse is "taken" and returned to the start. The taker is then allowed another throw.

Double pieces If a horse lands on a circle already occupied by one of his own or his partner's horses, the horses may be moved together as a "double piece" in subsequent moves.

Pachisi

Dice

Pachisi is thought to have originated several thousand years ago and was the forerunner of many contemporary racing board games. Several older forms of the game are still played in Asia and South America. The game described here is that played in the Indian subcontinent.

Board The traditional Indian board is either woven, or made of cloth with the playing area marked out in embroidery. The playing area is in the shape of a cross and is divided into small squares, 12 of which are distinctively colored to identify them as "resting" squares (where any number of pieces is safe from capture).

Board

a Starting squares

b Resting squares

c Finish

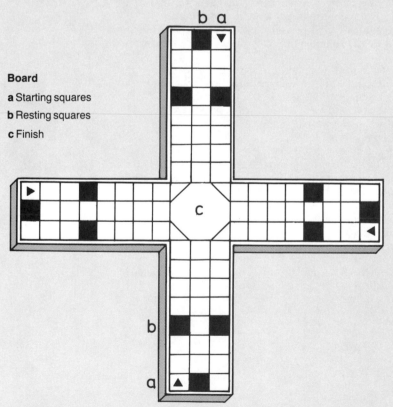

Pieces Each player has four shells, stones, or other objects that must be easily identifiable from those of his opponents.

Dice Traditionally, six cowrie shells are used. They are thrown from the hand and the position they adopt indicates the number of squares a piece must be moved, as follows:

Pieces

two shells with their openings uppermost, two;
three shells with their openings uppermost, three;
four shells with their openings uppermost, four;
five shells with their openings uppermost, five;
six shells with their openings uppermost, six.

If only one shell falls with its opening uppermost, the player moves forward ten squares.

If all the shells fall with their openings facing down, the player moves forward 25 squares.

If a player throws a 6, 10, or 25 he is allowed another throw.

Players Two, three, or four may play.

Objective In this race game, each player tries to be the first to get all four of his pieces around the board from the starting point to the finish.

© DIAGRAM

Play Each player in turn throws the cowrie shells, and moves one of his pieces the number of squares indicated by the shells. Pieces are moved in a clockwise direction around the board (see diagram).

At the start of the game each player's first piece may enter the race with any throw, but subsequent pieces (or the first piece if it has to repeat the route) may only enter the game if a 6, 10, or 25 is thrown.

A player may have one, two, three, or all of his pieces on the board at any one time.

After the players have each had one turn, they may – if they wish – miss a turn or decline to move a piece after making their throw.

Taking If a piece lands on any square other than a "resting" square already occupied by an opponent's piece, the opponent's piece is obliged to return to the start. It may only re-enter the game with a throw of 6, 10, or 25.

The player who took the opponent's piece is allowed another throw.

Once a piece has reached the central column of its own arm, leading to the finish, it cannot be taken.

Double pieces If a piece is moved onto a square occupied by another piece belonging to the same player, both pieces may be moved together as a "double piece" on subsequent moves. A double piece may never be overtaken by other pieces – whether the player's or an opponent's – and can only be taken if an enemy piece of equal strength lands directly on its square.

End of play The finish can only be reached by a direct throw. If, for example, a piece is seven squares away from the finish and the player throws more than a 7, he is obliged to await his next turn, or move one of his other pieces.

As soon as a piece lands on the finish, the piece is removed from the board.

The winner of the game is the first player to get all four of his pieces to the finish, and the game may be continued to determine the finishing order of the other players.

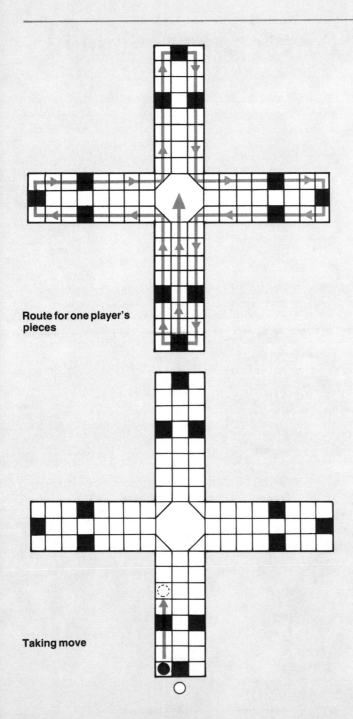

Route for one player's pieces

Taking move

© DIAGRAM

Party games: blindfold

In these games the blindfolded player's movements are a
source of much amusement. It is a good idea if an adult ties on
the blindfold and checks that it is tied neither so tightly as to be
painful nor so loosely that the "blind man" can peep out.

BLIND MAN'S BUFF
Objective A blindfolded player tries to catch and identify
another player.
Play A blind man is chosen and blindfolded. He is turned
around three times in the center of the room and then left on
his own.
The other players dance around, taunting him and dodging out
of his way to avoid capture.
When the blind man catches someone, he has two or three
guesses at the name of his prisoner. If he guesses correctly, the
prisoner becomes the new blind man. If wrong, he continues to
be the blind man and tries to catch another player.

TEN STEP BUFF
Objective As in Blind man's buff, a blindfolded player tries to
catch and identify another player.
Play The blind man stands in the center of the room. The other
players scatter around him and stand still.
The blind man takes ten paces and stretches out his hands. If he
touches a player, that player becomes the blind man. If not, he
takes another ten paces and tries again.

Blind man's buff

SQUEAK-PIGGY-SQUEAK

Objective A blindfolded player attempts to identify another player by getting him to squeak.

Play One player is blindfolded, given a cushion, and turned around three times in the center of the room. The others sit down around the room.

The blind man must then place his cushion on another player's lap and sit on it. He then calls "squeak-piggy-squeak" and the person he is sitting on squeaks like a pig. If the blind man recognizes the person, he changes places with him.

Once the new person is blindfolded, the players all change seats before he tries to sit on a player's lap.

BLIND MAN'S STICK

Objective A blind man tries to identify a player from the noises he makes.

Play One player is blindfolded and given a stick. The others form a circle and slowly move around him.

If the blind man touches a player with his stick, the player must grasp the stick. The blind man then asks the player to imitate a noise – for example a creaking door.

If the blind man guesses the player's name, that player becomes the new blind man. If he guesses incorrectly, the blind man must touch another player.

BLIND JUDGMENT

Play One player is blindfolded and placed on a "seat of judgment."

Another player then stands quietly in front of him, and the player in the judgment seat gives a brief description of whoever he thinks might be standing in front of him.

If the other players think that the "blind judgment" was reasonably accurate, the player in front of the blindfolded player becomes the new blind man.

If his judgment was inaccurate, the original blind man must pass judgment on another player.

BLIND MAN'S TREASURE HUNT

This game is an excellent way of giving out small presents at a party.

Objective Each player chooses a parcel by touch and tries to identify the contents before opening it.

Preparation Objects of different shape and feel are wrapped up – one parcel per player. The parcels are piled on a table.

Play Each player in turn is blindfolded and led to the table to choose a parcel. He then takes off his blindfold and waits until all the players have chosen a parcel. Each player then guesses what is in his parcel before opening it.

©DIAGRAM

BLIND POSTMAN

Objective A blindfolded player tries to sit in a vacant seat while two players are changing places.

Preparation One person is chosen to be postmaster. All the others choose a town, and the postmaster makes a list of their choices.

Play One player is blindfolded and becomes the first postman. All the other players sit in a circle. The postman stands in the center of the circle, and is turned around several times by the postmaster.

The postmaster then announces that a letter has been sent between two of the towns on his list, for example from Cambridge to Birmingham. The two players whose towns are called then try to change places before the postman sits in one of their empty seats.

If the postman gets a seat, the player without a seat becomes the new postman. More than one letter may be sent at a time.

Mode of travel The postmaster can also say how the letter traveled – and so indicate how the players should move. For example, if the letter went:

a) by air, they hop;
b) by sea, they walk backward;
c) by train, they crawl; and
d) by Pony Express, they bunny hop.

THIEVES

Objective A blindfolded player tries to catch players stealing from him.

Play One player is blindfolded and given a rolled newspaper to hold in his hand.

The blindfolded player sits in the middle of a circle made by the other players, and a pile of treasure – necklaces, brochures, bracelets, etc – is placed in front of him.

Players in the circle quietly take it in turns to steal a piece of treasure. If the blindman hears a thief, he strikes at him with the newspaper and calls "thief, thief."

If he touches a thief, the thief must return empty-handed to his place to await his next turn. The thief who collects most treasure wins the game.

JAILER

This is similar to Thieves except that the blindfolded man is guarding a bunch of keys.

The organizer names a player, who then has to take the keys from the jailer and carry them around the outside of the circle and back to his place.

The jailer listens for the thief and if he hears him points at him. If the jailer locates the thief the thief takes over as jailer.

Pin the tail on the donkey

PIN THE TAIL ON THE DONKEY

Objective Blindfolded players try to pin a tail in the correct position on a drawing of a tailless donkey.

Preparation The organizer draws a large picture of a donkey without a tail and fastens it onto a pinboard propped upright. He also makes a donkey's tail out of cardboard or wool and sticks a large pin through the body end.

Play Each player in turn is blindfolded and turned around so that he is in front of and facing the donkey. He is then given the tail and attempts to pin it on the correct part of the donkey. The organizer marks the position of each player's attempt. The player who pins nearest the correct place is the winner.

ELEPHANT'S TAIL

This is similar to Donkey's tail but instead of pinning on a tail players draw one. Each blindfolded player is given a crayon and draws a tail on a picture of an elephant (or any other animal).

MURALS

Preparation The organizer cuts out large pieces of paper for drawing on.

Play Each player in turn is blindfolded, given a crayon, and asked to draw a picture on a piece of paper pinned on the wall. The subject of the picture is chosen by the other players – good examples are a house, a person, or some kind of animal. The artist feels the edges of the paper and has one minute in which to draw the chosen subject. When everyone has had a turn, the drawings can be judged by an adult or by all the players together.

SWEET TOOTH

Objective Each player tries to identify foods that he has eaten while blindfolded.

Play Each player sits down and is then provided with a plate of foods such as chocolate, fudge, nuts, licorice, and pieces of orange.

When all the players have eaten or tasted all their foods, any leftovers are taken away and the blindfolds are removed.

The players then write down what they think they have eaten. If the players are too young to write, they can whisper their answers to an adult.

BLIND MAN'S SORT OUT

Objective Blindfolded players race to sort a collection of objects into categories.

Preparation The organizer collects a selection of buttons, screws, nails, beans, beads, etc.

Play The game is usually organized as an elimination contest – with two players competing at a time.

The objects are divided into two similar piles. The first two players are then blindfolded and each is placed in front of a pile of objects.

When the organizer calls "Go!" each of the blindfolded players starts sorting his objects into groups of buttons, screws, etc. The first player to finish sorting his objects into categories goes forward into the next round of the contest.

All the other players then compete in pairs, and the winners all go into the next round.

Further rounds are held until only two players remain for the final. The winner of the final wins the game.

BLINDFOLD OBSTACLE WALK

Blindfold obstacle walk

Preparation Everyone lays out obstacles – a pile of books, a glass of water, cushions, etc – from one end of the room to the other.

Play Several of the players volunteer to walk the course. They then leave the room to be blindfolded. Meanwhile the others quickly and quietly remove all the obstacles.

Each of the blindfolded volunteers is then brought in one at a time.

The blindfolded player then attempts to walk across the room without hitting the obstacles. To add to the fun all the onlookers utter appropriate gasps and shudders.

When he has completed the "course" the blindfold is removed.

NELSON'S EYE

This game plays on a blindfolded person's heightened imagination.

Play Several volunteers who do not already know the game are asked to leave the room. They are blindfolded and brought back into the room one at a time.

One of the other players begins by asking the blind man to feel "Nelson's good leg" – and the blind man's hands are guided so that he can feel someone's leg.

He is then asked to feel Nelson's bad leg – and his hands are guided to a chair leg.

Next the blind man must feel Nelson's good arm – and feels someone's arm. Then he must feel Nelson's bad arm, which can be a stuffed stocking.

This is followed by Nelson's good eye, which can be a marble. Finally he is asked to feel Nelson's bad eye – and is presented with a squashy pickled onion or a soft flour and water mixture. The blind man usually becomes rather squeamish at this point – much to the amusement of the other players!

Nelson's eye

MURDER IN THE DARK

Although players are not blindfolded for this game, a "detective" attempts to identify an unseen "murderer." The opening stages of play take place in the dark.

Preparation One small piece of paper per player is folded and placed in a hat. One is marked with a cross, another with a D, and all the others are blank.

Play Each player draws a piece of paper from the hat. The player who gets the paper with the cross is the murderer and the one with the D the detective. The detective first leaves the room and the lights are switched off.

The other players then dance slowly around the room in the dark. The murderer catches a victim and puts his hands on the victim's shoulders. The victim must scream and fall to the ground. The lights are then switched on and the detective is called in.

The detective tries to identify the murderer by questioning everybody except the victim. All the players except the murderer must answer his questions truthfully.

After the questioning the detective accuses his prime suspect of the murder, saying "I charge you (name of suspect) with the murder of (name of victim)." If the accusation is correct, the murderer must admit his guilt.

Party games: contests

In these games players perform various feats of skill. Some of the games are a test of physical strength or ability, others need ingenuity in order to outwit opponents. It is a good idea in case of dispute for someone to act as referee.

Balloon flights

BALLOON FLIGHTS
Objective Each player tries to flick a balloon the farthest distance.
Play Players form a straight line. Each person balances a balloon on the palm of one hand. Balloons should all be a different color, or marked with the players' initials.
The referee counts "One, two, three, go," and each player then flicks his balloon with the first finger and thumb of his other hand. The player whose balloon makes the longest flight is the winner.

STATIC ELECTRICITY
Objective Each player tries to have the most balloons clinging to a wall at the end of a time limit.
Preparation Plenty of balloons are inflated and their necks tied.
Play The balloons are placed in a pile in the center of the room and each player is allocated an area of wall.
On the word "Go," each player takes a balloon, rubs it on his clothing to create static electricity, and then tries to make it cling to the wall.
If he succeeds, he takes another balloon and does the same, and so on with as many balloons as possible. If the balloon falls off the wall any player may use it again.
End At the end of a time limit, the player with the most balloons still clinging to the wall wins.

HOPPIT
Objective Each player tries to hop the farthest while making progressively larger hops.
Play Using strands of yarn, two straight lines are marked on the floor. The lines are about 1ft apart at one end of the room and fan out to about 5ft apart at the other.
Players take turns at hopping back and forth across the two lines. They start at the narrow end and move down the room. The player who gets the farthest down the line before failing to hop right across the two lines is the winner.

SINGING HIGH JUMP
This is a test of vocal range – each player aims to sing the most widely spaced low and high notes.
Play The referee stands by a "take-off" line ready to score each player's attempt.
In turn, each player runs up to the take-off line, stops, and sings two notes: the first as low as possible, the second as high as possible. The player who makes the highest musical "jump" is the winner.

APPLE ON A STRING

This game is an old favorite for Halloween. Players try, without using their hands, to eat apples suspended from strings.

Play A piece of string is hung across the room, well above head height. One apple (or cookie) per person is suspended from it, also on a string.

The players try to eat their apples or cookies without using their hands. The first player to eat the apple down to its core, or to finish eating the cookie, is the winner.

APPLE PARING

Objective Each player tries to peel the longest unbroken paring from an apple.

Play Each player is given an apple, a knife, and a plate. All the apples and all the knives should be of similar quality.

The players then peel their apples. The winner is the one to produce the longest and narrowest paring.

CANDY WRAPPER

This game is similar to apple paring, but instead of fruit the players get a candy to eat.

Objective Each player aims to tear a candy wrapper into a long, thin, spiral strip.

Play Each player is given a candy, which he unwraps. While eating the candy, he tears its wrapping paper, starting at the outer edge and tearing round and round toward the center. The player with the longest unbroken strip of paper wins.

Apple on a string

HAPPY TRAVELERS
Each player tries to be the first to sort the pages of a newspaper into the correct order.

Preparation For each player the pages of a newspaper are put together in the wrong order – some pages may be upside down or back to front – and then folded.

Play Players sit facing each other in two rows. They should sit very close together like passengers on a crowded train.
Each player is given one of the newspapers. At the word "Go!" each player tries to rearrange the pages of his newspaper into the correct order. The first player to succeed wins the game.

PRINTERS' ERRORS
In this game players try to set out jumbled lines of a printed article into their correct order.

Preparation A jumbled article is needed for each player. The organizer makes as many copies of the article as he needs and then jumbles each one by cutting it into pieces after each line.

Play Each player is given his jumbled article. When the organizer gives the signal players start to sort out their articles. The winner is the first player to put his article into the correct order.

CARD AND BUCKET CONTEST
Objective Players try to flick all their cards into a bucket or other large container.

Play Each player is given ten playing cards – preferably old ones – and writes down which ones they are.
The players then form a large circle around a bucket. At a call of "Go!" each player tries to flick his cards into the bucket. When all the players have flicked all their cards, the cards in the bucket are identified.

The winner is the player who gets most cards into the bucket. Several rounds may be played.

Card and bucket contest

GRANDMOTHER'S FOOTSTEPS

Objective Each player tries to be the first one to creep up behind the "grandmother" without her seeing him move.

Play One person is chosen as the grandmother and stands, with shut eyes, facing a wall.

The other players line up against the opposite wall. When everyone is ready, the players start to creep up behind the grandmother – but whenever she looks round they must "freeze" into statues.

The grandmother may look round as often as she likes. If she sees anyone moving, she points to him and he has to go back to the start. The grandmother turns round to face the wall, and the players move forward again.

The first player to touch the grandmother's wall wins – and takes the next turn at being grandmother.

LIMBO

Originally a West Indian acrobatic dance, this is a test of suppleness and sustained contortion.

Play Two people gently hold a long stick horizontally and at chest height.

Each player in turn bends backward and edges himself under the stick. He must neither touch the floor with his hands nor touch the stick.

If a player, after two attempts, fails to pass under the stick he is eliminated. After each round the stick is lowered a little. The last person to stay in the game is the winner.

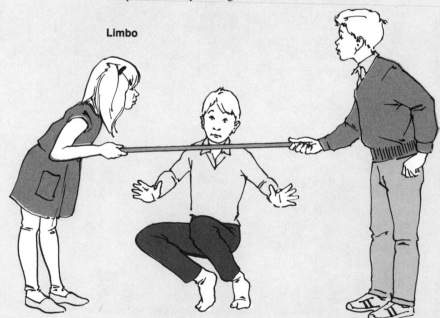

Limbo

TWO-MINUTE WALK

Objective Each player tries to walk from one end of the room to the other in exactly two minutes.

Play Players line up along one wall. On the word "Go," they set off across the room. Without using a watch or a clock, each player tries to reach the other side of the room in exactly two minutes. The organizer times the players' walks.

When all the players have finished, the player whose time was nearest two minutes wins.

Two-minute walk

©DIAGRAM

RUMORS

This is a competitive form of the popular old game of Chinese whispers.

Objective Each player tries to pass on a message that has been whispered to him.

Play Players divide into two equal teams and each team sits down in a circle. Players take it in turns to be team leader. The organizer decides on a message and whispers it to the two leaders.

Each leader then whispers the message to the player to his right. This player then whispers the message as he heard it to the player to his right, and so on around the circle. Whisperers are not allowed to give the message more than once.

The last player of each team tells the leader the message as he heard it. The leader then tells the message as it began. The team that kept the message most intact wins the game.

STORK FIGHTING CONTEST

Play Two players tie their left ankles together with a scarf, and hop on their right feet.

Each player then tries to make his opponent's left foot touch the ground – without putting down his own left foot.

If a player's left foot touches the ground, his opponent scores a point.

The winner is the player with the most points at the end of a time limit.

COCK FIGHTING CONTEST

Play Two players crouch on the floor facing each other.

Each brings his knees together under his chin and clasps his legs with his arms. A walking stick is then passed under his knees and over his arms.

The two players then try to tip each other over.

The first player to succeed in making his opponent fall over is the winner.

Cock fighting

TRIANGULAR TUG-OF-WAR

This is a game for three players.

Play A circle is made from a rope about 3yd long. Three players space themselves around the rope and hold it taut, forming a triangle. A handkerchief is placed at each corner of the triangle, out of reach of the players.

On the word "Go!" each player tries to pick up the handkerchief nearest him without letting go of the rope. The first player to pick up his handkerchief is the winner.

Triangular tug-of-war

ARM WRESTLING

Play Two players sit facing each other at either side of a table. Resting their right elbows on the table and with crooked arms, they clasp each other's right hands. (Both players may use their left arms if they prefer.)

On the signal to begin each player tries to force his opponent's right hand back until it touches the table. Elbows must be kept firmly on the table. The winner is the first to succeed.

Arm wrestling

©DIAGRAM

Party games: goal scoring

Although goal scoring games are often based on energetic
outdoor sports, they can safely be played in the home if a
balloon, soft ball, or large rag is used. Playing with balloons is
particularly enjoyable as they are difficult to control and
unlikely to cause damage.

AVENUE GOALS

Players try to score goals by patting a ball or balloon so that it
goes beyond their opponents' end of the avenue.
Players The players form two lines about 5ft apart, and sit or
kneel facing each other on the floor.
Counting from one end, the odd-numbered players in one line
belong to the same team as the even-numbered players in the
other line.
Each team is allotted one end of the avenue as its goal.
Play The organizer puts the ball into the center of the avenue.
Each team tries to score by patting the ball by hand down the
avenue into its opponent's goal. Players are not allowed to
hold or throw the ball. The ball is put back into the center of
the avenue after each goal. The winning team is the one with
most goals at the end of a time limit.

OVERHEAD GOALS

Players try to score goals by patting a balloon over their
opponents' heads.
Players The players form two teams in rows about 4ft apart,
and sit facing each other on the floor.
Play The organizer tosses the balloon into the center.
Each team tries to score goals by knocking the balloon over the
heads of the opposing team and onto the ground behind them.
The winning team is the one with most goals at the end of a
time limit.

Avenue goals

©DIAGRAM

BALLOON VOLLEYBALL

In Balloon volleyball players hit a balloon over a piece of string held taut by two players standing on chairs.

Players The players divide into two teams, one on either side of the string. Players within a team take turns at serving (hitting the balloon into play at the start of play or after a break).

Play Players hit the balloon back and forth over the string with the aim of making a shot that their opponents will not be able to return.

A team scores a point whenever it hits the balloon over the string onto the floor on its opponent's side. If the ball goes under the string, the opposing team serves it.

The winning team is the one with most points at the end of a time limit.

BLOW VOLLEYBALL

This is played in exactly the same way as Balloon volleyball except that the balloon is blown rather than hit, and the string is held lower.

Balloon volleyball

ASTRIDE BALL

This is a goal-scoring game without teams.

Players One player stands in the center of a circle formed by the other players standing with their legs apart.

Play The center player has a ball to be rolled along the ground. If he rolls it between the legs of a player in the circle, he "scores a goal" and changes places with that player.

The players in the circle should keep their hands on their knees except when trying to prevent a goal.

HOCKEY RAG TIME

In this game team members take turns at trying to shoot a goal.

Players The players form two rows about 6ft apart and sit facing each other on the floor. Each team member is given a number, starting with one.

A rag and two walking sticks are laid on the floor between the two rows of players. A chair is placed at each end of the avenue as a goal. Each team is allotted one of the goals.

Play The organizer calls out a number. Each player with that number picks up a walking stick and uses it to maneuver the rag into his opponent's goal. The successful player scores a point for his side.

The rag and walking sticks are replaced and the organizer calls another number.

The winning team is the one with most goals at the end of a time limit.

Astride ball

©DIAGRAM

Party games: musical

These are all active games in which players move around to music. When the music stops, the players must immediately stand still or change what they are doing. All the games require someone to organize the music.

MUSICAL CHAIRS
Preparation Chairs are placed around the room in a large circle. There should be one chair fewer than the number of players.
Play The players stand in the circle and, when the music starts, all dance around.
When the music stops, each player tries to sit on a seat. The player left without a seat is eliminated.
One chair is then removed from the circle and the music is restarted. The last person to stay in the game is the winner.

MUSICAL BUMPS
This is like Musical chairs, except that it is played without the chairs. When the music stops, players sit down on the floor. The last person to sit down is out.

OWNERSHIP MUSICAL CHAIRS
In this version of Musical chairs there is one chair per person. Before the music starts each player sits on a chair and marks it as his own.
When the music starts, the players dance around the circle in the same direction.
When the music stops, the players continue moving around the circle. As each player comes to his own chair he sits down. The last player to sit on his chair is out and remains seated.
The organizer may vary the game by calling directions to the players as they move around – eg walk backward, or turn to the right.
The last person to stay in the game is the winner.

MUSICAL BLACKOUT
This is played like Musical chairs except that when the music stops, the lights are switched off for five seconds. When the lights are switched on again, any player who has not found a chair is eliminated.

HIGH STEPPERS

Preparation Pairs of chairs with their fronts touching are placed around the room to form a circle of hurdles.
Play The players space themselves around the room in pairs. When the music starts, they march around the room and must climb over the hurdles as they come to them. When the music stops, any pair touching a hurdle is eliminated.
The music starts again and the game continues. The winning pair is the last one left in the game.

MUSICAL HOTCH POTCH

In this game, players race for objects instead of chairs.
Preparation A pile of objects, numbering one fewer than the number of players, is placed in the center of the room.
Play When the music starts, players hop or dance around the pile.
When the music stops, each player dives for an article from the pile. The larger the objects, the less likely are the players to bump their heads!
The player left without an object is out. One object is removed from the pile and the game continues.

Musical chairs

MUSICAL ISLANDS
Preparation Small mats, newspapers, pieces of cardboard, etc are scattered over the floor to form "islands."
Play When the music starts, players walk around in a circle. When the music stops, players must stand on an island. More than one player may stand on one island.
Anyone unable to get onto an island or falling off into the "water" is eliminated. The music starts again and the game continues.
Islands are gradually removed during the game. The last player left in the game is the winner.

MUSICAL MAGIC CARPET
The organizer chooses a part of the floor as a "magic patch" but keeps its position a secret.
Play When the music starts the players dance in pairs. When the music stops, they stop dancing.
The pair nearest the magic patch wins a prize, and the game continues until all the prizes are won.
Alternatively, the game can be played for points. The pair nearest the magic patch scores a point, and the game is won by the pair with most points after an agreed time.

MUSICAL RINGS
This is a game for a large room and many players.
Play Players space themselves around the room. When the music starts, they dance around.
When the music stops, the organizer announces a number and players quickly arrange themselves into groups of this size. Any spare players unable to form a group of the right size are out. The game ends when only two players remain. These players are the winners.

GODS AND GODDESSES
This is a game requiring fairly slow and gentle music.
Preparation Each player is given a book.
Play When the music starts, the players walk around the room balancing the books on their heads.
When the music stops, each player goes down on one knee. If a player's book falls off, he is eliminated.
The music starts again and the game continues. The last player left in the game is the winner.

MUSICAL STATUES
This game is an enjoyable "quiet" alternative to Musical chairs.
Play Players dance around the room to music. When the music stops, the players immediately stop dancing and stand as still as statues.
Any player seen moving after the music stops is eliminated. The music is started again fairly quickly and the game continues.
Eliminated players can help to spot moving statues. The last player to remain as a dancer is the winner.

Musical statues

©DIAGRAM

Party games: observation

In addition to games of pure observation, such as Memory game, this group includes a wide variety of hunting games. Many hunting games involve searching for hidden objects, whereas in Hide and seek and its entertaining alternative, Sardines, it is other players who must be hunted.

MEMORY GAME
This is an excellent test of the players' powers of observation. excellent test of the players' powers of observation.
Preparation The organizer puts about 20 small objects on a tray. He then covers them with a cloth until play begins.
Play The organizer uncovers the objects and allows the players about 3 minutes in which to memorize them. The players are not allowed to make any notes.
At the end of the time limit the organizer covers the tray with the cloth and gives each player a pencil and paper. The players are then asked to write down as many of the objects as they can. The winner is the player who remembers most objects.

Memory game

MISMATCHES

This is a team observation game, in which one team tries to spot all the "mismatches" made by the other.

Play Players divide into two teams. One team leaves the room while the other makes its mismatches by altering things in the room.

For example the team making the mismatches might change the position of objects – such as turning a vase upside down – or might change something about a person – such as putting a cardigan on inside out.

At the end of a time limit the other team returns and tries to spot the mismatches. At the end of another time limit, any mismatches that have not been noticed score one point for the team that made them.

The teams then change roles, and the winning team is the team that scores most points.

WRONG!

In this game players try to spot deliberate errors in a story that is read to them.

Preparation The organizer writes a short story in which there are numerous errors of fact – for example he might say that he went to the antique shop and bought a new clock.

Play The organizer reads out the story. If a player spots a mistake he shouts "Wrong!" The first player to call out a mistake scores one point. A player who shouts when there has been no mistake loses one point. The player with most points at the end of the story wins the game.

CUT-OUT PAIRS

This is a good game for introducing players to each other at the start of a party.

Preparation All sorts of pictures are cut out of magazines, comics, etc. Each picture is pasted onto cardboard and cut into two oddly shaped pieces. (Picture postcards may be used to save time.) There should be one picture for each pair of players.

Play Each player is given one piece of a picture. He then tries to find the player with the other half of the same picture. When two players have a complete picture they write a suitable caption for it. Pictures and captions are displayed and the writers of the funniest caption may win a prize.

MOTHERS AND BABIES

This is another pairing game along the lines of Cut-out pairs. For this game players are given a card showing a mother or a baby animal – for example a cow or a calf, a frog or a tadpole. Players then have to find the player with the card showing the other member of their family.

HUNT THE SLIPPER

In this game one player tries to find which of the others is holding the slipper. A little acting greatly adds to the fun.

Play All the players but one sit with their feet touching in a circle on the floor. These players are the cobblers.

The other player has a small slipper (or shoe) which he says is in need of repair. He then gives the slipper to the cobblers and asks them to mend it.

He walks away and returns several times to see if it is ready. Each time the cobblers pretend that it is not quite finished. Finally, however, they admit that they have lost it.

The hunt The cobblers now pass the slipper from one to another under their knees. The customer tries to touch a cobbler while he is holding the slipper. When he succeeds, the slipper is "found" and the customer and the cobbler holding the slipper change places.

HUNT THE RING

This is another game in which one player tries to find which of the others is holding an object.

Preparation A curtain ring is threaded onto a long piece of string. The two ends of the string are then tied together with a knot that is small enough to allow the ring to pass easily over it.

Play One player stands in the middle of the room and the others form a circle around him. The players in the circle each hold the string with both hands – and one of them also holds the ring so that the player in the middle cannot see it.

When the player in the middle says "Go!" the others pass the string through their hands – passing the ring from hand to hand at the same time.

The player in the center tries to locate the ring by touching any hand he thinks conceals it. A player must open his hand if it is touched. If it concealed the ring, he must change places with the player in the center. If his hand is empty, the original player stays in the middle.

UP JENKINS!

This game is similar to Hunt the ring but is played with any small object instead of a ring on a string.

Play One player sits on the floor in the middle of a circle formed by the other players sitting around him. The players in the circle sit with their hands behind their backs and one of them holds the small object.

When the player in the middle says "Go!" the players in the circle all pass, or pretend to pass, the object around the circle behind their backs.

When the player in the middle says "Up Jenkins!" the players in the circle, including the one with the object, must all raise their clenched fists.

When the player in the middle says "Down Jenkins!" the players in the circle must put their hands palms down on the ground – and the player with the object must, of course, do his best to keep the object concealed at this stage of the game. The player in the middle then tries to identify which of the players is hiding the object.

Up Jenkins!

©DIAGRAM

Hunt the thimble

HUNT THE THIMBLE
This very popular game is usually played with a thimble, but any other small object will do just as well.
Play All the players but one leave the room while this player hides the thimble somewhere in the room or on his person. He then calls the other players back into the room to look for it. The game is won by the first player to find the thimble and take it to the player who hid it. The finder then has a turn at hiding the thimble.

SIT DOWN HUNT THE THIMBLE
This is played in the same way as the last game except that when a player sees where the thimble is hidden he sits down on the floor.
The last person to see the thimble and sit down must pay a forfeit. The player who sat down first has the next turn at hiding the thimble.

SINGING HUNT THE THIMBLE
This is played like Hunt the thimble except that only one player leaves the room while one of the others hides it.
On his return, the players who stayed in the room try to guide him to the thimble by singing. They sing more loudly as he moves closer to the thimble and more quietly as he moves away.

HOT AND COLD THIMBLE
As in Singing hunt the thimble, only one player leaves the room while the thimble is hidden.
The other players help him find the thimble by telling him how "hot" he is in different parts of the room. If he is in the wrong part of the room he is "very cold" or "cold." As he approaches the thimble he is "getting warmer" – until he becomes "warm," "hot," and finally "very hot" just before he touches the thimble.

BEAN HUNT
Preparation The organizer hides a large quantity of beans around the room. A small container such as a paper cup is needed for each player.
Play Each player collects as many beans as he can within a given time limit. The player who finds most beans is the winner.

Butterfly hunt

BUTTERFLY HUNT
This game is played in the same way as Bean hunt except that players look for paper butterflies hidden by the organizer. The winner is the player who finds most butterflies after an agreed time limit.

JIGSAW HUNT

Preparation One "jigsaw" is needed for each player. The organizer makes the jigsaws by cutting picture postcards into four irregular pieces. Three pieces from each jigsaw are hidden in the room.

Play Each player is given one of the jigsaw pieces that was not hidden. The first player to find the three pieces missing from his jigsaw wins the game.

Jigsaw hunt

PRESENT HUNT

Each player is given a piece of paper with a written clue to guide him to his present.

COLOR HUNT

This game is played in the same way as Present hunt except that each player is given a small piece of wrapping paper and then hunts for and keeps the present wrapped in the same sort of paper.

Easter egg hunt

EASTER EGG HUNT

Each player hunts for a chocolate Easter egg wrapped in a particular color of paper. Alternatively, a tag with the name of one of the players may be attached to each hidden egg.

CARD HUNT

In this game players form two teams and look for playing cards hidden around the room.

Preparation Two decks of playing cards are needed. The cards from one deck are hidden around the room within reach of the players.

The other deck is divided into two piles – one of red cards and one of black cards.

Play Each member of one team is given a black card and each member of the other team is given a red one.

Each player searches for the hidden card that matches the card he has been given. When a player finds the card he is looking for he takes it to the organizer who gives him another card of the same color.

Play continues in this way until one of the teams has found all its cards.

Card hunt

© DIAGRAM

HIDDEN OBJECTS
In this game players look for objects hidden all around the house.

Preparation The organizer hides about 20 objects in different rooms. It should be possible to see the objects without moving anything. A list of the objects is prepared for each of the players.

Play Each player is given a list and tries to locate the objects, noting down wherever he finds one.

The game is won by the first player to locate all the objects and take his list to the organizer.

DETECTIVE TREASURE HUNT
This game requires more preparation and ingenuity than most hunting games.

Preparation The organizer draws up a series of clues in such a way that the solution of each clue will lead players to the hiding place of the next one.

The solution of the last clue may lead to:
a) a prize for the first player or pair to find it;
b) a pile of presents, one for each player; or
c) the table bearing the party food.

Play Sometimes players take part on their own. Alternatively they may play in pairs.

The organizer gives each player or pair the first clue. As the other clues are discovered, they should be left in their places for the other players to find.

STOREKEEPERS
This is an enjoyable team hunting game. It is best if there are about four teams each with three of four members. Each team represents a different store.

Preparation The organizer takes a number of plain cards and writes the name of a commodity on each one. These commodities should be items sold in the stores that will be represented. There should be an equal number of cards for each store. These cards are hidden around the room.

Play The players form teams and each team is given the name of a store – for example the bakery or the grocery store. The players are told how many commodities are missing from the stores.

Each team chooses a "storekeeper," who stands in the middle of the room. The other players then look for the cards and when they find a card for their own store take it to their storekeeper.

The game is won by the team that first finds all its hidden commodities.

HIDE AND SEEK

Children enjoy organizing this game themselves.

Play Players choose somewhere to be "home" – for example a chair or a door. They also choose someone to be the first "seeker." The seeker then shuts his eyes and counts to 40 while all the other players hide.

When he reaches 40, he shouts "Ready!" and goes and looks for the other players. When he finds a player, that player must try and reach home before the seeker can touch him.

The first player to be touched on the way home becomes the next seeker.

SARDINES

This is a type of Hide and seek usually played in the dark. The more rooms that can be played in the more exciting the game becomes.

Play One player is chosen as the first sardine. He then leaves the room and finds a place to hide – preferably somewhere big enough for most of the others to squeeze in too.

When the first sardine has had time to hide, the other players split up and look for him. When a player finds the hiding place he creeps in and hides with the first sardine.

The last sardine to find the others usually becomes the first sardine for the next game.

Hide and seek

© DIAGRAM

Party games: parcel

Everyone loves to unwrap a parcel and find a present inside. Pass the parcel is an old party favorite and is enjoyed by children of all ages. There are also a number of entertaining variations on the parcel-opening theme.

PASS THE PARCEL
Preparation A small present is wrapped in layer after layer of paper. Each layer should be secured with thread, glue, or a rubber band. Music – to be started and stopped by someone not taking part in the game – is also needed.
Play Players sit in a circle and one of them holds the parcel. When the music starts, players pass the parcel around the circle to the right.
When the music stops whoever is holding the parcel unwraps one layer of wrapping. The music is then restarted and the parcel passed on again.
The game continues in this way until someone takes off the final wrapping and so wins the present.

FORFEITS PARCEL
This game is the same as Pass the parcel except that a forfeit is written on each layer of wrapping. A player who is holding the parcel when the music stops must carry out the next forfeit before taking off the next layer of wrapping.

Pass the parcel

©DIAGRAM

MYSTERY·PARCEL

Preparation A parcel is prepared as for Pass the parcel but with a message written on each layer of wrapping. Typical messages are "Give to the player with the whitest teeth!" and "Pass to the person to your left!" Music is needed.

Play The parcel is passed around to the music as in Pass the parcel. When the music stops, the player holding the parcel reads out the message and hands the parcel to the player who fits the description in the message. This player then unwraps the next layer of paper before the music is restarted.

HOT PARCEL

Preparation A present is given a single strong wrapper. Music is needed.

Play is as for Pass the parcel except that when the music stops the person holding the parcel drops out of the game. The last player left in the game unwraps the parcel and wins the present.

LUCKY CHOCOLATE GAME

Preparation A chocolate bar is wrapped in several layers of paper. Each layer should be secured with thread.
The parcel and a knife and fork are then put on a breadboard on a table. A chair with a hat, scarf, and gloves on it is then placed at the table. One die is also needed.

Play The players sit in a circle on the floor and take it in turns to throw the die.
If a player throws a 6, he puts on the hat, scarf, and gloves, sits on the chair, and uses the knife and fork to remove the wrappings.
If another player throws a 6 he changes places with the player at the table.
When the chocolate is unwrapped, players at the table use the knife and fork to eat the chocolate. The game continues until all the chocolate has been eaten.

Lucky chocolate game

©DIAGRAM

Party games: trickery

In these games players try to trick others into carrying out some action for which they will be penalized. The usual penalty in most of these games is for a player to drop out if he makes a mistake. Alternatively, players may be allowed to stay in the game if they carry out a forfeit.

My little bird

MY LITTLE BIRD

This game is played in countries all over the world. Other names for it include Flying high and Birds fly.

Play One player is the leader and the others stand in a row in front of him. Alternatively everyone sits around a table.

The leader starts by saying "My little bird is lively, is lively," and then goes on to name something followed by the word "fly" – for example he might say "eggs fly."

If whatever he names can fly – for example cockatoos – the players raise their arms and wave them about. If it cannot fly – as with eggs – the players should remain still.

A player who makes a mistake is out. The last player left in the game wins.

YES-NO BEANS

In Yes-no beans players must guard against being tricked while at the same time trying to trick others.

Play Each player starts with five beans or any other unit of exchange.

The players circulate round the room, asking each other questions and replying to any questions that another player asks them. Players must not use the words yes or no in any of their replies.

Whenever a player succeeds in tricking another into saying yes or no, he gives that player one of his beans. The first player to get rid of all his beans wins the game.

LAUGHING HANDKERCHIEF

This game is often a riot of infectious laughter. It will be won only by a player who can start and stop laughing at will.

Play One player is the leader and stands in the center of a circle formed by the others.

The leader has a handkerchief which he drops as a signal for the other players to laugh. They must start laughing as soon as he lets go of the handkerchief and must stop when it touches the floor.

A player is out if he does not laugh the whole of the time that the handkerchief is falling or if he continues laughing after it has landed.

The last player left in the game wins and becomes the next leader.

©DIAGRAM

SIMON SAYS

Simon says is an old party game that remains a great favorite. It is sometimes called O'Grady says.

Play One player is the leader and the others spread around the room in front of him.

The leader orders the others to make various actions – such as touching their toes or raising their arms. Whether or not they must obey his orders depends on how the orders are given.

If the leader begins the order with the words "Simon says," the players must obey. If he does not begin with these words, they must not make the action.

If a player makes a mistake he is out of the game. The leader encourages mistakes by:

a) giving rapid orders;

b) developing a rhythm with a repeated pattern of movements and then breaking it;

c) making the actions himself for the others to follow.

The last person left in the game is the winner and becomes the next leader.

Simon says

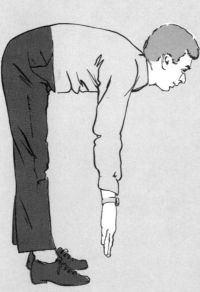

DO THIS, DO THAT!

This is played like Simon says except for the way in which the leader gives his orders. If the leader says "Do this!" the players should mimic his action. If he says "Do that!" they should remain still.

IN THE DITCH

This game is simpler than Simon says but calls for a lot of energy.

Play A line is marked along the floor with cushions or two parallel strands of yarn.

One player is the leader and the others space themselves out down one side of the line. One side is called "the bank" and the other side "the ditch."

The leader orders the players to jump from side to side by calling out "In the ditch!" or "On the bank!" He can try to trick the players by calling the orders very quickly and repeating an order instead of alternating them.

A player must drop out if he makes a mistake. The winner is the last person left in the game.

Party races: individuals

Races of many different kinds are suitable for indoor parties.
Here we begin with a few ideas for races in which individuals
compete on their own behalf rather than as members of a team.
None of these races requires any athletic ability!

NEWSPAPER WALK
Each player tries to be the first to walk the length of the room
on two sheets of newspaper.
Play Players stand in a line at one end of the room. Each player
is given two sheets of newspaper to stand on, one sheet under
each foot.
At the word "Go!" he starts to move across the room on his
newspaper. If he touches the floor with any part of his body he
must go back to the beginning again.

Newspaper walk

TORTOISE RACE

Each player tries to be the last to finish.

Play Players line up along one side of the room. At the word "Go!" they each start to move across the room as slowly as possible. They must head straight for the opposite wall.

A player is disqualified if he stops moving or changes direction.

FISHERMEN

Each player tries to be the first to wind in his "fish."

Preparation Each player requires a fishing line and fish – made by tying a teaspoon to a length of strong thread wrapped around a spool.

Play Players stand in a line at one end of the room. Each player is given a spoon and spool. He places the spoon on the floor and then unwinds the thread in a straight line to the other end of the room.

At the word "Go!" each player starts to wind in his spoon by turning the spool round and round in his hands. He is not permitted to hold the thread in one hand and wind it around the spool.

RABBIT RACE

Each player tries to be the first to jerk his "rabbit" along his piece of string.

Preparation One rabbit shape for each player is cut out of heavy card. A small hole is made in its center and a piece of string about 6ft long threaded through the hole and tied to a chair.

Play Each player holds the free end of one of the pieces of string and moves the rabbit to that end. At the word "Go!" each player, without touching his rabbit, must jerk it along the string to the chair.

BOTTLE FISHING

Each player tries to be the first to ring his bottle.

Preparation Several bottles of the same size and shape are needed, together with an equal number of rings large enough to slip over the necks of the bottles. Each ring should be tied to a length of string.

Play Players sit or stand in a line, with a bottle in front of each of them. Each player then tries to "catch" his bottle, by getting his ring over his bottle's neck.

Party races: pairs

This second group of party races is for people competing as one
of a pair. Back to back race, piggy back race, and three-legged
race are all quite energetic and are best held in a large room.
The races on pp. 262–263 call for different kinds of skills.

BACK TO BACK RACE
Pairs of players try to be the first to run the course.
Play Players form pairs and line up at one end of the room.
Each pair of players stands back to back with their arms linked.
At the word "Go!" the linked players race to the other end of
the room. Pairs who become unlinked must go back to the
beginning and start again.

Piggy back race

Back to back race

PIGGY BACK RACE

This is another race in which pairs of players try to be the first to run a course.

Play Players form pairs and line up at one end of the room. One player from each pair gets on the other's back to be carried. At the word "Go!" the pairs race to the other end of the room, where they must change places so that the carrier becomes the carried.

They must then race back to the original end of the room. If a player touches the floor while he is being carried, that pair must start again.

THREE-LEGGED RACE

Pairs of players try to be the first to run from one end of the room to the other.

Play Players form pairs and line up at one end of the room. A scarf is needed for each pair so that the right leg of one of the players in the pair can be tied to the left leg of his partner. At the word "Go!" pairs race to the other end of the room.

Three-legged race

©DIAGRAM

PATCHES

Players race to sew patches on their partners' clothes.

Preparation A square of material, a needle, and thread are needed for each pair of players.

Play Each player finds a partner and one of them is given a square of material, a needle, and a length of thread.

At the word "Go!" a player from each pair quickly sews his patch on his partner's clothes. (Big stitches are allowed!)

The first player to finish wins the heat. The other player in each pair then has a turn at sewing.

NECKLACE RACE

Each pair tries to be the first to thread all its beads.

Preparation 12 beads on a saucer, a needle, and a length of thread are needed for each pair of players.

Play Players line up in pairs along one side of the room. Each saucer of beads is placed opposite a pair of players at the other end of the room. One player in each pair is given a needle and length of thread.

At the word "Go!" each player with needle and thread must thread his needle and tie a large firm knot at one end of his thread. At the same time his partner runs to the saucer, picks up two beads, and returns with them.

When the first player in each pair has threaded his needle he takes the two beads from his partner and threads them while his partner goes back to the saucer for two more beads.

Play continues in this way until all 12 beads have been threaded. If any beads are dropped they must be picked up and threaded normally.

When a player has threaded all 12 beads, he removes the needle and ties the bead necklace around his partner's neck. The game is won by the first pair to finish its necklace.

Necklace race

DUMB ARTISTS

Each pair tries to be the first to have one player recognize an animal drawn by the other. Players are not allowed to speak to each other.

Play Players form pairs, and partners stand opposite each other at different ends of the room. The players at one end are each given a pencil and a card with the name of an animal written on it.

At the word "Go!" each of these players runs to his partner and, with the animal's name face down, tries to draw the animal.

When his partner thinks that he recognizes the drawing, he takes the pencil and writes down the animal's name. If his answer is correct, his partner nods his head and both players run to the other end of the room.

If the answer is incorrect, his partner shakes his head, takes the pencil back, and continues drawing.

The game is won by the first pair to reach the other end of the room after the animal has been guessed.

Dumb artists

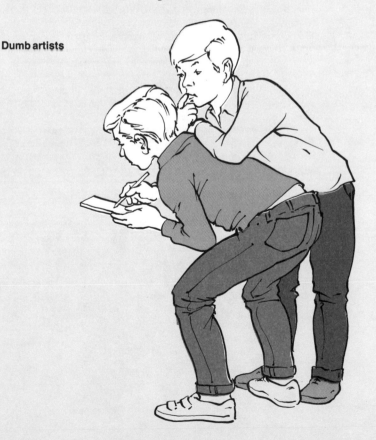

©DIAGRAM

Party races: teams

There is a fantastic variety of party races for competitors divided into two or more teams. Some races are organized on a relay basis, with each team member in turn being required to perform a particular activity. Other races involve individual team members competing separately for points.

NUMBER PARADE
Objective Each team tries to be the first to parade a number called by the organizer.
Preparation Single digits from zero to nine are drawn on separate pieces of card. The digits should be several inches high. There may be either one or two cards for each player but there should be the same set of digits for each team.
In addition, a list of numbers using the digits available to each team is drawn up.
Play The teams form lines and each player is given either one or two of the cards.
The organizer calls out a number – for example he might call "469."
Immediately the players in each team with the digits 4, 6, and 9 rush to the front and line up holding their digits so that they read "469."
The first team to parade the number correctly scores a point. Players return to their teams and another number is called.
To make the game more interesting the organizer can set easy sums for the players to solve and parade.

Number parade

WORD PARADE

This is played like Number parade except that letters are written on the cards and words are called out to be spelled and paraded by the players.

MYSTERY NUMBERS

Objective Each team's players try to be fastest at solving clues and running around their teams.

Preparation It is a good idea to prepare a list of clues indicating particular numbers. If there are seven players in a team, clues for numbers one through seven will be needed. For example for number six the clues might be: half a dozen, a hexagon, an insect's legs, June, the sides of a cube.

Play Players line up behind their leaders and sit down. In each team players are numbered off starting with the leader as number one.

The organizer calls out a clue. As soon as a player recognizes that it refers to his number, he jumps up, runs around his team, and sits down in his place again.

The first player back scores a point for his team. When all the players are seated again, the organizer calls out another clue.

End The team with the most points at the end of a time limit wins the game.

SIMPLE NUMBERS

This is played in the same way as Mystery numbers except that the numbers are not hidden in clues. The organizer simply calls out each number.

LADDERS

Ladders can be played like either Mystery numbers or Simple
numbers (p. 265). The difference is that the teams sit in two
rows facing each other. It is recommended that players take
off their shoes for this game. Each player sits with his legs
outstretched and his feet touching those of the opposing player
with the same number as himself.

When a player's number is called or indicated he runs up
between the lines over the other players' legs, back down
behind his team, and then up between the lines to return to his
place.

MY MOTHER'S CAKE

This is played in the same way as Ladders except that players
are given the name of an ingredient instead of a number.
The organizer then tells a story about how the cake was made
and while telling it he mentions all the various ingredients.
When a player hears the name of his ingredient he must race
around as in Ladders.

Ladders

YARN TANGLES
Teams of four players try to be first to untangle balls of yarn
wrapped around chairs.

Preparation A chair and four different colored balls of yarn are
needed for each team.

Play Players form into teams of four. Each team is given four
balls of yarn and a chair.

Teams are then allowed about one minute in which to tangle
their yarn around their chairs. They are not allowed to lift up
their chairs or to make deliberate knots in the yarn.

At the end of the time limit the organizer calls "Stop!" and
teams must move around to a different chair.

At the word "Go!" teams start to disentangle the yarn from
their new chair. Each player winds one of the balls of yarn.
Players are not allowed to pick up the chair or deliberately
break the yarn.

The game is won by the first team to untangle the yarn into four
separate balls.

CROCODILE RACE
This is an amusing race for teams of players.

Play Players divide into teams and line up behind their leaders
at one end of the room. Players then squat on their heels, each
with his hands on the shoulders or waist of the player in front of
him.

At the word "Go!" the "crocodiles" move forward by little
jumps or bounces. If a player loses contact with the player in
front of him, his team must stop and reassemble. For
reassembling, the hind end of the crocodile must stay where it
is while the front end moves back to join it.

The first team to reach the other end of the room intact wins
the race.

Crocodile race

Flying fish

FLYING FISH

Objective In this game (also known as Kippers) teams race each other at fanning "fish" across the room.

Preparation A "fish" about 10in long is made for each player out of fairly thick paper – the plumper the fish, the better it will "fly." Each team is given a folded newspaper or magazine.

Play Players line up behind their leaders at one end of the room. A plate is placed on the floor at the other end of the room opposite each team.

At the word "Go!" each leader places his fish on the floor and fans it with the newspaper, down the room and onto the plate. As soon as he has done this, he races back to his team and hands the newspaper to the next player in line.

Each player in turn fans his fish across the room and onto the plate, and the first team to finish wins the game.

BURST THE BAG

Objective Teams race each other to be the first to blow up and burst paper bags.

Play Players line up behind their leaders. Paper bags, one for each player, are placed on chairs opposite each team leader.

At the word "Go!" each leader runs to the chair, takes a paper bag, blows it up, and bursts it with his hands.

As soon as he has done this, he runs back to his team and touches the next player. As soon as this player is touched, he takes his turn at bursting a bag.

Play continues in this way until each player has burst a bag – the first team to finish being the winners.

SURPRISE SENTENCES

Objective Each team tries to write a sentence, with each player in the team writing one word of it.

Preparation For each team, a large sheet of paper is attached to a wall or to a board propped upright.

Play Each team lines up opposite its sheet of paper and the leader is given a pencil.

At the word "Go!" he runs up to his paper and writes any word he likes. He then runs back to his team, hands the pencil to the next player, and goes to the end of his team.

As soon as the next player gets the pencil, he goes to the paper and adds a second word either in front of, or behind, the leader's word.

Play continues in this way with each player adding one word. The words should be chosen and put together so that they can be part of a grammatically correct sentence.

Each player, except the last, must avoid completing the sentence. The last player should be able to complete the sentence by adding just one word, and he also puts in the punctuation.

Players may not confer and choose a sentence before writing their words.

End The first team to construct a sentence with one word from each player wins the game.

NOSE IN THE MATCHBOX

Play Players divide into teams and line up beside their leaders. A matchbox lid is given to each leader.

On the word "Go!" he lodges it on his nose and passes it onto the next player's nose without using his hands.

In this way the matchbox lid is passed down the line. If a player touches the lid with his hands or drops it, it is returned to the leader to start again.

End The first team to succeed in passing the matchbox lid down the line wins.

©DIAGRAM

DOUBLE PASS

Objective Players in each team try to pass objects behind them and in front of them in two directions.

Preparation Two identical piles of objects are collected, one for each team. Alternatively, a deck of cards may be divided between the teams.

Play Players divide into teams and sit in a line to the left of their leaders. One pile of objects, or cards, is placed beside the leader.

On the word "Go!" he starts passing the objects, one after the other, down the line.

Only right hands are used until the object reaches the end of the line. Then only left hands are used to return the objects behind the players' backs.

As objects arrive back at the beginning again, the leader makes a pile of the returned objects.

End The first team to return all the objects wins.

SWITCHBACK

Objective Each team tries to be quickest at passing through a hoop.

Play Players divide into teams and line up behind their leaders. A hoop is given to each leader.

On the word "Go!" the leader puts the hoop over his head, drops it to the ground, and steps out of it. The next player steps into the hoop, lifts it over his head, and hands it to the next player.

The hoop is passed down the line in this way, players putting the hoop over their heads and stepping into it alternately.

When the last player has passed through the hoop, he runs with it to the front of the line and passes it back as before. This continues with each player taking a turn at the head of the line.

End The first team with its leader at the front again wins.

Hat and scarf

HAT AND SCARF

Objective Players of each team try to be the quickest at dressing up and running around the team.

Preparation A hat, a scarf, a coat, and a pair of gloves are collected for each team.

Play Teams line up behind their leaders and a set of clothes is placed on a chair in front of each team.

At the word "Go!" each leader runs to the chair, puts on the clothes, and runs around his team.

He then takes off the clothes and gives them to the next player to dress up in.

Play continues in this way down the line. When the last player has run around his team, he places the clothes on the chair.

End The first team with its set of clothes back on the chair wins the game.

EMPTYING SOCKS

Emptying socks

Objective Each team tries to be the first to remove a variety of objects in their correct order from a long sock.

Preparation Identical groups of small objects are put into long socks, one sock for each team. There should be only one item of each kind in each group. The objects might be buttons, beans, coins of different sizes, hairpins, pebbles, etc.

Play Teams line up opposite their leaders. Each leader is given a sock to hold. The organizer announces the first object to be found.

Immediately the first player in each team runs to his leader and puts his hand in the sock. He feels for the object and picks it out of the sock. If he makes a mistake, he returns the object that he took and tries again.

If he takes out the correct object he gives it to the organizer and is told the next object to be retrieved. He returns to his team, tells the next player what to search for and stands at the back of his team.

As soon as the next player knows what to find, he takes his turn at feeling for an object in the sock.

Play continues in this way until each object has been retrieved, and the first team to finish wins.

FRUIT COLORS

Objective Each team tries to be the first to color in pictures of fruit.

Preparation For each team, outlines of fruit (one per player) are drawn on a large sheet of paper. The drawings should be the same for each team. The sheets of paper are attached to a wall or laid out on a table.

Play Teams line up behind their leaders at the opposite end of the room to the drawings. Each leader is given a box of crayons.

At the word "Go!" he runs to his team's sheet of paper and colors in one of the pieces of fruit. He then goes back to his team, hands the box of crayons to the next player and stands at the back of his team.

As soon as the second player gets the crayons, he goes and colors in another fruit and so on down the line of players. If a crayon is dropped on the floor, the player with the box must pick it up.

End The first team to color in all its fruit wins.

Balloon pass

BALLOON PASS
Objective Each team tries to be quickest at passing a balloon overhead.

Play Players divide into teams and form lines behind their leaders. Each leader is given a balloon.

On the word "Go!" he passes it over his head to the player behind him. This player in turn passes the balloon back over his head. In this way the balloon is passed down the entire line. When the last player gets the balloon, he runs to the front of his line and passes the balloon back in the same way as before. Thus each player takes a turn at the head of the line.

The end The winning team is the first one to have its leader at the front of the line again.

TUNNEL BALL
This is played like Balloon pass except that players stand with their legs apart and pass the balloon back between their legs.

BALLOON HOP
Objective Teams try to be the first to find and inflate all the balloons belonging to them.

Preparation Balloons of as many different colors as there are teams should be bought, and each player in each team will need a balloon.

Play Players line up behind their leaders. Each team is allotted a color. The balloons are placed in a pile at the end of the room.

At the word "Go!" each leader hops across the room, finds a balloon of his team's color and hops back with it to his team. When he returns, the next player hops across the room to find a balloon; and so on, until each player has a balloon.

When players return to their teams, they inflate the balloons and fasten the necks. If a player has a lot of difficulty tying his balloon, another player in his team may help him.

End The first team with all its balloons blown up and tied wins.

EGG CUPS

Objective Each player tries to blow a table tennis ball from one egg cup to another.

Play Players divide into teams and line up beside their leaders. Two egg cups and a table tennis ball are given to each leader. At the word "Go!" the leader blows the table tennis ball from one egg cup to the other. He may hold the egg cups so that they touch, but he may not merely tip the ball from one cup to the other.

As soon as the leader has finished, he hands the cups and the table tennis ball to the next player; and so on down the line, until each player has blown the ball from one egg cup to the other.

If the ball falls from the egg cups, or is handled or tipped instead of blown, it is returned to the leader who must start again.

End The first team whose players have all correctly blown the table tennis ball from one cup to the other wins.

Egg cups

HURRY WAITER!

Objective Players try to keep a table tennis ball balanced on a plate while weaving in and out of a line of their teammates.

Play Players divide into teams and stand in a line behind their leaders. Each leader is given a table tennis ball on a plate. At the word "Go!" he weaves in and out between the players in his team as quickly as he can without dropping the table tennis ball.

When he reaches the end of the line, he runs straight to the head of the line again and hands the plate and ball to the next player, saying "Here is your breakfast, Sir (or Madam)" as he does so.

This procedure is repeated, with each player beginning at the head of the line and returning to his place as soon as he has handed the "breakfast" to the next player in turn.

If a player drops the ball, he must go back to the head of the line and start again. The first team to finish wins the game.

PICK AND CUP

Objective Each team tries to be the first to pass assorted objects down its line of players.

Preparation Identical piles of various objects – eg fruit, beans, buttons, pebbles, etc – are collected together, one pile for each team.

Play Players divide into teams and sit down beside their leaders. One pile of objects is placed beside each leader.

On the word "Go!" each leader picks up an object and drops it into the cupped hands of the player next to him. The third player in the line picks the object out of the cupped hands and places it into the fourth player's cupped hands.

This continues down the line to the last player, who puts the object on the floor. The leader can then pick up the next object and pass it down the line as before.

End The first team to transfer all the objects down the line wins.

PALMS

Objective Each team tries to be quickest at passing coins while keeping their hands flat.

Play Players divide into teams and form rows to the left of their leaders. Each leader is given six large coins, which he holds in his left hand.

On the word "Go!" he places one coin on the flat palm of his right hand and slaps it onto the flat palm of the next player's right hand.

In this manner each coin is passed down the row. If a coin is dropped, it is returned to the leader to start again.

End The first team to succeed in passing all six coins from one end to the other wins.

STRAWS AND BEANS

Objective Each team tries to be quickest at using straws to pass beans from player to player.

Play Players divide into teams and sit in a line beside their leaders. A saucer with six beans on it is placed next to each leader, and an empty saucer is placed at the other end of each team. Every player is given a drinking straw.

On the word "Go!" the leader picks up a bean and transfers it from his hand to the next player's cupped hand by sucking the bean onto the end of his straw and holding his breath.

In this manner all the beans are passed down the line and placed in the empty saucer. If a bean is dropped, it is returned to the beginning again.

End The first team to transfer all its beans wins.

SUGAR AND SPOONS

This is played like Straws and beans except that players hold teaspoons in their mouths and tip sugar lumps from spoon to spoon.

PASSING THE ORANGE

Objective Seated players try to pass an orange down the line using their feet, or (in an alternative version) by using their chins!

Play Players divide into teams and sit in a line on the floor beside their leaders. Each leader is given an orange and, with his legs together, cradles it on his feet.

On the word "Go!" he passes the orange onto the feet of the next player.

(Alternatively, the leader tucks the orange under his chin. The next player takes the orange from him, also using his chin – neither player may use his hands.)

Using either one of these ways, the orange is passed from player to player. If the orange drops onto the floor, or if a player uses his hands, the orange is returned to the leader to start again.

End The first team to pass the orange down the line wins.

Sugar and spoons

©DIAGRAM

Pencil and paper games

Pencil and paper games need only the simplest equipment, yet they can provide great scope for the imagination, increase a player's general knowlege, and – above all – be a highly enjoyable way of passing time. Pencil and paper games fall basically into two categories: word games and games in which pictures or symbols are drawn.

KEYWORD
Keyword, sometimes called Hidden words, can be played by any number of people.

The players choose a "keyword" containing at least seven letters. Each player then tries to make as many words as possible from the letters in the keyword. The letters may be used in any order, but a letter may be used in any one word only as many times as it appears in the keyword.

Generally, proper nouns (capitalized words) or words with fewer than four letters are not allowed; nor are abbreviations or plurals.

The game may be played just for interest, with players working together; or it may be made into a contest, with individuals competing to find most words in an agreed length of time.

CROSSWORDS
This intriguing game can be adapted for play by any number of people. If up to five are playing, each of them draws a square divided into five squares by five on a sheet of paper. If more people take part, or if players wish to lengthen the game, the number of squares can be increased to, say, seven by seven.

Each of the players in turn calls out any letter of the alphabet. As each letter is called, all players write it into any square of their choice, with the objective of forming words of two or more letters reading either across or down.

Generally, abbreviations or proper nouns (names, etc) may not be used. Once a letter has been written down, it cannot be moved to another square.

Players continue to call out letters until all the individual squares have been filled.

The number of points scored is equal to the number of letters in each word (one-letter words do not count). Thus a three-letter word scores three points. If a word fills an entire row or column, one bonus point is scored in addition to the score for that word.

No ending of a word can form the beginning of another word in the same row or column. For example, if a row contains the letters "i, f, e, n, d" the player may score four points for the word "fend" but cannot in addition score two points for the word "if."

Each player adds together each of his horizontal and vertical totals; the winning player is the one with the highest score.

ACROSTICS

Acrostics is a popular word-building game. A word of at least three letters is chosen.

Each player writes the word in a column down the left-hand side of a sheet of paper; he then writes the same word, but with the letters reversed, down the right-hand side of the page.

The player fills in the space between the two columns with the same number of words as there are letters in the keyword – and starting and ending each word with the letter at either side.

For example, if the keyword is "stem," a player's words might read: scream, trundle, earliest, manageress.

The winner may be either the first person to fill in all the words, or the player with the longest or most original words.

Crosswords

Acrostics

CATEGORIES

One of the best-known pencil and paper games, Categories can be played at either a simple or a sophisticated level.

Preparation Each player (there may be any number) is given a pencil and a piece of paper.

The players decide on between six and a dozen different categories; these may be easy ones for children (eg girls' or boys' names, animals, colors) or more difficult for adults (eg politicians, rivers, chemicals). Each player lists the categories on his piece of paper.

One of the players chooses any letter of the alphabet – preferably an "easy" letter such as "a" or "d" if children are playing. Experienced players can make the game more challenging by choosing more difficult letters such as "j" or "k."

Players may decide to play to an agreed time limit of say 15 minutes.

Play The players try to find a word beginning with the chosen letter for each of the categories (eg if the chosen letter is "p" all the words must begin with that letter). They write down their words next to the appropriate category, trying where possible to think of words that none of the other players will have chosen.

Scoring Writing must stop as soon as the time limit is up, or as soon as one player has finished.

Each player in turn then reads out his list of words. If he has found a word not thought of by any of the other players, he scores two points for that word. If, however, one or more of the other players has also chosen the same word, each of them scores only one point. If the player could not find a word at all, or if his choice of word did not correctly fit the category, he gets no points. (Any disagreement about the relevance of a word to a category must be solved by a vote among the other players.) The winner is the player with the highest score for his list of words.

Subsequent rounds Any number of rounds may be played, using either the same or different categories; the chosen letter, however, must be different for each round. Players may take it in turns to choose a letter at the start of a round.

Players make a note of their scores at the end of each round. The winner is the player with the highest points total at the end of the final round.

GUGGENHEIM

Guggenheim is a slightly more complicated version of
Categories. Instead of choosing only one letter for each round
of play, the players choose a keyword of about four or five
letters.

The letters of the keyword are written spaced out to the right of
the list of categories, and players try to find words for each of
the categories begininning with the letter heading each
column.

Categories

CATEGORIES	P.	S.
Color	Pink	Scarlet
Boy's name	Paul	Stephen
City	Paris	Sydney
Country	Portugal	Spain
Island	Pitcairn	Seychelles
Mountain	Pilatus	Stromboli
Composer	Paderewski	Strauss

CATEGORIES	G.	A.	M.	E.
Color	Green	Amber	Magenta	Emerald
Boy's name	George	Andrew	Martin	Ernest
City	Glasgow	Amsterdam	Monbassa	Essen
Country	Greece	Austria	Morocco	England
Island	Galapagos	Arran	Malta	Ellice
Composer	Grieg	Albinoni	Mozart	Elgar
Girl's name	Glenda	Anne	Mary	Edna

©DIAGRAM

TRANSFORMATION

Two words with the same number of letters are chosen. Each player writes down the two words. He tries to change the first word into the second word by altering only one letter at a time, and each time forming a new word.

For example, "dog" could be changed to "cat" in four words as follows: dog, cog, cot, cat. It is easiest to begin with three or four letter words until the players are quite practiced – when five or even six letter words may be tried.

The winner is the player who completes the changes using the fewest number of words.

ANAGRAMS

This game is also called Jumbled words. Any number of players may take part. One of them prepares a list of words belonging to a particular category (eg flowers, cities, poets) and jumbles up the letters in each word.

Each of the other players is given a list of the jumbled words and their category, and tries to rearrange the letters back into the original words. For example, "peilmidhun" should be "delphinium" and "wodronsp" should be "snowdrop."

The first player to rearrange all the words correctly, or the player with most correct words after a given time, wins the game.

More experienced players may like to make up anagrams of their own by rearranging the letters in a word to make one or more other words, eg "angered" is an anagram of "derange."

SYNONYMS

A list of 10 to 20 words is prepared, and a copy given to each player. The objective is to find a synonym (word with the same meaning) for each word on the list. If a player can think of more than one synonym for any word he should write down the shortest one.

After an agreed length of time, the players' lists are checked. The winner is the player who finds a synonym for the most words, or, if two or more players have an equal number of synonyms, the player with the lowest total of letters in his synonyms.

FILL INS

A list of 30 to 40 words is prepared and kept hidden from the players.

Each player is then given the first and last letters and the number of letters missing from each word on the list. The winner is the first player to fill in all the blanks correctly. Alternatively, the players may be allowed an agreed length of time and then the winner is the player with the most correct words.

TELEGRAMS

Players are given or make up a list of 15 letters, and must use each of them – in the order given – as the initial letter of a word in a 15-word telegram.

(Alternatively, the players are given or select a word of about 10–15 letters, eg blackberries, so that the first word must begin with "b," the second with "l," and so on.)

The telegram may include one or two place names and may – if the player wishes – have the name of the "sender" as the last word. Stops (or periods) may be used for punctuation.

The winner is the first player to complete his telegram, or, if a time limit has been set, the player whose telegram is judged to be the best at the end of the time set.

Telegrams

BLACKBERRIES

BRING LAMP AND CHISEL STOP KNOW

BEST ENTRY ROUTE STOP REST IS EASY

STOP   SID

GEOGRAPHY RACE

This game is a good test of geographical knowledge. Players try to write down the name of a town or city that lies in a specified direction from another town or city.

Players form two teams of equal size, and if possible the teams should sit in parallel rows. The first member of each team needs a pencil and paper. The game is organized by an umpire.

Play The umpire chooses the name of any well-known town or city and specifies in which compass direction the other towns must lie. For example, he might say "Towns to the east of Berlin." He gives a start signal, and the first person in each team must write down a town that lies to the east of Berlin. The player then hands the pencil and paper to the next person in his team, who writes down a town to the east of the town chosen by the first player.

Play continues in this way until the last member in the team has written down a town.

Scoring As soon as one team has finished, the umpire checks both teams' answers.

The team that finished first scores a bonus of five points. In addition, each correct answer scores one point, and one point is deducted for each incorrect answer.

The team with the highest number of points after one or more rounds wins.

©DIAGRAM

CONSEQUENCES

Consequences is a favorite among children and is a game purely to be enjoyed – there are no winners or losers. Any number of players can take part, and each of them is provided with a sheet of paper and a pencil.

The objective is to write as many stories as there are participants, with each person contributing to each of the stories.

Play One person is chosen as "caller" (this does not exclude him from taking part). He calls out the first part of the story. Each person writes down an appropriate name, phrase, or sentence, making it as humorous as possible. He then folds over the top of the piece of paper to hide what he has written, and passes the paper to the player to his left.

The caller then says the next part of the story, and the players write something on the paper they have just received from their neighbors.

Consequences

PICTURE CONSEQUENCES

This game has similarities with standard Consequences, but instead of writing words the players draw parts of an animal or a person dressed in funny clothing – starting with the head and finishing with the feet.

When the pieces of paper are folded over, a part of the last drawing is left showing, so as to give a lead to the next player. For example, after drawing the head, the paper should be folded so that the edge of the neck is showing.

After drawing the feet, players may write down the name of the person whom they want the figure to represent!

This procedure is repeated until the story is complete. Any theme may be used, but the one described here is perhaps the best known.

1) "A girl . . ." (players write the name of someone known to them, or alternatively a famous personality or fictional character);
2) "met a boy . . ." (again, the players may choose any name of their choice);
3) "at . . . beside . . . in . . ." (the players may choose any location);
4) "he said . . .";
5) "she said . . .";
6) "the consequence was . . .";
7) "and the world said . . ."

When the story is complete, each player passes the piece of paper on which he wrote the last sentence to the person to his left. The pieces of paper are unfolded and the stories read out one by one – they may not be fictional masterpieces but are sure to provide a lot of fun!

Picture consequences

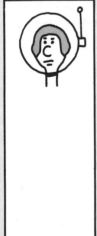

© DIAGRAM

PICTURES

Pictures is best played by two teams of at least three players each. In addition, there must be an organizer who belongs to neither team.

The organizer makes a list of half a dozen or so book titles, proverbs, or other subjects (they need not be in the same category).

The organizer whispers the first title on the list to one player from each team. This player returns to his team (the teams should preferably be in separate rooms) and must draw a picture representing the title. He may add to his drawing or make further drawings – until one of his teammates has correctly guessed the answer. (No verbal clues may be given, however!)

As soon as one player has guessed the title, he may go to the organizer for the next title on the list.

The winning team is the first one to guess all the titles on the organizer's list.

HANGMAN

Hangman is a popular game for two or more players. One person thinks of a word of about five or six letters. He writes down the same number of dashes as there are letters in his word.

The other players may then start guessing the letters in the word, calling one letter at a time. If the guess is a successful one, the letter is written by the first player above the appropriate dash – if it appears more than once in a word it must be entered as often as it occurs.

If the guess is an incorrect one, however, the first player may start to draw a hanged man – one line of the drawing representing each wrong letter.

The other players must try to guess the secret word before the first player can complete the drawing of the hanged man.

If one of the players guesses the word (this should become easier as the game progresses) he may take a turn at choosing a word. If the hanged man is completed before the word is guessed, the same player may choose another word.

To make the game more difficult, longer words may be chosen. Alternatively, the player may choose a group of words making a proverb or the title of a book or film – and should give the other players a clue as to the category.

Hangman

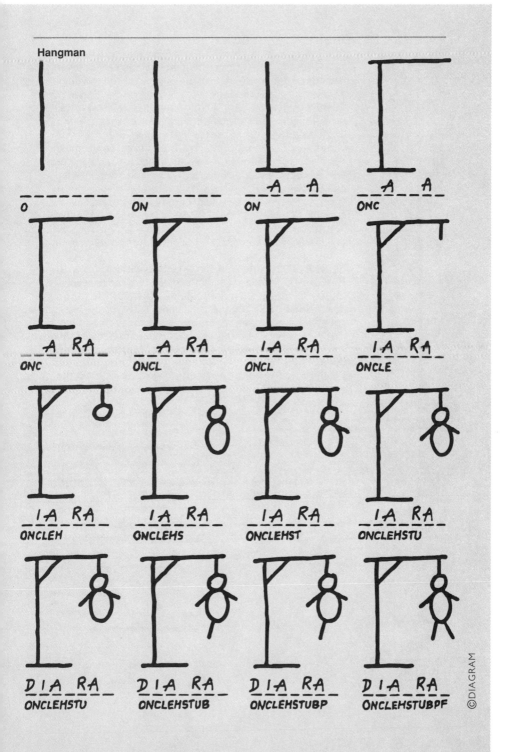

**Tick-tack-toe:
sample play**

TICK-TACK-TOE / NOUGHTS AND CROSSES

A favorite for generations, this game for two people is sometimes over in a matter of seconds!

Two vertical lines are drawn with two horizontal lines crossing them, forming nine spaces. Players decide which of them is to draw noughts (circles) and which of them crosses.

Taking alternate turns, the players make their mark in any vacant space until one of them manages to get three of his marks in a row (either horizontally, vertically, or diagonally). He then draws a line through his winning row and the game comes to an end.

If neither player succeeds in forming a row, the game is considered drawn.

As the player who draws first has a better chance of winning, players usually swop their starting order after each game.

THREE-DIMENSIONAL TICK-TACK-TOE

Based on the standard game, the three-dimensional version offers a lengthier and more challenging alternative. Three-dimensional Tick-tack-toe can be bought as a game, but can equally well be played with pencil and paper.

The cube may be represented diagrammatically by 64 squares – as shown. For actual play, each "layer" of the cube is drawn out individually.

Playing procedure is similar to standard Tick-tack-toe, but the winner is the first player to get four of his marks in a row (see illustrations).

**Three-dimensional
tick-tack toe: squares
making up the cube**

Three-dimensional tick-tack-toe: examples of winning rows

1st layer	2nd layer	3rd layer	4th layer

BOXES

This is a simple but amusing game for two players. Any number of dots is drawn on a piece of paper – the dots are drawn in rows to form a square. Ten rows by ten is a good number.

Players take alternate turns. In each turn they may draw a horizontal or vertical line to join up any two dots that are next to each other.

The objective is to complete (with a fourth line) as many squares or "boxes" as possible. Whenever a player completes a box he initials it and may draw another line. He may continue his turn until he draws a line that does not complete a box.

As soon as there are no more dots to be joined – all the boxes having been filled – the game ends. The player with the highest number of initialed boxes is the winner.

Another way of playing is to try to form the lowest number of boxes – the players join up as many lines as they can before being forced to complete a box. The winner is the player with the fewest initialed boxes.

Boxes: sample play

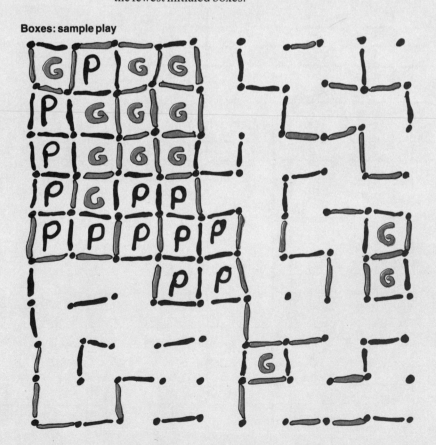

SPROUTS

Sprouts has certain similarities with Boxes, but needs rather
more ingenuity to win!

Two players take part. About six or so dots are drawn – well
spaced out – on a sheet of paper (more may be drawn for a
longer game).

Taking alternate turns, each player draws a line joining any
two dots or joining a dot to itself. He then draws a dot
anywhere along the line he has just made, and his turn ends.
When drawing a line, the following rules must be observed:

a) no line may cross itself;
b) no line may cross a line that has already been drawn;
c) no line may be drawn through a dot;
d) a dot may have no more than three lines leaving it.

The last person able to draw a legitimate line is the winner.

Disallowed sprouts

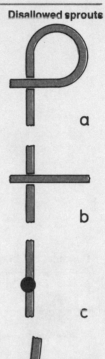

a

b

c

d

Sprouts: sample play

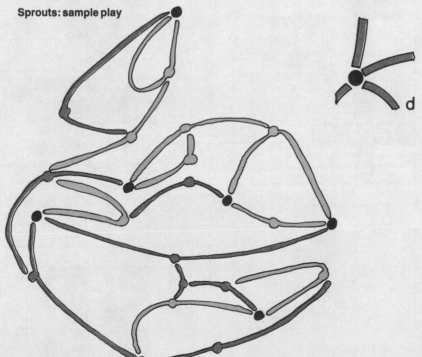

©DIAGRAM

CRYSTALS

In this sophisticated pattern visualizing game, each player tries to form symmetrical shapes known as "crystals."

Equipment All that is needed is a sheet of graph paper and as many different colored crayons as there are players.

The number of squares used for each game depends on the number of players: if two take part (the best number) about 20 rows of 20 squares each would form a suitable area.

Objective Each player attempts to "grow" crystals on the paper with the aim of filling more squares than his opponent. A player does not score points for the number of crystals he grows, but for the number of squares his crystals cover.

A crystal is made up of "atoms," each of which occupies a single square. In growing crystals, players must observe certain rules of symmetry that determine whether or not a crystal is legitimate.

Examples of allowed crystals

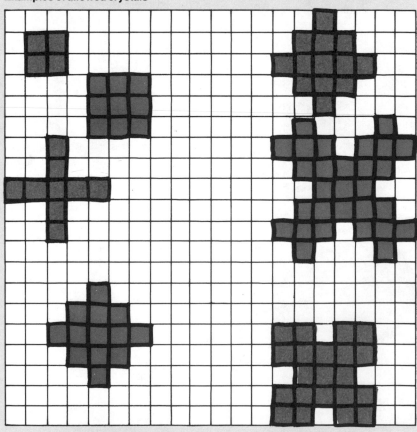

The symmetry of a crystal can be determined by visualizing four axes through its center: horizontal, vertical, and two diagonal axes. Once the axes have been "drawn," it should theoretically be possible to fold the crystal along each of the four axes to produce corresponding "mirror" halves that, when folded, exactly overlay each other (ie are the same shape and size).

Examples of disallowed "crystals"

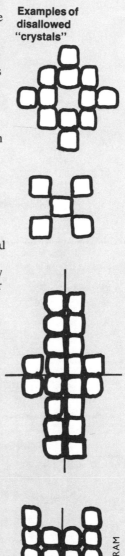

In addition to the rules of symmetry, players must observe the following:

a) a legitimate crystal may be formed from four or more atoms drawn by one player only;

b) the atoms forming a crystal must be joined along their sides – they may not be connected only by their corners;

c) a crystal may not contain any empty atoms (ie holes).

Play Players decide on their playing order and each one in turn shades in any one square of his choice – each player using a crayon of a different color.

In the first few turns, players rarely try to grow a crystal. Instead, they place single atoms around the playing area in order to establish potential crystal sites. As play progresses, players will see which atoms are best placed for growing crystals and add to them as appropriate.

When a player thinks he has grown a crystal, he declares it, and rings the area that it covers.

A player with a winning advantage will try to retain the lead by either blocking his opponents' attempts at growing crystals, or by growing long narrow crystals that – although not high scoring – restrict the playing area.

Play ends when no blank squares are left, or when the players agree that no more crystals can be formed.

Scoring Players work out which of the crystals are legitimate, and count the number of squares each crystal covers.

Any crystal that does not demonstrate symmetry around each of the four axes is not legitimate and does not score.

The number of squares in the legitimate crystals that each player has grown are added, and the player with most squares wins the game.

BATTLESHIPS

This is an extremely popular game for two players, each of whom needs a pencil and a sheet of graph paper.

The players should sit so that they cannot see each other's paper. Each of them draws two identical playing areas, ten squares by ten squares in size.

In order to identify each square, the playing areas have numbers down one side and letters across the top (thus the top left-hand square is A1; the bottom left-hand square is A10, etc).

Each player marks one playing area his "home fleet" and the other playing area the "enemy fleet."

Each player has his own fleet of ships that he may position anywhere within his home fleet area.

His fleet comprises:

a) one battleship, four squares long;

b) two cruisers, each three squares long;

c) three destroyers, each two squares long; and

d) four submarines, each one square only.

HOME FLEET   ENEMY FLEET

He "positions" his ships by outlining the appropriate number of squares.

The squares representing each ship must be in a row, either across or down. There must also be at least one vacant square between ships.

The players' objective is to destroy their opponent's entire fleet by a series of "hits." Players take alternate turns. In each turn, a player may attempt three hits: he calls out the names of any three squares – marking them on his enemy fleet area as he does so.

His opponent must then consult his own home fleet area to see whether any of these squares are occupied. If they are, he must state how many and the category of boat hit.

In order to sink a ship, every one of its component squares must have received a hit. The game continues with both players marking the state of their own and their enemy's fleets – this may be done by shading or outlining squares, or in some other chosen manner.

There is no limit to the number of hits each player may attempt – the game comes to an end as soon as one player destroys his opponent's fleet.

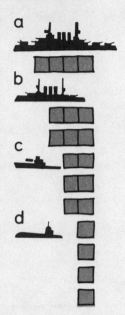

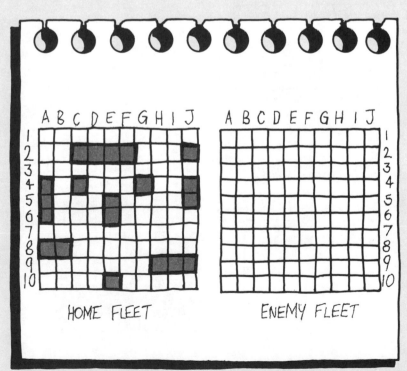

BURIED TREASURE

This is a much simpler version of Battleships (p. 292) and is particularly suitable for young children. It is a game for two, with a third person needed to help at the beginning of the game.

Each player draws an area nine squares by nine and marks it in the same manner as for Battleships, so that each square has a name.

The third person designates any four of the letters from A to I to one player, and any four of the remaining letters to the other player; he then does the same thing with the numbers from 1–9.

Neither player may know which letters and numbers have been designated to his opponent, nor which letter and number are left over – this is the square in which the treasure is "buried" and which the players must try to identify.

Players take turns to ask each other whether they hold a particular letter or number. Although a respondent must always give a truthful answer, a player may – if he wishes – enquire about a letter or number that he holds himself, so as to mislead his opponent.

The first player to locate the treasure by this mixture of bluff and elimination wins the game.

Buried treasure

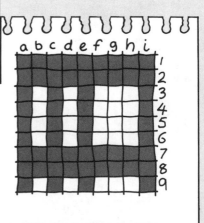

SQUIGGLES

This is a game for two people, each of whom should have a
piece of paper, and a pencil different in color from the other
player's.

Each player scribbles very quickly on his piece of paper – the
more abstract the squiggle, the better.

Players then exchange papers and set themselves a time limit
of, for example, two minutes, in which they must use every bit
of the squiggle to make a picture. Ingenuity is more important
than artistic ability – a third person could be asked to judge
which of the players has used his squiggle more inventively.

Squiggles: stage 1

Squiggles: stage 2

©DIAGRAM

AGGRESSION

Aggression is a game in which players fight imaginary battles in a bid to occupy the maximum amount of territory.

Two players are ideal – though the game can also be played by three or more, who may choose to form teams. Each player must have a crayon of a different color.

Playing area A large sheet of paper is used. One player begins by drawing the boundaries of an imaginary country; each player in turn then draws the outline of an imaginary country adjoining one or more other countries.

Any number of countries may be drawn (20 is an average number if two play) and they can be any shape or size.

When the agreed number of countries has been drawn, each is clearly marked with a different letter of the alphabet.

Armies Each player is allotted 100 armies. Taking turns with his opponent, he chooses a country that he intends to occupy and writes within it how many armies he is allocating to it. (Once a country has been occupied, no player may add further armies to it.)

This procedure continues until all the countries have been occupied, or until each player has allocated all his armies.

Drawing the boundaries

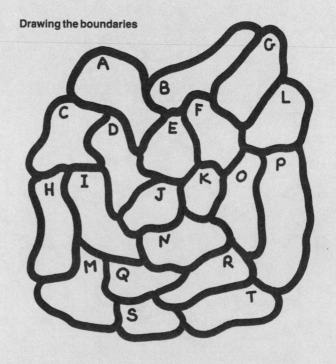

Play The player who chose the first country has the opening move. His objective is to retain more occupied countries than his opponent; to achieve this he "attacks" enemy armies in adjacent countries. (Adjacent countries are defined as those with a common boundary.) A player may attack with armies from more than one country – provided they are all in countries that have a common border with the country under attack.

If the number of armies located in the attacking country or countries is greater than those located in the defending country, the defending army is conquered – its armies are crossed off and can take no further part in the game. (The armies used to conquer a country may be reused.)

Players take it in turns to conquer countries until one or both of them cannot mount any further attacks.

Scoring At the end of the game the players total the number of countries each of them retains. The winner is the player with the highest number of unconquered countries – he need not necessarily be the player who made the greatest number of conquests.

Conquering
L conquers G
but is then
conquered by OP

Positioning the armies

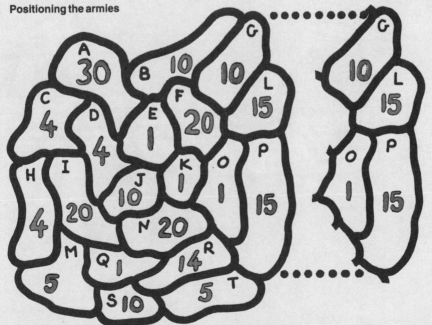

©DIAGRAM

Queen's guard

Queen's guard is an interesting old board game for two players. It can be played with counters on an improvised board. Players attempt to position their pieces in the winning pattern.

The board is in the shape of a hexagon, with 91 small hexagons in alternating dark and light bands.

Pieces There are two sets of pieces. Each set is a distinctive color and consists of one "queen" and six "guards."

Objective The game is won when one player succeeds in positioning his "queen" on the center hexagon and his six guards in the hexagons immediately surrounding it.

Board and pieces

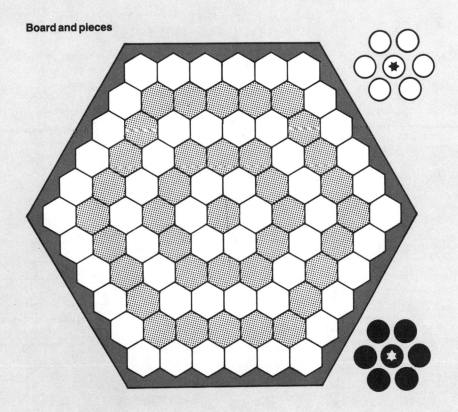

©DIAGRAM

Start of play There are two methods of starting play:
1) the pieces are positioned as shown in the diagram right;
2) each player positions his pieces in turn, one at a time,
anywhere he likes on the board.

Play Each player moves one piece in a turn. A piece may only
be moved into a vacant hexagon.

A player who touches one of his pieces must move that piece or
forfeit his turn.

Except when a piece is trapped between opposing pieces, it
may be moved one hexagon sideways or toward the center of
the board (**a**).

If a "guard" is trapped between two opposing pieces (**b**), its
owner must in his next turn move it to any hexagon in the
outside band.

If a "queen" is trapped between two opposing pieces (**c**), its
owner must in his next turn move it to any vacant square that
his opponent requires.

If more than one piece is trapped, the player must move them
back one in each turn. "Guards" may be moved back in any
order, but a "queen" must always be moved before a "guard."

Only a "queen" may be placed in the center hexagon. A player
forfeits the game if, when the center hexagon is empty, he
positions all his six guards in the band immediately
surrounding it.

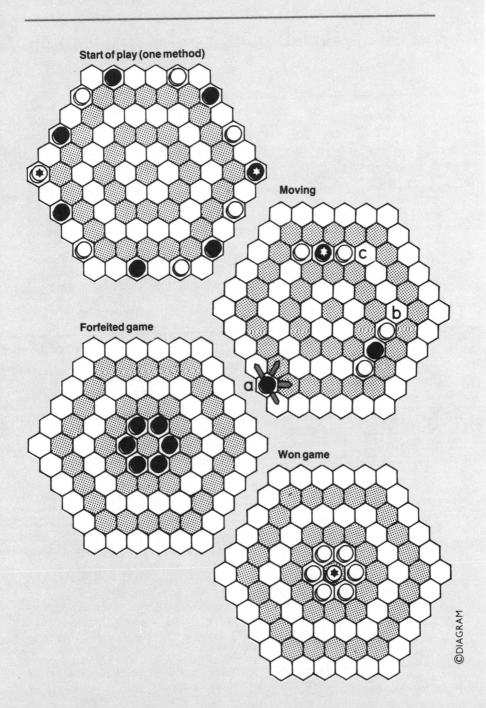

Start of play (one method)

Moving

Forfeited game

Won game

©DIAGRAM

Reversi

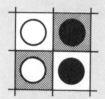

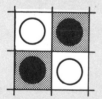

This game of strategy was invented in the late nineteenth century and has recently been revived.

Board Bought boards have 64 playing circles with interconnecting lines. Reversi can also be played on the 64 squares of a standard checkerboard.

Pieces 64 pieces are needed. Each piece must have two easily distinguishable faces.

Pieces can be improvised by:

a) sticking or drawing symbols (eg stars and circles) on the two faces of 64 checkers; or

b) sticking counters of two different colors (eg black and white) together to make a set of double-faced counters. Before play starts the players decide which of them will play with which face of the pieces up.

Objective Play ends when there is a piece on every square; the winner is the player who has the most pieces with his face up at the end of the game.

Turns alternate. In his turn each player attempts to place one piece on the board with his color or symbol face up.

First four pieces Each player's first two plays must be in the center four squares of the board, giving four possible starting patterns.

Taking After the first four pieces are placed, each player attempts to make one move in each turn.

Only taking moves are permitted, and if a player is unable to make a taking move he loses his turn. (Both players are, however, limited to a maximum of 32 plays.)

A taking move is made by positioning a piece so that:

a) it is in a square next to a square containing an opposition piece; and

b) it traps at least one opposition piece in a line in any direction between itself and another of the taker's pieces.

(In the example shown, blacks could be positioned in the squares marked B and whites in those marked W.)

When a piece is taken it is turned over to show the other player's symbol or color. A piece may be turned over many times during a game as it passes from one player to the other. Pieces are never removed from the board when they are taken.

Multiple takes By positioning a single piece a player may simultaneously take several pieces in more than one line (eg if a black were placed in the square marked T in the situation illustrated). Note that pieces may not be taken if a line is completed only when a piece is turned over.

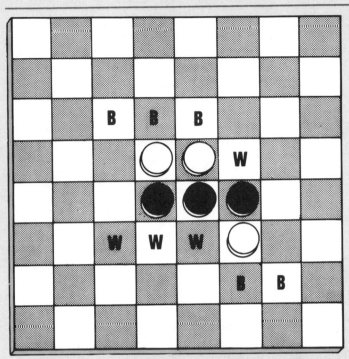

Taking move

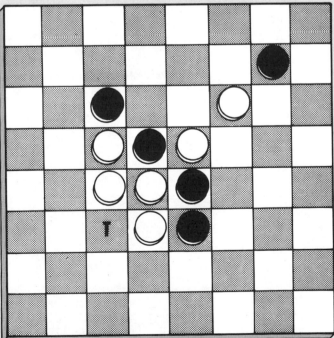

Multiple take

© DIAGRAM

Ring target games

Several good games can be played with small rings and different types of target. Best known of these games is the game known as Ringboard or Hoopla, but Ring the bull and Ringolette are enjoyable alternatives.

RINGBOARD/HOOPLA

This has been a popular indoor target game for many years.
Boards of different shapes and sizes are generally easy to buy – or may be made by the do-it-yourself enthusiast from plywood, hardboard, or chipboard.

Most bought boards are diamond- or shield-shaped, about 18in high, and decorated with brightly colored patterns or illustrations.

Screwed into the boards are a number of hooks – usually between 12 and 16. A figure below each hook indicates the number of points scored whenever a player throws a ring onto the hook.

At the back of the board is a thin rope loop for hanging the board on a wall or door.

Rings At least six rings should be provided. Bought rings are usually made of rubber, and are about 3in in diameter. They are similar to those used on jars of homemade preserves – which could easily be substituted. Other ideas for improvised rings are large curtain rings, or rings made from string or heavy card.

Play The players throw as individuals, or may form into teams. At his turn, each player stands an agreed distance from the ringboard and throws six rings.

Scoring At the end of his turn, a player scores the designated number of points for each ring on a hook. The game is won by the player or team with most points after an agreed number of throws.

RING THE BULL

This game was played in England during the reign of Queen Victoria. It is an amusing game and calls for more agility and control than first meets the eye.

The board can be made by:

painting a bull's head on a piece of plywood, hardboard, or chipboard;

attaching a rod, about 18in long, to the board above the bull's head;

screwing hooks into the board, one in the nose and one in each horn;

tying a piece of string, about 30in long, to a ring and then fastening the other end of the string to the rod.

Play Each player in turn makes an agreed number of attempts to throw the ring onto the hook on the bull's nose.

A player scores one point each time he succeeds. There is no score for throwing a ring onto the hooks on the bull's horns. The winner is the player with most points. (A re-throw may be held if a game is drawn.)

RINGOLETTE

Ringolette is another Victorian target game played with rings.

Equipment Victorian ringolette sets usually contained 10 or 12 small skittles and a similar number of wooden rings. A figure on each skittle indicated its points value.

The game can easily be played with improvised materials – rings like the ones described on p.304, and bottles instead of skittles.

Play The game is for two players or teams.

At his turn each player stands an agreed distance from the targets and throws all the rings, attempting to get each one over a different target.

For a target with one ring over it at the end of his turn, a player scores that target's points value. If any target has more than one ring over it, the player's opponent is awarded the points value of that skittle for each extra ring.

The game is won by the player or team scoring most points.

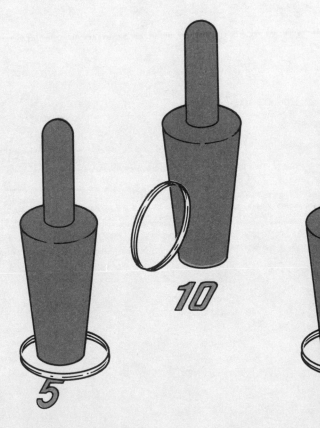

© DIAGRAM

Ringo

Ringo is a game of strategy for two people. Invented in Germany, it is played on a circular board and in some ways resembles Fox and geese (p. 154). One player (the "attacker") attempts to capture the central area of the board known as the "fortress," while the other player (the "defender") tries to ward off the attack.

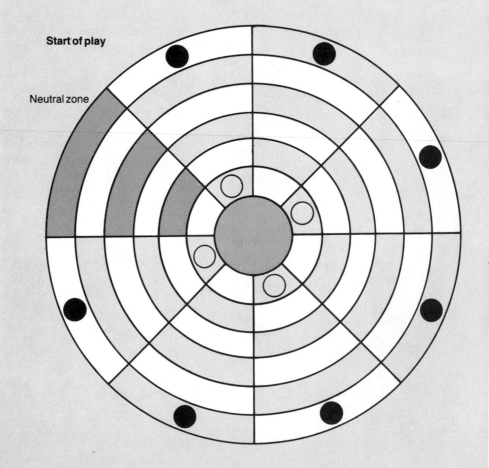

Start of play

Neutral zone

The playing area may be drawn on a sheet of paper. It comprises a large circle divided into eight segments of equal size. One of the segments is distinctively colored and is called the "neutral zone."

The central circle or fortress is also distinctively colored. Six concentric rings spread out beyond it, and the resulting sections are alternately light and dark colored (ie each segment has three light and three dark colored sections).

Pieces Each player has counters (or other suitable objects) distinguishable from his opponent's. The defender has four pieces and the attacker seven.

Objective Each player tries to capture or immobilize as many enemy pieces as possible in order to achieve his objective. The attacker's objective is to capture the fortress by getting two of his pieces into it; the defender's objective is to prevent him from doing so.

Start of play The defender's pieces are positioned around the fortress (but not in the neutral zone), and the attacker's pieces on the outermost ring.

Moving

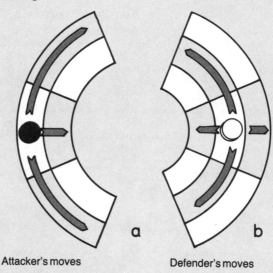

a
Attacker's moves

b
Defender's moves

Play The players decide which of them is to attack and which to defend. The attacker has the first move, and thereafter players take alternate turns.

The attacker may only move his pieces forward (ie toward the center) or sideways (**a**).

The defender – although having fewer pieces – has the advantage of being able to move them in any direction except diagonally (**b**). He may not actually enter the fortress, although he is allowed to jump over it when capturing.

When moving sideways (ie into another segment) pieces must remain on the same ring as the one on which they were standing.

Both players may move their pieces into the neutral zone – although the attacker may only have as many pieces in the neutral zone as the defender has on the board. For example, if the defender has only two pieces left on the board, the attacker may only have two pieces within the neutral zone.

Capturing Both players may capture enemy pieces, although there is no compulsion to do so. A piece is captured by jumping over it from a touching section onto a vacant section beyond (**a**). The captured piece is then removed from the board.

As in ordinary moves, the attacker is restricted to capturing in a forward or sideways direction, while the defender may also capture in a backward direction.

Capturing

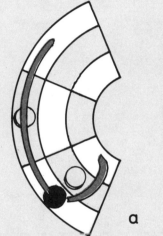

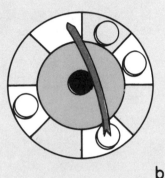

a

b

Capturing moves

Capture of an
attacker in the
fortress

When the player makes a sideways capture, the taking piece
and the piece being captured must be on the same ring.
A player may capture only one piece in a move.
All pieces are safe from capture when within the neutral zone.
However, it is permissible for a piece to use the neutral zone as
its "take-off" or "landing" area in a capturing move.
Although the defender may not actually enter the fortress, he
may jump over it in order to capture an enemy piece within it,
provided the section directly opposite is vacant (**b**).
End play The attacker may enter the fortress from any segment
(including the neutral zone). Should a defending piece be
positioned on the innermost ring, an attacking piece may jump
over it into the fortress (thereby capturing the defending
piece).
If the attacker gets one of his pieces into the fortress, it is still
prone to capture by a defending piece. Should the attacker
succeed in getting two of his pieces into the fortress, however,
he wins the game.
The defender wins the game if he either captures all but one of
the attacker's pieces or immobilizes the attacker's pieces so
that he is unable to get two pieces into the fortress.

© DIAGRAM

Salta

This game was invented in about 1900 and takes its name from a Latin word meaning jump.

Board The game is played on a Continental checkerboard, 10 squares by 10.

Pieces There are two sets of 15 pieces. Each set is of a different color, eg red and white, and has pieces numbered 1 through 15. Sets can easily be made by drawing or sticking numbers on checkers pieces, though original sets have stars on pieces 1 through 5, moons on pieces 6 through 10, and suns on pieces 11 through 15.

Objective The game is won by the first player to move all his pieces onto the corresponding squares originally occupied by his opponent's pieces (eg white 4 onto the square that was occupied by red 4).

Start of play Players position their pieces as shown, with pieces 1 through 5 on the black squares of the first row, 6 through 10 on the second row, and 11 through 15 on the third row.

Start of play

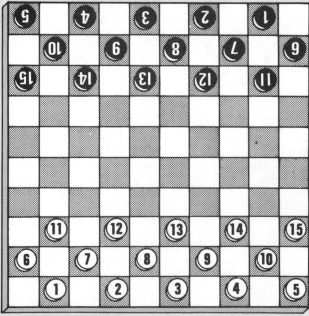

Moving A player may make only one move in a turn. The following moves are permitted:

a) one square diagonally forward or backward, or

b) a jumping move diagonally forward or backward over one piece of either color that has a vacant square beyond it. Multiple jumps are not permitted in this game, and no jumped piece is removed from the board. If a player can make a jumping move rather than an ordinary move he must do so – hence the strategic importance of forcing a player to jump his pieces back toward his own starting line.

120-move rule Some players like to play to the 120-move rule. By this rule, play automatically ends after 120 moves. Each of the players then calculates how many moves he would need to achieve his objective. The winner is the player who is nearest his objective when play ends.

Moving

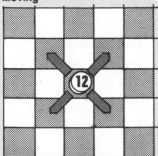
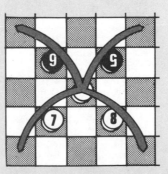

Sap tim pun

Sap tim pun, or Ten and a half, is a gambling game popular among the Chinese in Malaysia. It is played with Mah jongg tiles but has similarities with card games of the Blackjack family.

Sample hand

10½ points

Players Sap tim pun is a game for two or more players, one of whom acts as banker.

Tiles One standard set of 144 Mah jongg tiles is used. The tiles have the following point values:
a) suit tiles count their numerical face value;
b) dragons, flowers, seasons, and winds are each worth ½ point (except that special rules apply if an east wind tile is picked up in the first draw).

Objective Each player tries to get a hand with a point count that is higher than that of the banker – though not in excess of 10½.

Building the walls The tiles are turned face down on the table, shuffled, and then built into four walls. Each wall is 18 tiles long and two tiles high, as at the start of a game of Mah jongg (see p. 188).

Turns pass counterclockwise around the players, as in standard Mah jongg and Chinese domino games.

First draw and betting
1) The banker for the round declares the maximum stake.
2) Each player in turn draws one tile from the wall, with the player to the banker's right drawing first and the banker drawing last. Each player looks at his tile and then lays it face down in front of him.
3) Players other than the banker place a stake beside their tile and then turn the tile face up.
4) If the banker has drawn an east wind tile, he now turns it over and takes all the stakes on the table. He then discards the east wind tile and replaces it with another tile from the wall.
5) If any other player has drawn an east wind tile, and provided that the banker has not also drawn an east wind, the player receives his stake from the banker, replaces the east wind tile with another tile from the wall, and places a new stake beside it.

Drawing additional tiles Each player in turn has the opportunity of drawing an additional one or two tiles (to make a maximum of three tiles in his hand).
A player must draw a further tile if his hand with one or two tiles is worth less than 6 points; he has the choice of drawing or standing if his hand is worth 6 points or more.

The drawn tiles are kept concealed unless the player's hand totals more than 10½ points – in which case he throws in his tiles and passes his stake to the banker.

Banker's hand When all the other players have drawn or stood, the banker turns over his first tile and then draws or stands according to the same rules as other players.

Settlement

a) If the banker's hand exceeds 10½ points, he pays the stake of all players still in the game.

b) If his hand totals exactly 10½, he receives all stakes laid.

c) If his hand is less than 10½, he receives the stakes of all players with fewer points and pays all players with more points.

Rotating bank After each round the bank passes one player to the right.

© DIAGRAM

Shogi

Shogi is a member of the Chess family from Japan. It is very popular there and supports professional players. There have been many forms of Shogi since its introduction in about the eighth century. A feature peculiar to Shogi since the sixteenth century is that captured pieces join the capturing side and can be returned to any position on the board.

The board is nine squares by nine, giving 81 squares in all. The "squares" are in fact slightly oblong, and the board is placed between the two players so that they are facing each other down its longer length.

Black dots mark the two "promotion lines."

The notation used for referring to squares on the Shogi board is shown in the diagram below.

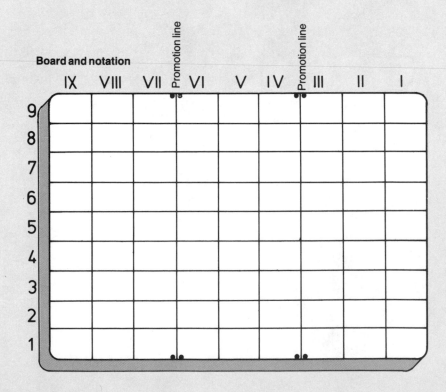

Board and notation

The pieces Each player begins with 20 pieces. Using Western Chess names as far as possible and with Western notation in brackets, these pieces are:

a king (K);
a rook (R);
a bishop (B);
two gold generals (G);
two silver generals (S);
two knights (Kt);
two lances (L);
nine pawns (P).

Shogi pieces are all the same shape and color: they are distinguished only by size and by the Japanese characters written on them.

The two players' pieces are distinguished on the board by being pointed toward the opposing player.

The objective is to "checkmate" the enemy king. A king is checkmated when, in the next enemy turn, it could be captured either on its present square or on any square to which it could move.

Pieces

King

Rook

Bishop

Gold general

Silver general

Knight

Lance

Pawn

© DIAGRAM

Pieces and their moves Pieces are only permitted to move on the board in certain ways. Each piece has a different move:

a) the king (K) can move one square in any direction;

b) the gold general (G) can move one square in any direction except diagonally backward;

c) the silver general (S) can move one square directly forward or one square in any diagonal direction;

d) the pawn (P) can only move one square directly forward (unlike the pawn in Chess, the pawn in Shogi makes the same move when capturing);

e) the knight (Kt) can move, in a single turn, one square directly forward and then one square diagonally forward (the square directly forward may be vacant or occupied, but if it is occupied by an enemy piece that piece is not captured);

f) the rook (R) can move an unlimited number of squares in any direction except diagonally;

g) the bishop (B) can move an unlimited number of squares in any diagonal direction;

h) the lance (L) can move an unlimited number of squares but only directly forward.

Pieces that can move an unlimited number of squares (the rook, bishop, and lance) must halt:

if they reach a piece belonging to their own side (in which case they can go no farther than the last vacant square before they reach that piece); or

if they reach an enemy piece (in which case the enemy piece is captured).

Value of pieces Players trying out a game of Shogi will probably be helped by a rough guide to the value of the pieces. As a game ends when a king is checkmated, the king is obviously the most important piece. The rook is the most powerful piece on the board and its importance increases as the game progresses. The bishop is almost as powerful as the rook and is most useful in the game opening.

The gold and silver generals are the intermediate pieces, with the gold slightly more useful especially in defense. The knight and lance are minor pieces, roughly equal in value and of real use only in attack. Pawns are of very little importance and, unlike in Chess, a one pawn advantage is seldom significant.

Moves

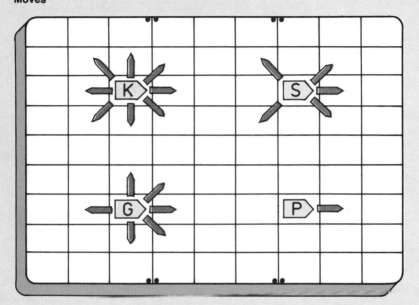

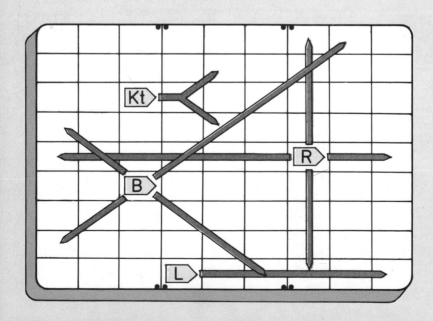

Start of play The pieces are placed on the board as shown. When a game is being described, the players may conveniently be referred to as "black" and "white," even though their pieces are not distinguished by color. Pointers at the side of the board in our diagrams indicate each player's direction of play. Players usually draw lots, and the player drawing black has the first turn.

Play The two players make alternate moves. In a move a player may either:

a) move one of his pieces on the board to a vacant square;
b) capture an enemy piece; or
c) replace a previously captured piece on the board.

Capture A player captures an enemy piece by moving one of his own pieces to the square occupied by that piece.

When a player captures a piece it becomes part of his own side, and in any future turn can be returned to the board on any vacant square.

In the capture illustrated it is black's turn to play. He moves by capturing the white pawn with his bishop.

Start of play

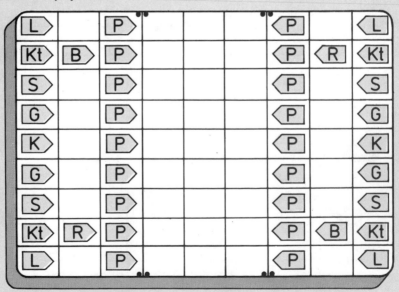

Capturo

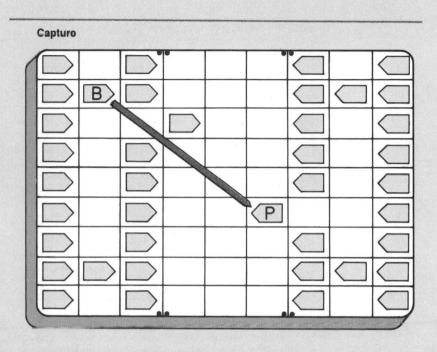

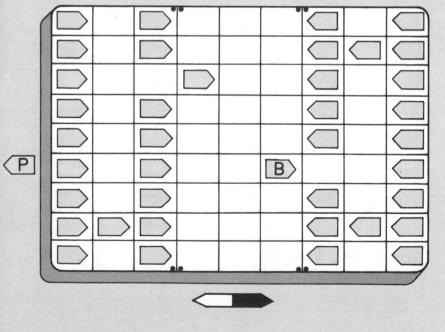

Promotion When a piece crosses the far "promotion line," its powers of movement may be changed if its player wishes. Promoted pieces move as follows:

a) a rook keeps its original move and adds the power to move one square at a time in any diagonal direction;

b) a bishop keeps its original move and adds the power to move one square at a time in any non-diagonal direction;

c) a silver general, a lance, a knight, and a pawn are all promoted to gold generals.

A gold general does not acquire any new powers on promotion. In play, promotion is shown by turning the piece over to expose a different Japanese character underneath. In diagrams of a game, promotion is shown by drawing a circle around the original piece.

Once a piece has been promoted, it retains its new powers even if it retreats so that it is not beyond the far promotion line.

A piece receives its promotion in the turn in which it crosses the promotion line, or in any subsequent turn, according to the player's wishes. Its new powers become available to it in the next turn after promotion.

A lance or pawn that reaches the last rank must be promoted; so must a knight that reaches the last two ranks. (Since these pieces cannot be moved backward, promotion is essential if they are to be moved again.)

A promoted piece loses its promotion when captured. For example, if black captures a promoted white pawn, it joins his side as a pawn not as a gold general.

Promotion

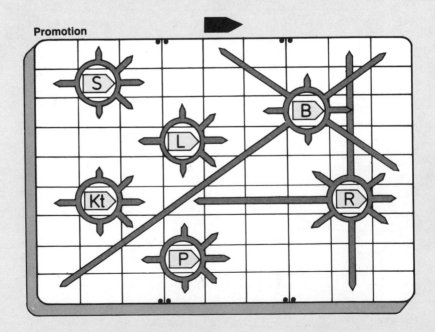

©DIAGRAM

Use of captured pieces A captured piece is removed from the board and becomes the property of the player who made the capture.

In any turn, instead of moving a piece already on the board, a player may place a piece that he has captured on the board on any vacant square. This is called a "drop." The piece is placed so that it points in the same direction as the player's other pieces.

A dropped piece, placed on the board beyond the far promotion line, does not receive promotion as soon as it is placed on the board but must first make a move on the board. Therefore a player must not place a pawn or a lance on the last rank, or a knight on one of the last two ranks, since these pieces would not be able to move again.

There are two restrictions on pawn drops:

a) a player must not place a pawn on the same file as one of his own unpromoted pawns;

b) a player cannot checkmate the enemy king by placing a pawn on the square directly in front of the king.

(It is because of the power of the drop as a maneuver that the king in Shogi almost always stays in one corner of the board surrounded by a heavy guard.)

Attacking the king A king is "in check" when it is exposed to capture – ie when it is on a square onto which the opposing player could move one of his pieces in his next turn. If a player's king is in check he must immediately escape check:

a) by moving the king to a square that is not being attacked;

b) by taking the attacking piece with the king; or

c) by taking the attacking piece with another piece.

Whatever he does, however, his turn must not end with his still being in check from any enemy piece.

It is "checkmate" when a player's king is exposed to capture and there is no move that he can make that does not leave it so exposed.

©DIAGRAM

Examples of checkmate

a) Basic checkmate: the gold general moves to 9viii and so mates the king. (If the gold general moved to 8viii the king would have been in check but the gold general, unprotected by the bishop, would have been taken in the king's next move.)

b) Checkmate by promoting: the knight moves to 6viii, is promoted, and so mates the king.

c) Checkmate by not promoting: white chooses not to promote his silver general, moves it to 2ix, keeps it unpromoted, and so mates the king. (If the silver general had been promoted to gold general it would have been unable to attack along the reverse diagonal.)

d) Checkmate by forced exchange: white's silver general moves to 9ii, giving check and forcing black's silver general to take it; black's silver general is in turn taken by white's gold general, which, covered by white's lance, then mates black's king.

e) Checkmate by promoting and then retreating: the promoted rook returns from beyond the promotion line to 2iv and so mates the king. (The rook needs the additional power given by promotion in order to mate.)

Examples of checkmate

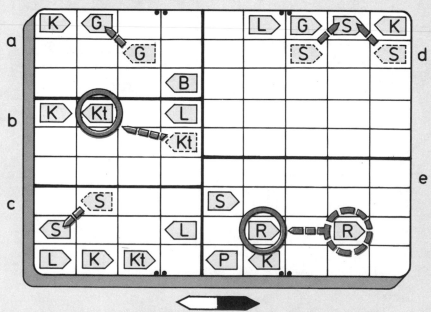

Checkmate by drop

a) Black takes white's gold general with his bishop, promotes it, and so gives check. White's king must take black's bishop to escape check.

b) Each player now has a captured piece in hand alongside the board: black has the gold general and white the bishop. Black drops the gold general onto 8ii – and so mates white's king.

Checkmate by drop

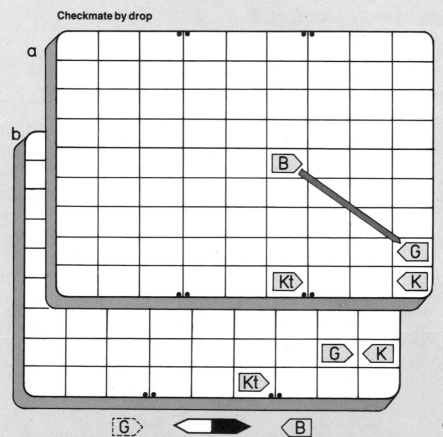

Shove soccer

Shove soccer is a table game for two players or teams based on the rules of Soccer. Players use a wood or plastic ruler to propel larger coins – "players" – into a smaller coin – the "ball." Goalposts are marked at each end of the table. The game is won by the team that scores most goals.

Table The game can be played on any rectangular table.
Equipment Players need:
a) a wood or plastic ruler for propelling the coins;
b) a small coin or disk for the "ball";
c) larger coins, marked according to team;
d) matches, pencils, or some other means of marking the goalposts.
Players Shove football can be played by:
two players with two or more coins each;
two teams with one or two coins per player.
(The game is probably best with a maximum of eight coins representing "players.")
Playing the ball A player uses his ruler to shove any of his team's "players" into the ball.
Duration A game consists of two halves of an agreed length of time – usually 2–5 minutes. Teams change ends at half time.
Turns The first turn goes to the team that wins the toss of a coin; the other team has the first turn in the second half. Otherwise turns alternate between teams, with team members playing in the same order throughout.
Kick off The ball is kicked off from the center of the table:
at the start of each half;
after each goal.
Players may position their "players" by hand before a kick off. No "player" may be within 3in of the "player" taking the kick.
Play A player is allowed only one kick in a turn unless:
he has been awarded a free kick – in which case he takes the free kick and then his ordinary turn;
he earns an extra kick by hitting the ball into another of his "players."
Fouls The following fouls are penalized by a free kick to the opposition:
a) touching the ball directly with the ruler;
b) touching an opposition "player" with the ruler;
c) hitting a "player" into an opposition "player" before hitting the ball;
d) moving a "player" by hand except when specifically allowed in the rules;
e) playing out of turn;

f) interfering with the game in any other way.

Free kick A free kick after a foul is taken from where the offense occurred.

The player taking the free kick may reposition any of his "players" by hand. Opposition "players" may not normally be moved, except that a "player" less than 6in from the ball must be moved to that distance.

Kick on The opposition is awarded a "kick on" (a free kick 2in from where the ball went out of play) if:
the ball is sent over the side edge of the table;
the ball is sent over the opposition's goal line (back edge of the table) without touching an opposition "player."
Both players may reposition any of their "players" for a kick on. Other "players" must be at least 3in from the "player" taking the kick.

Corner kick The attacking side is awarded a corner kick if the ball goes over the opposition goal line after last touching an opposition "player." The attacker takes a free kick from the corner of the table nearest where the ball went off.
Both players may reposition their "players" by hand. No "player" may be within 3in of the "player" taking the kick.

Scoring A goal is scored when the ball is pushed through the goalposts. After a goal, play is restarted with a center kick by the team who scored.

The game is won by the team scoring the most goals.

Shove ha'penny

Shove ha'penny is an old English game sometimes played in public houses. Two players or pairs attempt to position ha'pennies or metal disks on a marked board. A game is won by the first side to "shove" three ha'pennies into each of the board's nine "beds."

The board Shove ha'penny is usually played on a special board, but can be played on a tabletop marked with chalk or pencil. A strip of wood under the board keeps it steady when placed over the edge of a table or other level surface. Boards are 2ft by 1ft 2½in and are made of hardwood or slate. Wood boards have the grain running lengthways and the lines marked by shallow grooves.
Ten lines running across the board at 1¼in intervals mark out the nine "beds," and two lines at right angles to them mark the edges of the scoring area.
The squares along the edges of the board are used for recording the players' scores. Some boards have three holes in each square to hold small scoring pegs.
Ha'pennies The game was played in Britain long before decimalization of the currency in 1971. The old ha'penny was 1in in diameter. Players use very highly polished old ha'pennies or metal disks of the same diameter. Each player has five ha'pennies or disks.
Players Shove ha'penny is a game for two players or pairs.
Turns Choice of playing order may be decided by the toss of a coin, or by a preliminary shove for the nine bed (using only one ha'penny except in case of a tie). Each player shoves five ha'pennies in a turn.

Shoving

"Shoving" The ha'penny is placed partly over the edge of the board and is then shoved as illustrated. A sharp, light tap is most effective.
Shoving one ha'penny into another ("cannoning" or "caroming") is an important feature of the game.
Objective The game is won by the first side to shove three scoring ha'pennies into each of the board's nine beds.
Short shoves
a) A ha'penny that comes to rest on the nearest line of the first bed must be left in position, but may later be cannoned into the beds by another ha'penny.
b) A ha'penny that fails to reach the nearest line of the first bed after hitting a ha'penny on that line must also be left in place.
c) A ha'penny that fails to reach the nearest line of the first bed without hitting a ha'penny on that line may be retaken.

Dead ha'pennies must be immediately removed from the board and may not be retaken. A ha'penny is dead if:

d) it goes wholly beyond the far line of the ninth bed;

e) it stops wholly or partly beyond the side lines in the area used for keeping the score.

Ha'penny on another If a ha'penny stops wholly or partly on top of another, both are left on the board. If a ha'penny is on top of another at the end of a turn, neither can be scored.

Scoring A player's turn is scored only after he has shoved all his five ha'pennies – hence the importance of cannoning.

A ha'penny is scored if it lies completely within one of the beds for which the player needs a score (**f**). There is no score for a ha'penny on a line (**g**), however slight the overlap.

Scores may be made in any order, but good players usually fill the far beds first.

If a player scores more than three times in any bed, the extra scores may be claimed by the opposition – but not if this gives the opposition the final score needed to win the game.

Penalties A player loses all five shoves for the turn if he: touches a played ha'penny before all are played; or removes his ha'pennies before recording his score.

A player who plays out of turn is allowed no score for that turn and must miss his next turn.

©DIAGRAM

Shovelboard

Table shovelboard is the ancestor of Shove ha'penny (p. 330) and of the Shovelboard or Shuffleboard game played on ships' decks and outdoor courts. Players attempt to score points by propelling coins or disks into marked scoring areas. The game can easily be adapted for modern play.

Equipment Each player requires:
a) four coins or disks about 1in in diameter;
b) an implement such as a wood or plastic ruler for propelling the coins or disks.

Table In medieval times Shovelboard was played on very long, narrow tables – perhaps 30ft long and 2ft wide. The higher scoring area extended 4in from the end of the table and the lower scoring area 4ft in front of that.

It is, however, possible to play a form of Shovelboard on almost any rectangular or square table – by marking off an out of play area and scaling down the dimensions of the scoring areas.

Players Shovelboard is a game for two players or two teams of equal number.

Turns In team games, each player normally plays a round against an opponent from the other team. The two opponents in a round propel one coin alternately.

Playing a coin Players use their rulers to give the coin one push toward the scoring area.

All coins, except those more than half over the out of play lines, are left on the table until the end of the round. This makes hitting one coin into another an important feature of the game.

Scoring Players score:
a) three points for any coin partly over the far edge of the table;
b) two points for any coin completely in the far scoring area;
c) one point for any coin completely in the near scoring area;
d) one point for any coin on the line between the near and far scoring areas.

Results In singles games, the winner is the first person to score an agreed number of points – for example 11.

Team games can be decided in several ways:
the team winning most rounds;
the team with most points after an agreed number of rounds;
the first team to score an agreed number of points.

Snakes and ladders

Snakes and ladders is a development of earlier games such as the Game of goose (p.156), and has become a top favorite family game. Like many other race board games its outcome is entirely dependent on chance.

The board is divided into 100 squares. Snakes and ladders – usually about ten of each – are arranged around the board. Although the positioning of the snakes and ladders may vary from board to board, the snakes' heads are always on a higher number than their tails.
The board is often decorated with scenes of children encountering hazards or having fun.
Other equipment comprises one die, and one different colored counter for each player.
Objective Players move their counters around the board – hoping not to be "swallowed" down to a lower number by a snake but instead to be given a helping hand up a ladder to a higher number. The first player to land on the hundredth square wins the game.

Play Each player in turn moves his counter along the squares in numerical order, in accordance with the number obtained by the throw of the die.

If a player's counter lands on a square bearing the foot of a ladder, the player may move his counter up the ladder to the square at its top – thus "jumping" the intermediate squares.

If a counter lands on the head of a snake, the counter must go down the snake to the square at its tail.

End play The game continues with players throwing the die in turn until one of them reaches the hundredth square with an exact throw.

If a player's throw is higher than the number needed for his counter to land on the last square, he has to count the difference in descending order. For example, if the counter is on square 97 and the player throws a 5, he must move forward three squares to 100 and back two squares to square 98.

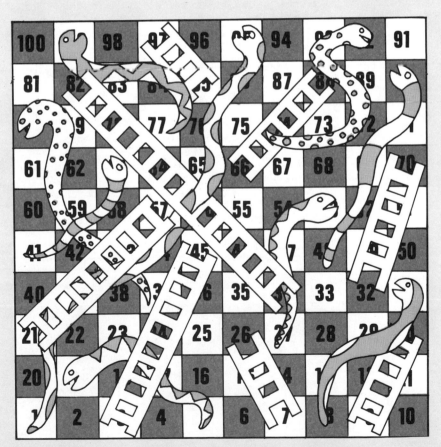

©DIAGRAM

Solitaire board games

Solitaire board games are an excellent diversion for one person. Board solitaire originated in France, where it is said to have been invented by an imprisoned nobleman. It was introduced into England in the late 1700s and has since spread to other parts of the world.

The objective of some solitaire games is to clear the board of all the pieces; in other games the player tries to position the pieces in a specific pattern.

Equipment Solitaire is played with a special board and a set of pegs or marbles made of ivory, bone, wood, or plastic.

The traditional French board is octagonal and has 37 holes to accommodate the same number of pegs.

Traditional English boards are circular and have 33 hollows to hold 33 marbles. A channel running around the edge of the board holds pieces eliminated from the game.

Some solitaire games require all the pieces – others only a certain number of them. The pieces are positioned before the start of play.

(The boards illustrated have been numbered, so that the solutions to the different games can be given.)

Play Pieces are moved in the same manner in all solitaire games. Each peg or marble is "jumped" over an adjoining piece to an empty hole beyond – the piece that has been jumped over is then removed from the board. Pieces may only be moved horizontally or vertically.

Result A game is considered won only if its objective has been exactly met. For example, the standard game is a success only if the board has been completely cleared of all but one of the pieces.

Although some games can be won by more than one method, a player will usually have to make numerous attempts until he has worked out a winning solution.

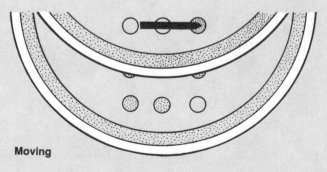

Moving

English board

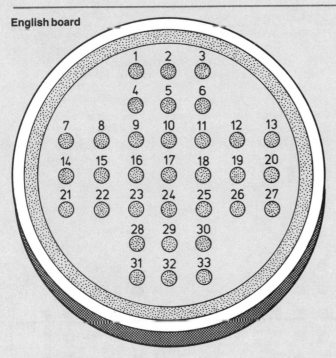

French board

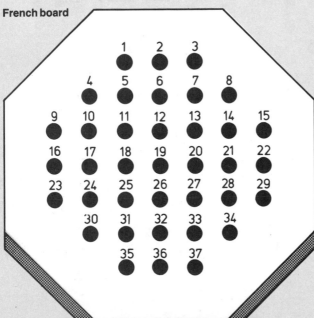

©DIAGRAM

STANDARD SOLITAIRE

The objective of the basic solitaire game is the same whichever type of board is used. The player tries to clear the board so that at the end of the game only one piece is left – either in the central hole or in some other hole predetermined by the player.

Play starts from the center of the board, after the middle piece has been removed. It is vital that no pieces are left isolated from the others during play, as they cannot then be cleared. If the player wishes, the board can be cleared from some other chosen starting point – leaving the center hole filled and removing a piece from elsewhere on the board in order to make a starting space.

Standard solitaire: start

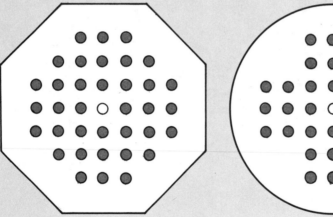
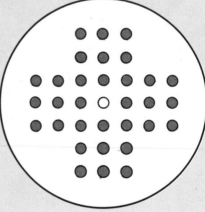

The cross: start

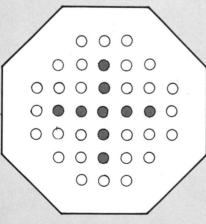
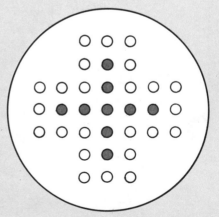

SOLITAIRE VARIANTS

There are numerous variations of the standard Solitaire game, particularly for play on a French board. A player may wish to devise a variant of his own – which will require patience, persistence, and plenty of time. Every move of every attempt to make a certain pattern must be noted until an exact solution has been found. The following are a selection of existing solitaire games.

THE CROSS

The cross is played using only nine pieces, positioned as shown. The object is to remove eight of the nine pieces from the board, leaving only one at the center. (The cross can be played on either the French or the English board.)

© DIAGRAM

THE CORSAIR

At the start of the game all the 37 holes of a French board are
filled. Any one peg at an angle of the board is then removed (ie
1, 3, 15, 29, 37, 35, 23, or 9).

The objective is to remove all the pieces except one – which
should end up in the hole diametrically opposite the starting
hole. For example, if the game were begun at hole 37 the last
peg should be in hole 1.

The corsair: start

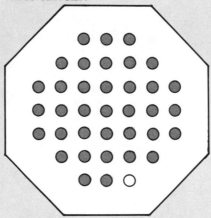

THE OCTAGON

This is another game using a French board. All the holes
except those at the angles of the board are filled (ie not 1, 3, 15,
29, 37, 35, 23, and 9). The player tries to end the game so that
only one piece – at the center of the board – remains.

The octagon: start

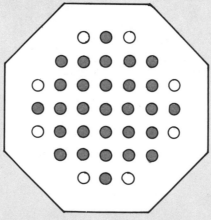

PATTERN FORMING GAMES

Many pattern forming games are designed for play on a French board. All the examples included here begin with all 37 pieces in position. The central piece is then removed, and the player tries to end the game by forming the patterns shown.

The world: objective

The apostles: objective

The letter E: objective

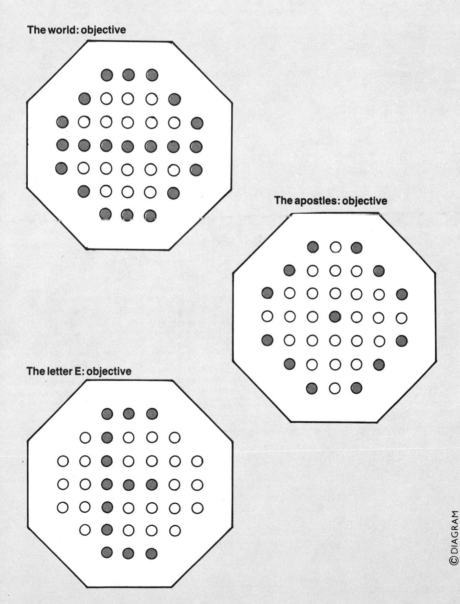

© DIAGRAM

SOLUTIONS

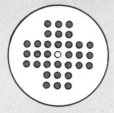 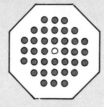 

Standard solitaire (English)
5–17
12–10
3–11
18–6
1–3
3–11
30–18
27–25
24–26
13–27
27–25
22–24
31–23
16–28
33–31
31–23
4–16
7–9
10–8
21–7
7–9
24–10
10–8
8–22
22–24
24–26
19–17
16–18
11–25
26–24
29–17

Standard solitaire (French)

No known solution

The cross (French)
12–2
26–12
17–19
19–6
21–19
2–12
12–26
32–19

The corsair
35–37
26–36
25–35
23–25
34–32
20–33
37–27
7–20
20–33
18–31
35–25
5–18
18–31
29–27
22–20
15–13
16–18
9–11
20–7
7–5
4–6
18–5
1–11
33–20
20–18
18–5
5–7
36–26
30–32
32–19
19–6
2–12
8–6
12–2
3–1

The cross (English)
10–2
24–10
15–17
17–5
19–17
2–10
10–24
29–17

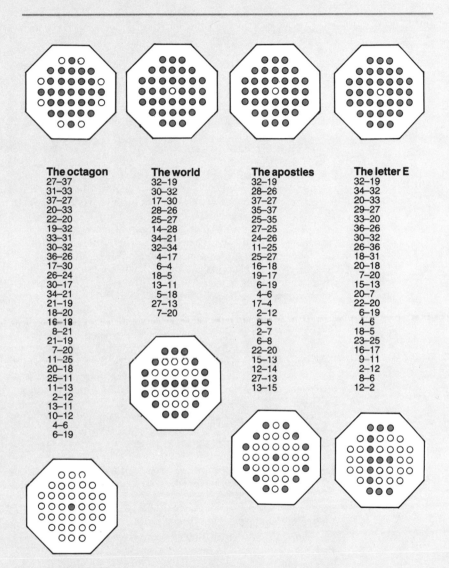

The octagon
27–37
31–33
37–27
20–33
22–20
19–32
33–31
30–32
36–26
17–30
26–24
30–17
34–21
21–19
18–20
16–18
8–21
21–19
7–20
11–25
20–18
25–11
11–13
2–12
13–11
10–12
4–6
6–19

The world
32–19
30–32
17–30
28–26
25–27
14–28
34–21
32–34
4–17
6–4
18–5
13–11
5–18
27–13
7–20

The apostles
32–19
28–26
37–27
35–37
25–35
27–25
24–26
11–25
25–27
16–18
19–17
6–19
4–6
17–4
2–12
8–6
2–7
6–8
22–20
15–13
12–14
27–13
13–15

The letter E
32–19
34–32
20–33
29–27
33–20
36–26
30–32
26–36
18–31
20–18
7–20
15–13
20–7
22–20
6–19
4–6
18–5
23–25
16–17
9–11
2–12
8–6
12–2

Spellicans

This game, which originated in China, is also called Spillikins. Players try their skill at removing straws or small sticks from a pile, one at a time and without disturbing any of its neighbors. Any number of players can take part.

Equipment Spellicans is played with a set of about 30 thin strips of ivory, wood, or plastic. These strips, called spellicans, have carved heads representing animals, people, etc. There is also a carved hook for moving the strips.

Start of play The order of play is determined by the throw of a die or some other means. The last person in the playing order then takes all the spellicans in one hand and drops them onto the table or floor. He must not interfere with any spellican after it has left his hand.

Play At his turn, each player takes the carved hook and attempts to remove a spellican from the pile without disturbing any of the others.

Once a player has started moving a particular spellican he is not permitted to transfer his attack to a different spellican.

If he successfully removes a spellican from the pile, he keeps it and tries to remove another spellican from the pile. A player's turn continues until he disturbs a spellican other than the one that he is attacking.

Play continues in this way until all the spellicans have been taken.

Scoring Each spellican has a points value, and a game is won by the player with the highest score.

Spellicans that are generally fairly easy to move have a low value, and more elaborate and difficult to move spellicans have a correspondingly higher value.

PICK-UP STICKS

This game is similar to Spellicans. Alternative names are Pick-a-stick, Jackstraws, Jerkstraws and Juggling sticks.

Equipment Pick-up sticks is played with about 50 wood or plastic sticks or straws. These are about 6in long, rounded, and with pointed ends, and colored according to their points value.

Play The rules are the same as for Spellicans except that players remove the sticks with their fingers or, in some versions of the game, may use a stick of a specified color after they have drawn one from the pile.

Squails

Squails is a type of table bowls that was popular in Britain in the last century. Players are divided into two teams and seek to position wood disks, called "squails," as near as possible to a metal target, called the "process" or "jack." The game can easily be played with improvised equipment.

Table Squails can be played on any kind of table, but a fairly strong, round one is best.

Squails The game was formerly played with wood disks about 1½in in diameter and raised at the center. Coins, wood counters, coasters, or plastic tiddlywinks can be substituted. Each team's squails should be clearly differentiated by color or a number. Each player has an equal number of squails.

Target Old targets were usually made of metal – eg a small medal or a stumpy lead cylinder. The target is placed in the center of the table at the start of a round.

Players Squails is a game for any even number of players, but four to eight is probably best. Players are divided into two teams, and team members take alternate places around the table.

Turns Choice of playing order goes to the player who gets his squail nearest the target in a preliminary play.

Turns pass clockwise around the table, alternating between teams. Each player plays one squail in a turn.

Playing a squail The player places his squail partly over the edge of the table and then pushes it with the palm of his hand – as in Shove ha'penny (p. 330).

Objective Players attempt to position their squails as near as possible to the target.

Playing one squail into another to move it forward or away from the target is permitted.

Moved target If a squail pushes the target more than 6in away from the center of the table, the target must be put back in its original position.

Two points are generally awarded to the opposition if a player knocks the target off the table or within 3in of the table edge.

Dead squails A squail that goes off the table or stops within 3in of the table edge is dead for that round.

Scoring Points are scored after all the players have played all their squails for a round. The squail farthest from the target scores one point, next farthest two points, and so on to the squail nearest the target.

A game consists of an agreed number of rounds.

Squails

Tiddlywinks

In the standard game of Tiddlywinks, each player attempts to put small disks or "winks" into a cup by shooting them with a larger disk called a "shooter." Variations include games based on sports such as Tennis and Golf.

Playing area Games are played on the floor or on a table. Any shape of table may be used but a square or round one is best if there are more than two players. The table should be covered with a thick cloth or piece of felt.

Shooter

Winks

Winks and shooters must be slightly pliable and are usually made of bone or plastic. Winks are usually about $^5/8$in and shooters about 1in in diameter. Each player's winks and shooter should be a different color.

Target cups are made of plastic, wood, or glass and are usually $1^1/2$in across and 1–2in high.

STANDARD GAME

Players The standard game is usually played by two, three, or four players.

Equipment Each player usually has a shooter and four winks. A target cup is also needed.

Objective The game is won by the first player to get all his tiddlywinks in the cup.

Start of play The cup is placed in the center of the playing area, and each player places his winks in a line in front of him.

Turns Order of play is often decided by a preliminary shot – the first shot of the game going to the player who gets his wink nearest the cup. Play is then usually clockwise around the players.

Each player shoots one wink in a turn plus one extra shot each time he gets a wink into the cup.

Shooting

Shooting A player shoots a wink by stroking and pressing the edge of the shooter against the edge of the wink and so making the wink jump into the air. A wink is shot from where it lies after the player's previous turn.

Out of play Any wink that is partly covered by another is out of play. A player whose wink is covered by an opponent's wink must either wait until the opponent moves his wink or must attempt to remove the opponent's wink by hitting it with one of his own winks.

Any wink that stops against the side of the cup is out of play until it is knocked level onto the table by another wink.

A wink that is shot off the table does not go out of play. It must be replaced on the table at the point where it went off.

Scoring Tiddlywinks may be scored in two ways:
a) players count the number of games they win;
b) players score one point for each wink in the cup when each game ends.

PARTNERSHIP TIDDLYWINKS
Tiddlywinks can be played by partners in the same way as the standard singles game except that:
players pair up with the player sitting opposite;
partners play alternately and may play either their own or their partner's winks.

FORFEIT TIDDLYWINKS
An interesting variation of the standard game is played by drawing six concentric circles around the cup. Play is the same as for the standard game except that any wink that lands in one of the circles is forfeited and immediately removed from the table.

TARGET TIDDLYWINKS GAMES

These variations involve shooting winks at numbered targets.
Typical layouts are:
a) a target with concentric circles each worth a set number of
points;
b) a raised target with numbered scoring areas.
Target tiddlywinks games are played in the same way as the
standard game except that:
players score a set number of points for landing their winks on
different parts of the target (a wink touching two scoring areas
always scores the lower number);
a wink may not be shot again once it has landed on any part of
the target, but may be knocked by another wink.

TIDDLYWINKS TENNIS

The lines of a tennis court should be marked on the floor or the
tiddlywinks cloth. (Dimensions for the court should be varied
to suit the skill of the players and the height of the net.) An
improvised net can be made with folded paper or card, or with
a row of books.
Players shoot a wink back and forth over the net – gaining
points whenever their opponent fails to get the wink over the
net or shoots it so that it goes outside the limits of the court.
The game can be played by two players (singles) or four players
(doubles). In the doubles version, partners take alternate turns
to shoot the wink from their side of the net.
Rules for service can be modified to suit the skill of the players
– eg extra shots allowed to get the wink over the net or no
restrictions on where in the opponent's court the wink must
land.
A match is scored in games and sets as in ordinary tennis.

TIDDLYWINKS GOLF

Tiddlywinks golf sets, with tiddlywinks, greens, obstacles, and
holes, are produced by various toy manufacturers.
The game can also be played on an easily improvised course.
Nine "holes" should be positioned at intervals around the
course. Holes can be egg cups, napkin rings, or just circles
drawn on the tiddlywinks cloth.
The course is then made more interesting by the addition of
obstacles – such as rumpled or corrugated paper under the
cloth to make rough ground, upturned books to make raised
ground, and box or jar lids for water obstacles.
The game can be scored by "stroke" or by "hole" as in real
golf. In the first, each player counts the number of shots he
takes to complete the course. In the second, players score one
for each hole won and a half for each hole tied.

Target tiddlywinks

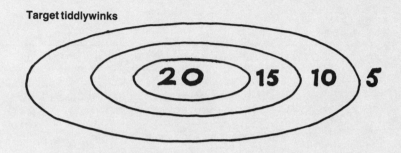

Tiddlywinks tennis

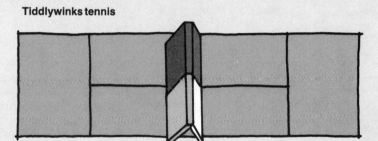

Tiddlywinks golf

Word games: acting

Play with words is one of the most popular forms of amusement. Games in this first group all require players to act, most often in mime, words that other players must guess. There is no need for any great acting ability, but a lively imagination will prove extremely useful!

Players Acting guessing games can be played by any number of players divided into two teams.

One team chooses a word or phrase according to the rules of the particular game and then the other team attempts to guess it. The teams change roles whenever a correct guess is made.

Costumes and other props are not necessary for these games, but they can add to the players' enjoyment.

CHARADES

Charades is probably the best known and most popular of all word games involving acting.

The objective is for one team to guess a word with several syllables that is acted out in mime by the other team.

Play The acting team leaves the room and decides on a suitable word. Usually words of three syllables are chosen, but players may choose words of only two syllables or of four or more. This word is then presented to the other team in mimed scenes representing the different syllables, and then in a final scene representing the whole word.

Usually there is one scene for each syllable, although players may choose to represent two syllables in a single scene. (For example, the word "decorate" could be broken down as "deck-or-rate" or as "decor-ate.") One of the actors must announce the number of scenes before miming begins.

The actors usually leave the room between scenes and the guessing team is then free to discuss its ideas. It is advisable for players to agree on a time limit for guessing words after the final scene.

An example of the sort of word that might be chosen is "nightingale," which was used in a charade scene in the book Vanity Fair by the nineteenth-century English novelist, William Thackeray. Nightingale breaks down into three syllables and could be represented by:

a) a "night" scene with people going to bed or sleeping;
b) an "inn" scene with people drinking and making merry;
c) a "gale" scene with people being blown down a street;
d) a "nightingale" scene with people flapping their arms and imitating bird song.

CATEGORY CHARADES

This game is played in the same way as standard Charades
except that teams must choose words that belong to a
previously agreed category and there is no miming of the full
word.
Ideas for categories are:
a) towns (eg "came-bridge," "prince-ton");
b) people's names (eg "rob-in," "car-row-line");
c) animals (eg "lie-on," "buff-a-low");
d) flowers (eg "snow-drop," "butter-cup").

PROVERB CHARADES

Proverb charades is played in the same way as standard
Charades except that teams choose a proverb or well-known
quotation, which they then act out word by word or in groups
of several words. A good proverb for this game would be
"a bird in the hand is worth two in the bush."

SPOKEN CHARADES

This game is played in the same way as standard Charades
except that the actors speak. Instead of miming scenes
representing the syllables and then the full word, players must
mention them while acting in the different scenes. This game is
easier to play than most Charades games, and for this reason is
particularly popular with younger children.

© DIAGRAM

THE GAME
This is a fascinating variation of Charades. It is called "The game" because its early enthusiasts claimed that it was truly the game of all games.

The players are divided into two teams, and each team nominates a different person to be its actor for each round.

Objective Using conventional gestures and free mime, the actor must convey to his teammates a well-known phrase chosen by the opposing team. The teams compete on a time basis.

Categories Phrases for this game must belong to one of a number of categories previously decided by both teams. Typical categories are the title of a book, play, television series, song, or painting, or a quotation, slogan, or proverb.

Play One team chooses a phrase and whispers it to the actor from the other team. The actor then begins miming, and a person appointed as timekeeper makes a note of the time. The actor should use conventional gestures where possible.

His teammates are allowed to speak, and make guesses as the acting proceeds. The actor, however, is only allowed to reply to their guesses with gestures.

If a correct guess is made, the timekeeper records the time and the teams change roles. (It is advisable to have a time limit, after which the teams must change roles even though the phrase has not been guessed.)

Gestures Players may improvise in their miming, but The game is characterized by the use of previously agreed gestures.

Firstly the actor indicates the category of the phrase. For example he can mime holding a book (**a**) for a book title.

To indicate the number of words in the phrase the actor then holds up that number of fingers (**b**).

If the actor is going to mime the entire phrase he forms a circle, either with his thumb and forefinger (**c**) or with his arms.

If he wishes to mime only part of the phrase, he indicates a word by tapping the appropriate finger (**d**). He then counts his fingers to shown how many letters there are in this word (**e**).

If he wishes to use only part of a mimed word, he must make chopping actions to divide the word into syllables.

When his team makes a correct guess, the actor nods his head. If a guess is along the right lines, he beckons; if totally wrong, he makes a brushing away gesture.

Scoring The game is always scored on the basis of the time taken to guess the phrases. There are, however, two different scoring systems:

a) a round is won by the team that guesses its phrase most quickly and a game is won by the team that wins the most rounds;

b) times for the different rounds are added together and the game is won by the team with the shortest total guessing time.

The Game: gestures

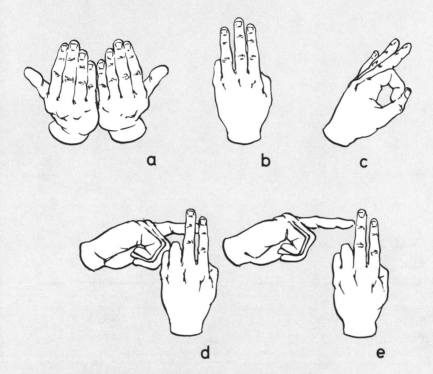

a   b   c

d   e

THE GAME (SIMULTANEOUS)
Some players prefer to have both teams acting the same phrase
simultaneously. In this case it is necessary to appoint a referee,
who thinks of a phrase, writes it on two slips of paper, and
hands the slip to an actor from each of the teams.
Acting takes place in different rooms – so that players cannot
hear the guesses of the opposing team.
A round is won by the team that is first to guess the phrase
correctly. A game is won by the team that wins the most
rounds.

THE GAME (RELAY)
This is played in the same way as the simultaneous version
except that it is organized like a relay race.
The teams must be of equal size and each team member has a
turn at being the actor. As soon as a team guesses a phrase, its
next actor goes to the referee, tells him the last phrase, and is
given a new one.
A game is won when a team guesses its final actor's phrase.

©DIAGRAM

DUMB CRAMBO

Dumb crambo is a very old game of the Charades family. It was particularly popular in the nineteenth century.

Objective After receiving a rhyming clue, a team attempts to guess and mime a word, usually a verb, chosen by the opposing team.

Play The first team chooses a word, for example "feel," and then tells the second team a word rhyming with it, for example "steal."

It is obviously best for this game to choose a word that has several words rhyming with it. For example, other words that rhyme with "feel" are "heal," "keel," "reel," "deal," and "peel."

The second team then attempts to guess the chosen word and must mime its guesses. A maximum of three guesses is allowed. If a guess is incorrect, members of the other team hiss or boo; if a guess is correct, they clap their hands.

A team scores one point each time it guesses a word. Teams change roles after a word is guessed or after three incorrect guesses. The game is won by the team with most points when play ends.

IN THE MANNER OF THE WORD

This is an amusing acting game in which players attempt to guess adverbs.

Play One player chooses an adverb, such as rapidly, quietly, or amusingly. The other players, in turn, then ask him to carry out some action "in the manner of the word." For example, a player might say: "eat in the manner of the word," "walk in the manner of the word," or "laugh in the manner of the word."

The player who chooses the adverb must do as the other players ask, and the other players may make guesses as soon as acting begins.

The first player to guess an adverb correctly scores one point. If no one guesses the word after each of the players has asked for an action, the player who chose the adverb receives one point.

The game is won by the player with most points after each of the players has had a turn at choosing an adverb.

Word games: guessing

Games in this second group of word games require players to identify what another player is thinking. Many of them can be made either easy or difficult to suit the ages and abilities of the people taking part.

I-SPY

I-spy is an excellent game for children learning to spell. It is also fun for older children, who can try and outwit each other by "spying" inconspicuous objects.

Objective Each player tries to be the first to guess which visible object one of them has spied.

Play Two or more people can play, and one of them is chosen to start. He says "I spy, with my little eye, something beginning with . . ." and gives the first letter of an object that he has secretly chosen, and that is visible to all the players. (They may have to turn their heads in order to see the object, but they should not need to move about.)

For example, if he chose a vase, he would give the letter V or, if he chose a two-word object, the first letter of each word (eg PF for picture frame).

If the player chooses an object such as a chair, of which there may be more than one in the room, the other players must guess the particular chair he has in mind.

The game ends as soon as someone has spotted the object that was chosen – he may then spy the next object.

Variation I-spy may be played by very young children if colors rather than first letters are given. For example, a player may say "I spy, with my little eye, something red" and the others then look for the red object that he has in mind.

I-spy

ANIMAL, VEGETABLE, OR MINERAL

Sometimes called Twenty questions, this game is one of the oldest and most familiar word guessing games. Players try to guess an object thought of by one of the others.

Players The game needs two or more players, or two teams. It is often helpful to have a non-playing person to act as referee.

Play One of the players thinks of an object. It may be general (eg "a ship"), specific (eg "the Lusitania"), or a feature (eg "the bridge of the Lusitania").

He then tells the others the composition of his chosen object (ie animal, vegetable, or mineral). The three categories may be defined as follows:

1) animal: all forms of animal life or anything of animal origin, eg a centipede, a tortoiseshell comb;

2) vegetable: all forms of vegetable life or anything of vegetable origin, eg flax, a wooden mallet;

3) mineral: anything inorganic or of inorganic origin, eg soda, a mirror.

Objects are often a combination of categories, for example a can of beer or a leather shoe. (The referee may be consulted if the player is unsure as to the category of an object.)

The player usually indicates the number of words in the object – excluding the definite or indefinite article.

The other players then ask anything up to to 20 questions to try to guess the object. They should ask questions of a general nature rather than make random guesses, until they feel confident that they are near to knowing the object.

As each question is put to the player, he must reply either "Yes," or "No," or "I don't know" as appropriate. The referee may intervene if he feels the player has given a wrong or misleading answer; he may also be consulted for guidance on a particular point.

End The first player to guess the object correctly may choose an object for a new round of play.

If no one has guessed the object by the time 20 questions have been asked (usually the referee keeps a count) the players are told what it was, and the same person may choose an object for the next round, or – if two teams are playing – a person in the other team may choose.

MAN AND OBJECT

In Man and object, a player thinks of a person and something identified with him. The person may be someone known personally to all the players, or a famous personality or fictional character. Examples might be an eskimo and his igloo, or Dante and the inferno.

Playing procedure is the same as for Animal, vegetable, or mineral – except that the players may be allowed to ask more than 20 questions.

COFFEEPOT

Coffeepot is a word substitution game that is easily learned and a lot of fun.

One player leaves the room while the others choose a verb or participle describing an activity – for instance "laugh" and "eat" or "laughing" and "eating."

The player then returns to the room and tries to guess the activity by asking questions in which he substitutes the word "coffeepot" for the unknown word. He puts a question to each of the players in turn, saying something like "Do you often coffeepot?" The players must answer truthfully, with either a straight "Yes" or "No," or with answers like "Only sometimes" or "When it rains."

As the guesser does not know what the activity is, some of the questions will be hilarious – which is why the game is such fun. If he manages to guess the word, the player whose answer enabled him to do so becomes the next guesser. If he cannot guess the word within a reasonable time, he must take another turn at guessing.

TEAKETTLE

As in Coffeepot, one of the players leaves the room while the others think of a word for him to guess.

The choice of word might be quite tricky, as it must be one with several meanings. Examples are: rain, reign, rein; or way. weigh, whey.

The player comes back into the room and listens to the others as they make conversation; he may join in if he likes. Sentences must have "teakettle" in place of the chosen word, so that a player might say: "It always seems to teakettle (rain) when I take my baby for a walk."

As soon as he guesses the word, another player takes a turn at guessing a new word.

A variation of Teakettle is for the first player to select the word, and the other players to guess what it is as he makes up different sentences. The first person to guess the word correctly may then take a turn at choosing a word.

JOIN THE CLUB

This game needs players who have not played it before. Only when they guess a secret solution, known only to the leader, are they allowed to "join the club."

The leader says: "Mrs Pettigrew doesn't like tea, what does she like?" The other players suggest different things and the leader tells them whether they are right or wrong – if they are wrong they must drop out.

Play continues until all the players have dropped out, or until one of them guesses the solution; "tea" is really the letter T, so that any answer given should not contain it. For example, answers like "chocolate," "tomatoes," or "tequila" would eliminate a player.

If a player guesses the solution, the leader says "Join the club!"
Other questions the leader could ask are:
"Our cook doesn't like peas, what does he prefer?"; or
"The stung man doesn't like bees, what does he like?"

PROVERBS
In this guessing game, one player has to discover a proverb
hidden in the other players' answers to his questions. (It is
sometimes called Hidden proverbs, or Guessing proverbs.)
The player who is to be first guesser leaves the room while the
other players select a proverb. The guesser then returns to the
room and asks each player in turn a question – it may be about
anything at all, such as "What did you have for breakfast today?"
Each answer must contain one word from the proverb in the
correct order. As soon as all the words have been used up, the
players begin again with the first word of the proverb.
The questioner may make as many guesses at the proverb as he
likes within a time limit of, say, ten minutes. If he cannot guess
the proverb, he is told the answer and another player takes
over as guesser in the next round.

Proverbs

©DIAGRAM

WHAT IS MY THOUGHT LIKE?

This is a game for those with a lively imagination and the ability to bluff. Any number of players may take part. One of them thinks of a thing or a person and asks the other players "What is my thought like?"

Each of them then makes a totally random guess (as no clues have been given) as to the object thought of.

Once all of the players have made their guesses, they are told the object and are given a moment or two in which to think of a way of justifying the relationship between the object and their own guesses.

For example, if the object were a tiger and the first player had suggested a fire engine, he might legitimately explain "A fire engine is like a tiger because they both roar down the road!" As some of the explanations may be rather farfetched they may be discussed among the other players. Any player whose explanation is disallowed must pay a forfeit. If all the players give satisfactory answers, the questioner must pay a forfeit. A different questioner is chosen for each subsequent round.

WHO AM I?

This is a fairly simple game, in which one player does all the guessing. He leaves the room while the other players think of any well-known personality – real or fictional, dead or alive. The guesser returns to the room and asks "Who am I?" The other players each reply with a clue to the character's identity. If the character is Napoleon, for example, answers might be:
"You are rather short and stout,"
"You are a great strategist at war,"
"You underestimated the Russian winter."
When each of the players has given a reply, the guesser may make three guesses as to the identity of the person. If he fails to guess correctly, he is told the answer.
Another player is always chosen for the next round.

BOTTICELLI

This game requires a good general knowledge.

One person chooses a famous person, and tells the other players the initial of his surname. For example, he might say "M" for Groucho Marx.

Taking turns, each player must think of a character whose name begins with that letter, and give a description of him without naming the person he has in mind. If he thought of Mickey Mouse, he would ask "Are you a Walt Disney cartoon character?"

If the first player recognizes the description, he answers "No, I am not Mickey Mouse," and another player may make a guess.

If the first player does not recognize the description, however, the player who gave it may then ask a direct question that will give him and the other players a lead, such as "Are you in the entertainment business?" The first player must give a truthful "Yes" or "No" reply.

The first person to guess the personality wins the round and may choose the next character. If nobody succeeds in guessing the personality after a reasonable length of time, the first player tells them the answer and may choose again for the new round.

Botticelli

©DIAGRAM

SCISSORS, PAPER, STONE

This ancient game, also known as Hic, haec, hoc and by many other names, is played all over the world. It is a game for two players.

Three objects (scissors, a piece of paper, and a stone) are indicated by different positions of the hand:

a) two fingers making a V shape represent scissors;
b) an open hand represents a piece of paper; and
c) a clenched fist represents a stone.

Each player hides one hand behind his back and adopts one of the three positions. One of the players calls "One, two, three" (or "Hic, haec, hoc") and as the third word is called the players show their hands.

The winner of a round is decided with reference to the following statements: scissors can cut paper, paper may be wrapped around a stone, and a stone can blunt the scissors. Thus if one player chooses scissors and the other player paper, the player who chooses scissors wins the round. If both players decide on the same object, the round is a draw.

Players usually play a pre-determined number of rounds.

Scissors, paper, stone: gestures   **Scissors, paper, stone: play**

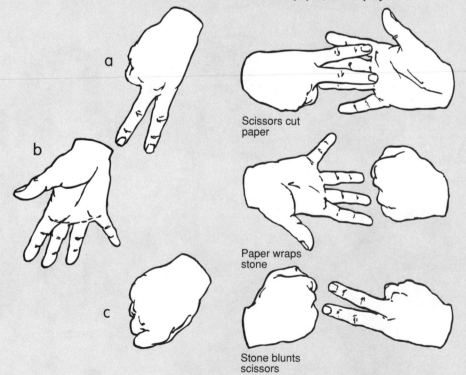

Scissors cut paper

Paper wraps stone

Stone blunts scissors

MORA

Mora, also known as Fingers, is another finger guessing game for two players. The object of the game is to guess the number of fingers that will be "thrown" (displayed).

The players stand facing each other, each with a closed fist against his chest. At a given signal they throw a chosen number of fingers (or extend their clenched fist to indicate zero) and simultaneously call out the total number of fingers that they think will be thrown by both players (thumbs count as fingers). A call of "Mora!" indicates that the player is betting on ten fingers.

If neither player guesses correctly, the round is considered void. If one player guesses correctly he wins that round; if both players guess the right number, the round is a draw. A game usually comprises 10 or 15 rounds.

Mora: gestures

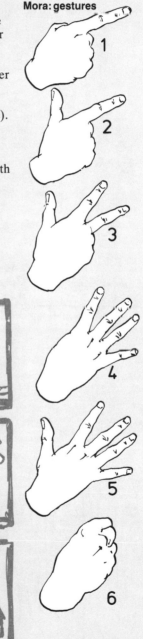

SHOOT

Shoot is rather like Mora (p. 365), except that the two players must guess not the number of fingers thrown, but whether it will be an odd or even total. The players may throw the fingers on one or both hands (ie each player may throw any number from zero through ten).

As they show their hands, the players call out "Odds!" or "Evens!" The fingers are counted (zero is considered an even number) and the winner is determined as in Mora.

SPOOF

This is an intriguing game of bluff for at least two players, in which each person tries to guess the total number of objects the players are concealing in their hands.

Each player requires three small objects, such as coins or matches. He hides any number of them (or none if he wishes) in his outstretched fist.

One by one, in a clockwise direction, the players call out the number of objects they think are contained in the players' hands – but no two players may say the same number.

When all the players have guessed, they open their fists and the objects are counted. The player who guessed correctly, or whose guess was nearest the correct number, wins the round. Obviously, much depends on the ability to determine whether a player is bluffing when he calls a number. For example, guessing high might indicate that the caller has a full hand of three objects (especially if he happens to be the first caller in a round). Similarly, guessing low could mean a low number of objects – or an attempt to deceive the other players as to the contents of a hand.

Spoof: two players

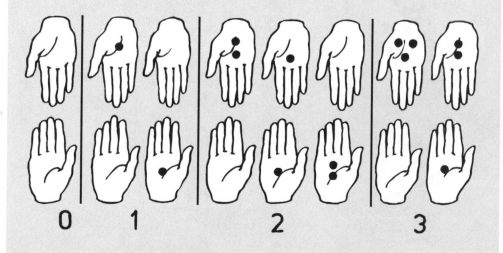

0   1   2   3

Shoot

Word games: vocabulary

These games range from simple spelling games to more
complex games requiring considerable verbal dexterity. Most
can be played by any number of people.

SPELLING BEE
One person is chosen as leader, and the other players sit facing
him. The leader may be given a previously prepared list of
words or he may make one up himself. It is a good idea to have
a dictionary to hand in case of disputes.
The leader then reads out the first word on his list and the first
player tries to spell it. He is allowed ten seconds in which to
make an attempt at the correct spelling.
If he succeeds, he scores one point and the next word is read
out for the next player. If he makes a mistake, the leader reads
out the correct spelling. The player does not score for that
word, and the next word is read out for the next player.
(Alternatively, the player is eliminated from the game for an
incorrect answer.)
Play continues around the group of players until all the words
on the list have been spelled.
The winner is the player with the most points at the end of the
game.

GREEDY SPELLING BEE
In this version of Spelling bee, whenever a player spells a word
correctly he is given another word to spell. Only when he
makes a mistake does the next player take a turn – and he starts
with the incorrectly spelled word.
One point is scored for each correct spelling, and the player
with the highest score at the end of the game wins.

BACKWARD SPELLING BEE
In this more difficult version of Spelling bee, players must spell
their words backward. Scoring is the same as in the standard
game.

RIGHT OR WRONG SPELLING BEE

The players should form two teams of equal size, and get in line opposite each other.

The leader calls out a word to each player in turn, alternating between teams. Each time a player spells a word, the player standing opposite him must call out "Right" or "Wrong." If he calls a correctly spelled word wrong or a misspelled word right, he is eliminated from the game and must leave the line. (Players may move around once their numbers have been depleted, so that there is a caller for each player in the other team.) If the caller makes a correct call, he gets the next word to spell.

The last team to retain any players wins the game.

Spelling bee

©DIAGRAM

GHOSTS

Concentration and a good vocabulary are needed to win this game. Players take it in turns to contribute a letter to an unstated word, while trying to avoid completing any word. The first player begins by thinking of any word (eg banana) and calls out the first letter (B). The next player then thinks of a word beginning with B (eg beetle) and calls out its second letter (E). Play then continues in this way until one of the players is unable to contribute a letter that does not complete a word. Whenever a player completes a word – and the other players notice – that player loses a "life." This is true even if he completes a word by accident because he was thinking of another word.

If a player is unable to think of a suitable word he may try to bluff his way out of the situation by calling out a letter of an imaginary word. However, if he hesitates for too long or the other players suspect that he has no particular word in mind they may challenge him. The challenged player must state his word, and if he cannot do so he loses a life. If his explanation is satisfactory, however, the challenger loses a life.

Whenever a player loses his first life he becomes "a third of a ghost." Losing a second life makes him "two-thirds of a ghost," and if he loses a third life he becomes a whole ghost and must drop out of the game.

The game is won by the player who survives longest.

GRAB ON BEHIND

Also called Last and first or Alpha and omega, this is a good game for a lot of players.

Players decide on a specific category, such as flowers, cities, or insects. The first player calls out a word in the chosen category. The next player then follows with another word in the category – but it must begin with the last letter of the previous word. Play continues in this way around the group. For example, if the category were flowers the words might be: mimosa, anemone, edelweiss, sweet pea, and so on.

Players have only five seconds in which to think of a word and may not repeat a word that has already been called.

Anyone failing to think of a word or calling an incorrect word drops out of that round. The last player to stay in wins.

INITIAL LETTERS

The players sit in a circle. One of them puts a question – it may be as farfetched as he likes – to the others. Each of them in turn must reply with a two-word answer, beginning with the initials of his or her name. Players have only five seconds in which to think of an answer.

For example, if the question were "What is your favorite food?" Bruce Robertson could reply "Boiled rice," and Robert Chapman might say "Roquefort cheese." When all the players have answered, the second player asks a question.

Any player who fails to answer after five seconds or who gives a wrong answer drops out of the game; the winner is the last person to stay in.

INITIAL ANSWERS

This is a good game for a large group of people. The players sit in a circle and one of them starts by thinking of any letter of the alphabet (eg S). He must then think of a three-letter word beginning with that letter and give a definition of his word, for example "S plus two letters is a father's child."

The second person in the circle has to try and guess the word ("son"), and he then thinks of a word of four letters also beginning with S. He might choose "soup" and define it as "S plus three letters makes a tasty start to a meal" for the person sitting next to him to guess.

This next person, after guessing the word correctly, must think of a five-letter word – perhaps "snail" – defining it "S plus four letters carries a house on its back."

The game continues in this way, with each person having to think of a word beginning with the chosen letter, and each word having one letter more than the previous word.

Any player who fails to think of an appropriate word, or who fails to guess a word must drop out. The last person left in the game is the winner.

A different letter of the alphabet should be chosen for the next round.

©DIAGRAM

TRAVELER'S ALPHABET

In this game the first player says "I am going on a journey to Amsterdam," or any other town or country beginning with A. The next person then asks "What will you do there?" The verb, adjective, and noun used in the answer must all begin with A; for example, "I shall acquire attractive antiques." The second player must then give a place name and an answer using the letter B, the third player uses the letter C, and so on around the players. Any player who cannot respond is eliminated from the game.

If the players wish to make the game more taxing, they may have to give an answer that is linked with the place they have chosen. For example, a player might say "I am going to Greece to guzzle gorgeous grapes."

If a player gives an inappropriate answer he may be challenged by another player. If that player cannot think of a more fitting sentence, the first player may stay in the game. Should the challenger's sentence be suitably linked, the first player is eliminated.

I LOVE MY LOVE

In I love my love, players have to think of an adjective beginning with each letter of the alphabet to complete a given statement.

The first player starts by saying "I love my love because she is . . ." using any adjective beginning with A. The next person repeats the phrase, but his adjective must begin with B, the next person's with C, and so on through the alphabet.

Alternatively, each player must make a different statement, as well as using an adjective with a different letter. Examples of suitable statements are:

"Her name is . . ."

"She lives in . . ."

"And I shall give her . . ."

Players may write down the chosen statements if they wish, but there must be no hesitation over the answers. Any player who hesitates or gives an incorrect answer drops out of the game, and the winner is the last person left in.

A WAS AN APPLE PIE

This is a similar game to I love my love, but players must think of a verb instead of an adjective.

The first player says: "A was an apple pie. A ate it," and other players might add "B baked it," "C chose it," "D dropped it," and so on.

I WENT ON A TRIP

Each player tries to remember and repeat a growing list of items.

One of the players chooses any article he likes – for example an umbrella – and says "I went on a trip and took my umbrella." The next player repeats that sentence and adds a second item after "umbrella." In this way the players gradually build up a list of articles.

Each time his turn comes, a player repeats the list and adds another item. Whenever a player cannot repeat the list correctly, the list is closed and the next player in the group begins a new list.

CITY OF BOSTON

City of Boston is very similar to I went on a trip, but in this game players must add to a list of items for sale. Thus the first player might say "I shall sell you a bunch of violets when you come to the City of Boston." Each of the other players then repeats that sentence and adds an item that he will sell.

ONE MINUTE PLEASE

One minute please calls for quick wits and imagination as players try to speak for one minute on a given topic. One player is chosen as timekeeper, and also picks a topic for each player to talk about.

When it is his turn to speak, the player is told his topic. This may be anything from a serious topic such as "The current political situation" to something frivolous like "Why women wear hats."

The player may choose to treat the subject in any manner he pleases and what he says may be utter nonsense, provided he does not deviate from the topic, hesitate unduly, or repeat himself.

Other players may challenge the speaker if they feel he has broken a ruling. If the timekeeper agrees, then that player must drop out and the next player is given his topic.

The winner is the player who manages to speak for an entire minute. If two or more players achieve this, the others decide which of the speeches was the best, or alternatively further rounds may be played.

ASSOCIATIONS

Associations needs quick thinking, as the slightest hesitation eliminates a player from the game!

One person starts by saying any word (preferably a noun). As quickly as possible, the player next to him says the first word that the first player's word brought to mind, and so on around the group, beginning again with the first player.

If a player hesitates before saying a word, he drops out – if he manages to stay in the game longer than all the other players, he wins.

ASSOCIATION CHAIN

This game can be played as a continuation of the last game. As soon as the chain has been formed, the last player to have called out a word starts to repeat the chain backward. If he makes a mistake, he drops out, and the player before him continues to unravel the chain. This goes on until either the first word is reached, or only one player is left.

The more obvious or striking the associations, the easier it is to unravel the chain.

NUMBER ASSOCIATIONS

Number associations needs a person to call out any number between 1 and 12.

As soon as he has said a number, the players call out an appropriate association. For example, if the number called is seven, a player could call "Deadly sins."

The first player to call out a correct association scores one point. Other players may challenge a reply if they feel it is inappropriate. If the leader agrees with the challenge, that player loses one point from his score.

An association may not be repeated. At the end of the game, the winner is the person with the highest number of points.

TABOO
In Taboo – sometimes called Never say it – players try to avoid saying a particular letter of the alphabet. One player is the questioner and chooses which letter is to be "taboo."
He then asks each of the players in turn any question he likes. The respondent must answer with a sensible phrase or sentence that does not contain the forbidden letter – if he does use the taboo letter, he is out.
The last player to stay in the game wins and becomes the next questioner.

BUZZ
This game should be played as briskly as possible for maximum enjoyment.
The players sit in a circle. One player calls out "One," the next player "Two," the next "Three," and so on.
As soon as the number five, or any multiple of five, is reached, the players must say "Buzz." If the number contains a five but is not a multiple of five, only part of it is replaced by buzz. (For example, 52 would be "buzz two.")
If a player forgets to say buzz or hesitates too long, he drops out; the last player to stay in the game is the winner.

FIZZ
This is played exactly like Buzz, except that players say "Fizz" for seven or multiples of seven.

BUZZ-FIZZ
Buzz-fizz combines the two games, so that 57, for example, becomes buzz-fizz.

1 2 3 4 *BUZZ* 6 *FIZZ* 8
9 *BUZZ* 11 12 13 *FIZZ*
BUZZ 16 1 *FIZZ* 18 19 *BUZZ*
FIZZ 22 23

©DIAGRAM

Section 2
General card games

General rules

The origin of playing cards is a mystery. Chinese playing cards, it seems, grew out of a marriage between divinatory arrows and paper money. Such cards may have reached Europe via the Crusades or the China trade. Alternatively Western playing cards may have had a separate European origin – seeming to have appeared quite suddenly, around 1370, in almost their present form.

THE CARDS
The deck The standard international deck of playing cards consists of 52 cards, divided into four suits of 13 cards each. Many decks also contain two jokers, sometimes used as wild cards.
The suits are named hearts, diamonds, spades, and clubs, and each card of the suit bears the appropriate symbol, as shown. Hearts and diamonds bear red symbols, spades and clubs black symbols.

Complete deck of cards

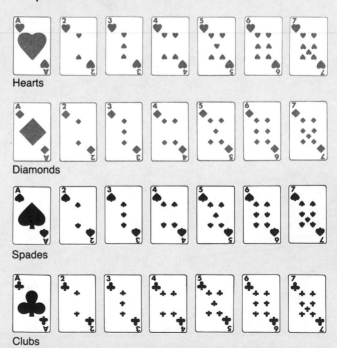

Hearts

Diamonds

Spades

Clubs

The cards in any one suit are all of different denominations:
nine are numbered from 2 to 10; three are "face" cards (jack,
queen, king); the remaining card is the "ace," which is the "1"
but is often the most powerful card of the suit.

The denomination of numbered cards is shown both by
numbers and by the appropriate number of suit symbols.
The ace is shown by an "A" and a single large suit symbol.
Face cards are shown by stylized drawings and by initial
letters, which vary according to the country of origin of the
deck. In English language countries these letters are "J" (for
jack), "Q" (for queen), and "K" (for king).

The rank of cards is usually either:
2 (low), 3,4,5,6,7,8,9,10,j,q,k,a (high); or
a (low), 2,3,4,5,6,7,8,9,10,j,q,k (high).
In either list, a card beats any card listed before it.
These rankings are referred to in the text as "cards rank
normally, ace high," and "cards rank normally, ace low."

A meld is a scoring combination of cards in certain games. It is
usually either:
a) three or more cards of the same denomination; or
b) three or more cards in consecutive order of rank and of the
same suit.

Trumps In games with tricks (see p 383), it is often ruled that certain cards are made trump cards (trumps). If so, any trump card ranks above any other card.

Usually, all the cards of one suit are chosen as trump cards (trump suit). But in some games only some cards of one suit are the trump cards; or in other games there are other trump cards in addition to the trump suit.

Within a trump suit, cards rank in the standard order for the game being played.

Choice of trump suit The method depends on the game being played.

Some games use a permanent trump suit, chosen by agreement or convention at the beginning of the game. But usually a suit has the role of trump suit for only one deal at a time. In this case, the trump suit for a deal is decided in one of the following ways, depending on the game being played:

a) by competitive bidding among the players;

b) by chance, ie turning a certain card face up – the suit revealed becomes trumps;

c) by set order of rotation among the suits.

PREPARING AND DEALING

Choice of partners for partnership play is usually by an initial draw. Each of the four players draws one card from the deck; the two players with the two highest ranking cards form one partnership and the other two players form the second.

Choice of first dealer

a) By high cut. Any agreed player acts as temporary dealer and shuffles the cards. Any other agreed player cuts them.
Each player then cuts the deck, beginning with the player to the temporary dealer's left, going clockwise, and ending with the temporary dealer.
Each cut consists of lifting a section of cards from the top of the face-down deck. The card cut by the player is that at the bottom of this section.

The section is held so all players can see this card.
After each cut, the two sections of cards are restacked in their original order, before passing to the next player.
The player cutting the highest denomination card becomes the first dealer. Cards rank normally; ace ranks high or low according to the game played. Players who cut equal highest, cut again until a decision is reached between them.

b) By deal of cards. Any agreed player acts as temporary dealer and shuffles the cards. Any other agreed player cuts them.
The temporary dealer then deals one card face up to each player, including himself, beginning with the player to his left and going clockwise, until the first card of a specified denomination is dealt (eg the first ace). The player receiving this card becomes the first dealer.

Shuffling

Shuffle and cut are often required before every deal. The dealer shuffles. Any other player also has the right to shuffle, but the dealer has the right to shuffle last.
The procedure of shuffling is not governed by rules – providing that an adequate shuffle is given to the cards in some way. One simple and satisfactory procedure is illustrated here.
The player to the dealer's right is offered the cards to cut. If he declines the player to his right is offered the cut, and so on. If no player wishes to cut, the dealer must cut.
A cut consists of lifting a section of cards from the top of the deck, placing it on the table, and placing the other section on top of it.
Cards remain face down and unexposed throughout.
There must be at least five cards in each section.

The deal Unless otherwise stated, the dealer gives one card at a time to each player, beginning with the player to his left and going clockwise. This rotation is repeated until each player has the required number of cards. The deal must be from the top of a face-down deck.

Deal in packets is a deal in which each player receives more than one card at once. It is required for certain games.

On the deal, the dealer gives each player a specified number of cards (eg three cards), before going on to the next player. Otherwise the deal follows normal procedure.

Sometimes the number of cards specified changes during the deal. For example, in solo whist:

when the dealer goes around the circle of players for the first, second, and third times, he gives each player three cards each time;

when he goes around the fourth (last) time, he gives each player one card, as in a normal deal.

A widow is a batch of cards dealt in addition to the players' hands. Its role varies from game to game.

The stock is, in certain games, the part of the deck which remains undealt after the deal is complete but which becomes available to players in the course of play.

ROTATION OF PLAY

Unless otherwise stated, play begins with the player to the dealer's left, and continues with the other players in clockwise rotation.

TRICKS

A trick signifies, in certain games, one round of cards during play – one card being contributed by each active hand.

It also means the cards themselves when gathered together.

On each trick one player plays first ("has the lead"), and the other players follow in clockwise rotation.

Each player's action consists of taking one card from his hand and placing it face up in the centre of the table.

The lead is held, in most games:

a) on the first trick after a deal – by the player to the dealer's left;

b) on the remaining tricks of the deal – by the player who won the previous trick.

Choice of cards The lead may play any card he wishes. The other players must "follow suit" if possible, ie each must play a card of the same suit as the lead card if he has one. If a player cannot follow suit, he may play any other card that he has.

A trick is won by the highest ranking card of the suit led – providing that no trump is played. If one or more trump cards are played, it is won by the highest ranking trump card.

A player may usually only play a trump card if he cannot follow suit.

The player playing the winning card takes the trick: he gathers the cards together, and places them face down on the table, usually near his (or his partner's) position.

Revoking A player who has failed to follow suit when he in fact had a card of the required suit is said to have "revoked." Penalties for this vary from game to game.

IRREGULARITIES

Rules on irregularities in play vary from one game to another. But the following rules are general.

A misdeal should be declared:

a) if, during a deal, a card is found face up in the deck; or

b) if the rules of shuffling, cutting or dealing are broken.

Imperfect deck If the deck is found to have cards missing, or added, or duplicated, the hand being played is immediately abandoned. However, any scores made so far on that hand are valid.

Winning a trick

Trumps

Lead

King wins

Trump wins

©DIAGRAM

All fives

All fives is a similar game to seven up, but has a different scoring system. It is a game for two or three players.

Cards A standard deck of playing cards is used. Cards rank normally, with ace high.

Deal Players cut for the deal; highest card deals.
Each player is dealt six face-down cards in packets of three. The next card is turned face up to denote trumps. The deal passes clockwise around the table.

Rank

Trumps If the player to the left of the dealer is happy to play with the trump suit designated by the face-up card, he says "Stand" and play begins.
If the player to the dealer's left would prefer a different trump suit, he says "I beg." The dealer can then choose whether or not to change trumps.
If the dealer chooses to keep trumps as they are, he says "Take one"; the player to his left then scores one point, and play begins.
If the dealer agrees to change the trump suit, he sets aside the face-up card, deals three more cards to each player, and then turns the next card face up to denote trumps. If this card shows a different suit from the first face-up card, play begins with this suit as trumps.
If the new face-up card belongs to the same suit as the first face-up card, the dealer gives another three cards to each player and turns up another face-up card; this procedure is repeated until a new trump suit is determined. If the deck is used up before a new trump suit is found, the entire deck is shuffled and redealt.

Play Rules of play are as for whist

Scoring At the end of each round the tricks are turned face up for scoring. Points are scored for trump cards in tricks won:
a) ace of trumps, four points;
b) king of trumps, three points;
c) queen of trumps, two points;
d) jack of trumps, one point;
e) 10 of trumps, ten points;
f) 5 of trumps, five points.
Game is 61 points.

Auction pitch

This game is derived from seven up and is especially popular in the United States. It is also called setback. It is a game for two to seven players.

Cards A standard deck of playing cards is used. Ace is high.
Deal Players cut for the deal, highest card dealing. Each player is dealt six face-down cards in packets of three.
Objective Each player tries to score the number of points needed to win the game.
Bidding Each player in turn, starting with the player to the dealer's left, makes a bid of one, two, three, or four – or passes. A bid indicates the number of points the bidder intends to make. A bid of four is called "shoot the moon," "slam," or "smudge."
Each bid must be higher than the previous bid, except that the dealer may hold (ie take over) the previous bid if it is under four.
The highest bidder, or the dealer if he held a previous bid, is called the "pitcher."
Play The pitcher leads to the first trick and his card denotes trumps for the deal.
In a trump suit players must follow suit or, if they cannot, must discard one card. In a plain (non-trumps) suit, players may either follow suit or play a trump card – if they can do neither, they discard.
The winner of a trick leads to the next.

Scoring Players other than the pitcher score points exactly as in seven up, ie:

a) "high," one point for the player dealt the highest trump;

b) "low," one point for the player dealt the lowest trump;

c) "jack," one point for the player who takes the jack of trumps in a trick;

d) "game," one point for the player who takes the highest total value of cards in tricks (for which purpose, cards are valued four for an ace, three for a king, two for a queen, one for a jack, ten for a 10).

The pitcher only scores if his score is equal to or greater than his bid. If he fails to make his contract, he is set back by (ie loses) the number of points he bid.

Game is usually seven points, but players can decide to play for 10,11, or 21 points.

If the pitcher ties with another player, the pitcher is the winner. For ties between other players, points are counted in the order: high, low, jack, and game.

AUCTION PITCH WITH JOKER

A joker is added to the deck for this version of auction pitch. It ranks as the lowest card of the trump suit in play.

If the pitcher leads the joker to the first trick, spades are trumps.

The player who takes the joker in a trick scores one point.

"Low" is scored by the player who is dealt the lowest trump card above the joker.

Game is 10 points. If there is a tie, the order for counting points is: high, low, jack, joker, and game.

Rank

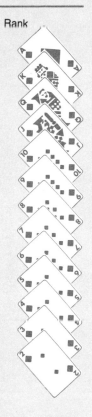

Bezique

Rank

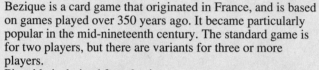

Bezique is a card game that originated in France, and is based on games played over 350 years ago. It became particularly popular in the mid-nineteenth century. The standard game is for two players, but there are variants for three or more players.

Pinochle is derived from bezique.

TWO-HANDED BEZIQUE

The deck comprises a double piquet deck, or two standard 52-card decks from which the 2s,3s,4s,5s, and 6s have been removed – making a total of 64 cards in play.

The cards rank: a (high), 10,k,q,j,9,8,7.

The objective of the game is to make winning melds or declarations, and to take tricks containing certain scoring cards known as brisques.

Deal Players cut for deal. The dealer gives eight cards to each player, dealing three, two, and three cards at a time.

The next (the seventeenth) card is placed face up on the table and indicates the trump suit for that hand. If this card is a 7, the dealer scores 10 points.

The remaining cards are turned face down in a pile, forming the "stock."

Play is in two stages.

The first stage lasts as long as there are cards in the stock.

The non-dealer leads first; thereafter the winner of each trick leads to the next one.

After each trick the winner may make any declaration, and then both players draw cards from the stock to replenish their hands, the winner of the trick drawing first.

The winner of the last trick takes the last stock card, and the loser takes the exposed trump card.

During this stage the players are not obliged to follow suit.

A trick is taken by the higher card of the suit led or by a trump card. If cards of equal value are played, the card that led takes the trick.

Declarations

Trumps

a	b	c	d	e
20 points	40 points	40 points	40 points	60 points

The second stage begins when the stock is exhausted.
The players must follow suit for these last eight tricks, except
they may trump if they cannot follow suit. A player must win a
trick if he is able to.

The winner of the last trick scores 10 points.

Declarations may be made after winning a trick.

The cards of each meld must be laid face up in front of the
player, but they may be played to tricks as if they were still in
the hand.

The possible declarations are as follows:

a) common marriage: king and queen of the same suit, except
trumps, 20 points;

b) royal marriage: king and queen of the trump suit, 40 points;

c) bezique: queen of spades and jack of diamonds, 40 points
(when spades or diamonds are trumps, some players prefer to
make "bezique" the queen of clubs and jack of hearts);

d) any four jacks, 40 points;

e) any four queens, 60 points;

f) any four kings, 80 points;

g) any four aces, 100 points;

h) sequence: a,10,k,q,j of the trump suit only, 250 points;

i) double bezique: both queens of spades and both jacks of
diamonds, 500 points;

j) exchanging the 7 of trumps for the face-up card, 10 points
(the holder of the other 7 of trumps scores 10 points when he
plays it, which does not count as a declaration).

A player may make only one declaration after winning a trick.
But if his exposed cards show a second possible declaration, he
can announce that he will declare it when he next takes a trick.
No card may form part of a second similar declaration. For
example, a queen of spades in "four queens" cannot form part
of a second declaration of "four queens," but can form part
of a "bezique," "double bezique," "royal marriage," or
"sequence."

The cards used to form a "bezique," can be used again to form
part of a "double bezique," but neither card can be used with a
fresh partner for a second "bezique."

Brisques are every ace and every 10 taken in tricks, and they
count 10 points each.

The brisques are counted up by each player examining his tricks
at the end of the game.

© DIAGRAM

f	g	h	i	j
80 points	100 points	250 points	500 points	10 points

Game is either 1000 or 2000 points up.

Penalties If a player draws out of turn, his opponent scores 10 points.

If a player holds more than eight cards, his opponent scores 100 points, provided he himself has the right number of cards.

A player who plays to the next trick without having drawn a card during the first stage forfeits 10 points to his opponent.

A player who revokes (fails to follow suit although able to) during the last eight tricks, or fails to take a trick if he is able to do so forfeits all eight tricks to his opponent.

Scoring is most easily done using special bezique markers; but it can also be done with pencil and paper, counters, or with a cribbage board (each hole on the board counting as 10).

THREE-HANDED BEZIQUE

Three-handed bezique is the same as ordinary bezique except that 96 cards (three piquet decks) are used. Each player plays for himself. Triple bezique scores 1500 points.

RUBICON BEZIQUE

Rubicon bezique is a popular two-player variation of the standard two-handed game. It is similar to standard bezique, with the following differences.

The deck consists of 128 cards, or four piquet decks.

The deal consists of nine cards to each player, dealt either singly or in threes.

Trumps are established by the first sequence or marriage declared by either player. No stock cards are turned up, and the 7 of trumps has no value.

Play is the same as for standard bezique, except that the last trick counts 50 points.

Declarations are as in standard bezique, with the following additions.

a) Carte blanche: worth 50 points, and scored if either player is dealt a hand not containing a face card. The hand must be displayed.

If, after drawing a further card, the player's hand still does not contain a face card, carte blanche may be scored again, and this continues until a face card is drawn.

Once a player has held a face card, carte blanche cannot be scored.

Rubicon: declarations

Trumps

50 points

150 points

1500 points

4500 points

b) Ordinary sequence/back door: a sequence not of the trump suit, 150 points;

c) triple bezique: three queens of spades and three jacks of diamonds, 1500 points;

d) quadruple bezique: four queens of spades and four jacks of diamonds, 4500 points.

Cards may be reused to form the same combinations. For example, if "four queens" are declared and one queen is played, a fifth queen may be laid down to form "four queens" again. Two marriages of the same suit may be rearranged to form two more marriages.

Brisques are only counted if there is a tied score, or to save a player from being "rubiconed," ie failing to reach 1000 points. If one player chooses to count brisques, the other player's brisques are also scored.

Game is a single deal. The player with the higher score wins 500 points plus the difference between his and the loser's score. If the loser is rubiconed, the winner gets 1000 points, plus the sum of his and the loser's scores, plus 320 points for all brisques. (This applies even if the winner himself has scored fewer than 1000 points.)

If the loser fails to score 100 points, the winner scores an extra 100 points.

Any fractions of 100 points may be ignored in scoring, except if the players' scores are very close.

SIX-DECK BEZIQUE

Six-deck bezique, also known as Chinese bezique, is a variant of rubicon bezique. The rules are the same as for rubicon bezique, with the following changes.

The deck is 192 cards (six piquet decks shuffled together).

The deal is 12 cards to each player, dealt singly or in threes.

Trumps are indicated by the first declared marriage or sequence.

Brisques do not count at all.

Declarations can be made as in rubicon bezique, reusing cards in similar scoring combinations.

In six-deck bezique, carte blanche (**a**) is worth 250 points, as is winning the last trick. Declarations in addition to those in rubicon bezique are, in the trump suit only:

b) four jacks, 400 points;

c) four queens, 600 points;

d) four kings, 800 points;

e) four 10s, 900 points;

f) four aces, 1000 points.

Bezique varies according to which suit is trumps, as follows:
hearts, queen of hearts and jack of clubs;
diamonds, queen of diamonds and jack of spades;
clubs, queen of clubs and jack of hearts;
spades, queen of spades and jack of diamonds.

Six deck: declarations

Trumps

250 points

400 points

600 points

800 points

900 points

1000 points

©DIAGRAM

Game is a single deal. Scores are calculated as for rubicon bezique, except that:
the winner gets a game bonus of 1000 points instead of 500; and the rubicon point is 3000 instead of 1000.

Eight-deck: declarations

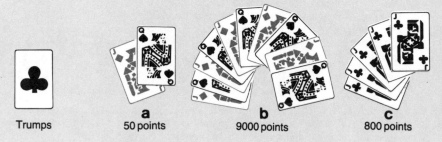

Trumps   **a**   50 points   **b**   9000 points   **c**   800 points

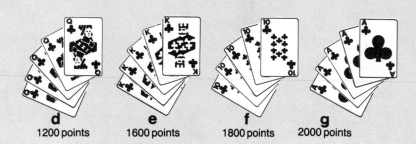

d   1200 points   **e**   1600 points   **f**   1800 points   **g**   2000 points

EIGHT-DECK BEZIQUE
Eight-deck bezique is played like six-deck bezique, with the following variations.
The deck consists of 256 cards, or eight piquet decks.
The deal is 15 cards to each player.
Declarations are as in six-deck bezique, with the following changes and additions:
a) bezique, 50 points;
b) quintuple bezique, 9000 points.
In the trump suit only:
c) five jacks, 800 points;
d) five queens, 1200 points;
e) five kings, 1600 points;
f) five 10s, 1800 points;
g) five aces, 2000 points.
A player is rubiconed if he fails to score 5000 points.

FOUR-HANDED BEZIQUE

Four-handed bezique is similar to rubicon bezique, but the game is played with 192 cards (six piquet decks). The players play in partnership, two against two.

The deal is nine cards to each player; the player on the dealer's left leads to the first trick.

Declarations may be made by any player after winning a trick; alternatively he may allow his partner to make the declaration. A player may use both his own cards and any of his partner's declared cards to make a declaration.

Scoring is as in rubicon bezique, with the following variations and additions:

a) double carte blanche: both players in a partnership being dealt a hand without a face card, 500 points;

b) any four jacks, 400 points;

c) any four queens, 600 points;

d) any four kings, 800 points;

e) any four 10s, 900 points;

f) any four aces, 1000 points;

g) quintuple bezique, 13,500 points;

h) sextuple bezique, 40,500 points.

Four-handed: declarations

Trumps

a 500 points

b 400 points

c 600 points

d 800 points

e 900 points

f 1000 points

g 13,500 points

h 40,500 points

©DIAGRAM

Boston

Rank

This game developed from whist and is itself an ancestor of the now more popular solo whist. It was very popular at the time of the American Revolution.

Players The game is for four players, each playing for himself.
Cards Two standard decks are used: one in play and the other for determining the "preference" and "color" suits. (If the preference and color suits are determined before the deal the game can be played with only one deck.) Cards rank normally, with ace high.
Chips A large number of chips are required for scoring purposes. (To make settlement simpler, players sometimes use chips of different values.)
Objective Each player tries to contract and fulfill a bid.
Choice of first dealer is by high cut, with ace low.
Pool Before each hand, each player pays 10 chips into a pool. If the pool exceeds 250 chips, the excess is put aside for the next pool.
Deal The dealer deals out all the playing deck, beginning with the player to his left and going clockwise. The cards are dealt three at a time, with a final round of single cards.
If there is a misdeal, the dealer must pay 10 chips into the pool. The deal then passes one player to the left.
Determining preference and color suits After the deal, the second deck is cut by the player sitting opposite the dealer. The top card of the bottom section is turned face up and denotes the preference suit. The other suit of the same color is called the color suit.
Bidding Each player in turn, beginning with the player to the dealer's left, may make a bid or pass.
The bids are ranked in the following order, with each outbidding the one before:
a) "Boston," ie a bid to win five tricks with one of the plain suits as trumps;
b) six tricks;
c) seven tricks;
d) "little misery," ie a bid to lose 12 tricks, playing with no trumps and after each player has discarded one card face down;
e) eight tricks;
f) nine tricks;
g) "grand misery," ie a bid to lose every trick, playing with no trumps;
h) 10 tricks;
i) 11 tricks;

j) "little spread," ie a bid to lose 12 tricks, playing with no trumps and the hand exposed;
k) 12 tricks;
l) "grand spread," ie a bid to lose every trick, playing with no trumps and the hand exposed;
m) "grand slam," ie a bid to win all 13 tricks.

Trumps There are no trumps for misery and spread bids. For other bids the player chooses his own trump suit, usually stating what it is only when his bid has been accepted.

However, if two or more players wish to make a bid for the same number of tricks, the bids are ranked as follows according to the proposed trump suit: preference suit (high), color suit, plain suits (low).

No bid hands If all players pass, each one throws in his cards and pays 10 chips into the pool. The deal then passes one player to the left.

Play The player to the left of the dealer leads to the first trick. Play is as for whist (p 126).

A player who revokes loses the hand and must pay 40 chips into the pool.

Settlement If a player fulfills his bid he receives chips from each of the other players and, if his bid was for seven tricks or higher, he also receives the chips in the pool.

If a player fails to fulfill the bid he pays to each of the other players and must also double the chips in the pool.

For misery and spread bids the bidder pays or receives chips as follows: 20 for little misery; 40 for grand misery; 80 for little spread; 160 for grand spread.

If a player fulfills any other bid he is paid according to table A.

If a player fails to fulfill any other bid he pays according to the number of tricks by which he fails – as given in table B. A player is said to be "put in for" the number of tricks by which he fails.

Table A

Tricks bid	5	6	7	8	9	10	11	12	13
Payment	10	15	20	25	35	45	65	105	170

Table B

Tricks bid	Number put in for												
	1	2	3	4	5	6	7	8	9	10	11	12	13
	Payment												
5	10	20	30	40	50								
6	15	25	35	45	55	65							
7	20	30	40	50	60	70	80						
8	25	35	45	55	70	85	100	115					
9	35	45	55	65	80	95	110	125	140				
10	45	55	70	80	95	110	125	140	155	170			
11	70	80	95	110	125	140	155	170	185	200	220		
12	120	130	145	160	180	200	220	240	260	280	300	320	
13	180	200	220	240	260	280	300	320	340	360	390	420	450

©DIAGRAM

Bridge

For many people bridge is the most fascinating of card games: it is played in homes, clubs, and tournaments throughout the world. Its origins can be traced back some 400 years to the development of whist in England, but it was only in 1896 that the game of bridge itself evolved.

CONTRACT BRIDGE
This form of bridge was developed in 1925, and within a few years had become by far the most popular form of the game.

General rules

Cards A standard deck of 52 cards is used. By convention a second deck, with contrasting backs is also used, so that while one player deals another can shuffle in readiness for the next deal.

The cards rank: ace (high) through 2 (low). The 2 is commonly called a "deuce," and the 3 a "trey."

Players As in whist, there are four players, each pair forming a partnership. Partners sit opposite each other. One partnership is usually called North-South, the other East-West.

Objective Each partnership aims to win a "rubber," by winning the most points in the best of three games.

A game is won by scoring 100 points, earned by taking tricks that have been contracted for.

Honors are the high-ranking cards in the trump suit, from the ace down through and including the 10. In "no trump" games, the four aces are honors.

Suits For the purpose of bidding the suits are ranked as follows: spades (highest), hearts, diamonds, clubs (lowest).

The draw At the beginning of a bridge game, one deck is spread out face down on the table, and each player draws one card from the deck.

The two players who draw the highest cards form one partnership; the other two players form the second. The player with the highest card becomes the first dealer and chooses his seating position; his partner sits opposite him.

If cards of the same denomination appear on the draw, they are ranked according to suit, as for bidding.

Shuffle and cut The player to the left of the dealer shuffles the deck; the player to the dealer's right cuts the deck.

As the cards are being dealt, the alternate deck is shuffled by the dealer's partner.

The deal begins with the player to the dealer's left. The cards are dealt in a clockwise direction, one at a time and face down, until each player including the dealer has 13 cards.

Rank of cards

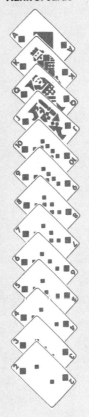

Rank of suits

Honors

©DIAGRAM

Bidding

The auction begins once players have had a chance to study their cards. It opens with the dealer and continues in clockwise rotation. Each player, according to his hand, makes a "call," which may be a bid, pass, double, or redouble.

If a player passes, he may still make another call at a later stage in the bidding. But when a bid, double, or redouble is followed by three passes in succession, the auction ends.

If there are four passes at the opening of bidding, one from each player, the cards are "thrown in" to the center of the table and shuffled. A new hand is then dealt by the next dealer.

A pass indicates that a player does not choose to make any other call at that time in the bidding.

A bid is a statement of a number and a trump suit, eg "three clubs," or "five no trumps." It offers an undertaking that if that suit is trumps (or if there are "no trumps") the bidding player's partnership will take a certain number of tricks.

Bidding refers to the number of "odd" (ie additional) tricks that a bidder undertakes to make over six tricks.

A bid of "one club," for instance, means that a player thinks that his partnership can make seven tricks in all, if clubs are trumps.

A bid of "four no trumps" offers the undertaking to make ten tricks in all, if no suit is trumps.

Continuing the bidding As the auction continues, each successive bid must be higher than the preceding bid – either by calling a greater number of tricks or by naming a higher ranking suit.

For instance, a bid of "two spades" is higher than two hearts, diamonds, or clubs.

A no trump call ranks above all suits. So, for example, a bid of "two no trumps" is higher than two spades. The next player to bid would have to bid at least "three clubs."

The contract The highest bid of the auction becomes the "contract." The players in the partnership making that bid must, in play, make as many tricks as they have contracted for, or more. Their opponents have only to prevent them from doing this – it does not matter what they themselves have bid.

The first six tricks taken by the contracted bidders are commonly referred to as "making the book."

Slam The maximum number of tricks in any played hand is 13. This gives a maximum bid of "seven," when one side believes it can take all the tricks: the book (of six), plus seven odd tricks. If a side succeeds in bidding and winning 13 tricks, this is known as a "grand slam."

A "small slam" occurs if a side bids and wins a total of 12 tricks.

Doubling If a player says "Double" after any of his opponents' bids, it means that he believes he could prevent them from making their bid, if it became the contract.

A bid that has been doubled need not become the contract: it can be overbid in the usual way, by either partnership. If,

Sample deal and bidding

Deal by South

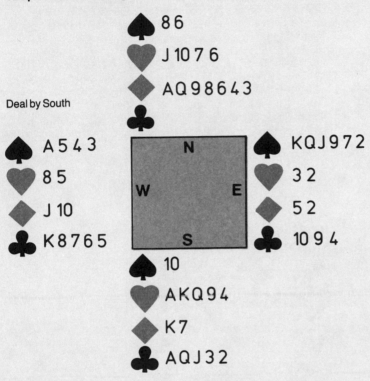

Bidding

S	W	N	E
1 ♣	double	1 ♦	1 ♠
2 ♥	2 ♠	3 ♦	double
3 ♥	pass	pass	3 ♠
4 ♥	pass	pass	pass

The contract is four hearts:
North-South have bought the
contract and South is declarer

©DIAGRAM

however, it does become the contract and succeeds, the contracting players' score is doubled. Should the bidders "go down" (ie not make their contract) the side that doubled gets at least twice the score that it would otherwise have had.

Redoubling If a bid has been doubled, either player of the bidding partnership may say "Redouble." This confirms his confidence in the bid, and – as in doubling – the scoring is affected whether or not the contract is made (see the section on scoring, p 402).

A bid that has been redoubled can be overbid in the usual way.

The declarer The player in the contracting side who first made a bid in the trump suit of the contract (spades, hearts, diamonds, clubs, or no trumps), is referred to as the "declarer." He plays both hands of the contracting partnership's game.

Beginning play

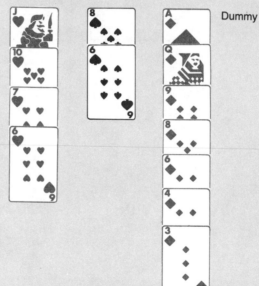

Dummy

South dealt and also made the contract (p 399). West leads. North (dummy) then lays out his hand.

Play

A trick consists of four cards, one played from each player's hand, in clockwise rotation. The player who must play first is called the "lead."

The lead The opening lead is held by the player to the dealer's left. He plays the first card after the bidding ends. After this, the winner of each trick makes the next lead.

A player may lead any card, and the other three players must follow suit if possible. If a player cannot follow suit, he may play any other card in his hand.

Winning the trick If none of the four cards is a trump, the trick is won by the highest card played in the suit led. If one or more of the four cards is a trump, the trick is won by the highest trump.

No trump When a "no trump" bid becomes the contract, all suits have equal rank and the highest card in the suit led always wins the trick.

Dummy As soon as the opening lead has been made, declarer's partner lays down his cards face up on the table, sorted out by suit, with trumps to his right.

The exposed cards, and declarer's partner himself, are referred to as "dummy" for that hand.

Only declarer can choose the cards to play for the dummy hand. The dummy partner may not participate in that hand, other than physically to play a specified card at declarer's request.

Plays from a dummy must be in correct order of rotation, ie following a card played by the player to declarer's left.

Declarer must play a card in dummy that he touches (except when rearranging the cards or touching a card next to the one to be played).

Gathering won tricks is done by either player of the side winning the trick.

The four cards are gathered together and placed face down on the table.

All declarer's and dummy's tricks are placed in front of declarer; all the opponents' tricks are placed in front of one opponent.

The arrangement of gathered tricks must show clearly how many tricks have been won and in which order. Common procedure is to bunch the first six of declarer's tricks into one group, so that it is clear how many odd tricks have been made.

A trick may be inspected by the declarer or by either opponent, until a player of the inspecting side has led or played to the following trick.

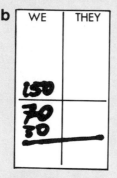

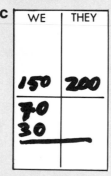

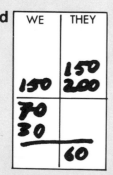

Scoring

It is important to master the scoring in contract bridge as this strongly affects the game's strategy.

Both sides should keep score in case of disagreement.

A scoring pad has a central vertical line dividing "we" (one partnership) from "they" (its opponents).

A horizontal line is initially drawn across the scoring pad, and a partnership can score points either "below the line" or "above the line."

Trick points are entered below the line. Only declarer's side can score trick points on a hand, and only if the contract is made. Only the odd tricks contracted for can be scored below the line. Trick points show each side's progress toward winning the current game.

Premium points are scored above the line, and may be scored by both sides in any hand. They are won for:
a) overtricks;
b) successful doubling or redoubling;
c) bidding and making a slam;
d) having a certain number of honors cards in one hand in the deal; or
e) winning the final game of a rubber.

Undertricks If declarer's side fails to make the contract, the number of tricks it has failed by are known as "undertricks." These are credited to the opponents' premium points and scored above the line.

Vulnerable A partnership is "vulnerable" if it has won its first game toward the rubber. (It is therefore possible for both partnerships to be vulnerable.)

Winning a game The first side to reach a score of 100 or more, either in one or in several hands, wins the game.

A horizontal line is then drawn below the trick scores of both sides. Trick scores for the next game are entered below this line, both sides beginning again from zero.

Winning the rubber When one side has won two games, the rubber ends.

This side earns 700 premium points if its opponents have won no game, and 500 premium points if its opponents have won one game.

All trick and premium points are then totalled, and the side with the higher total wins the rubber.

The back score indicates an individual player's standing. It is used in any competition in which partners rotate.

After a rubber, the difference between the two sides' final scores is calculated by subtracting the lower from the higher. This difference is rounded to the nearest 100 (50 and above become 100), and divided by 100. For example, 753 becomes 800, giving 8. Each player of the winning partnership is then given a score of plus 8 and each opponent a score of minus 8. In subsequent rubbers, with different partnerships, the same procedure is followed. The player with the highest plus score at the end is the overall winner.

Contract bridge scoring table

Trick score: scored by declarer below the line

	♣	♦	♥	♠	NT
First trick over six bid and made	20	20	30	30	40
Subsequent tricks bid and made	20	20	30	30	30
Doubling doubles trick score					
Redoubling doubles doubled score					

Premium score: scored by declarer above the line

	Not vulnerable	Vulnerable
Small slam	500	750
Grand slam	1000	1500
Each overtrick undoubled	Trick value	Trick value
Each overtrick doubled	100	200
Each overtrick redoubled	200	400
Making a doubled or redoubled contract	50	50

Rubber, game, and partscore: scored above the line

	Points
For winning rubber, if opponents have won no game	700
For winning rubber, if opponents have won one game	500
For having won one game in an unfinished rubber	300
For having the only partscore in an unfinished rubber	50

Honors: scored by either side above the line

	Points
Four trump honors in one hand	100
Five trump honors in one hand	150
Four aces in one hand, no trump contract	150

Undertricks: scored by opponents above the line

	Undoubled	Doubled	Redoubled
First trick, not vulnerable	50	100	200
Subsequent tricks	50	200	400
First trick, vulnerable	100	200	400
Subsequent tricks	100	300	600

Explanation of scoring diagrams

a) "We" score 70 trick points.
b) "We" score 30 trick points and 150 premium points. "We" win the first game and are now vulnerable.
c) "We" go under by two tricks. "They" score 200 undertrick points.
d) "They" score 60 trick points and 150 premium points.

DUPLICATE CONTRACT BRIDGE

Duplicate contract bridge is very popular among advanced bridge players. It is the only form played in international tournaments. All groups of players are presented, in turn, with the same deal of cards. In this way, the game relies more on skill than on luck of the deal.

Equipment:
1) one table for every four players in the tournament;
2) the same number of duplicate boards or trays as tables;
3) one deck of cards for each board.

Players Competing units may be individuals, pairs, or teams of four or six, depending on the nature of the tournament. In individual events, partnerships change during the tournament; in team events, partnerships change at half-time; and in pairs matches, the same partnerships are preserved throughout.

A duplicate board is used at each table. Each board has four pockets, an arrow or label indicating North's side, and markers indicating the dealer and the vulnerability or otherwise of partnerships.

Before the tournament the boards are arranged so that a quarter have North-South vulnerable, a quarter East-West vulnerable, a quarter both pairs vulnerable, and a quarter neither pair vulnerable.

Within each category, the position of dealer is distributed equally between the pairs.

Basic procedure Each board maintains the same deal of cards throughout the tournament.

The boards and players move from table to table in a specified way.

The tournament ends, according to the system used, either:
a) when all North-South players have met all East-West players; or
b) when all players have played with and against all other players.

Deal For the first hand at each board, the designated dealer shuffles and deals the cards in the usual way.

Thereafter, following each hand, this original deal is preserved. Each player's cards are placed in the appropriate board pocket, in readiness for the next set of players.

The auction for any hand takes place in the usual way, commencing with the player indicated as dealer.

If all players pass, there is no redeal.

Play on any hand proceeds as in contract bridge, except that after each trick is completed the cards are not gathered together.

Each player takes back his card, and turns it face down on the table in front of him. He points the card lengthwise toward the partners who won the trick; this allows players to keep track of the number of tricks won by each side.

Scoring a hand No points are given for winning a rubber.

If a side bids and makes a contract that gives it a game (100 trick points), it gets 500 premium points if vulnerable, 300 if not. Additional premium points for making a grand slam are 1500 if vulnerable, 1000 if not; and for a small slam 750 if vulnerable, 500 if not.

If a side bids and makes a contract less than game, it gets 50 premium points.

A score made on one board cannot be carried forward to affect scoring on the next.

Unless cumulative tournament scoring is used, no premium points are given for holding honors in one hand.

Scoring the tournament

a) Match point procedure is always used if the competing units are individuals. It can also be used for pairs.

The comparison is between scores made at the same board, ie success in playing the same deal.

Each score is given two points for each lower score made in the same position on that board, and one point for each exactly equal score.

Each individual in an individual event receives points for the score made by his partnership.

The individual or pair with the highest number of match points wins the competition.

b) International match point (imp) scoring is usually used for teams. Each partnership's surplus (or deficit) of points over its opponents is calculated for each hand, and added together at the end to give a team total. This is then converted into match points on the basis of an established scale.

c) Cumulative (total point) scoring is still sometimes used for team competitions.

©DIAGRAM

AUCTION BRIDGE

A forerunner of contract bridge, auction bridge evolved from the game of whist.

Except for the scoring – which greatly affects the strategy of the game – its rules are as for contract bridge.

Major differences The two major differences in scoring are as follows:

1) In auction bridge there is no concept of vulnerability. If one partnership has won a game there is no extra penalty (as in contract bridge) for failure to make a contract.

2) All odd tricks, whether contracted for or not, are scored "below the line." They contribute to winning the game, provided that declarer has succeeded in making the minimum number of tricks named in the contract.

Trick points	♣	♦	♥	♠	NT
Undoubled	6	7	8	9	10
Doubled	12	14	16	18	20
Redoubled	24	28	32	36	40

Game The first side to score 30 points below the line wins a game. A horizontal line is drawn across the scoring pad, as in contract bridge, to indicate that a game has been completed.

Rubber The first side to win two games out of three wins the

rubber and is awarded an additional 250 points.

Honors If either side has three or more honors in the trump suit (or aces at no trumps) then – whether or not that side is declarer – the following scores are given above the line:
three honors or aces, 30 points;
four honors or aces, divided, 40 points;
five honors, divided, 50 points;
four honors, one hand, 80 points;
five honors, divided four to one, 90 points;
four aces, one hand 100 points;
five honors, one hand, 100 points.

Bonuses 50 points are given above the line if a doubled contract is bid for and made. In addition, declarer's side gets 50 points for each trick in excess of the contract.

If declarer succeeds in making a redoubled contract, both the bonuses mentioned above are raised to 100 points each.

Undertricks If declarer's side fails to make its contract, the opponents are given the following points (above the line) for each undertrick:
undoubled contract, 50;
doubled contract, 100;
redoubled contract, 200.

Slams If either side makes a small slam (12 tricks), it receives 50 points above the line – regardless of the bidded contract.
If a grand slam (13 tricks) is won, 100 points are awarded.

©DIAGRAM

Calabrasella

Rank

Calabrasella is an interesting and fast-moving card game for three players. Its characteristic features are a stripped deck, unusual ranking of cards, and the absence of a trump suit.

Cards A standard deck of playing cards with the 8s, 9s, and 10s removed is used.

The cards rank 3 (high),2,a,k,q,j,7,6,5,4 (low).

Players This is a game for three.

Objective Each player tries to take certain tricks.

Deal Players cut for the deal and lowest card deals.

The dealer gives each player 12 face-down cards in packets of four. The four remaining cards are placed face down in a pile in the centre of the table as the widow (extra hand).

Bidding Starting with the player to the left of the dealer, each player in turn may choose either to play or pass.

The first player to choose to play is opposed by the other two players in partnership for that round.

If none of the three players wishes to play, the hand is thrown in and the cards are redealt.

Widow The player who decided to play may discard, face down, up to four of his cards and replace them with cards from the widow, turned face up. The discarded cards, if any, and any remaining widow cards are then placed face down in a pile. These four cards will go to the winner of the last trick.

Play The player to the left of the dealer leads to the first trick with any card he likes. In turn, each of the other players must follow suit if possible, or discard if not.

The winner of each trick leads to the next.

Scoring Players score for taking cards in tricks as follows:
aces, three points each;
3s,2s,ks,qs, and js, one point each.

The player who takes the last trick scores an extra three points, and also scores for the four spare (widow or discard) cards. Thus the maximum possible score is 35 points.

Each side totals its score, and the difference between them is the final score for that hand.

Payoff If the single player wins, each of the opponents pays him the final score in counters or points.

If he loses, he pays each opponent the final score.

If one side scored the maximum of 35 points, the payoff is 70 points or counters.

Game is 100 points. Alternatively, play can continue until one player has lost all his counters.

Canasta

Canasta is a partnership game of the rummy family.
Originating in Uruguay, it reached the United States in 1949
and in the early 1950s became one of the biggest fads in the
history of card playing.

Cards Two standard decks of 52 cards and four jokers are used,
shuffled together.
The cards are not ranked.
There are 12 wild cards: the four jokers and all eight deuces
(2s). Wild cards can be given any denomination that the holder
wishes.

Players In the standard game there are four players divided into
two partnerships.

The objective is to be the first side to score 5000 points over a
series of hands. Points are mainly scored by making melds.

A meld is a set of at least three cards of the same denomination.
They can be all natural cards, or a mixture of natural and wild
cards. But whatever the size of the meld, there must be at least
two natural cards and not more than three wild cards.
Melds score according to the cards they contain (see table A,
p 413).

Cutting for partners Each player cuts a card from the deck, and
the two who cut the highest cards play against the other two.
For this purpose, cards rank normally (ace high) and suits rank
spades (high), hearts, diamonds, clubs (low).
Players cutting a joker or exactly equal cards cut again.
The player cutting highest becomes first dealer and has choice
of seats.

Shuffle and cut are normal

The deal begins with the player to the dealer's left.
The cards are dealt one at a time and face down in a clockwise
direction until each player including the dealer has 11 cards.
The remaining cards are then placed face down on the table as
the stock. The top card of the stock is turned face up alongside
to start the discard pile.

Play starts with the player to the dealer's left.
In a normal turn a player first takes the top card of the stock.
He then makes any melds that he can, or adds to those that he
or his partner have already laid out on the table.
Finally he discards by placing one card from his hand face up on
the discard pile.

The initial meld of a partnership after each deal must total at
least a certain number of points – how many depends on their
score so far (see table B, p 413).
Once either partner has made this first meld, both partners can

Wild cards

Melds

Natural   Mixed   Canasta

make new melds of any value and can add to melds that they have already laid out on the table.

A player may add to either his own or his partner's melds.

A canasta is a meld of seven cards.

A natural canasta consists of seven cards of the same rank and has a bonus value of 500 points on top of the card score.

A mixed canasta has natural cards and one to three wild cards, and has a bonus value of 300 points.

Once a canasta is completed, the cards are gathered into a pile.

A natural canasta has a red card placed on top for identification, and a mixed canasta a black card.

Further cards may be added to a canasta. But a mixed canasta may not receive a fourth wild card and a natural canasta loses its value if a wild card is added.

Taking the discard pile In place of taking the top card from the stock, a player may in his turn take the upcard from the discard pile – but only if he has in his hand at least two natural cards of the same denomination.

He must lay the appropriate hand cards face up on the table and meld the upcard with them.

He then also takes all the remainder of the discard pile, and immediately uses as many cards as possible by adding to existing melds or laying out new ones. Any cards that he cannot use become part of his hand.

The player ends his turn by discarding one card to start a new discard pile.

Provided it is not "frozen," a player may also take the discard pile:

a) if he can meld the upcard with one card of the same denomination and one wild card; or

b) if the upcard matches an existing meld of his partnership.

100 points

800 points

Frozen discard pile The discard pile is frozen as follows.

1) It is frozen for a partnership that has not made its initial meld.

2) It is frozen for a player if a black 3 is the upcard. In this case it is no longer frozen after the player has drawn from the stock and discarded.

3) It is frozen for all players if the discard pile contains a red 3 or a wild card. In this case further discards are placed crosswise on top of the freezing card. The discard pile remains frozen until one player unfreezes it by melding the upcard or wild card with two natural cards from his hand.

Red 3s are bonus cards counting 100 points each (**a**). They cannot be melded.

If a player draws a red 3 from the stock, he must lay it face up on the table and draw another card from the stock.

If he is dealt a red 3 he must lay it face up on the table and draw a card from the stock in addition to his regular draw.

If a red 3 is taken as part of the discard pile, it must be laid face up on the table without any extra card being drawn from the stock.

If a partnership holds all four red 3s, these cards count 200 points each, ie 800 points in all (**b**).

All red 3 points count against a partnership if it has not made an initial meld when play ends.

Black 3s may only be melded when a player is going out. They can never be melded with wild cards. Their main use is as "stop cards" to freeze the discard pile.

Going out occurs when a player is able to meld all his cards, providing that when he has gone out his side has made at least one canasta. A player can go out without discarding if he wishes.

Concealed going out occurs when a player melds all his cards when he has not previously melded any cards.

Note that a player must always meld a canasta unless his partner has already melded one.

Permission is usually asked to go out, in the form of "May I go out partner?" A yes or no answer is required and is binding. This procedure is generally used as a warning to a partner to meld as many cards as possible, so that the requesting player can go out in his next turn.

Scoring Each partnership receives the total of all bonus points earned in the hand (see table C), plus the total point value of all melded cards, less the value of any cards remaining in the hands of either player in the partnership at the end of play.

(Note that the low bonuses for going out make the completion of high-scoring melds more significant than being first to go out.)

If one partnership has failed to meld at all, the value of any red 3s it has laid down count against it.

It is possible for a partnership to make a minus score on a hand.

Hands continue until one side has made a total of 5000 points and wins the game.

For each successive hand the deal passes clockwise.

Variant rules The following variations on the standard rules are widely accepted.

1) Even if the discard pile is not frozen, a player may not take the upcard to add it to a completed canasta of his own side.

2) When taking the upcard from the discard pile to make a new meld, a player must always have a natural pair to match it (ie not a matching card and a wild card).

Table A

Card	Points for each card in meld
Joker	50
Deuce (2)	20
Ace	20
8,9,10,j,q,k	10
4,5,6,7	5
Black 3	5
Red 3	see text (p 46)

Table B

Accumulated score of partnership	Value required for initial meld
Any minus score	15
0–1495	50
1500–2995	90
3000 or more	120

Table C

	Bonus points
Natural canasta	500
Mixed canasta	300
Going out	100
Concealed going out	100 extra
Red 3s	see text (p 46)

©DIAGRAM

Casino

Casino can be traced back to the fifteenth-century gambling games of France. In the United States, its era of greatest popularity was eclipsed by the gin rummy boom of the 1930s. Although appearing comparatively simple, casino is in fact a game of considerable mathematical skill.

CASINO: BASIC GAME

Players The game can be played by two, three, or four players.
A deck of standard playing cards is used.
Face cards have no numerical value; aces count 1; and other cards count their face value.

Objective Each player tries to "capture" certain cards during play and to score the most points.

Deal Players cut for the deal and the lowest card deals. If there are two players, two cards are dealt face down to the nondealer, then two cards face up to the center of the table, then two cards to the dealer. This procedure is repeated, so that each player has four cards and there are four face-up cards in the center of the table.

If there are three or four players, the dealer deals two cards to each player including himself, two face-up cards to the center of the table, two more cards to each of the players, and then two more cards to the center.

Each time the players have played the cards in their hands, they are dealt a further four cards in packets of two – no more cards are dealt to the center.

Players take it in turns to deal the whole deck.

Play Beginning with the player to the left of the dealer, players take it in turns to play one card. Each player may "capture," "build," or "trail" with each card.

Capturing Cards are captured in the following ways.

a) Pairs: if a face-up card has the same numerical value as a player's card, the player may capture the face-up card. He does this by placing his card face down on the face-up card, and then moving the pair toward him. For example, a 7 of spades may capture a 7 of diamonds.

If two or more face-up cards match a single card in the player's hand, he may capture them all at the same time.

b) Groups: if the combined value of two or more face-up cards is equal to the numerical value of a player's card, the player may capture all the face-up cards involved. He puts the face-up cards in a pile in front of him and places his own card face down on top of them. For example, a 9 could capture a 2,3, and 4 from the centre.

If one of a player's cards has the same numerical value as both a single face-up card and a group of face-up cards, he may capture all the cards involved at the same time.

For example, a 9 of spades could capture both a 9 of diamonds and a group of cards (eg a 2,3, and 4) totalling 9.

c) Court cards: if a player holds a face card, he may either capture one matching face-up face card, or alternatively three matching face-up face cards if he holds the fourth.

This means that if, for example, he holds a queen and there are two face-up queens, he can only capture one of them in a turn (but had there been three face-up queens, he could have captured all of them in a turn).

© DIAGRAM

Building may be in either one of two ways: single or multiple.
Single build A player may build a card face up onto a central
face-up card provided:

a) the combined numerical value of the cards does not exceed
ten; and

b) he holds another card that is of equal value to the build he is
making, so that in his next turn he would be able to take that
build.

For example, if a player holds a 4 and a 7, he may build the 4
onto a face-up 3 (ie 4+3=7) and say "Building 7."

A build may be increased by either player with a card from his
hand, provided that the total of all the cards in the build still
does not exceed ten, and that he holds a card equal in value to
the build he is making.

For example, if the opponent holds an ace and an 8, he may
build the ace onto an existing build of 7, saying "Building 8."

Multiple build A single build can be changed to a multiple build
by duplicating the single-build value with other cards.

For example, a player may add an ace from his hand to a build
of 7 in order to make a build of 8 (ie 3+4+1=8), and add to
that build another build of 8 (eg 2+6) and say "Building 8s."

Once a multiple build has been established, its stated value
cannot be altered.

A multiple build is captured by a card equal in value to its stated
value (8 in the example above).

Next turn If a player makes or adds to a build, unless his
opponent plays to the build immediately, he must in his next
turn either:

a) capture it himself (placing the captured build face down in
front of him):

b) make a new build; or

c) add to a build.

Trailing If in his turn a player cannot build or capture, he
simply places one card from his hand face up on the table.

End of a round When all the cards have been dealt out, the last
player to capture cards takes all the remaining face-up cards for
scoring.

Scoring Points are scored for capturing cards as follows:
one point for the 2 of spades ("little casino");
two points for the 10 of diamonds ("big casino");
one point for each ace;
one point for seven or more spades;
three points for 27 or more cards.

In addition, one point is scored for capturing all the center
face-up cards in any single turn during the course of play; this
is known as "making a sweep."

Game Players may either: count each deal as a separate game
(the player with most points being the winner), or end the
game as soon as one player (the winner) has made a set
number of points (usually 21).

ROYAL CASINO

This differs from casino in that the court cards are given numerical values and can be included in builds and captured in tricks like other cards.

A jack counts 11, a queen 12, and a king 13. Aces may count either one or 14 as the player chooses.

DRAW CASINO

In draw casino only the first 12 cards are dealt. Thereafter, each player draws a card from the stock every time he plays a card. Otherwise, play is the same as in casino.

SPADE CASINO

Spade casino is played like the basic game, but has additional scoring as follows:

jack of spades, two points;

2 of spades, two points;

other spades, one point each.

Game is 61 points.

Single build

Multiple build

Cribbage

Cribbage is reputed to have been invented by Sir John Suckling, an English poet and courtier who lived in the early 1600s. Six-card cribbage for two players is the most popular form of the game today, but there are also five- and seven-card forms as well as adaptations for three and four players.

Cards All forms of cribbage are played with one single standard deck of 52 cards.

Card values Face cards count 10 each, and all other cards count their face value.

Cribbage board The score can be kept with pencil and paper, but it is easier to use a special cribbage board.

Most cribbage boards are made of wood and measure about 10in by 3in.

There are four rows of 30 holes, two rows for each player, and additional game holes at one or both ends of the board.

Each player has two pegs, usually red or black for one player and white for the other.

When there are four game holes, the players usually put their pegs in them for the start of play.

A player marks his score by moving his pegs first along his outer row and then back along his inner row of holes.

Moving pegs Both pegs are used to score in the following way:

a) a player marks his first score by moving one peg that number of holes from the start;

b) his second score is marked by placing his second peg that number of holes beyond his first peg;

c) his third score is marked by placing his first peg that number of holes beyond his second peg;

d) scoring continues in this way until a player's forward peg has passed all the scoring holes to end in one of the game holes.

Moving pegs

a
b
c
d

Cribbage board

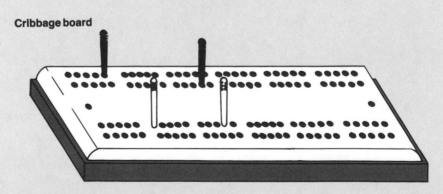

SIX-CARD CRIBBAGE

Players The basic game is for two players.

Objective The game is won by the first player to score 121 points, ie to go "twice around the board."

The deal Players cut for deal. The player with the lower cut (with ace low) deals first, and then the deal alternates between players.

The deal is six cards, one at a time, to each player. The remaining cards are placed face down to one side.

The crib is an extra hand scored by the dealer. It is formed by each of the players discarding two cards and placing them, face down, to the dealer's right. Each player is thus left with a hand of four cards.

The cut After the discards the non-dealer cuts the deck, and the dealer turns up the top card of the remaining stack.

This card is placed face up on the stack for the rest of the game. It is known as the "start" or "starter."

If the start is a jack, the dealer scores "two for his heels."

Scoring Points are scored both during the playing of a hand and when the hands are shown after play.

Combinations of cards score as follows:

a) A pair, two cards of the same rank, scores two points.

b) A pair royal, three cards of the same rank, scores six points (two points for each of the possible pairs to be made).

c) A double pair royal, four cards of the same rank, scores 12 points.

d) A sequence or run is a series of cards in face order (ace low) and scores one point for each card. The cards do not have to be of the same suit.

e) A flush is four or five cards of the same suit and scores one point for each card. If a flush is also a run, points are scored for both features.

f) Fifteen is any combination of cards with a face value totalling that number. It scores two points.

a

2 points

b

6 points

c

12 points

d

4 points

e

4 points

f

2 points

©DIAGRAM

Play begins with the nondealer. He places a card face upward in front of him and calls out its face value as he does so. Face cards are called as 10.

The dealer then places one of his cards face upward in front of himself and calls out its value.

Whenever a pair, pair royal, double pair royal, sequence, or fifteen (but not a flush) is formed during play, the player putting down the card that forms it scores the appropriate points.

If the non-dealer lays down a 5 and the dealer follows it with another 5, the dealer would say "ten for a pair" and score two points. If a third 5 is played, the non-dealer would say "fifteen for eight," the eight points being made up of a fifteen and a pair royal.

A sequence of cards scores regardless of the order in which it is played. Thus if cards are played in the order ace, 2, 5, 4, 3, the player putting out the 3 can count a run of five cards. Should the second player be able to add a 6 he can score a run of six cards, and so on.

When the count during play reaches 31, the cards are turned face down and the player whose card brought the total to 31 scores two points.

If a player at his turn is unable to play a card that is within the limit of 31, he says "Go." His opponent then plays any of his cards that are low enough to be within the limit. If they make 31 he scores two points; if less than 31 he scores one point and also says "Go."

Play then resumes with the remaining cards in hand, and proceeds until all the cards are played or 31 is again reached. Playing the last card of a hand scores "one for last."

The show After all the cards have been played, each player picks up his own cards from in front of him.

The non-dealer shows and scores his hand first, which gives him an advantage if he is very near reaching 121. The start is taken into the reckoning as part of each hand.

A card may be ranked for scoring in any number of different combinations. Thus two 10s and two 5s would give a score of eight points for fifteens plus four points for pairs – giving a total of 12 points. The combination 4,4,5,6,6 scores eight points for fifteens, four points for pairs, and 12 points for sequences – giving a total of 24 points (see illustration).

If a player holds a jack of the same suit as the start, he scores "one for his nob."

A flush of four cards in hand scores four points. If the start is of the same suit the player scores five points, but a flush of four cards including the start scores nothing.

After the non-dealer has declared his score, the dealer shows and scores his own hand. After which, he shows and also scores for the crib.

The crib is scored in the same way as the hands, except that the only flush allowed is a five-card one.

Muggins If a player overlooks a score, whether in his hand or in play, his opponent may call "Muggins" and claim the score for himself. (This rule may be dropped.)

Lurch If a player reaches 121 before his opponent is halfway around the board, he scores a lurch and counts two games instead of one.

Errors If an error in dealing is noticed during the deal, there should be a redeal.

If an error in dealing is found after play has started, the non-dealer scores two points and the error is rectified either by a redeal or by drawing additional cards from the stack.

If after "Go" is called a player fails to play his additional cards, he may not subsequently play those cards and his opponent scores two points. Errors in counting during play are not penalized.

4 points
for pairs

FIVE-CARD CRIBBAGE

This is an earlier form of the game than six-card cribbage. Except as specified, the rules are as for the six-card game.

Objective Game is 61 points.

The deal is five cards to each player.

The crib consists of two cards from each player.

Play Non-dealer pegs three points before play begins, to compensate for not having the crib.

Hands are not played out after 31 is reached or "Go" is called. Hands are shown and scored; then there is a new deal.

SEVEN-CARD CRIBBAGE

This version is played in the same way as six-card cribbage, except that:

a) game is 181 points;

b) the deal is seven cards each (of which two go to the crib).

THREE-HANDED CRIBBAGE

The game is adapted as follows for three-handed play.

Game is 61 points.

The deal is five cards to each player and one to the crib. Each player then gives one card to the crib.

Play begins with the player to the left of the dealer, and passes to the left. The player who leads also has the first show.

FOUR-HANDED CRIBBAGE

This is a partnership form of the game. Partners sit opposite each other, and play begins with the player to the dealer's left.

Game is 121 points.

The deal is usually five cards to each player (of which one goes to the crib).

12 points
for sequences

©DIAGRAM

Ecarté

Ecarté is a card game for two players that first became popular in France in the early 1800s. Its name is the French word for "discarded."

Deck A 32-card deck is used: a standard 52-card deck with the 6s,5s,4s,3s, and 2s removed.

Cards rank: k (high), q,j,a,10,9,8,7.

Rank

Objective Each player tries to take tricks and to score points.

Deal Players cut for deal, highest card dealing first (the cards rank as in play). The dealer gives each player five face-down cards, in packets of either two then three, or three then two. Whichever system is used must be kept throughout the game. The deal passes clockwise around the table.

Trumps The eleventh card is placed face up beside the stock and indicates trumps.

Exchanging cards The non-dealer may propose an exchange of cards. To do this he says "Cards."

If the dealer accepts, the non-dealer exchanges as many cards as he wishes for cards drawn from the stock. The dealer may then do likewise.

The non-dealer may repeat the proposal, and players go on exchanging cards until the stock is exhausted.

But if the dealer refuses at any time by saying "Play," there is no more exchanging.

If the non-dealer does not wish to exchange at any time, he says "I play."

The dealer cannot propose an exchange.

Play The non-dealer leads first. Players must follow suit if they can, and may trump if they cannot.

A player must always take a trick if he can. The winner of a trick leads to the next trick.

Deal

Player 1   Player 2

Trumps    Stock

Scoring is as follows:
a) "point" or "the trick" (three tricks won), scores one point;
b) "the vole" (all five tricks won), scores two points;
c) king turned up to indicate trumps, scores one point for the dealer; and
d) king of trumps held in the hand, scores one point if it is declared before the holder plays his first card.
Game is five points.

Penalties If a player has refused to exchange and fails to make at least three tricks (point), his opponent scores an extra point if he makes point.
There is no penalty if the opponent scores vole.

©DIAGRAM

Euchre

Euchre is a derivative of écarté and dates back at least to the 1800s. For a time it was the national game of the United States. It is a game for two to six players depending on the version played; perhaps most popular is four-handed euchre.

Rank in plain suits

FOUR-HANDED EUCHRE

Four people play in partnerships of two. Each player sits opposite his partner.

Deck A 32-card deck is used: a standard deck with the 6s,5s,4s,3s, and 2s removed. Ace ranks high, and 7 low.

Trumps The jack of trumps, called the "right bower," ranks as the highest trump. The other jack of the same color, called the "left bower," ranks second. For example, if diamonds are trumps, the jack of hearts is the left bower.

Thus the trump suit ranks: rb (high), lb,a,k,q,10,9,8,7 (low).

Objective Each partnership tries to win the most tricks.

Deal Players draw for first deal, lowest card dealing.

Each player is dealt five face-down cards, in packets of three and two. The dealer then turns the next card face up to indicate trumps. The deal passes clockwise around the table.

Nominating trumps Each player, beginning with the player to the dealer's left, has the option of accepting the suit of the face-up card as trumps, or refusing it in the hope of nominating a different suit.

To accept, the dealer's opponents say "I order it up"; the dealer's partner says "I assist"; and the dealer says nothing but indicates his acceptance by discarding one card, and adding the face-up card to his hand.

To refuse, the non-dealers say "I pass," and the dealer puts the face-up card under the stock.

Once one player has accepted, play begins.

If all four players refuse, there is a second round in which each player in turn has the right to nominate the trump suit or pass. Once a player has nominated a suit, play begins.

If all players pass, the hands are thrown in and the cards are dealt by the next dealer.

Play The player who nominated trumps is called the "maker." Before play begins, he may decide to play the hand without his partner, in which case he says "I play alone."

His partner then lays his hand face down on the table. Although he does not play the hand, he shares in any stakes.

Rules of play are the same as in whist

Scoring If the maker and his partner win all five tricks, this constitutes a "march," and scores two points. If the maker is playing alone, he scores four points for a march.

If the maker and his partner win four or three tricks, they score one point; if they win fewer than three tricks they are said to be "euchred," and their opponents score two points.

Players may use counters to keep the score, but it is customary to use a 3 and a 4 from the unused cards as markers, one card being face up, the other face down, as illustrated:

a) the 3 exposed with the other card across it signifies one point;
b) the 4 exposed with the other card across it is two points;
c) the 3 on top of the other card is three points;
d) the 4 on top is four points.

Game is generally five points, but some players prefer to set a target of seven or ten.

RAILROAD EUCHRE
In this variation of four-handed euchre, the joker is used as an additional trump, ranking above right bower.

TWO-HANDED EUCHRE
The deck is reduced to 24 cards by discarding the 8s and 7s. Rules are the same as for four-handed euchre, except that there is no need for a declaration to play alone.

THREE-HANDED EUCHRE
In three-handed euchre (also called cutthroat euchre) the maker plays on his own, with the other two players in partnership against him. The maker scores three points for march; otherwise scoring is as in the four-handed game.

CALL-ACE EUCHRE
This is a version for four, five, or six players, each playing for himself. The rules are as for four-handed euchre, with the following differences.

Calling The maker has the right to decide whether to play on his own or with a partner. To choose a partner he says "I call on the ace of . . ." and nominates a suit. If a player holds the ace named, he plays as the maker's partner, but does not declare his partnership until he plays the ace. As the ace may in fact not have been dealt, the maker may find he is playing alone!

Scoring A lone maker wins points as follows:
a) march, as many points as there are players;
b) four or three tricks, one point.
A partnership wins points as follows:
a) march, two points for each player if there are three or four players, and three points for each player if there are five or six;
b) four or three tricks, each partner scores one point.
If the maker, with or without partner, is euchred, the other players score two points each.

Keeping the score

1 point

2 points

3 points

4 points

Rank in trumps

©DIAGRAM

Five hundred

Five hundred is related to euchre and also has certain similarities to bridge and whist. The basic game is for three players.

THREE-HANDED FIVE HUNDRED

Deck 33 cards are used: a standard deck excluding the 6s,5s,4s,3s, and 2s; plus a joker. Ace ranks high, and 7 low. In the trump suit cards rank, in descending order, as follows: joker, right bower (jack of the trump suit), left bower (other jack of the same color), a,k,q,10,9,8,7.

Rank in plain suits

In no-trump hands, there are no right and left bowers. The holder of the joker may then nominate it to represent any suit he pleases; the joker automatically ranks as the highest card of that suit and takes any trick to which it is led or played.

Objective Each player aims to make a contract by bidding and to win enough tricks to fulfill it.

Deal Players cut for deal (king ranks high, ace low, and joker lowest): lowest card deals.

Ten face-down cards are dealt to each player, in packets of either three, two, three, two; or three, three, three, one. The remaining packet of three cards constitutes the "widow," and is placed face upward on the table.

The deal passes clockwise around the table.

Scoring table for five hundred					
Tricks bid	♠	♣	♦	♥	*No trumps*
6	40	60	80	100	120
7	140	160	180	200	220
8	240	260	280	300	320
9	340	360	380	400	420
10	440	460	480	500	520

Bidding Each player in turn makes a bid, starting with the player to the dealer's left. Each player specifies the number of tricks he intends to take and his choice of trumps.

The lowest number of tricks that can be bid is six, and the highest ten. For bidding the calls are ranked: no-trumps (highest), hearts, diamonds, clubs, spades (lowest).

Any player who passes cannot make a further bid in that round of play.

Widow The player who wins the contract adds the three widow cards to his hand and discards face down any three cards of his choice.

Play Rules of play are the same as in whist.

If a player leads the joker in a no-trump hand, he cannot nominate it to a suit in which he has either declared himself void or that he has failed to follow when able.

The winner of a trick leads to the next trick.

Scoring The players opposing the contract play as partners, but each always scores ten points for each trick he makes.

The bidder scores points according to the table, provided he has made his contract.

If he fails to score sufficient tricks, he loses the value of the contract.

Bonuses There are no bonuses for overtricks (ie tricks over the number bid).

However, a player who has made a contract of less than eight clubs but has scored "grand slam" (all ten tricks), receives a total of 250 points.

(There is an optional system for when grand slam is scored after a bid of eight clubs or better. In this system, the successful player scores a bonus equal to the contract.

For example, a bid of eight diamonds that results in a grand slam is worth 280 points plus a bonus of 280.)

Players losing contracts may well find their scores going into minus figures.

Game is 500 points. If two players reach this total in the same deal, the player who reached 500 first wins.

TWO-HANDED FIVE HUNDRED

This is played in the same way as the three-handed game, except that a third hand, known as a "dead-hand," is dealt. It remains face down throughout the game, and adds a degree of uncertainty to the bidding and play.

FOUR-HANDED FIVE HUNDRED

This game is also played like the three-handed game, but facing players act as partners. The deck is increased to 43 cards by adding the 6s, 5s, and two 4s – one of each color.

Rank in trumps

©DIAGRAM

Forty-five

This game is related to loo and spoil five. Cards have the same unusual ranking as in spoil five, but in forty-five there is a different scoring system and no pool. It is a game for two, four, or six players, divided into two equal and opposing sides.

Cards A standard deck of playing cards is used. The cards are ranked, in descending order, as follows.

Spades and clubs
Plain suits (ie non-trump): k,q,j,a,2,3,4,5,6,7,8,9,10.
Trump suits: 5,j,a of hearts, a of spades or clubs, k,q,2,3,4,6, 7,8,9,10.

Hearts
Plain suit: k,q,j,10,9,8,7,6,5,4,3,2.
Trump suit: 5,j,a,k,q,10,9,8,7,6,4,3,2.

Diamonds
Plain suit: k,q,j,10,9,8,7,6,5,4,3,2,a.
Trump suit: 5,j,a of hearts, a of diamonds, k,q,10,9,8,7,6,4,3,2.

Objective Players try to win tricks and to prevent their opponents from doing so.

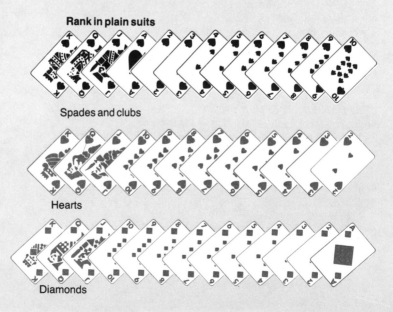

Rank in plain suits

Spades and clubs

Hearts

Diamonds

Deal Players draw for deal, using standard ranking with ace high and 2 low. The player drawing the lowest card deals. Five face-down cards are dealt to each player in packets of two then three, or vice versa. The next card is turned face up to indicate trumps. The deal passes clockwise around the table.

Exchanging If the face-up card denoting the trump is an ace, the dealer may, before the first card is led, exchange this face-up card for any card in his hand.

Any player who has been dealt the ace of trumps has the option of exchanging any card in his hand for the face-up card. If he does not exchange a card, he must announce that he has the ace at his first turn of play. Failure to announce that he has the ace of trumps means that this card becomes the lowest trump for the round.

Play Rules of play are as in whist, except as follows.

If a card of a plain suit is led, a player may choose either to trump or to follow suit; he may discard another plain suit card only if he can neither follow suit nor trump.

If a card of the trump suit is led, a player must usually follow suit; he is not, however, obliged to play any of the top three trumps if the leading card was a lower trump.

Scoring Points are scored by the winning player or partnership. According to one scoring system, 5 points are scored for making three or four tricks and 10 points for making five tricks. An alternative scoring system gives 5 points for three tricks, 15 points for four tricks, and 25 points for five tricks.

Whichever scoring system is used, the game is won by the first side to score 45 points – a fact that gives the game its name.

Rank in trumps

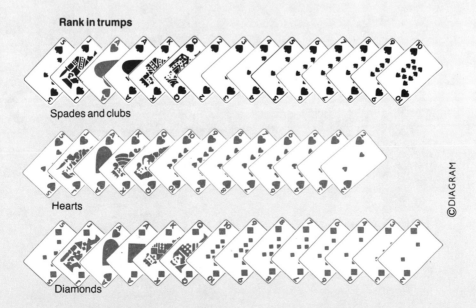

Spades and clubs

Hearts

Diamonds

©DIAGRAM

AUCTION FORTY-FIVE

Auction forty-five is very popular in parts of Canada. Its basic rules are the same as for spoil five, with the following variations.

Players Four or six people play in partnerships of two or three respectively. Each player sits between two players of the opposing side.

Bidding The player to the left of the dealer bids first, followed by each player in turn to his left.

The bids, indicating the number of points each side is contracted to make, are 5,10,15,20,25, and 30. Each bid must outbid the previous bid.

The dealer has the option of "holding," ie outbidding, the previous bid without increasing it. Each of the other players

who bid may then bid again; but the dealer has the option of holding a second time.

Trumps are nominated by the highest bidder.

Discards Each player may exchange as many cards as he likes for cards drawn from the top of the stock.

Play The player to the left of the highest bidder leads first.

Scoring Each trick counts five points, and the highest trump in play scores five extra points for whichever side takes it.

If a side fulfills its contract it scores the number of points bid plus the points scored with its tricks.

If it fails, it loses the number of points bid.

The side that did not make the contract scores all the points it makes in play.

Game is 120 points.

©DIAGRAM

Grand

Grand is a combination of whist, euchre, and hearts. Each hand is played like one of these three games or according to rules for a fourth – "grand" – option, depending on the choice of the bidder.

Players Four people play, in partnerships of two.

Deck A standard deck of playing cards is used. The rank of the cards depends on the type of game being played.

Objective Each partnership aims to make and fulfill a contract.

Deal Players cut for the deal (ace ranks low), and highest card deals. Cards are dealt in a clockwise direction, one at a time and face down, until each player has 13 cards.

Bidding Each player in turn, starting with the player to the left of the dealer, has one chance to either bid or pass.

The bids are five and multiples of five, and indicate the number of points the bidder expects to score in that hand if he is the highest bidder.

At the end of bidding the highest bidder names which game (whist, grand, euchre, or hearts) will be played for that round. If the first three players pass, the dealer must make a bid.

General play Unlike whist, euchre, and hearts, the bidder always leads to the first trick.

Whist

If whist is chosen, the bidder names the trump suit. Play is the same as in whist.

Scoring Each trick more than six counts five points. For example, on a bid of 25 the bidding partnership needs to take 11 tricks to score.

If the bidding partnership makes a grand slam (winning all 13 tricks), it scores for all 13 tricks, making 65 points.

No points are scored for honours.

Setbacks If the bidding partnership fails to make its bid, the entire amount of its bid is deducted from its previous score. In addition, the opposing partnership wins five points for each trick that it takes above six tricks.

Grand

If grand is chosen, play is the same as in whist, except that there are no trumps.

Scoring Each trick more than six scores nine points.

A grand slam also scores 40 points for the first six tricks, making a total of 103 points. If either partnership makes a grand slam, it wins the game – regardless of its score.

Setbacks are scored in the same way as in the whist option, except that each trick counts nine points.

The opponents also win nine points for each trick they take over six tricks.

Euchre

Euchre can only be chosen on a bid of 25 or less. The bidder
names the trump suit. Each player then discards eight cards
face down – he may not keep any trumps lower than 8.

Play is the same as in euchre with the following differences.
If the bidder calls less than 20 he cannot play alone. If he bid 20,
he may choose whether or not to play alone. If he bid 25, he
must play alone.

If playing alone, the bidder may exchange any one of his cards
for the best card in his partner's hand. The bidder's partner puts
his cards face down on the table.

Scoring Points are scored by either partnership as follows:
three tricks, 5 points;
four tricks, 10 points;
five tricks if made in partnership, 20 points;
five tricks if made by lone hand, 25 points.

Setbacks If the bidding partnership fails to make its bid, the
amount bid plus 20 points is subtracted from its score. If a lone
hand fails to make his bid, he loses twice the amount bid.

Hearts

Hearts is only allowed on a bid of 50 or less. Play is as in hearts.
Scoring If the bidding partnership does not take any tricks
containing hearts, it wins 50 points.
Setbacks If the partners do take tricks containing hearts, the
amount bid plus one point for each heart taken is subtracted

from their score. The opponents are set back one point for each heart they take.

Heart bid option If the first bidder passes when the dealer's partnership has a score of less than 70, it is generally regarded as an indication that he is prepared to play hearts.

If the dealer's side has 70 or more points, the first bidder may determine that hearts are played by leading a heart and saying "Hearts."

Game is 100 points, but the game may finish at the end of a time limit or after a set number of rounds. The scores at the end of play are used to calculate the final result.

1) The difference between 100 and the lowest score at the end of play stands as a separate score for the side with the highest score at the end of play.

2) The difference between the number of times each side has been set back is multiplied by ten. This stands as a separate score for the side with the fewer setbacks.

3) The result of this final scoring indicates the winner.

For example, if at the end of play side A has a score of 80 with seven setbacks and side B has a score of 60 with five setbacks, then the final result is calculated as follows:

1) $100-60=40$ (awarded to side A):

2) $(7-5)\times10=20$ (awarded to side B):

3) so side A wins with a total of 40 against side B's total of 20.

Hearts

Hearts is one of the avoidance games – meaning that it is based on the principle of not taking penalty cards rather than of winning tricks. It evolved in the nineteenth century, since when many interesting variants have appeared.

HEARTS: BASIC GAME

Penalty cards

Players Three to seven people can play. There are no partnerships.

Cards A standard deck of 52 playing cards is used.

2s are discarded as follows:

one 2 with three players;

none with four players;

two with five players;

three with seven players;

If possible, the 2 of hearts is not discarded.

The cards rank normally, with ace high. There are no trumps.

Choice of first dealer is by low cut

Deal The dealer deals out all the cards one at a time and face down, beginning with the player to his left and going clockwise.

Play The player to the dealer's left leads to the first trick. Thereafter the winner of one trick leads to the next.

Each player after the lead must follow suit if he can. If he cannot, he may play any card he likes.

A hand ends when all the hearts suit has appeared in play.

Revoking If a player fails to follow suit when he is able to, he may correct his mistake without penalty if he does so before the trick is picked up.

Otherwise he scores 13 penalty points and the hand ends. No other players can score penalty points on that hand.

Scoring Each player scores one penalty point for each card of the hearts suit contained in tricks taken by him.

Continuing play After each hand, the deal passes one player to the left.

The winner is the player with the fewest penalty points after an agreed number of hands.

Alternatively, the winner is the player with the fewest penalty points when one player reaches a set number of points (eg 50 points).

SPOT HEARTS

Also called chip hearts, this game is played in the same way as basic hearts except that each heart card counts as many penalty points as its face value. The king counts 13, the queen 12, and the jack 11.

(Almost any hearts variant can be scored in this way.)

BLACK LADY HEARTS

In this popular version the queen of spades is an extra penalty card, scoring 13 penalty points. Each heart card counts one penalty point.

Sometimes it is ruled that a player must take the first possible opportunity to discard the queen of spades.

13 points

GREEK HEARTS

In this variant the penalties are the same as for black lady hearts, but play and scoring differ in the following ways.

Exchanging Before play begins, each player, after looking at his cards, passes three cards of his choice face down to the player to his right. No player may look at the cards he is receiving until after he has passed on his own cards.

Scoring Each heart is scored as in spot hearts, and the queen of hearts counts 50 penalty points. Except that if one player takes all the penalty cards he does not score at all for this hand and instead all the other players score 150 penalty points each.

50 points ©DIAGRAM

DOMINO HEARTS

The penalty values are as in the basic hearts game, but play varies as follows.

Deal Six cards are dealt to each player, and the remainder are placed face down to form the stock.

Play If a player cannot follow suit he draws cards one at a time from the top of the stock until he can follow suit. Drawn cards of other suits remain in his hand to be played later. When the stock is exhausted players may discard as in the basic hearts game.

Each player drops out when he has played all his cards. The last player left in scores one penalty point for each heart card left in his hand as well as for those in his tricks.

If a player wins a trick with his last card, the lead passes to the next player to the left.

The winner is the player with the lowest score when one player reaches 31 points.

JOKER HEARTS

In this hearts game, the 2 of hearts is discarded and a joker used.

5 points

The joker ranks between the 10 and jack of hearts, and wins any trick in which it is played, regardless of the suit led, unless a higher heart also appears in that trick – in which case the higher heart takes the trick.

A high heart played when the joker is not played is a discard as usual, unless hearts were led.

The joker counts five penalty points.

HEARTSETTE

In this variant of hearts a widow hand is dealt face down in the center of the table.

The 2 of spades is not used if there are three or four players. The size of the widow depends on the number of players:
with three or four players, three cards;
with five players, two cards;
with six players, four cards.

All other cards are dealt out to the players.

Play and penalties are as in the basic hearts game except that the winner of the first trick adds the widow to it and scores penalty points for any penalty cards it contains.

TWO-HANDED HEARTS

This is an adaptation of the basic game for two players.

It is played like basic hearts except that 13 cards are dealt to each player and the remainder are placed face down to form a stock.

After each trick the winner takes the top card from the stock and the loser takes the next card.

The game continues until all the cards have been played.

BLACK MARIA

This very popular version of hearts is also known as Slippery Anne.

Play is as for basic hearts except as follows.

Penalty cards As well as hearts (one point for each card), there are three penalty cards:

the queen of spades (Black Maria), 13 points;

the king of spades, 10 points;

the ace of spades, seven points.

Exchanging occurs before play as in Greek hearts.

Each hand ends when all the penalty cards have been played.

13 points

10 points

7 points

Imperial

Rank

This game resembles piquet, but there is a trump suit and the cards rank differently. It is a game for two players.

Cards A 32-card "piquet" deck is used – a standard deck with the 2s, 3s, 4s, 5s, and 6s removed.
Cards rank k (high), q,j,a,10,9,8,7 (low).
"Honors" are the k,q,j,a, and 7 of trumps.
Chips are used for scoring: 12 white chips and eight red. One red chip is worth six white. At the beginning of the game all chips are placed together in a central pool.
Objective The aim is to be the first to win five red chips.
Shuffle is normal
Cut is by the non-dealer. There need be only two cards in each section. Otherwise the cut is normal
The deal is in packets of three cards, face down. When both players have 12 cards each, the 25th card is placed face up in the centre of the table to denote trumps for the hand. The undealt part of the deck is placed to one side, out of use for the remainder of the hand.
Scoring procedure Scoring occurs before, during, and after each hand of play.
Whenever a player scores, he takes the appropriate chip or chips from the central pool. Whenever a player has collected six white chips, he exchanges them immediately for one red chip from the pool.
Whenever a player gains a red chip in any way, his opponent must put back into the pool any white chips that he holds.
Scoring before play occurs in the following order:
1) the dealer scores one white chip if the turned up (25th) card is an honor card;
2) either player scores one red chip if he has been dealt carte blanche, ie a hand containing no king, queen, or jack;
3) players declare and score for combinations – point, sequences, and melds – held in their hands;
4) players declare and score for sequences and melds that use the turned up card in addition to cards in their hands.
Declarations Combinations are declared in the order: point, sequences, melds. A player may include any card in more than one combination.
To avoid revealing more information than necessary, players use the same formal dialogue used in piquet (see Announcing the declarations, p 464). In imperial, all winning combinations must be declared and shown.

Point This term refers to a player's longest suit (ie the suit of which he holds most cards).

The player with the longest suit scores the point and takes one white chip for each card that he holds in that suit. If players have suits of equal length, the point goes to the player whose relevant cards have the highest face value (counting ace 11, court cards 10 each, and other cards at their numerical face value). If the players still tie, the non-dealer scores.

Sequences These are consecutive cards belonging to the same suit. They may be of three or four cards but may contain only kings, queens, jacks, and aces. A four-card sequence beats a three-card sequence. Three card sequences rank according to the top card. The player with the best sequence scores one red chip. If the players tie, the non-dealer scores.

Melds These are cards of the same rank. Only fours of kings, queens, jacks, aces, and 7s are counted – ranking in that order, with king high. Threes do not count. The player with the best meld scores one red chip.

Combinations using the turned up card

1) Players declare any sequence that includes the turned up card. The higher ranking sequence wins one red chip.

2) A player declares if he has a meld of four using the turned up card. If so, he wins one red chip.

Honors

Play The non-dealer leads to the first trick; thereafter the winner of each trick leads to the next one.

In every case, the second player to a trick must take it if he can. He must follow suit if possible. If he cannot follow suit he must use a trump if he has one; only if he has no trump may he discard.

Cards are not collected in tricks. Each player puts the cards he has played face up in front of him, and is free to examine them at any time.

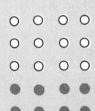

Chips

Scoring during play

1) A player taking the jack of trumps by leading the king or queen wins one red chip.

2) A player taking the ace also wins one red chip.

3) A player takes one white chip for each trump honor contained in tricks that he wins.

Scoring after play If one player takes more tricks in a hand than his opponent, he wins one white chip for every trick in excess of his opponent's total.

Thus if a player wins all 12 tricks – referred to as "capot" – he wins two red chips.

The winner is the first player to win five red chips. Hands continue until one player does this, with the deal alternating between players.

If a player gains five red chips in the middle of a hand, the hand is abandoned at once.

© DIAGRAM

Kalabriasz

This excellent game is also known as klaberjass, clab, and clobber. It is essentially the same as the French game, belote.

Players The basic game is for two players.
Cards Play is with a standard deck of cards from which the 2s,3s,4s,5s, and 6s have been removed.
The cards ranks as follows:
a) in plain suits, a (high), 10,k,q,j,9,8,7 (low).
b) in the trump suit, j (high), 9,a,10,k,q,8,7 (low);
Objective Players aim to meld sequences and to take certain scoring cards in tricks.
Choice of dealer for the first hand is by high cut, with ace low.
First deal The dealer gives each player six cards face down in packets of three. He then places the next card face up in the center of the table, and places the rest of the deck – the stock – face down in a pile beside it.
Determining trumps Players make bids to determine the trump suit.
1) The non-dealer opens with a bid of "Accept," "Schmeiss," or "Pass."
If he bids to accept, the suit of the central face-up card becomes trumps for the hand.
A bid of schmeiss is a proposal for a new deal. The dealer then has the opportunity of agreeing to a new deal or of accepting the suit of the central face-up card as the trump suit.
If the non-dealer says "Pass," the dealer has a turn at bidding.
2) The dealer may now either: accept the suit of the central face-up card as trumps; bid "Schmeiss," in which case the non-dealer must agree to the new deal or accept the suit of the face-up card as trumps; or pass, in which case there is a second round of bidding.
3) If both players pass in the first round of bidding, the non-dealer may then either: nominate any trump suit that he wishes, in which case play will be with this suit as trumps; or pass, in which case the dealer may nominate trumps, or pass.
If both players pass in the second round of bidding, the cards are thrown in and a new first deal made.
The player who actually determines the trump suit is called the "maker."
Second deal Once the trump suit has been established, each player is dealt three more cards, one at a time and face down. The dealer then takes the bottom card of the stock and places it face up on top of the stock.
If the suit of the central face-up card was accepted as trumps, a

player holding the 7 of that suit may exchange it for the central face-up card if he wishes. The 7 of trumps is called the "dix."

Declaring sequences usually takes place before play begins, but may be after the non-dealer has led to the first trick. By their declarations players establish who holds the highest sequence.

Sequences All cards in a sequence must be consecutive and of the same suit. There are two kinds of sequence:

a) a sequence of three cards, worth 20 points; and

b) a sequence of four or more cards, worth 50 points.

For sequences cards rank in the order a (high), k,q,j,10, 9,8,7 (low).

Sequences of equal value are ranked according to their highest card. Note that a sequence of four cards beats a longer sequence provided that the four-card sequence is headed by the highest card.

If sequences are of equal value and are headed by cards of the same rank, a sequence in the trump suit is higher.

If equal sequences headed by cards of the same rank are both in plain suits, some versions of the game rule that the non-dealer's sequence is higher while others rule that the sequences are equal and neither player may score.

Declaration procedure The non-dealer begins by announcing "Sequence of 50" if he has a sequence of four or more cards, or "Sequence of 20" if he has a three-card sequence.

The dealer then replies "Good" if he cannot beat it, "Not good" if he can beat it, or "How high?" if he has a sequence with the same points value.

If the dealer replies "How high?" the non-dealer states the rank of the card that heads his sequence, and then the dealer replies "Good" if he cannot beat it, or "Not good" if he can.

Sequences

20 points

50 points

Rank in plain suits

Rank in trumps

©DIAGRAM

Scoring of sequences Only the player with the highest sequence scores any points at this stage of the game. He scores for his highest sequence after first showing it to his opponent. He also scores for any other sequences that he is prepared to show.

Play Non-dealer leads to the first trick.

Players must follow suit if they are able, and if they cannot follow suit must play a trump if they have one. If a trump is led the opposing player must take the trick if he can.

The winner of a trick places it face down in front of him and leads to the next trick.

Bella is a meld comprising the king and queen of trumps. It is worth 20 points to any player who holds it, and is scored automatically when the second of these cards is played.

Scoring during play Players score points as follows for cards taken in tricks:

a) "jasz" (jack of trumps), 20 points;
b) "menel" (9 of trumps), 14 points;
c) each ace, 11 points;
d) each 10, 10 points;
e) each king, four points;
f) each queen, three points;
g) each jack but jasz, two points.

The player who takes the last trick scores a further 10 points.

The final score for each hand is calculated as follows.

a) If the player who determined the trump suit (the maker) has a points total higher than his opponent, each player scores his own total.

b) If the opposing player has a higher total, he scores both his own points total and that of the maker. This is called "going bate."

c) If the players have an equal number of points, the maker scores no points and his opponent scores his own points total. The maker's opponent is said to have gone "half bate."

Game is usually 500 points. If both players reach the agreed game total in the same hand, the one with most points wins.

Trumps

Scoring during play

a 20 points

b 14 points

c 11 points

d 10 points

e 4 points

f 3 points

g 2 points

THREE-HANDED KALABRIASZ
In the three-handed game turns pass clockwise around the
table. The maker must score more than both his opponents
together, or go bate. Players score their own sequences and
points won in play, but opponents share the maker's points if he
goes bate.

PARTNERSHIP KALABRIASZ
This differs from the basic game as follows.
All but the last card are dealt out so that the dealer has seven
cards and the other players eight each.
The last card becomes the central face-up card. Before play, the
player with the dix exchanges it for the face-up card, and the
dealer takes the dix to complete his hand.
After one player has established the highest sequence, his
partner may also score for any sequences.
Partners keep their tricks together and score as a side.

Knaves

This game combines the principles of trick-taking and of avoidance games. Players score points for taking tricks, but must then subtract points for any tricks containing jacks.

Penalty cards

a

4 points

b

3 points

c

2 points

d

1 point

Players Knaves is a game for three players.
Cards A standard deck of 52 cards is used.
Objective Each player tries to win tricks without taking any jacks.
Deal and play are as for whist (p 492).
Tactics Each player plays for himself, but if one player is winning, the other two often act as a temporary partnership to try to reduce his lead.
Scoring At the end of each hand, each player scores one point for each trick he has taken.
If he has taken any jacks, he then subtracts points as follows:
a) jack of hearts, four points;
b) jack of diamonds, three;
c) jack of clubs, two;
d) jack of spades, one.
A player may have a minus score.
The winner is the first to reach 20 plus points.

POLIGNAC
This game is a French version of knaves. Players must avoid taking tricks containing jacks, especially the jack of spades, which is given the name Polignac.
Players Four to six can play.
Cards For four players a standard deck without the 2s,3s,4s,5s, and 6s is used.
For five or six players the two black 7s are also removed.
Deal and play are as in whist (p 492), except without trumps.
Scoring At the end of each hand, each player scores penalty points for each jack he has taken, as follows:
one point each for the jacks of hearts, diamonds, and clubs; two points for the jack of spades (Polignac).
"General" A player may decide to try and take all the tricks in a hand. This is known as general, and the player must announce his intention before the lead to the first trick.
If he succeeds, all the other players score five penalty points.
If he fails, he scores five penalty points and the jacks score penalty points in the usual way against the players who take them.
The winner is the player with the fewest points after an agreed number of hands.

Loo

Rank

Loo, or lanterloo as it is sometimes called, was once one of the most widely played card games in Europe. It has several variations but is always played for stakes.

THREE-CARD LOO

Players Three or more people can play, but about six is best.
Deck A standard 52-card deck is used. Ace ranks high.
Objective Each player tries to win at least one trick.
Deal Players cut for deal, lowest card dealing.

Each player is dealt three face-down cards, one at a time. An extra hand known as a "miss" is also dealt, as either the first or the last hand of each deal. The top card of the remaining cards is turned face up and denotes trumps.

The deal passes clockwise around the table.

Pool In an optional opening deal called a "single," no miss is dealt, and only the dealer puts three counters into a pool. In subsequent deals, or if no single has been played, a miss is dealt and each player contributes three counters to the pool.

The choice Beginning with the player to the dealer's left, each player in turn chooses one of the following:
a) to play with the cards he holds;
b) to throw in his own cards and play with the miss; or
c) to pass.

To indicate their choice, players say "I play," "I take the miss," or "I pass," as appropriate.

If a player passes, he throws in his cards and takes no further part in that deal. If everyone passes, the dealer takes the pool.

If only one player decides to play but has not taken the miss, the dealer must play him, using the cards in the miss. If the dealer loses, he does not pay, nor is he paid if he wins.

If only one player decides to play and has taken the miss, the dealer may either play him with standard scoring, or just let him take the pool.

Play The first player to choose to play leads to the first trick, with his highest trump if he has one.

Each player who did not pass plays a card to each trick. He must follow suit if he can, and if possible must play a higher card than any already played to that trick.

If a player cannot follow suit, he should trump the trick with a higher trump than any already played to that trick; if he cannot do this, he may discard.

The winner of a trick must lead with a trump if possible.

Scoring The winner of each trick takes one third of the pool.

Looing A player who has not won a trick is said to be "looed." In limited loo, a looed player pays an agreed amount (usually three counters) into the pool.

In unlimited loo, he pays as many counters as there were in the pool at the beginning of the hand.

Penalties A player is also looed for:

a) playing out of turn;

b) looking at the miss without taking it;

c) failing to take a trick when possible; and

d) failing to lead the ace of trumps when holding it.

Variations

a) The trump card is not turned up until a player cannot follow suit.

b) If a player is dealt three trumps, he collects the pool. The hands are thrown in, and the cards are shuffled and dealt for the next round.

FIVE-CARD LOO

This variant is played in the same way as three-card loo, except for the following changes.

Deal Each player receives five cards.

Pool Contributions to the pool are five not three counters.

Miss is never dealt.

Exchanges Each player may exchange up to five cards for the same number of cards drawn from the stock. A player who exchanges must then play his hand.

Pam The jack of clubs, called "pam," ranks as the highest trump regardless of suit. If a player leads the ace of trumps and says "Pam be civil," the pam cannot be played to that trick.

Flushes are five cards of the same suit, or four of the same suit plus pam. The holder of a flush exposes it before play and wins the pool. Each of the other players is then looed unless he also holds a flush or flush with pam.

If there is more than one flush, a trump flush wins over one in a plain suit, and if there is a clash between plain suit flushes, the highest card wins. If two or more plain suit flushes are equal, the pool is divided.

Blaze This is an optional winning hand, entirely made up of face cards. The same rules of precedence apply as with flushes, and a blaze outranks a flush.

IRISH LOO

This is played like three-card loo, with the following changes.

a) Miss is not dealt.

b) Exchanging is carried out in the same way as in the five-card game.

c) "Club law:" if clubs are trumps every player must enter the game.

Michigan

Michigan is a popular and fast-moving game usually played for low stakes. It is easy to learn but can also be a challenging game for the experienced player. Other names by which Michigan is known are boodle, Newmarket, Chicago, and Saratoga.

Players Any number from three to eight can play.
Cards In addition to one standard deck of playing cards, an ace, king, queen, and jack – each in a different suit – from a second deck of cards are used. These four cards are called "boodle" cards and are placed face up in the centre of the table.
Cards rank normally, with ace high.
Chips Each player is given a supply of betting chips or counters.
Objective Each player tries to play certain cards, thereby collecting chips, and to be the first to get rid of all his cards.
Ante Before each hand is dealt, every player must ante by putting one chip on each of the four boodle cards.
Deal Players cut for the deal, highest card dealing.
The dealer gives one face-down card at a time to each player and to an extra hand (widow) to the dealer's left.
Each player must have the same number of cards. Any card or cards left over at the end of the deal are placed face down on the table.

Boodle cards

Auction Before the start of play the dealer has the right to exchange his hand for the widow. If he does so, he discards his hand face down.
If the dealer chooses not to take the widow, the other players may bid for it. The highest bidder pays the dealer in chips, discards his hand face down, and takes the widow.
If no player wants the widow, it is left face down without being seen by any player.
Play begins with the player to the dealer's left. He places his lowest card in any suit face up in front of him.
The player with the next card higher in that suit (ie either the same or another player) plays it face up. This continues with cards played in sequence until either the ace is reached or nobody has the next card in the sequence.
Usually, players announce the rank and suit of cards as they play them.
Each player forms a pile of face-up cards in front of him. Once a card is covered, it cannot be inspected.
Stopped play At the end of a sequence play is said to be "stopped." The last person to have played a card starts a new sequence with his lowest card in any other suit. If he cannot do this, the next player to his left able to lead with another suit does so.

If none of the other players can lead another suit, the first
player may lead with his lowest card in the same suit as the
previous sequence.

Boodle winnings Whenever a player lays down a card that
matches one of the four boodle cards, he wins all the chips on
that card.

If no player claims the chips on a boodle card during a hand, the
chips remain on the card and carry over to the next deal.

Before each hand, each player antes one chip on each boodle
card.

Play ends as soon as one player has got rid of all his cards.
Every other player must then pay him one chip for each card
still in his hand.

Penalty If a player fails to play a card in sequence when able
to do so, he must pay one chip to each of the other players.

If by failing to play a card he prevented another player from
winning boodle chips, he must make up the loss to the
dispossessed player with his own chips. The chips on the boodle
card remain and are carried over to the next deal.

The winner of a game is either:

a) the first person to win an agreed number of chips; or

b) the player with the the most chips at the end of a set number
of deals or on the expiration of a time limit.

Napoleon

Rank

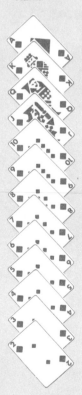

Also called nap, this game is in some ways similar to euchre. Any number of players from two to seven may take part. There are no partnerships.

Deck A standard 52-card deck is used; ace ranks high.

Objective Each player aims to contract a bid and take tricks to fulfil it.

Deal Players cut for deal, highest card dealing first. Each player is dealt five face-down cards, one at a time. The stock is then placed face down on the table.

The deal passes in clockwise rotation.

Bidding Beginning with the player to the dealer's left, each player can either pass or bid two, three, four, or "Napoleon" – indicating the number of tricks he intends to win. (Napoleon signifies five tricks.)

Each bid must be higher than the previous bid, and the player with the highest bid becomes the bidder.

There is only one round of bidding.

Trumps The bidder leads to the first trick, and the suit of his opening card denotes trumps.

Play is the same as in whist

Scoring Napoleon is played for stakes, the usual ones being:

two units for a bid of two;

three units for three;

four units for four; and

ten for Napoleon.

If the bidder wins his contract, each of the other players pays him the stake. If he fails to win his contract, he pays each of the other players the stake. If he fails on a bid of Napoleon, he pays only half the stake.

Optional bids The following optional bids are sometimes used.

a) "Wellington" is a declaration to win all five tricks at double stakes. It cannot be called unless Napoleon has already been called.

b) "Blücher" overcalls Wellington, and is for five tricks at triple stakes.

c) "Misère" or "misery" is a declaration to lose every trick. In the bidding it ranks between three and four, and carries the same stakes as three. There are no trumps in this bid.

PURCHASE NAP

The rules of purchase nap are the same as for Napoleon, except that each player may exchange any number of cards for fresh ones from the stock, on payment of one unit for each card. The payments are put in a kitty, won by the first player to make a bid of Napoleon.

SEVEN-CARD NAP

In seven-card nap, each player receives seven cards. Play is the same as for Napoleon, but bids of Wellington and Blücher are not permitted.

The order of bids with their stakes are as follows:

three bids, a stake of three;

four, stake of four;

nap and misère (optional), stake of 10;

six, stake of 18; and

seven, stake of 24.

Players losing nap, misère, six, or seven pay half stakes.

©DIAGRAM

Oh hell

Rank

Also known as blackout, this game has many features in common with whist. It is a game for three or more players, each playing for himself.

Cards A standard deck of 52 cards is used. Aces rank high.

Objective Each player tries to win the exact number of tricks he has bid.

Deal Each game involves a series of deals. Players cut for the first deal (highest card deals) and thereafter the deal passes in a clockwise direction around the table.

In the first deal, each player is dealt one card; in subsequent deals, the number of cards dealt to each player is increased each time by one card. When the size of the hand can no longer be increased by one card per player, the game is finished.

Thus with four players, the cards will be dealt 13 times, and with five players ten times.

At the end of each deal, the dealer turns the top card of the stock face up to denote trumps. If in the final deal there is no spare card to turn face up, the hand is played without trumps.

Bidding Starting with the dealer, each player in turn bids the number of tricks he expects to win, or "nullo" if he expects to lose every trick.

In the first deal, possible bids are one or nullo; the number of possible bids increases with the size of each hand.

Play is opened by the player to the dealer's left. He leads with any card, and the other players must follow suit; if unable to do so they may trump or discard. The winner of a trick leads to the next.

Scoring Every player who fulfils his bid exactly scores one point for each trick of his bid and a ten point bonus.

There is no standard score for making nullo; sometimes ten points are awarded, sometimes five, or five points plus the number of tricks in the deal. If a player wins more or fewer tricks than the number he bid, he neither scores nor pays a penalty.

Optional scoring A successful bid of small slam – winning all but one of the tricks in the hand – with a hand of more than five cards earns a 25 point bonus. Similarly, a successful bid of grand slam – winning all the tricks in the hand – earns a 50 point bonus.

The winner is the player with the highest cumulative score after all the deals have been played.

Pinochle

This game is derived from bezique and is widely played in North America. Its name is also spelled pinocle and sometimes penuchle.

Players The basic game is for two players.
Cards A 48-card deck is used: made from two standard decks excluding all the 2s,3s,4s,5s,6s,7s, and 8s. Cards rank a (high), 10,k,q,j,9 (low).

Rank

Objective Each player aims to take tricks containing certain cards. and to make melds.
Choice of first dealer is by high cut. Thereafter the deal alternates.
Shuffle and cut are normal (see p 381), except that the nondealer must cut.
Deal The dealer gives 12 cards to each player in packets of three or four.
The thirteenth card is then turned face up on the table, and its suit becomes trumps for that hand.
The rest of the deck, the "stock," is then placed face down on the table, half covering the trump card.
First stage of play This lasts as long as there are any cards in the stock.
The non-dealer leads to the first trick. Thereafter the winner of one trick leads to the next.
In this stage, players may play any card to a trick. This includes playing a trump when holding a card of a plain suit led.
Each trick is won by the highest trump, or, if no trumps appear, by the highest card of the suit led. If two cards of the same denomination and suit appear, the one played first wins.
The winner of a trick places it face down in front of him.
After each trick, the winner may make one meld (see the section on melding). Then, whether or not a meld has been made, the winner draws the top card from the stock and the loser draws the next card.
The winner then leads to the next trick.
Drawing after tricks continues until all the stock and the exposed trump card have been drawn. (It is often ruled that the player who draws the last face-down card must also expose it.)
Melding After each trick in the first stage, the winner of the trick may claim one meld.
A meld is claimed by placing the cards involved face up on the table, and stating the score.
A player can only score for one meld in a turn – even if the cards he exposes for that meld have also given him another scoring combination.

Melds

Class A

150 points

40 points

20 points

Class B

40 points

Trumps

Class C

100 points

80 points

60 points

40 points

Each card melded can also be used later to form another meld of a different class (see the section on melds) or one of a higher score in the same class. However, each new meld formed in this way requires a new turn and the addition of at least one card from the player's hand.

Any card that a player uses in a meld may still be played to a later trick, but once a card has been played to a trick it cannot then be used in further melds.

Melds There are three classes of meld. Points are scored as follows when the melds are put on the table.

Class A:
"sequence" (or "flush") – a,10,k,q,j of trumps – 150 points;
"royal marriage" – k and q of trumps – 40 points;
"marriage" – k and q of any plain suit – 20 points.

Class B:
"pinochle" – q of spades and j of diamonds – 40 points;

Class C:
four aces, 100 points;
four kings, 80 points;
four queens, 60 points;
four jacks, 40 points;
(Note that all "fours" must contain one card of each suit.)

The second stage of play, or "play out," begins with each player taking back into his hand any cards that he has melded.

The players then play for the remaining 12 tricks to use up the cards in their hands. The winner of the last trick in the first stage leads to the first trick in the second.

In this stage a player must follow suit if he can, and may only trump if he cannot.

If a trump is led, the following player must play a higher trump if he can. (Usually it is made a general rule for this stage that a following player must win any trick he can.)

Tricks are won as in the first stage, and the winner of one trick leads to the next. No melds are made in this stage.

The "dix" is the name given to the 9 of trumps.

If the card turned up to decide trumps is a 9, the dealer scores 10 points immediately.

If a player holds a dix during the first stage of play, he can declare it and win 10 points by placing it face up on the table after winning a trick. (Most players rule that a meld can also be made in the same turn.)

If the first dix to appear is one declared by a player, it is not left face up in front of him but is exchanged for the exposed trump card at the bottom of the stock pile. The player takes that trump card into his hand and puts the dix in its place.

Scoring of tricks Points for cards taken in tricks are scored at the end of each hand. Cards are scored as follows:

a) each ace, 11 points;
b) each 10, 10 points;
c) each king, four points;
d) each queen, three points;
e) each jack, two points.

The winner of the last trick in the second stage scores a further 10 points.

Points for tricks are rounded to multiples of 10 (only 7, 8, or 9 being rounded up) before being added to the player's total score.

Game is usually 1000 points. If both players reach 1000 or more after the same hand, play continues until one player reaches 1250. If the same happens again, play continues to 1500, etc.

The "dix"

10 points

Scoring of tricks

a   b   c   d   e

11 points   10 points   4 points   3 points   2 points

AUCTION PINOCHLE

In this version, players bid on how many points they expect to score. Chips are collected by successful players.

Players Three people play. Usually the game is played at tables of four, with the dealer taking no active part.

Cards The deck and rank of cards are as in basic pinochle.

Deal 15 cards are dealt to each player in five packets of three. After each player has been dealt one packet, a widow of three cards is dealt face down.

Bidding Each player in turn, starting with the player to the dealer's left, may make a bid as to the number of points he expects to score.

Bidding must start at an agreed minimum (usually 300) and must rise 10 points at a time.

A player must bid or pass. If he passes, he may not bid again in that hand. Bidding ends when two players have passed. The other player is then the "bidder," and his highest bid is his contract.

The other two players together try to prevent him making his contract.

Melding The bidder takes up the widow cards, shows them to the other players, and then adds them to his hand.

He then names the trump suit and lays down his melds. No other player is allowed to make melds at any time.

Melds and their scores are as in basic pinochle, except that the dix counts as a Class A meld scoring 10 points, and is scored only if the bidder places it on the table with his other melds.

Starting play The bidder begins by discarding three cards face down from those still in his hand. He then picks up his meld cards and leads to the first trick.

He may change his mind about his melds, discards, or trumps at any time before he actually leads to the first trick. But if he discards a meld card that he has scored for, he forfeits the game unless he corrects the mistake before leading to the first trick.

Tricks are won as in basic pinochle. Each player must follow suit if he can; and, if trumps are led, must try to win the trick if he can.

If a player cannot follow suit he must trump rather than discard. This still applies after a trick has been trumped, but he need not trump higher if he does not wish to.

The winner of each trick leads to the next.

Scoring of tricks may be as in basic pinochle. Alternatives are:

a) 10 points for each ace or 10, and 5 points for each king or queen; or

b) 10 points for each ace, 10, or king.

Whatever the points system, the bidder scores for any scoring cards contained in the three cards he discards, and there is a bonus of 10 points to the bidder if he wins the last trick.

Game Each hand is a complete game. If the bidder makes or exceeds his contract, he wins chips from each player. Typical amounts are:
a) 300-340 bid, three chips;
b) 350-390 bid, five chips;
c) 400-440 bid, 10 chips;
d) 450-490 bid, 15 chips;
e) 500-540 bid, 20 chips;
f) 550-590 bid, 25 chips;
g) 600 or more, 30 chips.
These amounts are doubled if spades are trumps.

A **kitty** usually features in auction pinochle. The following are typical rules.

1) Each player must put three chips into the kitty before play begins.

2) If all players pass on a deal, all pay three chips into the kitty.

3) If a bidder makes, or fails on, a contract of 350 or more, he collects from, or pays to, the kitty, as well as each other player. Amounts are the same as for settlements between players.

Piquet

Piquet is a card game for two players that allows great opportunities for skill. It has been known, under various names, since the middle of the fifteenth century. The present French name and terminology were adopted in English during the reign of Charles I of England, as a compliment to his French wife, Henrietta Maria.

Rank

Players The game is for two.

Objective Each player aims to score points, both with certain combinations of cards in his hand and by playing for tricks.

Cards A deck of 32 playing cards is used, commonly called a piquet deck. This is a standard 52-card deck from which all the 2s,3s,4s,5s, and 6s have been removed.

Usually two decks are used alternately, one being shuffled in readiness for the next hand while the other is being dealt into play.

The cards rank normally, from 7 low to ace high.

Choice of first dealer is by low cut (see p 381). The first dealer also has choice of seats.

Shuffle is normal (see p 381).

Cut is by the non-dealer.

There need be only two cards in each section. Otherwise the cut is normal

The deal is in packets of two cards, face down. The dealer gives two cards to his opponents, then two to himself, until each has 12 cards.

The remaining eight cards form the stock, which is placed face down in the center of the table. The stock is divided so that the upper five cards rest at an angle to the lower three.

Discards The dealer has the chance to discard first. Under American rules, he need not discard; under English rules, he must discard at least one card. In either case, the most cards he can discard is five.

If he is discarding, he places the discards face down beside him, and draws an equal number from the stock. (Players must draw cards in the order in which they are stacked in the stock.)

Even if the dealer does not draw, or does not draw all five, he may look at the cards that he could have drawn, and then replace them without showing them to his opponent.

Then the non-dealer discards at least one card and at most as many cards as remain in the stock.

He places his discards face down beside him and draws an equal number of stock cards, beginning with any left by the dealer.

The non-dealer may look at any cards in the stock that remain undrawn. But in this case the dealer may turn these cards face

up for himself to see also. (Sometimes it is ruled that the dealer may do this only after leading to the first trick.)

A player may inspect his own discards during play.

Scoring Points are scored in two ways. Some points are scored by "declaration," which occurs immediately after discarding and before play. Other points are scored during play.

Declarations Each player declares certain combinations of cards held in his hand, and scores points if his declaration ranks higher than his opponent's.

A player does not have to declare a potentially winning combination if he preferes not to – but he cannot then score points for it. This is called "sinking."

A player may include any card in more than one combination.

Scoring combinations

Point The player with the most cards of one suit scores one point for each card he holds in that suit.

If both players have long suits of the same length, the better point is the one with the higher face value. (Face value is calculated by counting the ace as 11, face cards as 10 each, and other cards as their numerical face value.) If the players tie, neither scores.

A player can only score for one point – even if he has more than one suit longer than his opponent's longest.

Sequence

Meld

Sequences The player with the most cards in rank order in one suit scores as follows:

tierce (three cards), three points;

quart (four cards), four points;

quint (five cards), 15 points;

sextet or sixième (six cards), 16 points;

septet or septième (seven cards), 17 points;

octet or huitième (eight cards), 18 points.

The holder of the highest sequence can also score for any other sequences he holds.

If players tie for the longest sequence, the sequence with the higher top card wins. If both sequences have the same top card, neither scores for any sequences.

Meld The player with the highest ranking meld, of three or four cards of a kind, scores as follows:

trio or "three" (three cards of the same denomination), three points;

quatorze or "fourteen" (four cards of the same denomination), 14 points.

But only aces, kings, queens, jacks, or 10s may be declared for melds (and sometimes it is ruled that 10s only count if a quatorze is held).

If both players have sets of equal length, the one with the higher ranking cards wins.

The winner also scores for any other melds he holds.

Announcing the declarations is by a formal dialogue, designed to reveal no more information than necessary.

The non-dealer makes the first declaration in each category of combination, following the order point, sequence, meld.

Declaring a point Non-dealer says: "A point of ———," stating whatever number of cards he holds in his longest suit.

Dealer replies:

"Good," if he concedes the point;

"Not good," if he holds a longer suit – stating its length;

"How many?" if he holds a suit of equal length.

If the reply is "How many?" the non-dealer must then declare the face value of his point. The dealer then replies "Good," "Not good" (stating the face value of his point), or "Equal" (in which case no one scores).

Whoever has won the point then states the length of his point again (adding the face value if that also had to be declared), and announces his score.

Declaring a sequence Non-dealer says: "A sequence of ———" (or "A tierce," etc), stating the number of cards in his longest sequence.

The procedure then follows as in declaring a point – except that when the dealer holds a sequence of equal length his reply is "How high?" The non-dealer then declares the top card of his sequence, and the dealer states "Good," "Not good," or "Equal."

Declaring a meld Non-dealer says "A three (or fourteen) of
——," naming the denomination.
(Alternatively he can use the words "trio" or "quartorze.")
The dealer cannot hold a meld of the same length and
denomination, and so must reply "Good" or "Not good."

A sample declaration
Non-dealer: "A point of five."
Dealer: "Good."
Non-dealer: "A point of five. I score five." Then he names his
best sequence: "A sequence of four" (or "A quart").
Dealer: "How high?"
Non-dealer: "Queen."
Dealer: "Not good. Ace. Also a tierce. I score seven."
Non-dealer (naming his best meld): "Three kings" (or "A trio
of kings").
Dealer: "Not good. Fourteen queens" (or "quatorze of
queens"). I score 14. I start with 21."
Non-dealer (playing the lead to the first trick and automatically
adding one point to his score – see below): "I start with six."

English style declaration
In this, the dealer only names his combinations after the
non-dealer has led to the first trick. For example:
Non-dealer: "A point of five."
Dealer: "Good."
Non-dealer: "A point of five. I score five. A quart."
Dealer: "How high?"
Non-dealer: "Queen."
Dealer: "Not good."
Non-dealer: "A trio of kings."
Dealer: "Not good."
Non-dealer (playing first card): "I start with six."
Dealer: "A quart to the ace. Also a tierce. Seven. And a
quatorze of queens: 14. I start with 21."

Showing combinations Sometimes it is ruled that all winning
combinations must be shown before they score. More usually,
winning combinations are shown only at the opponent's
request. A combination that is shown is replaced in the holder's
hand as soon as the opponent has seen it.

Play The non-dealer leads to the first trick. Each player must
follow suit to a lead if he can. If not he may discard any card.
The winner of a trick leads to the next.

Scoring during play A player scores for tricks; also players may
score additional points in various ways.

Scoring for tricks Each player scores as follows:
a) one point for leading to a trick;
b) one point for taking a trick that his opponent led to;
c) one point for taking the last trick; and
d) 10 points for taking seven or more tricks.
Each time a player scores he announces his total score so far.

Variation Sometimes it is played that:

a) a player scores for leading to a trick only if the card led is higher than a 9;

b) a player scores for winning a trick only if the winning card is higher than a 9.

Additional scoring Points may also be scored in the following ways.

a) Carte blanche is a hand devoid of face cards, and scores 10 points. It must be claimed by a player immediately before he discards after the deal. (Under English rules, it must be claimed before either player discards.)

b) Pique is scored by the non-dealer if he scores 30 points before the dealer scores anything. It scores 30 bonus points.

c) Repique is scored by either player if he scores 30 points on declaration, ie before the lead to the first trick. It is worth 60 bonus points.

d) Capot is scored by either player if he captures all 12 tricks in play. It is worth 40 bonus points, but the 10 standard points for taking a majority of tricks are not scored.

A game is known as a partie. It consists usually of six deals, though some players prefer to have a partie of four deals, with scores for the first and fourth deals counting double.

The turn to deal alternates between the two players.

Scoring the partie

a) The scores for the individual deals are added together to give a total for each player.

The procedure then depends on whether these totals exceed the "rubicon" of 100 points.

b) If both players have 100 or more points, the player with the higher total wins by the difference between the two totals plus 100 points bonus for the partie.

For example, if the dealer has totalled 120 and the non-dealer 108, the dealer wins and scores 112 points (120−108+100).

c) If either or both players have less than 100 points, the player with the lower total is said to be "rubiconed." The player with the higher total wins by the sum of the totals plus 100 points bonus.

For example, if the scores are 125 and 92, the player with 125 wins and scores 317 (125+92+100); if the scores are 98 and 92, the player with 98 wins and scores 290 (98+92+100).

PIQUET AU CENT

This version has different final scoring. Deals continue until one player totals 100 points or more. At the end of that deal, the player with the higher total scores the difference between his own and his opponent's totals – or double that difference if his opponent's total was below 50.

AUCTION PIQUET

This piquet variation puts more emphasis on the play of the hands.

Bidding takes place before the discard. The non-dealer bids or passes first. If both pass, the cards are dealt again by the same player. Once a bid has been made, bidding continues until one player passes.

The minimum bid is seven. A bid may be either "plus" (winning the stated number of tricks) or "minus" (losing that number). Plus and minus bids rank equally: to continue the bidding a player must bid a greater number of tricks.

The final bid is the "contract" as in contract bridge.

Other rules are as for basic piquet, with the following exceptions.

Discards Players need not discard at all.

Declarations may be made in any order.

Sinking is not allowed on minus contracts.

Pique is scored after 29 points in plus contracts and 21 points in minus ones.

Repique is scored after 30 points in plus contracts and 21 points in minus ones.

Scoring for tricks Each player scores one point for each trick that he takes (whoever led to that trick).

Players do not score for leading to a trick or for taking the last trick.

Scoring the contract If the contracted player exceeds his contract, he scores 10 points for every trick won (on plus contracts) or lost (on minus contracts) in excess of his contract. If he fails to make his contract, every trick by which he fell short scores 10 points for his opponent.

Doubling and redoubling are allowed, as in bridge, but affect only the scores for overtricks or undertricks.

Scoring the partie Rubicon is 150 points, and bonus for the partie is also 150 points.

Pope Joan

Pope Joan is a card game for three or more players and was invented by combining two earlier games, commit and matrimony. Contestants try to play their cards in such a way as to win as many counters as possible.

Cards A standard deck of 52 cards is used, but with the 8 of diamonds removed.

The cards are referred to in the usual way, except for the 9 of diamonds which is called Pope Joan. Aces count low.

Counters At the start of a game, each player should have an equal number of counters.

Betting layout A board or other betting layout is required for the game.

Layouts are usually circular or square, and are divided into sections labelled ace, jack, intrigue, queen, matrimony, king, Pope Joan, and game. Some traditional Pope Joan boards comprise a circular tray revolving on a central stand.

A layout can easily be drawn on a sheet of plain paper or material. Each section should be large enough to hold at least 20 counters.

Layout

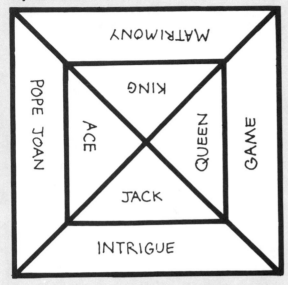

Betting

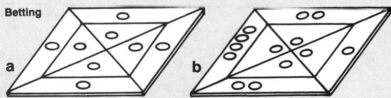

Objective Each player aims to win as many counters as possible by playing certain cards. Counters are also won by the first contestant to use all his cards.

Bet and deal Players decide upon a dealer.

Each player, including the dealer, then places counters in the different sections of the betting layout. This may be done in one of two ways, either:

a) each player, including the dealer, puts out the same agreed number of counters, dividing them equally between the different sections; or

b) each player, including the dealer, puts four counters in the pope section, two in matrimony, two in intrigue, and one in each of the other sections.

The dealer then deals one hand to each player including himself, and one extra hand.

He deals by giving one card to each player in a clockwise direction, beginning with the player to his left. The card for the extra hand is dealt just before he deals to himself.

All cards are dealt face down. The deal continues in this way until all the cards but one have been dealt; this card is placed face upward on top of the extra hand.

©DIAGRAM

The exposed card If the card dealt face upward is Pope Joan (the 9 of diamonds), the dealer wins all the counters in the pope and the game sections. (In an alternative version of play the dealer wins all counters on the layout.)

The round ends and the player to the dealer's left becomes the new dealer.

If any other card is dealt, its suit determines trumps for that hand.

Claiming counters

Trumps

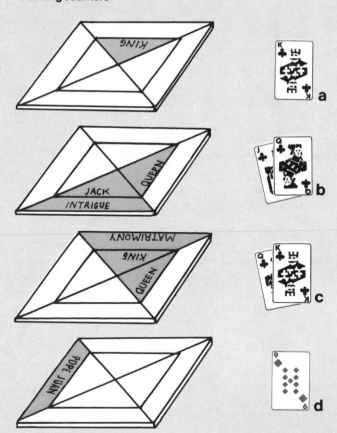

If the card dealt face upward is an ace or a face card, the dealer wins the counters on the section with the same name.

Play Each player examines his own hand, but no player may look at the extra hand.

The player to the dealer's left begins. He plays any one card from his hand face up onto the middle of the playing area and says its name, eg "3 of hearts."

The player with the 4 of hearts then plays it, followed by the player with the 5, the 6, and so on.

This continues until no player can add to the sequence because either:

a) the sequence has been completed by reaching the king;

b) the next card needed is the 8 of diamonds; or

c) the next card needed is hidden in the extra hand or has already been played.

At this point the cards already played in the sequence are turned face down, and whoever played the last card begins a new sequence by playing any card of his choice.

Claiming counters Anyone who plays the ace, jack, queen, or king of trumps receives all the counters in the section marked with the same name (**a**).

If a player plays the jack and queen of trumps in sequence, he wins all the counters in the intrigue section, as well as those on jack and queen (**b**).

If anyone plays the queen and king of trumps in sequence, he receives all the counters in the matrimony section, as well as those on queen and king (**c**).

A player putting out Pope Joan wins all the counters on that section (**d**).

It should be noted that these cards only win counters when played in the correct way, ie by starting or adding to a sequence. They win nothing if they are still unplayed at the end of a round.

Ending the round The round continues until any one player has played all his cards, when he may take all the counters in the game section.

All the other players have to give him one counter for every card still in their hand, with the exception of anyone holding the unplayed Pope Joan, who is exempted from paying for the cards left in his hand.

Unclaimed counters Any counters that are not won in a round remain on the betting layout until won in subsequent rounds. New counters are added as usual to all sections at the beginning of each round.

Any counters left at the end of a game are distributed by redealing the cards, face up, without an extra hand.

The players who receive the ace, jack, and queen of diamonds and the Pope Joan take any remaining counters in those divisions. Any counters in the matrimony section are divided between the holders of the king and queen, and those in the intrigue section between the holders of the queen and jack.

Pope Joan

Preference

This is a fairly straightforward game usually played for small stakes. Three players take part, each playing for himself.

Cards A standard deck with all the 2s,3s,4s,5s, and 6s removed is used.

The cards are ranked: ace (high), k,q,j,10,9,8,7 (low).
The suits, in descending order, rank: hearts (known as

Rank

"preference"), diamonds, clubs, spades.

Objective Each player tries to be the highest bidder and to fulfil the contract.

Preliminaries Before the start of play, each player puts an equal agreed number of chips into the pool.

Players must also decide:

a) how much a successful bidder should receive from the pool, depending on the rank of the trump suit; and

b) the payment to be made into the pool by an unsuccessful bidder.

Deal Any player may deal the first hand; thereafter the deal passes clockwise around the table.

The dealer gives ten face-down cards to each player, and also deals two cards face down in the center of the table as the "widow," making the deal as follows.

He first deals a packet of three cards to each player, then he deals the widow, then another packet of four cards to each player, and finally a packet of three cards to each player.

Bidding Each player in turn, beginning with the player to the dealer's left, either bids a suit or passes.

By bidding a suit, the player indicates that he intends to win at least six tricks of the possible ten, with the named suit as trumps.

Each player is permitted one bid only, and each bid must be in a higher ranking suit than the previous bid.

If all three players pass in the first round of bidding, there is a second round in which each player can either pass or put chips into the pool. The player putting most chips into the pool then wins the right to name the trump suit; he may also discard any two of his cards and take the widow into his hand.

If a player bids in the first round, the widow is not used.

Play The player to the left of the successful bidder leads to the first trick.

Every other player must follow suit if he can; if he cannot he may play a trump or discard any card.

The highest card in the suit led or the highest trump played takes the trick.

The winner of a trick leads to the next trick, and the game

continues until all ten tricks have been taken.

Settlement If the bidder fulfils his bid (takes at least six of the ten tricks) he wins the agreed number of chips from the pool, depending on the rank of the trump suit. If the bidder fails in his contract, he pays the agreed number of chips into the pool.

Rummy

Rummy is one of the most commonly played of all card games, second only to poker in popularity. Formerly known as rum poker, rummy developed in the saloons and gambling houses of late nineteenth-century America. Although its rules are easily learned, it nonetheless offers plenty of scope for skillful play.

Group

RUMMY: BASIC GAME

Cards A standard deck of 52 cards is used.

In play, the cards rank normally with ace low.

For scoring, the jack, queen, and king are each worth 10 points; all other cards are worth their face value.

Players Two to six may play. There are no partnerships.

Objective Each player attempts to be the first to go out through having "melded" all his cards. Cards are melded in either groups or sequences.

A group is three or four cards of the same rank (eg 4 of hearts, 4 of spades, and 4 of clubs).

Sequence

A sequence is three or more cards of the same suit falling in numerical order (eg 9, 10, and jack of diamonds).

Starting the game The player with the lowest cut or draw becomes dealer. The dealer shuffles, and the player to his right cuts the deck. The cards are dealt in a clockwise direction. The number of cards dealt varies according to the number of players:

two players, 10 cards each;

three to four players, seven cards each;

five to six players, six cards each.

After the deal, the remaining cards are turned face down to form the stock. The top card from the stock is turned face up beside it to start the discard pile (this card is called the upcard).

Play Players take their turns in a clockwise direction, beginning with the player to the dealer's left.

The player starts his turn by drawing the top card from either the stock or the discard pile. He may then meld a group or a sequence face up on the table.

He may also "lay off" (add) as many cards as possible to any matched sets already melded on the table, whether the original melds were his own or an opponent's.

He ends his turn by rejecting one card from his hand and placing it face up on the discard pile. If he began his turn by drawing a card from the discard pile, he is not permitted to end the turn by discarding that same card.

If the stock is used up before any player goes out, the discard pile is turned face down (unshuffled) to form a new stock.

Going out A player goes out – and wins the hand – if he succeeds in getting rid of all his cards, with or without a final discard.

Going rummy A player "goes rummy" if he goes out by melding all his cards in one turn without having previously melded or laid off any cards.

Scoring If a player goes out, the numerical value of all the cards then left in his opponents' hands is totaled to give the winner's score for the round. This score is doubled if the player went rummy.

Continuing play The deal passes to the next player to the left if there are more than two players. If there are two players, the winner of one round deals the next.

Game The first player to reach a previously agreed total wins the game.

©DIAGRAM

GIN RUMMY

This is probably the most popular of all rummy variations.
Cards Two standard decks of 52 cards are used. While one player deals, the other shuffles the second deck ready for the next deal.

The cards rank normally, with ace low. They are valued as for basic rummy.

Players Basic gin rummy is for two players. It can be adapted for any larger even number by dividing players into two equal sides, and holding separate but simultaneous games between pairs of players.

Objective As in rummy each player tries to meld his cards in groups or sequences. Unlike basic rummy, however, it is possible for a player to win a hand without melding all his cards.

Choice of first dealer The player cutting the higher card has the choice of seat, deck of cards, and whether he wants first deal.

Shuffle and cut are normal

Deal The dealer deals 10 face-down cards to each player, beginning with his opponent and dealing one card at a time. The twenty-first card is then turned face up and becomes the first card on the discard pile (the upcard).

The remaining cards are placed face down on the table alongside the upcard to form the stock.

Start of play The non-dealer decides whether or not he wants the upcard. If he decides not to take it, the dealer has the option of taking it. If the dealer does not want it, then the non-dealer must draw the top stock card.

Whichever player takes a card must then discard one.

Turn of play In subsequent turns a player takes the top card from either the discard pile or the stock, and then discards. Players do not lay melds on the table until one player ends the hand by "going gin" or "knocking."

Going gin. A player goes gin if he can meld all 10 of his cards in matched sets. He declares this when it is his turn, and lays all his cards face up on the table.

His opponent may then lay down his own melds, but he may not lay off any cards onto the winner's melds.

Knocking is an alternative way of going out. It may be done if the unmatched cards – deadwood – in a player's hand add up to 10 points or less.

A player can knock only when it is his turn. He draws a card in the usual way, knocks on the table, and discards one card face down. He then lays out all his remaining cards face up on the table, grouping them into melds and unmatched cards.

His opponent must then, without drawing, lay out his cards on the table. Cards should be grouped into melds and unmatched cards, but the player also has the opportunity of laying off cards onto the knocker's melds.

Each player's deadwood cards are then totalled, and the totals compared.

Scoring a hand

1) If a player goes gin he gets a 25 point bonus in addition to the value of his opponent's deadwood.

2) If a player knocks and his deadwood count is less than his opponent's, the knocker wins the hand and his score is the difference between the two counts.

3) If a player knocks and his opponent's deadwood count is lower than or the same as his own, the opponent has "undercut" the knocker and wins the hand. For this he scores a 25 point bonus as well as any difference between the deadwood counts.

"No game" The last two cards in the stock may not be drawn. If the player who draws the fiftieth card is unable to go gin or knock, the hand is a tie and no points are scored. The same dealer deals for the next hand.

Box (or line) A running total is kept of each player's score. When a player wins a hand, a horizontal line called a box (or line) is drawn under his score.

Game score The first player to score 100 or more points ends the game and has 100 points added to his score.

If his opponent has failed to win a hand, the winner then doubles his score (including the 100 point bonus).

Finally, for every hand a player has won — as shown by the boxes in his running score – he receives an additional 25 point bonus.

©DIAGRAM

Seven up

Seven up is a card game for two or three players and originated in England in the seventeenth century. Other names by which it is known are all fours, high-low-jack, and old sledge.

SEVEN UP: BASIC GAME

Deck A standard deck of cards is used. Ace ranks high.

Objective Each player tries to score seven points and so win the game.

Deal Players cut for the deal, highest card dealing. Each player is dealt six face-down cards in packets of three.

The next card is turned face up and denotes trumps, and if it is a jack the dealer scores one point.

The deal passes clockwise around the table.

Trumps If the player to the dealer's left is happy to play with the trump suit shown, he says "Stand" and play begins.

Should he prefer to play another trump suit he says "I beg," and the dealer can choose whether or not to change trumps. If the dealer chooses to keep the same trump suit he says "Take one" to the player, who scores one point. Play then starts.

If the dealer agrees to change the trump suit, he sets aside the face-up card, deals a further three cards to each player, and turns the next card face up to denote trumps.

If this card shows a different suit from the first face-up card, play begins with this suit as trumps – and if it is a jack, the dealer scores one point.

Should the face-up card be the same suit again, however, another three cards are dealt to each player and a third card is turned face up.

This procedure is repeated until a new trump suit is determined, and the dealer scores one point for each jack that is turned up, provided it is not of the same suit as the suit initially rejected.

If the deck is exhausted before a new trump suit is turned up, the entire deck is shuffled and redealt.

Discarding If the trump suit has been changed, each player discards face down a sufficient number of cards to reduce his hand to six.

Play is the same as in whist

Scoring At the end of each round the tricks are turned face up for scoring. Points are scored as follows:

"high," one point for the player dealt the highest trump;

"low," one point for the player dealt the lowest trump;

"jack," one point for the player who takes the jack of trumps in a trick;

"game," one point for the player who takes the highest total

value of cards in tricks. The cards arc valued as follows:
four for each ace;
three for each king;
two for each queen;
one for each jack;
ten for each 10.

Game The first player to make seven points wins the game. If more than one player reaches seven points in the same hand, the points are counted in the following order so as to determine the winner: high, low, jack, game.

FOUR-HANDED SEVEN UP

In this version four people play in partnerships of two. Each player sits opposite his partner.

Play is the same as in the basic game, except that the two players to the right of the dealer do not look at their cards until after trumps have been determined.

CALIFORNIA JACK

This variant of seven up is sometimes called draw seven or California loo. It is played by two people and differs from seven up in the following ways.

Trumps The first card turned face up denotes trumps.

After each trick, first the winner and then the loser of that trick take a card from the top of the stock. The next card of the stock is then turned face up and denotes trumps for the next trick. When the stock is exhausted, each player's remaining cards are played out using the last trump suit, and with the winner of each trick leading to the next.

Scoring One point is scored for taking each of the following in tricks: the highest trump, the lowest trump, and the jack of trumps. The first player to make 10 points wins.

Skat

Rank with no trumps

All suits

Skat developed in Germany in the early 1800s and its rules were codified in 1896. It has since flourished on both sides of the Atlantic, being one of the most skillful of all card games. The simplified variant described here – Rauber Skat – is gradually replacing the original game.

Players Three to five people can play, but only three play on any one deal.

With four players, the dealer sits out. With five, the dealer and the third player to his left sit out: the first, second, and fourth play.

The first player to the dealer's left is called "forehand," the next "middlehand," and the last player with cards "endhand."

Cards Skat is played with a standard deck from which all the 2s,3s,4s,5s, and 6s have been removed.

Rank of cards Most contracts require trumps.

The highest trumps are always the four jacks, which rank in the order clubs (high), spades, hearts, diamonds (low).

In addition there may also be a trump suit. If so, the rest of that suit rank below the lowest jack, in the order a (high), 10,k,q,9, 8,7 (low).

When play is with trumps, cards in plain suits also rank a (high), 10,k,q,9,8,7 (low).

When there are no trumps, all suits rank a (high), k,q,j,10,9,8,7 (low).

Objective Each player tries to win the right to choose the game that will be played, and then successfully to complete that game.

Choice of first dealer is by high cut. Thereafter the deal passes one player to the left after each game.

Deal A packet of three cards is dealt to each active player. Then a "skat" of two face-down cards is set aside. A packet of four is next dealt to each active player, and finally a further packet of three.

This gives three hands of ten cards each, and two cards in the skat.

Bidding The player who makes the highest bid wins the right to name the game. He then tries to fulfil his bid and the other two players try to prevent him.

A bid states only the number of game points that the player believes he can make if he wins the right to choose the game. The lowest permitted bid is 18; the highest practicable bid is about 100.

Bidding follows the deal.
Middlehand bids first, or passes.
If middlehand bids, forehand must reply. He must state either
"Pass" or "Hold."
"Hold" means that he makes the same bid as middleman.
By bidding hold, he retains the right to name the game, because
a player cannot lose this to a player to his left unless that player
has bid higher.
This continues with forehand holding bids and middlehand
raising bids until either player passes.
Then endhand must either raise the bid or pass; and if he bids,
the survivor of the first pair replies by passing or holding. This
continues as between the first pair, until one bidder gives in.
If both middlehand and endhand pass without bidding,
forehand may make a bid or may pass. Once a player has
passed, he may not make a bid.
The player who survives in the bidding will now be referred to
as the "bidder."
The skat The bidder begins by deciding whether or not to pick
up the two cards that form the skat.
If he picks up the skat, he must then discard any two cards from
his hand. These discards will eventually count toward his final
score.
If he does not pick up, this is referred to as "handplay." The
skat is then set aside for the duration of play. At the end of the
hand, the fate of the skat depends on the game that has been
played.
If the bidder chooses to pick up the skat, this limits his choice of
game for the hand (since for certain games it is ruled that the
skat may not be picked up).
The games The bidder then chooses which game will be played
in that hand. His choice is between "suits," "grand," "simple
null," "open null," and "reject."
(A bidder who has picked up the skat is not permitted to choose
simple null, open null, or reject.)
To fulfil his bid, he must not only successfully complete the
game he chooses (for example, by making sufficient trick points
if that is required), but must also score sufficient "game" points
to equal or exceed his bid.
Suits In this option, the bidder names a suit. All the cards in
that suit become trumps, together with the jacks.
The bidder's aim is to make at least 61 trick points by taking
tricks containing scoring cards.
Grand Only the four jacks are trumps. The bidder's aim is as in
suits.

Rank with trumps

Trump suit

Trumps

©DIAGRAM

Simple null There are no trumps. The bidder aims to lose every trick.

Open null As in simple null, but the bidder must play with all his cards exposed. He lays them face up on the table before the opening lead.

Reject This game may only be chosen by forehand, and he may choose it only if middlehand and endhand have both passed without a bid. He does not make a numerical bid, but simply states "Reject."

Only the four jacks are trumps.

Each player tries to take fewer trick points than any other player.

Open If the bidder has opted for handplay, and names suits or grand, he may increase the value of his game by declaring "Open."

The bidder must then play with all his cards exposed, laying them face up on the table before the opening lead.

Schneider or schwarz If the bidder has named suits or grand, he may, before the opening lead, declare:

a) "Schneider," ie he aims to win at least 91 trick points; or

b) "Schwarz," ie he aims to take every trick.

He need not declare either – in which case his goal remains 61 trick points.

Play Forehand leads to the first trick. Thereafter the winner of one trick leads to the next.

Other players must follow suit if possible. If unable to follow suit they may trump (if there are trumps in the game) or they may discard.

The highest trump played, or the highest card of the suit led if no trumps appear, wins the trick.

Scoring of trick points Cards taken in tricks score as follows:

each ace, 11 points;

each 10, 10 points;

each king, four points;

each queen, three points;

each jack, two points.

Scoring the skat After the last trick has been taken, the skat is allocated as follows:

a) at suits or grand, to the bidder (if he took the skat before play, he is given the cards he discarded);

b) at reject, to the winner of the last trick;

c) at null, to no one – the skat is discarded.

Whoever receives the skat (or discards) counts trick points for any scoring cards it contains.

Making the game Except at reject (see separate section on reject play, p 485), the bidder makes the game if he achieves that game's object (ie 61 trick points, 91 trick points, all tricks, or no tricks.)

He must, however, then consider if he has made the number of game points that he bid.

©DIAGRAM

Making the bid Except at reject, a bid is made if the bidder's game score equals or exceeds the number of game points stated in his bid. Game points are scored as follows:

a) At null games, the game value is fixed: 23 game points for making simple null, and 24 for making open null. Provided that the player's bid was not higher than this, he makes his bid.

b) At suits or grand, the game value has to be calculated – by multiplying a base game value by various multipliers. A player does not know how many multipliers he will qualify for until after play ends. The player makes his bid if the total game value (base x all multipliers) equals or exceeds his bid.

Base values for the games are:

diamonds, nine game points;

hearts, 10 game points;

spades, 11 game points;

clubs, 12 game points;

grand, 20 game points.

The multipliers are as follows:

a) automatic multiplier for having made game, one;

b) for holding "matadors" (see separate section), the multiplier varies but is at least one;

c) for choosing handplay, one;

d) for making schneider or schwarz (see separate section), the multiplier varies but is at least one.

The player adds all his multipliers together. The total will be between two and 14. He then multiplies the base value for his game by this total.

Matadors The jack of clubs and all other trumps in unbroken sequence in the bidder's hand (including the skat, whether or not it is used in play) are called matadors.

When the bidder holds the jack of clubs, his hand is said to be "with" a number of matadors.

When he does not hold the jack of clubs, his hand is said to be "without" a number of matadors.

The multiplier is the number of matadors that the bidder is with or without (it does not matter which).

Two examples are shown.

a) Spades are trumps, the player is with three matadors (the missing jack of diamonds breaks the sequence before the ace of spades). The multiplier is three.

b) Hearts are trumps, the player is without two matadors (the top two trumps are missing). The multiplier is two.

Multipliers for schneider and schwarz The bidder may only count one of the following multipliers:

a) schneider made but not predicted, one;

b) schwarz made but not predicted, two;

c) schneider predicted and made, three;

d) schneider predicted and schwarz made, four;

e) schwarz predicted and made, five.

Scoring Except when reject is played (see separate section), scoring is as follows. Only the bidder scores.

If he has made his bid, he scores the total of his game points (which may be higher than his bid).

If he has not made his bid:

a) at suits or grand, he loses the amount of his bid at handplay – or twice that amount if he took the skat;

b) at null, he loses the absolute game value.

Scoring of reject In this game, there is no bidder and no bid. Normally the player who makes the fewest trick points scores 10. But:

a) if he takes no tricks, he scores 20;

b) if two players tie for fewest trick points, the one who did not take the last trick receives the score of 10;

c) if one player takes all tricks, he loses 30 and the others score nothing;

d) if all players tie with 40 trick points, forehand alone scores 10 for naming the game.

Winning The scores are recorded on a piece of paper and totaled at the end of a session.

The winner is the player with the highest score.

Often, an average score is worked out – players above the average then collect money accordingly, while players whose score is below average must make the payments.

Matadors

Cards in hand

Trumps

Three matadors: the multiplier is three

Two matadors: the multiplier is two

© DIAGRAM

Solo whist

Temporary partnerships are formed in solo whist, but each player scores for himself. Basically play is as for whist, but the game has its own bidding and scoring systems.

Players Solo whist is a game for four players. At the start of each hand each player is on his own.

Cards A standard deck of 52 playing cards is used. Cards rank normally, with ace high.

Objective Each player tries to contract and fulfil a bid.

Choice of first dealer is by high cut, with ace low.

Shuffle and cut are normal.

Rank

Deal The dealer deals out all the cards, beginning with the player to his left and going clockwise. The cards are dealt three at a time, with a final round of single cards. All but the last card are dealt face down; the last card, dealt to the dealer, is dealt face up and indicates trumps for some bids. Rules for misdeals are the same as for whist.

Bidding Each player in turn, beginning with the player to the dealer's left, may make a bid or pass without making a bid. In certain circumstances players may have a second chance to bid.

The bids are ranked in the following order, with each outbidding the one before.

a) Proposal and acceptance, or "prop and cop," involves a temporary partnership of two players. A call of "I propose" or "Prop" indicates that the player will try to win eight tricks in partnership with any of the others. Play is with the trump suit indicated at the deal. In his turn, a subsequent bidder may call "Accept" or "Cop" to become the partner.

b) "Solo" is a bid to take five tricks playing alone against the other three. Play is with the trump suit indicated at the deal.

c) "Misère" or "nullo" indicates that the player will try to lose every trick, playing with no trump suit.

d) "Abondance" is a bid to take nine tricks, playing with a trump suit nominated by the bidder. He does not announce the trump suit until all remaining players have passed.

e) "Royal abondance" or "abondance in trumps," is a bid to take nine tricks, playing with the trump suit indicated at the deal.

f) "Misère ouverte" or "spread" indicates that a player will try to lose every trick, playing with no trumps and turning his remaining cards face up on the table after the first trick has been taken.

g) "Abondance declarée" is a bid to take 13 tricks, playing with no trump suit.

Second bids may be made in the following cases:
a) by the player to the left of the dealer to accept a proposal;
b) by any player who has been overbid and wishes to make a higher bid;
c) by a proposer who has not been accepted and wishes to amend his proposal to a higher bid.

No bid hands If all players pass, the cards are thrown in and the deal passes to the left.

Play The player to the dealer's left leads first, unless the bid is abondance declarée in which case the bidder leads.

The rules for making tricks and trumping are as for whist.

It is not always necessary to play a hand right out. For example after a misère bid the hand ends once the bidder takes a trick.

Revoke A revoke (see p 494) loses or wins three tricks depending on the bid and on which the player made the error. A hand is always played out after a revoke, and a bidder who revokes must pay for the three tricks even if he makes his bid without them.

Scoring Chips are usually used for scoring: red ones worth five points each and white ones worth one point. Alternatively a written record may be kept.

Scores are as follows. For a successful proposal and acceptance bid, one partner receives five points from one opponent, and the other partner the same from the other opponent. For an unsuccessful bid, partners pay instead of receive the points. For all other bids, the bidder receives points from each of the other players if successful, or pays each of them if unsuccessful. The number of points varies with the bids:

solo, 10 points;
misère, 15 points;
abondance, 20 points;
royal abondance, 20 points;
misère ouverte, 30 points;
abondance declarée, 40 points.

In addition, for bids other than misère, misère ouverte, or abondance declarée, one extra point changes hands at each payment for each overtrick (trick in excess of the bid) or undertrick (trick fewer than the bid).

Rank in three-handed solo

THREE-HANDED SOLO

The game can be adapted for three-handed play as follows.

Cards There are two alternative changes:
1) A 40-card deck is used – obtained by stripping the 2s, 3s, and 4s from a standard deck. 39 cards are dealt out and the 40th indicates the trump suit.
2) A 39-card deck is used – obtained by stripping out the whole of one suit. The trump suit is indicated by the last card dealt.

Bids There is no proposal and acceptance bid. Misère overbids abondance, and misère ouverte overbids abondance declarée.

Scoring Misère is worth 20 points, abondance 15 points, misère ouverte 40 points, and abondance declarée 30 points.

Spoil five

Spoil five is similar to loo but has an unusual and complex ranking system. It is especially popular in the Republic of Ireland.

Players Two or more people can play, but the game is best played with five or six. Each person plays for himself.

Deck A standard deck of playing cards is used. The cards are ranked, in descending order, as follows.

Spades and clubs

Plain suits (ie non-trump): k,q,j,a,2,3,4,5,6,7,8,9,10.
Trump suits: 5,j,a of hearts, a of spades or clubs, k,q,2,3,4, 6,7,8,9,10.

Diamonds

Plain suit: k,q,j,10,9,8,7,6,5,4,3,2,a.
Trump suit: 5,j,a of hearts, a of diamonds, k,q,10,9,8,7,6,4,3,2.

Hearts

Plain suit: k,q,j,10,9,8,7,6,5,4,3,2.
Trump suit: 5,j,a,k,q,10,9,8,7,6,4,3,2.

Note that the ace of hearts is always the third-best trump, regardless of suit; the 5 of the trump suit is highest; and the jack of the trump suit second highest.

Objective Each player tries to win three tricks and to prevent anyone else from doing so.

Deal Players draw for deal, using standard ranking with ace high and 2 low. Lowest card deals.

Five face-down cards are dealt to each player in packets of two then three, or vice versa. The next card is turned face up to indicate trumps.

The deal passes clockwise around the table.

Pool Each player puts an agreed number of counters into the pool. It is won by a player taking three tricks in one hand.

Exchanging If the face-up card denoting the trump suit is an ace, the dealer may exchange it for a card in his hand before the first card is led. This is called "robbing."

If a player has been dealt the ace of trumps he may, if he wishes, exchange any card in his hand for the face-up card.

If he does not exchange a card, he must announce that he has the ace at his first turn of play – otherwise the ace becomes the lowest-ranking trump for that round, even if it is an ace of hearts.

Play The player to the left of the dealer leads to the first trick and the winner of each trick leads to the next.

Rules of play are the same as for whist, with the following differences.

If a card of a plain suit is led, a player may either trump or follow suit. He may discard another plain suit card only if he can neither follow suit nor trump.

If a card of the trump suit is led, a player must follow suit if he can. He need not play any of the top three trumps if the leading card was a lower trump – holding back a card in this way is called "reneging."

Jinxing A player who wins three tricks may take the pool, and the hand ends.

Alternatively, he may call "Jinx," implying that he will try to win the remaining two tricks. Play continues, and if he wins the extra two tricks he takes the pool, plus a sum from each player equal to his original contribution to the pot. If he does not make both tricks he loses the pool and the hand counts as a "spoil."

Spoil is when nobody wins three tricks, or a winner fails to win all five after jinxing. The cards are dealt for a new hand but only the new dealer contributes to the pot. Only when the pot is won do all the players contribute to a new pot.

Rank in trumps

Rank in plain suits

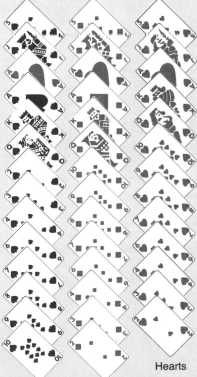

Hearts

Spades and clubs   Diamonds

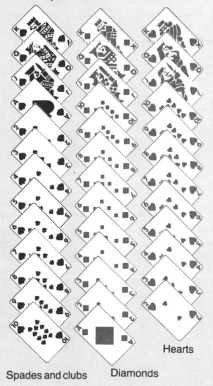

Hearts

Spades and clubs   Diamonds

© DIAGRAM

Vint

A member of the whist family, vint is a game for four players playing in partnerships of two.

Cards A standard deck of cards is used. The cards rank normally, with ace high. The suits rank no trumps (highest), hearts, diamonds, clubs, and spades (lowest).

Objective Each partnership aims to make and fulfill a bid by taking tricks.

Deal The entire deck is dealt out, one face-down card at a time to each player. The deal passes clockwise around the table with each round of play.

Bidding Starting with the dealer, each player in turn bids or passes.

Each bid indicates the intention to take six tricks plus the number called, in the suit named or with no trumps. Thus the lowest bid is one spade (ie taking seven tricks with spades as trumps); and the highest is seven no trumps (ie taking thirteen tricks).

Rank of cards

A bid is overcalled by a bid of more tricks in the same suit, or the same number of tricks in a higher ranking suit or no trumps. When a player is overcalled he may call higher when his turn comes round again, even if the only other bidder is his partner.

Play is opened by the player to the left of the highest bidder, and proceeds in a clockwise direction around the table. Each player must follow suit if able to do so; if he cannot, he either plays a trump or discards. The winner of a trick leads to the next trick.

Scoring Each partnership records its score on a scorepad or piece of paper divided into two sections by a horizontal line (as in bridge, p 402).

Game points are entered below the line. Each partnership scores for each trick taken – whether or not the bid is fulfilled. However, the number of tricks bid determines the value of each trick, ranging from ten points per trick for a bid of one, 20 points per trick for a bid of two, and so on up to 70 points per trick for a bid of seven.

The first partnership to score 500 game points wins the game – even if it reaches this score part way through a hand, and regardless of whether or not it won the bidding.

Bonus points are entered above the line. They are scored as follows:
a) winning a game, 1000 points;
b) winning a rubber (two out of three games), 2000 points;
c) "little slam" (12 tricks) made but not bid, 1000 points;
d) little slam bid and made, 6000 points;

e) "grand slam" (13 tricks) made but not bid, 2000 points;
f) grand slam bid and made, 12,000 points.

Honor points are scored above the line and comprise the a,k,q,j, and 10 of trumps and the other aces. In a trump suit, the ace is counted twice, both as an honor and as an ace. When playing no trumps, only the four aces are honors. The partnership holding the most honors scores ten times the trick value for each honor held in trumps, or 25 times the trick value for each honor (ace) held when playing no trumps.

For example, if the final bid is three trumps, each trick is worth 30 points and therefore each honor is worth 300 points (10x3=300).

If one partnership has a majority of aces and the other a majority of honors, those two majorities are compared, and the partnership that has the bigger majority scores for the difference.

For example, if side A has two honors and one ace, but side B has one honor and three aces, the two honors are deducted from the three aces and side B scores for one honor, worth ten times the trick value.

But if side A has three honors and one ace, and side B has one honor and three aces, neither side scores, as the three honors and the three aces cancel each other out.

If both sides hold two aces: at no trumps, neither side scores; at trumps, the side that wins most tricks scores for its honors.

Coronet Any player holding three aces or a sequence of three cards in a plain suit – known as a "coronet" – scores 500 points, entered above the line.

If a player holds the fourth ace, he scores a further 500 points; and each extra card in a sequence also scores a further 500 points.

If the sequence is in the trump suit, or in any suit when no trumps has been declared, coronet is worth double.

Unfulfilled bids If a partnership fails to make its bid, it is penalized for each undertrick by 100 times the value of each trick (entered above the line); but it also scores game points below the line for the number of tricks it took.

For example, if the bidding partnership made a bid of five no trumps (ie 11 tricks) and took only eight tricks (ie it failed by three tricks), scoring would be as follows:
a) 3×50×100=15,000 penalty points;
b) 8×50=400 game points;
c) the opponents score game points in the usual way for the number of tricks they took, ie 5×50=250 game points.

Rank of suits

Whist

Whist evolved in the eighteenth century from an earlier game called triumph. It has since given rise to a whole family of games, including the popular contract bridge and solo whist. The rules are comparatively simple, but a great deal of skill is needed to play really well.

Rank

Players Whist is a game for four players, two playing against two as partners. Partnerships are decided by draw (see p 381). Players sit around a table, with partners facing each other. By convention, players are referred to by the points of the compass, with North and South playing against East and West.

Cards A standard deck of 52 playing cards is used. Cards rank normally, with ace high.

The suits are not ranked, except that one suit is designated the trump suit for each hand. A card of the trump suit beats any card from any other suit.

Objective Players aim to win tricks. A trick consists of four cards, one played by each player.

Choice of first dealer is by high cut, with ace ranking low.

Shuffle and cut Any player has the right to shuffle, but the dealer has the right to shuffle last. The player to the right of the dealer cuts the cards and passes them to the dealer.

Deal Beginning with the player to his left and going clockwise, the dealer deals out all but one of the cards, face down and one at a time.

The remaining card is placed face up on the table and its suit indicates the trump suit. The dealer adds it to his hand when it is his turn to play.

Misdeal It is a misdeal if:

a) more or fewer than 13 cards are dealt to any player; or

b) any card other than the last one is exposed.

It is not a misdeal if a player is dealt two or more successive cards and the dealer rectifies the error at once.

If there has been a misdeal, players may agree to accept the deal after the error has been rectified.

Any player, however, has the right to demand a new deal until the first trick is completed. After that the deal must stand.

If there is to be a redeal, players throw in their cards and the deal passes one player to the left.

Play The player to the dealer's left leads by placing any one of his cards face up in the centre of the table.

Each of the other players in turn plays a card to the centre of the table.

If a player has a card of the same suit as the card led, he must play this card. This is called "following suit," and failure to do

so is penalized (see the section on revoking, p 494). If he does not have a card of the suit led he may play any other card.
The trick is won:
a) by the player of the highest trump card, or
b) if no trump cards have been played, by the player of the highest card of the suit led.
The winner of one trick leads to the next. Play continues in this way until all 13 tricks of a hand have been played.
The deal passes to the next player in a clockwise direction. The cards are reshuffled and cut for the new deal.

©DIAGRAM

Revoking is failing to follow suit when able to do so.

A player is not penalized if he corrects his error before the trick is turned over, and the partner of a player who fails to follow suit may caution him by asking if he does not have any cards of the suit led.

Once the trick has been turned over but before play to the next trick has begun, the opposing partnership may challenge and claim a revoke.

Points penalties for revoking vary with the different scoring systems for the game.

A partnership cannot win the game in any hand in which it revokes. If both partnerships revoke in the same hand, all cards are thrown in and a new deal is made.

Calling If a player exposes a card, other than when playing it to a trick, he must leave it face up on the table until one of his opponents "calls" on him to play it to a trick where it will not cause a revoke.

Scoring There are a number of ways of scoring, but the following systems are most common.

English whist uses a five-point game, including the scoring of honours. Games are grouped into rubbers.

There are three ways of scoring game points.

1) The first six tricks do not score. From the seventh trick onward, one game point is scored for each trick taken.

2) The honors are a,k,q, and j of trumps. A partnership scores four game points if it is dealt all four honors, and three game points if dealt any three.

However, if both pairs reach five game points in the same deal, the trick points from that deal take precedence over the honors points. At least one trick must be taken in the last deal before declaring game. After game, the losers' honors score, if any, is no longer counted in their game points total.

3) There are three alternative rulings concerning the penalties for revoking:

a) the revoking pair loses three game points;

b) the revoking pair transfers three game points to its opponents; or

c) the opponents gain three game points.

After each game, additional points are scored by the winners as follows:

a) three points if the opponents had no game points;

b) two points if the opponents had one or two game points; and

c) one point if the opponents had three or four game points.

A rubber consists of three games.

The winners of two out of three games score two extra points for the rubber. All points are then totaled, and the partnership with the highest score wins.

If the first two games of a rubber are won by the same pair, a third game is not played.

In America a seven-point game is usual, with two ways of scoring game points.

1) The first six tricks played do not score. Thereafter, each trick taken scores one game point.

2) Revoking also provides game points, as the pair that failed to follow suit transfers two of its game points to the other pair. The first pair to get seven game points scores the difference between seven and the losers' score.

TERMS USED IN WHIST

Finessing consists of playing the third-best card of a suit when also holding the best – trusting that the opponents do not hold the second best.

Forcing is playing a suit in which another player is void.

Long trumps are the remaining trump or trumps left in a hand after all other trumps in the deck have been played.

Loose card is a card of no value.

Quarte is any four cards of the same suit in sequence.

Quarte major is a sequence of a,k,q,j in the same suit.

Quinte is any five cards of the same suit in sequence.

See-saw occurs when each member of a partnership is trumping a suit, and each plays these suits to the other for that purpose.

Slam is winning every trick.

Tenace consists of holding the cards immediately above and below the opposing side's best in suit, for example ace and queen when the opponents hold the king.

© DIAGRAM

Section 3
Children's card games

Introduction

All the games in this section are fast-moving and fun for children to play. The easiest among them – games such as slapjack, snap, and beggar my neighbour – provide an excellent first introduction to games using standard playing cards. At the other end of the scale are games like racing demon, cheat, and concentration, which are challenging enough to be enjoyed by adults and children alike.

Card recognition The simplest card games using standard playing cards involve recognizing certain cards as they appear in play. Simplest of all is slapjack, in which only the jacks must be picked out. Slightly more elaborate is beggar my neighbour in which players must recognize face cards – kings, queens, jacks – and aces.

Matching cards by rank Many card games for children depend on matching cards of the same rank. In snap, menagerie, old maid, and memory, players must watch out for pairs – for example, two 7s or two queens. In donkey and go fish, players try to collect all four cards of the same kind. Other easy games that involve matching cards by rank include go boom, cheat, and snip-snap-snorem.

Following suit Another group of simple games requires players to know the four suits – hearts, diamonds, spades, and clubs. In my ship sails, the winner is the first player to collect seven cards belonging to the same suit – for example seven spades. For other games in this group, players must also know the usual rank order of cards – from ace (low), through 2, 3, 4, 5, 6, 7, 8, 9, and 10, to jack, queen, and king (high). It is then possible to play a whole variety of games. Some of these – like card dominoes, give away, play or pay, sequence, spit, and racing demon – involve building up sequences of cards in rank order. Others – like linger longer, knockout whist, and rolling stone – serve as a useful introduction to whist and other more complex games in which tricks must be won.

Beggar my neighbor

Beggar my neighbor is an easy and exciting game. No skill is required as the outcome depends on the luck of the deal.

Players There may be two to six players.

Cards Any deck of standard playing cards may be used, and it need not be complete. For more than three players it is a good idea to mix two decks together.

The objective is to win all the cards. But, as the game may go on for a very long time, the winner may be the player who has the most cards at the end of an agreed length of time.

Deal One player deals out all the cards in a clockwise direction – one at a time and face down. It does not matter if some players have one card more than the others.

Each player puts his cards into a neat pile face down in front of him.

Players are not allowed to look at their cards.

Play The player to the dealer's left turns up the top card in his pile and places it in the center of the playing area.

Each player in turn, in a clockwise direction, then places the top card from his pile face up on the central pile.

This continues until one player turns up an ace or face card (a jack, queen, or king).

Payment of cards The player next to him then has to "pay" him by placing a certain number of cards on the central pile:

a) four cards for an ace;

b) three cards for a king;

c) two cards for a queen;

d) one card for a jack.

If, however, one of the payment cards is an ace or a face card, the payer stops turning over his cards and the player next to him has to pay the correct number of cards.

This goes on until a player paying out cards turns over the correct number of cards with no aces or face cards.

When this happens, the last player to have turned over an ace or a face card may take the central pile and place it at the bottom of his own pile.

The player then starts a new round by playing his next card face up in the center of the playing area.

As soon as a player has no more cards, he is out.

Payment

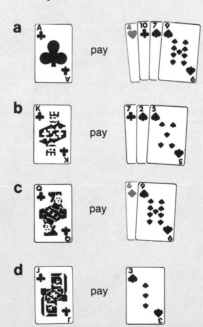

© DIAGRAM

Card dominoes

This game of luck and skill is also called sevens, parliament, and fan-tan. A player can increase his chances of winning by carefully choosing the order in which he plays his cards.

Sample play

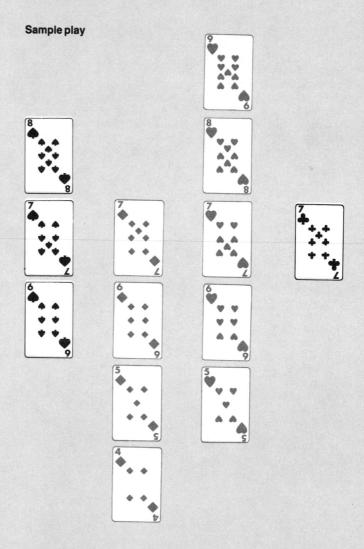

Players The game is for two or more players.
Cards One complete deck of standard playing cards is used.
Objective Each player aims to be first to play his cards onto a central pattern of cards in sequence.
Deal One player deals all the cards in a clockwise direction, one at a time and face down.
Play Each player looks at his cards and sorts them in his hand according to suit and sequence.
The player with the 7 of diamonds starts the game by putting it face up in the centre. The player to his left must then try to put down either the 6 or 8 of diamonds or another 7. If he plays the 6 or 8 of diamonds he puts it respectively below or above the 7. If he plays another 7 he puts it next to the 7 of diamonds.
If, however, he does not hold any of these cards he "passes" and the play then goes to the next player to the left.
Play continues in this way, with each player in turn adding a card to one of the sequences, putting down a 7, or passing. The sequences are built up from 7 through 8, 9, 10, jack, and queen to king, and down from 6 to ace.
End The game is won by the first player to put down all his cards, but play usually continues until every card has been played and there are four complete suit sequences.

©DIAGRAM

Cheat

Also known as I doubt it, this game is great fun for those who like taking risks and calling people's bluffs.

Players A minimum of three people is needed to play, but the more the better.

Cards One or two decks of playing cards are used.

Objective Each player aims to be the first to get rid of all his cards.

Deal One player deals out all the cards. Some players may have one extra card.

Play Players look at their cards. The player to the left of the dealer places one to four cards of the "same" rank (eg all 7s) face down in a pile in the center. He calls their rank as he does so. (In fact, the cards need not be what he claims – see cheating.)

Subsequent players must then play – or claim that they are playing – one to four cards of the rank one higher than those played by the preceding player.

Cheating There are at least two ways of cheating.

a) instead of putting down cards of the correct rank, a player can put down any other cards, so long as he pretends that they are all the same, and of the next highest value to those just played.

If a player does not have cards of the required value, he has no

alternative but to do this. It is important that a player should avoid giving the others reason to doubt him.

b) A player may put down more cards than he states. Again, he should avoid drawing people's attention to this.

Calling a player's bluff If a player suspects another of cheating, he can challenge him by calling "Cheat" or "I doubt it" before the suspect's cards are covered by those of the next player. The challenged player must then turn over his cards for inspection.

If the player who called "Cheat" or "I doubt it" is correct, the person who cheated picks up all the cards in the central pile and adds them to his hand.

If the player did not cheat, the challenger must pick up the central pile of cards.

The player who picks up the cards from the center starts the next round.

End The winner is the first person to succeed in playing his last card – ie either:

a) he withstands a challenge from another player; or

b) his cards are covered by the next player's before anyone has challenged him.

UP AND DOWN CHEAT

The only difference between this game and ordinary cheat or I doubt it is the rank of the cards that can be played. Instead of only claiming to play cards in ascending rank, a player may also claim that he is playing cards that are either of the same rank or one rank lower than the last player's cards.

Concentration

This card game for any number of players is also called pelmanism or memory. It is easy to play and is an excellent test of memory and observation.

Cards One or two standard decks of playing cards are used, depending on the number of players.

The cards should be clean and reasonably new, so that when they are lying face down they cannot be identified by creases, marks, or torn corners!

The playing area must be flat and as large as possible – the floor or a big table is best.

The deal One player shuffles the cards and lays them face down on the table – in all directions and so that no card is touching another.

Objective Each player tries to collect as many cards as possible by turning up pairs with the same rank (number or picture).

First player The player to the left of the dealer starts the game. He turns over two cards at random and allows the other players to see them.

If the rank of the two cards is the same, for example two aces or two kings, he takes them and may turn over two more cards.

He continues in this way until he turns over two cards that do not match.

If the cards that are turned over do not match, the player must put them face down in their original positions. His turn then ends.

Second player The person to the first player's left now turns over any two cards.

If the first card matches one that has already been turned over he must try to remember where that card is. If he is successful he takes the pair. He continues his turn until he fails to turn over a matching pair.

Successive players Play continues with the players taking their turns in a clockwise direction, until all the cards have been collected.

The winner is the player with most cards at the end of the game.

©DIAGRAM

Donkey

Donkey is a fast and noisy card game in which players are penalized with letters from the game's name.

Players Three or more can play.

Cards Special cards can be bought but donkey is usually played with sets of cards taken from an old deck of standard playing cards.

Each set consists of four cards with the same picture or number. The number of sets used is the same as the number of people playing. For example if there are five players, the aces, kings, queens, jacks, and 10s might be used.

Spoons, buttons, or some other unbreakable objects should be placed in the center of the table at the start of each round.

There must be one object fewer than the number of players.

The objective is to collect a set of four cards and at the same time to avoid being the "donkey" (ie the first player to lose six rounds of the game).

A player is penalized with one letter from the word donkey each time he fails to pick up an object at the end of a round.

Play Keeping his cards hidden from the other players, each player chooses one card that he does not want and places it face down on the table. All the players then pass their unwanted card to the player to their left.

Each player then looks at his new card and again chooses a card to pass to his neighbour.

He may pass the new card if he wishes.

The game continues in this way, as quickly as possible, until one player has a set of four cards of the same value. When a player has a set of cards, for example four 10s, he should quietly put them face up on the table and pick up an object from the table. As soon as any player does this, the other players must reach for an object whether they have a set of four cards or not.

The player who fails to pick up an object loses the round and is penalized with a letter.

Donkey The first player to be penalized with all the letters of the word donkey loses the game and must "hee-haw" three times.

PIG

Pig is a similar game to donkey. The number of players and the cards used are the same as for donkey, but in pig there is no need for any unbreakable objects.

The objective is to collect a set of four cards of the same value while also avoiding becoming the "prize pig."

Play is the same as for donkey, except that when a player has a set of cards he puts his finger to his nose. The last player to do so is pig for the round.

Prize pig The game is lost when one player becomes prize pig after losing ten rounds. As a forfeit, the prize pig must say "oink-oink" three times.

©DIAGRAM

Give away

Give away is a simple game that requires players to stay alert.
The faster it is played the better.

Objective Each player aims to be first to get rid of all his cards.
Players Two or more can play this game.
Cards A standard deck of playing cards is used.
Deal One player deals out all the cards in a clockwise direction –
face down and one at a time. It does not matter if some players
have one card more than others.
Players do not look at their cards but put them in a neat
face-down pile in front of them.
Play The player to the left of the dealer turns over the top card
of his face-down pile.
If it is not an ace, he places it face up by his face-down pile and
ends his turn.

If it is an ace, he puts it face up in the center of the table and turns over another card. His turn continues until he turns over a card that he is unable to play to the center – a card may be played to the center if it is an ace or if it can be built in rank order (a, 2, 3, 4, 5, 6, 7, 8, 9, 10, j, q, k) onto a center card of the same suit. When he turns over a card that cannot be played to the center he places it face up by his face-down pile and ends his turn.

Each player then plays in turn. As well as playing to the center a player may play a card onto another player's face-up pile – provided that it is one higher or lower in rank than the top card of that pile.

When a player plays his last face-down card onto his face-up pile, he waits until his next turn before turning over his face-up pile to start again.

If he plays his last face-down card into the center or onto another player's pile, he turns over his face-up pile immediately and continues his turn.

End The first player to get rid of all his cards wins the game.

Play

Play to centre

Play on
opponent's
face-up card

©DIAGRAM

Go boom

Go boom is a straightforward game for two or more players, which can be played by quite young children.

Cards A standard deck of playing cards is used.
Objective Each player aims to be the first player to get rid of all his cards.
Deal The players cut for deal; the one with the highest card (ace ranks high) deals out the cards in a clockwise direction, one at a time and face down, until each player has seven cards. Spare cards are placed face down in a neat pile in the center.
Play Each player looks at his cards and sorts them in his hand. Turns pass clockwise around the players, starting with the player to the dealer's left.
The first player chooses a card from his hand and places it face up in the center. Each of the other players in turn, making a central face-up pile, plays a card that is either :
a) of the same suit (eg all spades); or
b) of the same rank (number or picture) as the card put down by the person before him.
If a player cannot follow suit or rank, he takes cards one at a time from the top of the central face-down pile until he has a card that he can play onto the central face-up pile. If all the cards have been taken, the player says "Pass" and play moves on to the next player.
When each player has played a card or "passed," the cards are compared for the highest card (ace ranks high) and the player of the highest card starts the next round.
If two or more players tie for the highest card, the first one to play his card starts the next round.
End The winner is the first player to get rid of all his cards and shout "Boom."

SCORING GO BOOM

This is a variant of go boom that is made more interesting by the introduction of a scoring system. It is played in the same way as basic go boom, except that several rounds are played and points are scored for going boom.
When a player goes boom, he scores points for all the unplayed cards still in the other players' hands. Scoring is:
a) 10 points for each king, queen, or jack;
b) one point for each ace;
c) the numerical face value of all other cards.
A game is won by the first player to score an agreed number of points (usually 250).

10 points

1 point

CRAZY EIGHTS

Crazy eights is the same basic game as go boom except that the 8s are wild.

A player may play any 8 after any card, and then decides which suit should follow.

As in scoring go boom, the first player to play all his cards scores points for the unplayed cards still in the other players' hands.

Points are scored as follows:

a) 50 points for each 8;
b) 10 points for each king, queen, or jack;
c) one point for each ace;
d) the numerical face value of all other cards.

If the face-down pile of cards is exhausted before any player plays all his cards, the game is blocked and the player with the lowest count in his remaining cards scores the difference in count between his own hand and the other players' hands.

50 points

10 points

1 point

© DIAGRAM

Go fish

A group of
four 7s

To win at this popular game, players will need a mixture of skill and luck.

Players Fish can be played by two players, but it is better with more.

Cards A standard deck of cards is normally used, but young players may prefer to use happy families cards.

Deal One of the players deals out all the cards. As well as dealing a hand for each player, the dealer also deals a spare hand – so, for example, five hands are dealt if there are four players.

The spare hand is placed face down in the center of the table and is called the "fish pile."

Objective Each player tries to get rid of all his cards.

Play Each player looks at his cards and sorts them into groups with the same rank (number or picture). Players must take care not to let anyone else see their cards at any time.

When all the players are ready, the person to the dealer's left asks any player, by name, for a particular card (eg 7 of spades). He must already possess at least one card of the same rank (eg 7 of hearts).

If the person who is asked for a card has it, he must give it to the player who asked for it. The player who made the first request may then ask any player for another card, again provided he already has at least one card of the same rank. A player can go on asking for cards in this way until he asks someone for a card that he does not have. The person who does not have the card then tells the player who asked for it to "Go fish." The player who was told to go fish must then take one card from the top of the fish pile. The player who told him to go fish then takes over asking for cards.

Once a player collects all four cards in a group, he puts them into a pile face down in front of him.

End The winner is the first player to have no cards other than his completed groups. If two players finish at the same time, the one with most completed groups of four cards is the winner.

©DIAGRAM

Knockout whist

An easy-to-play member of the whist family, knockout whist is very popular with older children. It is a good way of learning about tricks and trumps. Players are eliminated until only one remains.

Players Two to seven people can play.
Cards A standard deck of playing cards is used.
Objective Each player aims to win all the tricks of a hand.
A trick contains one card from each player played into the centre.
Except when a trump has been played, a trick is won by the highest card belonging to the suit that was led – ie to the same suit as the first card played in that trick.
Aces are the highest cards, followed by kings, queens, jacks, and so on down from the 10s to the 2s.
A trump is a card belonging to the trump suit. The trump suit is determined before each game is played. A trump card beats any card belonging to the suit led.
Deal One player deals out the cards face down, one at a time, and in a clockwise direction until each player has seven cards. The remaining cards are put face down in a pile in the center. Each time the cards are dealt, the number dealt to each player is decreased by one.

Rank of cards

High

Low

Play The top card of the center pile is turned over and this determines the trump suit for the first hand.

The player to the dealer's left then starts the first trick by playing any card he chooses.

Each player in turn then plays a card, following suit if he can. If a player cannot follow suit, he may either play a trump or discard any other card into the centre.

The trick is won by the player who played the highest trump card or, if no trump was played, by the player who played the highest card of the suit led.

When all seven tricks have been played anyone who has not won a trick drops out of the game.

The dealer collects all the cards, shuffles them, and deals six cards to each remaining player.

The winner of the most tricks in the first round chooses the trump suit and plays the first card in the second hand.

Play continues in this way – with players without tricks dropping out at the end of each hand.

End The first player to win all the tricks in a single hand is the overall winner.

If play continues to the seventh hand, each player will have only one card. There will be only one trick, and the winner of this trick wins the game.

Tricks (four players)

Trump suit

Trick won by king

Trick won by 4 of trumps

©DIAGRAM

Linger longer

Linger longer is an ideal introduction to the principles of trump play that form the basis of many more complicated card games.

Players Three or more people can play. Four to six is best.
Cards A standard deck of playing cards is used.
Objective Each player tries to be the last person with cards in his hand. Players obtain new cards by winning tricks.
A trick comprises one card from each player played into the center. Unless a trump has been played a trick is won by the highest card belonging to the suit that was led – ie to the same suit as the first card played in that trick.
Aces are the highest cards, followed by the kings, queens, jacks, and so on down from the 10s to the 2s.
A trump is a card belonging to the trump suit. The trump suit is determined before each game is played. A trump card beats any card belonging to the suit led.
Deal One player deals out the cards in a clockwise direction, face down and one at a time, until each player has the same number of cards as there are players. For example, if there are four players, each one of them receives four cards.
The remaining cards are placed in the center in a face-down pile called the stock.
The last card dealt to the dealer is shown to all the players. The suit of this card is the trump suit for the game.
Play The player to the left of the dealer plays any card he likes face up in the center.
Each player in turn then plays one card into the center. (These cards together form a trick.) If possible, players must play a card of the same suit as the first card – this is called "following suit." If a player is unable to follow suit, he may play a trump card or any other card.
A trick is won by the player who played the highest trump card or, if no trump was played, by the player who played the highest card of the suit led. Ace ranks high for this game.
A player who wins a trick places these cards face down in front of him. He then draws the top card from the stock and adds it to the cards in his hand (no other player draws).
This player plays the first card of the next trick.
Players continue playing tricks in this way as long as they have any cards in their hand – ignoring the cards in any tricks that they have won.
A player with no cards in his hand must leave the game.
End The last player left in the game wins.

Rank of cards

High

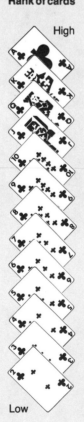

Low

Tricks

Trump suit

Trick won by
ace

Trick won by
6 of trumps

Menagerie

This hilarious and noisy game is similar to snap. It is sometimes called animals.

Players It can be played by two, but is better with more.
Cards One or two decks of standard playing cards are used.
Objective Players aim to win all the cards.
Choosing the animals Players first choose the name of an animal with a long and tongue-twisting name.
After checking that everyone has chosen a different animal, each player is given a small piece of paper on which he must write his animal's name. (An older person can help anyone who hasn't learned to write.)
All the pieces of paper are folded and then shaken together in a bag or hat. Each player then takes one piece of paper – and the name on that paper is his animal for the game.
Players should then learn the animal names of all the persons playing.
Deal One player deals out all the cards in a clockwise direction – one at a time and face down. It does not matter if some players have one card more than the others.
Each player puts his cards into a neat pile face down in front of him. Players are not allowed to look at their cards.
Play The player to the dealer's left turns over the top card of his pile and places it face up to start a face-up pile of cards next to his face-down pile. The next player to his left does the same, and so on around the players until any player sees that the cards on the top of any two face-up piles have the same value.
Whenever the top card on any two player's face-up piles are the same (eg two 7s), each of these two players must call out the other player's animal name three times.
The first player to do so wins the other player's face-up pile and adds these cards to the bottom of his own face-down pile.
Penalty If a player wrongly calls out a name, he must give all his face-up cards to the player whose animal name he called.

ANIMAL NOISES
This game is played like menagerie, except that:
a) players choose animals that make distinctive noises (eg dog, cat, or duck);
b) players imitate their opponents' animal noises instead of repeating their animal names.

©DIAGRAM

My ship sails

An easy game for beginners, my ship sails is also great fun when played at speed by those familiar with it.

Players Four to seven people may play.

Cards A standard deck of playing cards is used.

Objective Each player aims to be the first to collect seven cards of the same suit, for example seven spades.

Deal Each player cuts the cards and the one with the highest card (ace high) is the dealer.

He deals out the cards in a clockwise direction, one at a time

My ship sails!

and face down, until each player has seven cards. The
remaining cards are not used.

Play Each player sorts his cards into suits in his hand and
decides which suit he will try to collect. This will probably be
the suit for which he has most cards at the start of a round, but
he may change his mind during the course of play.

Exchange of cards Each player takes one card that he does not
want and puts it face down on the table. When all the players
are ready, they pass these cards to the next person to the right.
The players pick up their new cards, decide on another card to
discard, and then pass it in the same way.

End Players continue to exchange cards until one person
collects seven cards of the same suit. He then calls "My ship
sails," and wins the game. If two players call together, the first
to start calling is the winner.

Old maid

Old maid is a simple card game that is a great favourite with young children. Another name for this game is pass the lady.

Players This is a game for three or more players.
Cards One of the queens is removed from a standard deck to leave an odd queen – the "old maid."
Deal One player deals all the cards face down, one at a time, to all players. It does not matter if some players have one card more than the others.

Objective Each player aims to get rid of all his cards by discarding pairs of equal value. The player who is left with the old maid card when play ends is the loser. There are no winners in this game.

Play Each player looks at his cards, making sure that none of the other players can see them.

If he has any pairs – two matching character cards or two playing cards with the same value, eg two 9s or two kings – he lays them face down on the table.

A player with three cards of the same value may only put down two of them and must keep the third, but a player with four cards of the same value may put down all four as two pairs.

The player to the dealer's left fans out his cards, keeping their faces toward him, and offers them to the player to his left.

The player who is offered the cards must take any one of them. He then looks to see whether the new card pairs up with any of the cards already in his hand. If it does, he lays the pair face down on the table. If not, he adds the new card to the cards in his hand. He then fans out his cards and offers them to the player to his left.

Play continues in this way until all cards but the "old maid" have been played. The player holding the "old maid" is the loser, and all the other players call him "old maid" before a new game is started.

Variation To make the game last longer, cards may be considered as pairs only if their colour matches as well as their number, for example two red 7s or two black aces.

Old maid

One queen removed

Pair of queens

The old maid

Pairs

©DIAGRAM

Le vieux garçon

LE VIEUX GARÇON

This French game is similar to old maid.

It is played with a standard deck of playing cards, with the jacks of hearts, diamonds, and clubs removed.

The game is lost by the player left with the jack of spades – called "le vieux garçon" or "old boy."

Play or pay

Cards in sequence

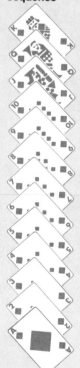

This easy game, sometimes called round the corner, is fun for players learning about the rank and sequence of playing cards.

Players Three or more can play.
Cards A standard deck of playing cards is used.
Counters Each player starts with 20 counters.
Objective Each player aims to be first to get rid of all his cards.
Deal One player is chosen as dealer. He deals out all the cards in a clockwise direction, one at a time and face down. It does not matter if some players have one card more than others.
Play The player to the left of the dealer chooses any one of his cards and places it face up in the center.
The next player to his left then looks at his cards to see if he has the next card "in sequence."
A card is in sequence if it belongs to the same suit as the last card that was played and follows the order a, 2, 3, 4, 5, 6, 7, 8, 9, 10, j, q, k. If the last card was a king, the next card in sequence for this game is the ace of the same suit. (This is called a "round the corner" sequence.)

If the player has the next card in sequence he plays it face up onto the card in the center.

If he does not have this card, he must pay one counter into the center.

Play continues with each player in turn either playing the next card in sequence or paying a counter.

When all the cards of a suit have been played, the player who put down the last card has an extra turn and may play any card that he chooses.

End The first player to get rid of all his cards is the winner of the round and takes all the counters from the center. Each loser must also pay him one counter for every card left in his hand. The winner of the game is the player with most counters after an agreed number of rounds.

Racing demon

Racing demon is a fast and noisy game in which players race to get rid of all their cards.

Players Any number can play.
Cards One complete deck of standard playing cards is needed for each player. Old decks with different backs are recommended.
Playing area This game requires a lot of space.
Deal Each player shuffles and deals his own deck.
After shuffling, each player first deals out 13 cards, face down, in a pile in front of him.
This pile is then turned over so that only the top card is visible. He then deals four cards face up, in a row alongside his pile of 13 cards.
His spare cards should be held face down in one hand.
Objective Each player aims:
a) to get rid of his pile of 13 cards;
b) to play as many cards as possible into the center.
Start of play One of the players is chosen to be the starter. When all the players have dealt out their cards, he starts play by shouting "Go!"
Play All the players play at the same time: there is no waiting to play in turn. Players may either play cards into the center or onto their own face-up cards.
Play into the center If a player has an ace among his face-up cards, he should place it face up in the center.
Once an ace has been played into the center, anyone with a face-up 2 of the same suit can play this onto the ace. A face-up 3 of the same suit can then be added by any player, and so on through to the 10, jack, queen, and king.
Playing on face-up cards As well as building up the piles in the center, a player can build piles of cards on the four cards alongside his original pile of 13.
Cards added to these piles must be in descending order and alternately black and red (for example a black 6 can be added to a red 7 and then a red 5 added to the black 6).
Cards added to these piles may be:
a) the top card from the player's original pile of 13;
b) a card, or a correct sequence of cards, from one of the player's other face-up piles.
Any space left by the removal of one of the four face-up piles should be filled with the top card from the player's original pile of 13.

Play

Play to centre

Play on face-up cards

Spare cards If a player is unable to play a face-up card into the center or to move any of his face-up cards, he turns to the cards that were spare after he first dealt out his cards.

These spare cards are turned over, three at a time, onto a separate pile, until one of them can be played into the center or onto a face-up pile.

When all the spare cards have been turned over, the player picks up the pile, turns it face down, and continues play.

End As soon as any player uses up all his cards from his original pile of 13, he shouts "Out!" and play ends.

Scoring The cards in the center are sorted into their separate decks.

A player's final score is the difference between the number of his cards in the center and the number of cards left in his original face-up piles.

The winner is the player with the highest score.

©DIAGRAM

Rolling stone

This popular game is highly unpredictable in its outcome. Just as a player is on the verge of winning he can get a new handful · of cards to play. It is also known as enflay or schwellen.

Players Four, five, or six people can play.
Cards A standard deck of playing cards is used, but with cards removed so that there are eight cards per player.
The following cards should be removed before play:
a) for four players, the 2s, 3s, 4s, 5s, and 6s;
b) for five players, the 2s, 3s, and 4s;
c) for six players, the 2s.
Objective Each player aims to be the first to get rid of all his cards.

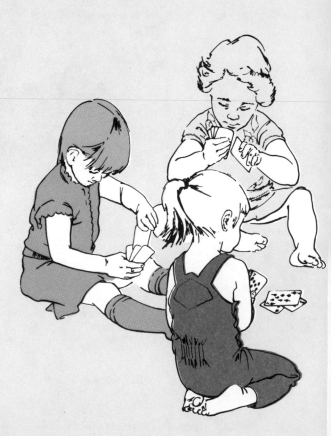

Deal Each player cuts the cards and the one with the highest card (ace high) is the dealer. He deals out all the cards in a clockwise direction, one at a time and face down.

Play Each player looks at his cards and sorts them into suits in his hand.

The player to the dealer's left starts play by choosing a card from his hand and placing it, face up, in the center.

The other players, in turn, then try to play one card of the same suit.

If all the players are able to "follow suit," these cards (called a "trick") are put to one side and are out of play for the rest of the game. The player who played the highest card (with ace high) then starts the next trick by playing another card into the centre.

If any player is unable to follow suit, he must pick up the cards already played for that trick and add them to his own hand. He then plays the first card of the next trick, but must not use any of the cards that he has just picked up.

End The winner is the first person to play all his cards.

Rank of cards

High

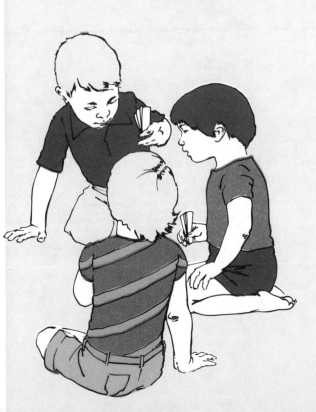

Low

©DIAGRAM

Sequence

A sequence

This game is easily learned but calls for a little skill in choosing which card to play when starting a sequence.

Players Two or more can play sequence but it is best with four or five players.

Cards A standard deck of playing cards is used.

Objective Each player aims to be first to get rid of all his cards.

Deal One player is chosen as dealer. He deals out all the cards in a clockwise direction, one at a time and face down. It does not matter if some players have one card more than others.

Play The player to the left of the dealer starts by putting his lowest card of any suit face up in the center. (2s count as the lowest cards and aces as the highest.)

The player with the next card in sequence then plays it face up onto the card in the center. A card is in sequence if it is of the same suit as the last card that was played and follows the order 2, 3, 4, 5, 6, 7, 8, 9, 10, j, q, k, a.

Play continues in this way until the ace is played and the sequence ends.

A player who ends a sequence starts another by playing any card from his hand.

When part of a suit has already been played, a sequence ends with the highest card yet to play. The following sequence is then started by the player who played this highest card.

End The first player to get rid of all his cards is the winner.

Scoring If more than one round is to be played, players may each start with 10 counters or beans.

At the end of every round each loser pays the winner one bean for every card still in his hand.

The winner is the player with most counters or beans after an agreed number of rounds.

©DIAGRAM

Slapjack

This is an exciting game that needs no skill. It can be enjoyed by the very young as the only requirement is that players can recognize a jack.

Players Two or more can play.
Cards Standard playing cards are used. If there are more than three players it is a good idea to mix two decks together. It does not matter if a few cards are missing.
Objective Players aim to win all the cards.
Deal One player deals out all the cards in a clockwise direction – one at a time and face down. It does not matter if some players have one card more than others.
Each player puts his cards into a neat pile face down in front of him. Players are not allowed to look at their cards.
Play The player to the dealer's left turns over the top card of his pile and places it face up in the center.
Turns then pass around to the left, with each player placing his card on top of the previous player's card.
Slapping a jack When a jack is turned up, each player tries to be the first to put his hand on the card – ie to "slap the jack."
The successful player wins the central pile of cards and shuffles

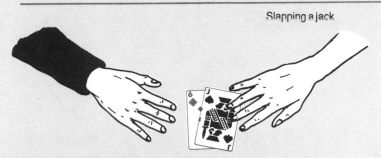

Slapping a jack

them with his own cards to form his new face-down pile.
The player to the winner's left starts the next round, placing a
card face up in the center.

If more than one player puts his hand on the jack, the winner is
the player whose hand is underneath.

If possible it is a good idea to appoint a referee to settle
arguments.

If a player loses all his cards he can stay in the game if he is first
to slap the next jack.

If he fails to slap the next jack he must retire from the game.

Penalty If a player slaps a card that is not a jack, he must give
his top card to the player whose card he slapped in error.

End The winner of the game is either:

a) the first person to collect all the cards; or

b) the player with the most cards at the end of a time limit set at
the start of the game.

Snap

Amusing and noisy, snap is among the most familiar of all children's card games.

Players Two or more can play.
Cards Special snap cards can be bought but the game is just as much fun with standard playing cards.
It is best to use old cards in case of damage, and it does not matter if any of the cards is missing.
If there are more than three players it is a good idea to use two decks of cards.
Objective Players aim to win all the cards.
Deal One player deals out all the cards in a clockwise direction – one at a time and face down. It does not matter if some players have one card more than the others.
Each player puts his cards into a neat pile face down in front of him.
Players are not allowed to look at their cards.

Play The player to the dealer's left turns over the top card of his pile and places it face up to start a face-up pile of cards next to his face-down pile.

The next player to his left does the same, and so on around the players until any player sees that the cards on the top of any two face-up piles have the same value (eg two 10s).

Snap The first player to shout "Snap" when there are matching cards on the top of two face-up piles, collects both these piles of cards and puts them at the bottom of his own face-down pile. Players now continue turning cards over as before, beginning with the player to the left of the last player who turned over a card.

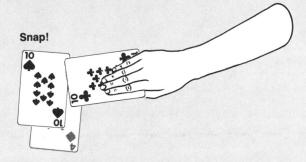

Snap!

Snap pool If two players shout "snap" together, the matching face-up piles are put face up in a pool in the center.

Players then continue to turn over cards, and the pool is won by the first player to shout "snap pool" when the top card of any player's face-up pile matches the top card of the pool.

No more cards When a player runs out of face-down cards he simply turns over his face-up cards when it is next his turn to play.

Penalty There are different rules for when a player calls "Snap" in error:

a) the player gives one card from his face-down pile to each of the other players;

b) the player's own face-up pile is put into a central pool to be won like an ordinary snap pool.

End The game ends when only one player has any cards.

EASY SNAP

This version is particularly suitable for very young children. Instead of having individual face-up piles, each player plays his cards onto a central face-up pile. Players shout "Snap" when the top two cards are of the same value.

SPEED SNAP

In this faster version of snap, players still turn their cards up one at a time but all players do so together.

©DIAGRAM

Snip-snap-snorem

Sample play

A game with funny words to say, snip-snap-snorem is noisy, fast-moving, and fun to play.

Players It is a game for three or more players.
Cards A standard deck of playing cards is used.
Objective Each player aims to be the first to get rid of all his cards.
Deal Each player cuts the cards and the one with the highest card (ace high) is the dealer.
He deals out all the cards in a clockwise direction, one at a time, and face down.
It does not matter if some players have one card more than the others.

Snip

Play Each player looks at his cards without letting any other player see them, and sorts them in his hand.
Turns pass clockwise around the players, starting with the player to the dealer's left.
The first player places any one of his cards face up in the center.
If the next player has a card of the same rank (eg another queen, if the first player played a queen), he places this face up in the center of the table and shouts "Snip" as he plays it.
If he has another card of the same rank he keeps it until his next turn.
If he does not have a card of the same rank, he says "Pass" and play moves on around the players.
The next player with a card of the same rank shouts "Snap" when he plays it, and the player of the fourth card shouts "Snorem!"
The player of the fourth card starts the next round.

Snap

End The winner is the first player to play all his cards.
Variation If a player has more than one card of the same rank, he must play them all in the same turn, saying the appropriate words.

Snorem!

JIG

This is played exactly like snip-snap-snorem except that instead of playing four cards of the same rank, a sequence of four cards is played.
For example, if the first player puts down a 5, this is followed by a 6, then a 7, and finally an 8.
The cards can be from different suits.
Players call out "Jiggety, joggety, jig" when playing the cards.

© DIAGRAM

Spit

Spit is an excellent game that calls for alertness and speed.

Players Two persons can play.
Cards A complete deck of standard cards is used.
Deal All the cards are dealt out equally between the two players.
Before play starts, each player lays out a row of cards in front of him, as follows:
1) starting from the left, he places three cards face down followed by a fourth card face up;
2) he places a second face-down card on each of the first two face-down cards and a face-up card on the third;
3) he places a face-down card on the first pile and a face-up card on the second;
4) he places a face-up card on the first pile.
Each player then places the rest of his cards face down in a pile to the left of his row.

Objective Each player aims to be the first to get rid of all his cards.

Start of play When both players are ready, either one of them calls "Spit!"

Immediately both players take the top card from their piles of spare cards and place them face up, side by side, in the center.

Playing into the center Each player then quickly plays as many cards as possible from his row of face-up cards onto either of the face-up cards in the center of the table.

A card may be played into the center if it has a numerical value either one higher or one lower than a central face-up card. (For example, a 9 or a jack can be played onto a 10. Either a king or a 2 can be played onto an ace.)

If playing a face-up card into the center exposes a face-down card in a player's row, this card should be turned face up.

Players continue to play cards onto the central piles in this manner until neither player can put out any more of his cards.

Spit If neither player can play any card from his row of face-up cards, one of the players shouts "Spit!"

Both players take the top card from the piles of spare cards and place them face up on their central piles.

If possible, players then resume playing cards into the center from their face up piles.

If players still cannot add any cards from their face-up rows, the other player calls "Spit!" and both players again play the top card of their spare piles. They continue in this way until either player can play a card from his row.

If a player wishes to call "Spit!" and the players' spare piles have been used up, each player takes his own central pile and turns it face down to form a new spare pile. The player then calls "Spit!" and play continues as before.

End of a round When a player has played all the cards from his face-up row into the center, he shouts "Out!" and wins the round. He then picks up his spare pile.

The other player then collects both central face-up piles, picks up the cards left in his row, and adds all these cards to the bottom of his spare pile.

Starting a new round Players lay out their cards as for the first round.

New rounds are played in the same way as the first round, except that if one player does not have enough cards for a spare pile he does without and both players play onto a single central pile.

End of game A game is won by the first player to get rid of all his cards.

Stealing bundles

As soon as a player can spot that two cards have the same rank (face value), he is old enough to play stealing bundles. Other names for this game are old man's bundle and stealing the old man's bundle.

Players Two or four people can play.
Cards A standard deck of playing cards is used.
Objective Each player tries to collect as many cards as possible.
Deal One person is chosen as dealer. He deals the cards in a clockwise direction, one at a time and face down, until each player has four cards.
The dealer then places four cards face up in a row in the center.
Play The player to the left of the dealer begins.
If he has a card of the same rank as one of the cards in the center, he captures that card. He places the captured card and his matching card face up in a pile in front of him. This is the beginning of his "bundle."

If two or three center cards have the same rank as one of the player's cards he may capture them all in the same turn.

If none of the player's cards matches a center card, he must place one of his own cards face up in the center. This is called "trailing."

Each player then plays one card in turn. In place of or in addition to capturing cards from the center, he may steal another player's bundle if his card matches the top card of that bundle.

Every time a player captures cards he places them in his bundle with the matching card face up.

If none of his cards matches any face-up card he must "trail" one of his cards.

Extra deals When all the players have played each of the four cards in their hands, the dealer deals out four more cards to each player. No cards are dealt to the center. Play then continues as before.

End The game ends when all the cards have been dealt and played.

The winner is the player with most cards in his bundle when play ends.

War

Rank of cards
High

Low

An easy game, war is a good way of introducing young children to card playing.

Players This game is for two people.
Cards A complete deck of standard playing cards is used.
Objective Each player aims to win all the cards.
Deal One player deals all the cards.
Each player puts his cards into a neat pile face down in front of him. Players are not allowed to look at their cards.
Play Both players turn over the top card of their piles, and place them face up, side by side, in the center.
The player who has played the higher card, regardless of suit, wins both cards and places them face down at the bottom of his pile.
Aces are the highest cards, followed by kings, queens, jacks, and so on down from the 10s to the 2s.
The "war" If the two cards turned up have the same value, the war is on.
Each player puts one card face down on top of his first card in the center. He then puts another card face up on top of this.
The two new face-up cards are compared, and the highest card wins all six cards in the center.
If the face-up cards match again, the war continues. Each player puts out another face-down card with a face-up card on top. Play continues in this way until someone plays a card higher than the other.
End The winner of the game is either:
a) the first player to win all the cards; or
b) the player with the most cards at the end of a time limit set at the start of the game.

"War"

Player A

Player B

Player B
wins all
six cards

WAR FOR THREE PLAYERS

This version of war is for three players.

Deal The cards are dealt out as for war for two, except that the last card is not dealt out. (In this way, all three players begin with the same number of cards.)

Play is the same as in war for two, except that:

a) when two cards of the same value are turned up, all three players engage in war;

b) when three cards of the same value are turned up, the players engage in double war.

In double war each player puts out two cards face down and then one card face up. If the cards still match, the three players then continue with single war.

PERSIAN PASHA

Persian pasha, also called pisha pasha, is a similar game to war.

Players It is game for two players.

Cards A complete deck of standard playing cards is used.

Objective Each player aims to win all the cards.

Deal Cards are dealt as for war.

Play Each player turns over his top card and places it on a face-up pile next to his face-down pile.

Players continue turning over cards until their top face-up cards are of the same suit.

The player with the higher card then takes all the other player's face-up pile and puts these cards at the bottom of his face-down pile.

Section 4
Gambling card games

Introduction

Included in this section are card games that are played primarily for gambling. This is not to suggest that some of them are any less interesting or demanding to play than some of the games included as general card games in section 1 of this book. Indeed, blackjack and poker in particular both call for high levels of skill from their players. A number of the games included here are professional games rarely found outside casinos and gambling clubs. Others are private games suitable for more general play.

Casino and gambling club games Depending on the game being played, betting in casinos and gambling clubs may be either against the house management acting as banker or against other players. As well as winning money by acting as banker in some games, managements charge players for the services of their officials and also take a percentage cut when money changes hands between players. Casino and gambling club games described in this section are: baccarat/chemin de fer, blackjack, card craps, faro, monte bank, poker, skinball, trente et quarante, and ziginette. Some of these games are also suitable for playing at home.

Private banking games In these games one player acts as banker, taking on the bets of all the others. He also has a different role to the other players in play. But unlike in casino banking games no one person is banker continuously. Instead, to equalize players' chances, the role of banker moves around – often after every hand. Private banking games included in this section are: ace-deuce-jack, banker and broker, Blücher, card put-and-take, Chinese fan-tan, hoggenheimer, horse race, lansquenet, monte bank (private version), Polish red dog, red and black, red dog (banking version), and slippery Sam.

Pool games In these private gambling games there is no banker. Instead, all players' bets take the form of contributions to a central pool. In many games the entire pool is then won by a single player – usually at the end of every hand – but in other games the pool acts as a reservoir of chips, from which payments are made to players according to their success. Pool games included here are: bango, brag, injun, Kentucky derby, red dog, thirty-five, thirty-one, and yablon.

NOTES ON BETTING

Betting chips When playing private gambling games, any counters, matchsticks, or other agreed objects may be used.

An ante is a contribution to a central betting pool made before a deal. It may be required from all the players or sometimes only from the dealer.

Odds The recognized forms in which payment odds are stated are:

a) "x to y" (eg 30 to 1, also written as 30-1), in which case the player's stake is returned in addition to the win payment (giving a player who staked one chip at 30 to 1 a return of 31 chips); or

b) "x for y" (eg 30 for 1), in which case the player's stake is returned as part of the win payment (giving a player a total return of 30 chips in our example).

©DIAGRAM

Ace-deuce-jack

The odds in this game are so heavily loaded that it is found only as a hustler's game. The hustler simply has to ensure that the sucker is on the wrong side of the particular version being played – in which case the sucker will on average lose his money in nearly 60 plays out of 100.

Equipment:
1) one standard deck of 52 cards;
2) money for betting.
Players Two or more can play. One player is banker.

WITH THE HUSTLER AS BANKER
Objective Players bet that none of the three cards exposed in play will be an ace, deuce (2), or jack.
Betting limits are agreed beforehand.
Shuffle and cut The banker shuffles. Any player has the right to shuffle but the banker has the right to shuffle last. Any player other than the banker then cuts the deck.
Preparation
1) The banker takes three cards face down from the bottom of the deck, making sure that no one sees their denominations. These three cards are ruled "dead," and are put to one side.
2) The banker then cuts two groups of cards from the deck, taking care that no one sees the bottom card of each cut. He places each group face down alongside the deck, so that there are now three groups of cards on the table.
Bet and play Each player but the banker may place a bet. The banker then turns the three sections face up, exposing the bottom card of each section.
Settlement If any one of the three cards is an ace, deuce, or jack, the banker takes all bets. If none of the cards is one of these denominations, the banker pays 1 to 1 on all bets.
Continuing play All cards in the deck are collected, shuffled, and then cut for the next turn of play.

Deal   Show

WITH THE SUCKER AS BANKER

Sometimes the sucker wants to be banker. The hustler then suggests the following version, in which players bet on which denomination will appear. "You bank, and we'll do the guessing too," says the hustler. "You can't help but win."

On a big hustle, with a planned victim, the hustler may set up this version from the beginning.

Objective Players bet that one of the three cards exposed in play will be one of three specified denominations.

Betting limits are agreed beforehand.

Shuffle, cut, and preparation are as for the version with the hustler as banker.

Betting Each player but the banker may place a bet. Sometimes the betting denominations are as in the first version, ie ace, deuce, jack.

But usually the three denominations change for each hand, and are chosen by the players as they place their bets.

This "guessing" process gives the banker the impression that the odds are with him.

Play The banker turns the three sections face up, exposing the bottom card of each section.

Settlement If none of the three cards is one of the three denominations bet on, the banker takes all bets.

But if any one or more of the denominations appear, the banker pays 1 to 1 on all bets. (Note that he pays only 1 to 1 even if two or three denominations appear.)

Continuing play is as in the first version.

Baccarat/Chemin de fer

Games of the baccarat and chemin de fer family originated in the baccarat that became popular in French casinos in the 1830s. In the present century they have travelled from Europe to the United States, from the United States back to Europe, and from both points to casinos throughout the world. This process has resulted in wide variations in playing rules, and what is called "baccarat" in one casino may more nearly resemble the "chemin de fer" of another. Three basic forms of play are described here.

Players: at least two, but usually seven or more. Often persons without seats may also bet.

Croupier The casino provides a croupier, who assists players in making and settling bets, advises on rules and odds, and takes the casino's cut. The croupier also plays the "bank" hand when the game is banked by the casino. The casino makes an hourly charge for the croupier and his assistants, and for supervising the game.

The objective is to bet on a winning hand, ie on a hand with a higher point value than the other hand(s).

Hands are of two or three cards.
Cards score as follows:
a) face (court) cards and 10s, zero;
b) aces, one point;
c) any other card, its numerical value.
When scoring a hand tens are ignored – eg five plus seven counts as two not 12. Hence the highest possible score for a hand is nine.

The basic sequence of play is:
1) placing of bets;
2) dealing of hands;
3) receipt of another card on request;
4) comparison of hands and settlement of bets.

Equipment Several standard decks of playing cards are used. Other equipment is:
a) a heavy table, padded and covered with green baize, and marked with a layout for nine or 12 players;
b) a card-holding box or "shoe," from which the cards are dealt one at a time;
c) a discard box, positioned beneath a slot in the table;
d) wooden palettes for distributing cards and payments to the players.

Card values

© DIAGRAM

CHEMIN DE FER

The distinctive features of the "chemin de fer" game are that:
the role of banker rotates rapidly among the players;
only a bank hand and one non-bank hand are dealt;
bets can only be placed against the bank.

Cards Six or eight standard decks of cards are used.

The shuffle

1) The croupier places the decks face down on the table.

2) Players and croupier take groups of cards and shuffle them, and then shuffle the groups of cards into each other.

3) The croupier gathers the cards, gives them a final shuffle in large groups, gathers them all into a single deck, and cuts the deck several times.

4) The croupier asks one of the players to make a final cut. (Often the croupier makes the actual cut, after the player has inserted an indicator (a blank or advertising) card at the point where the cut should be made.)

5) Often the croupier then inserts a second indicator card into the deck, around eight or ten cards from the bottom, to give warning of the end of the shuffled cards.

6) The croupier places the deck face down in the shoe.

7) The croupier deals three or four cards from the shoe, shows them, and discards them.

Chemin de fer layout

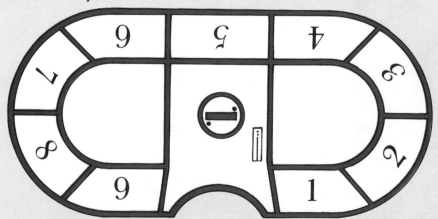

First choice of banker is either:

a) by lot;

b) by auction, with the players bidding the amounts they are prepared to put forward as the "bank";

c) by acceptance, the bank being offered first to the first player to the croupier's left or right (according to house rules), and then on around the table, clockwise or counterclockwise, until a player accepts the bank.

The croupier passes the shoe to the first banker.

Amount of the bank On the first play of a turn as banker, the bank is:

a) what the player bid for it if the bank was gained by auction;

b) any figure the banker wishes to put at risk if he gained the bank by lot or acceptance.

On all subsequent plays of a turn as banker, the bank is the amount stated on the first play plus subsequent winnings.

Betting takes place before any cards are dealt.

Players can only place bets against the bank – ie they bet that the bank will lose.

The total of bets on a single play is limited to the amount of the bank – the banker is never liable for payment of bets in excess of this.

The player to the banker's right (or left, according to house rules) has first bet. Any amount of the bank he does not "fade" (bet against), may be bet against by the next player in turn.

Betting passes around the table until the entire bank is covered by several bets, someone has called "Banco," or everyone has bet who wishes to.

Bystanders may bet if there is part of the bank left to cover or if one of them calls "Banco."

If the bank is not completely covered, the amount not faded is safe for the hand and is kept by the banker whether he wins or loses.

"Banco" A player or bystander who wishes to bet against the entire bank makes this known by calling "Banco." A call of "Banco" makes all other bets void.

When two or more wish to banco, a player who bancoed on the preceding hand has precedence over all others.

Otherwise, a seated player has precedence over a bystander and the order of priority among players belongs to the player who is earliest in the betting order.

Natural 8s

Natural 9s

Play is as follows.

1) The banker deals two hands of two cards each. The cards are dealt singly and face down, alternately to the table and to the banker himself. The "table" hand represents all players betting against the bank. It is played by whoever made the highest bet against the bank. If there are two equal bets, the player nearer the banker in the betting order has priority.

2) The player and banker examine their hands without showing them.

3) If the player's hand totals eight or nine, it is a "natural," and is immediately declared and turned face up. If it is an eight hand, the player calls "La petite"; if a nine he calls "La grande."

4) If the player's hand is a natural, the banker shows his own cards. If only the player's hand is a natural, all bets against the bank win. If both hands are naturals, a nine beats an eight. If both hands are naturals of the same number, it is a "stand-off" and all bets are returned.

5) If the player's hand does not contain a natural, he says "Pass." The banker then examines his own hand, and if it contains a natural he declares it immediately and wins all bets.

6) If both hands have been examined, and neither contains a natural, the player may "draw" (request another card, face up) or "stay" (not request another card). His decision must be based on the rules of mathematical advisability (see table), except that in some games a player who has bancoed is allowed to ignore these rules.

7) Whether the banker then draws another card or stays depends on the card that he has just given to the player (see table), except that in some games the banker is allowed the option when holding a five hand and having given a four. If a player has bancoed and is allowed to use his judgment, the banker may also ignore the rules for drawing or staying.

8) The hands are shown. If there has been any error, the banker must reconstruct the play as it should have been.

Winning The hand totalling nine or nearest nine wins.

a) If the totals are the same, all bets are returned.

b) If the banker has won, he collects all bets less any casino levy. In most countries the casino levies a percentage (usually 5%) on bankers' winnings. Sometimes the winnings on a player's first hand as banker are exempt from the levy. (In countries where a percentage levy is illegal, all casino profits come from the hourly rate charged by the casino.)

c) If the banker has lost, each player collects the amount of the bank that he had covered.

Keeping the bank If the banker has won a hand, he may keep the bank for the next hand.

In this case, the new bank comprises the original bank plus the winnings after any levy.

A player who keeps the bank is not permitted to remove any of his winnings between hands.

If the original bank plus winnings exceeds the house limit on bets, the excess is not at stake.

Passing the bank If the banker has won a hand but chooses not to keep the bank, he may take his winnings and pass the bank. In this case:

a) the bank is offered to the players in turn until one of them accepts it, after which the new banker decides the amount of his bank; or

b) the house croupier holds an informal auction, and the bank passes to a player who will put up a bank equal to the one that has just been passed.

Losing the bank If the banker loses a hand, the bank is offered to the players in turn – as when the banker chooses to pass the bank. (An auction is not held.)

Reshuffling The cards are not reshuffled until at least 5/6 of the deck has been used – and usually not until the last few cards are reached.

Player

Player holding	Action
0, 1, 2, 3, or 4	draw
5	optional
6 or 7	stay
8 or 9	face

Banker

After giving	Banker stays on	Banker draws on
0 or 1	4, 5, 6, 7	3, 2, 1, or 0
9	4, 5, 6, 7, (or 3)	2, 1, 0, (or 3)
8	3, 4, 5, 6, or 7	2, 1, or 0
7 or 6	7	6, 5, 4, 3, 2, 1, or 0
5 or 4	6 or 7	5, 4, 3, 2, 1, or 0
3 or 2	5, 6, or 7	4, 3, 2, 1, or 0
Player has stood	6 or 7	5, 4, 3, 2, 1, or 0

BACCARAT BANQUE

Also known as *baccarat à deux tables* (double table baccarat), baccarat banque is the oldest European form of the game.

The distinctive features of baccarat banque are that:

a) the role of the banker rotates more slowly among the players or may be held permanently by the casino or concessionaires;

b) one bank hand and two non-bank hands are dealt;

c) bets can be placed only against the bank.

Except when specifically described here, the rules are the same as for chemin de fer.

Cards Three standard decks are used.

Banker Sometimes the role of banker is held permanently by the casino – or by concessionaires who pay the casino a percentage of their takings.

Otherwise the procedure is as follows.

a) The bank is auctioned to the highest bidder, who pays 2½% of his bid to the casino.

b) The banker does not lose the bank if he loses a hand, but holds it until he loses the whole bank or passes.

c) The banker cannot withdraw any money from the bank unless he passes – but any part of the bank not bet against on a hand is not at risk.

d) When a bank is lost or passed, the bank is again auctioned. As before, the casino takes a 2½% cut from the winning bidder.

Baccarat banque layout

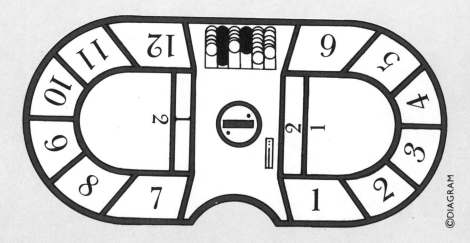

©DIAGRAM

Betting and play differ from chemin de fer in the following ways.

a) The banker deals three hands – one to his right, one to his left, and one to himself.

b) Bets against the bank may be placed on either the right or the left hand, or on both hands. Betting on both hands is called betting "*à cheval*" (on horseback).

c) Priority for betting on the right table hand begins with the player sitting to the banker's right; for the left table hand, with the player to the banker's left. Calling "Banco" is usually allowed, but not always.

d) Each hand is played by a player on the appropriate side of the table. The player playing the right hand always plays first. On the first deal, the hands are played by the players nearest the dealer on his right and left sides.

Thereafter, a player continues playing one of the table hands until he loses a hand. After a player has lost a hand, the right to play that side's hand passes to the next player in rotation.

e) Table players are bound by the same staying and drawing rules as in chemin de fer. The banker may stay or draw on any hand, and will obviously concentrate on beating the hand on which most money has been bet.

f) Players betting *à cheval* lose only if the bank wins both hands, and win only if the bank loses both hands. Otherwise their bets are returned.

BACCARAT-CHEMIN DE FER (LAS VEGAS)

The distinct Las Vegas form of the game may be called baccarat, chemin de fer, or baccarat-chemin de fer.

The distinctive features of the Las Vegas game are that:

a) the role of the banker is usually held permanently by the casino, although it may rotate slowly among the players;

b) one non-bank hand is dealt;

c) bets can be placed either with or against the bank.

Cards Six or eight standard decks are used.

Banker When the role of banker rotates among the players, the rules for the bank are the same as for baccarat banque.

More usually the casino keeps the bank, and the procedure is as follows.

a) The limit on bets on a hand is not the size of the bank but the house betting limit. (The house betting limit will, however, sometimes be raised when a player requests this.)

b) There is no banco bet and no need for rules of precedence in betting.

c) A single player can play.

d) The casino takes a cut (usually 5%) from winning bets that have bet the bank to win.

Betting Players may bet with or against the bank.

A player betting the bank to win places his bet on the appropriate numbered section at the table center.

A player betting the bank to lose places his bet on the numbered section in front of him.

A player may also back the bank to have a natural eight or nine, and if successful, he is paid the odds of nine to one.

Baccarat-Chemin de fer layout

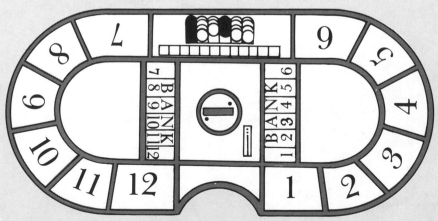

Play is as in chemin de fer, except that all players' and banker's options are removed to become draw plays. Thus:
a) a player must draw if holding a hand totaling five;
b) the banker must draw if holding a three hand when he has given a nine, or a five hand after giving a four.

Bango

In this card variant of the bingo played in bingo halls, players turn over playing cards instead of covering rows of numbers on a score card.

Equipment
1) two standard 52-card decks, with different backs;
2) betting chips.
Players The game is for three to ten players.
Objective Each player aims to be the first player to turn all his face-up cards face down.
Choice of first dealer is by deal: first ace to appear. (See p 381.)
Shuffle and cut The dealer and the player to his left each shuffle one deck of cards. Each deck is then offered separately to the player to the dealer's right to be cut as usual (see p 381).
Ante Before each deal, each player including the dealer puts an equal agreed amount into the pool.
Deal From one deck, the dealer deals five cards to each player

including himself, dealing them face up and one at a time. The rest of this deck is then put to one side out of play.

Play The players arrange their cards face up in front of them. The dealer then takes the second deck of cards and deals the top card face up onto the table, stating its rank and suit as he does so.

If any player including the dealer has the identical card from the first deck face up in front of him, he now turns that card face down.

The dealer then takes the next card from the top of the second deck and deals it face up onto the table, stating its rank and suit as he does so.

Play continues in this way until one player has turned all his cards face down. He announces this by calling "Bango."

Checking The dealer checks the hand of the player who called against the cards that have been dealt from the second deck, and if no mistake has been made that player wins the pool.

Change of dealer The deal passes one player to the left after each hand.

BANGO VARIANT

In this game players take into account only the rank of the cards turned up by the dealer. The dealer calls the rank and players turn face down all cards of that rank in their hands.

Deal

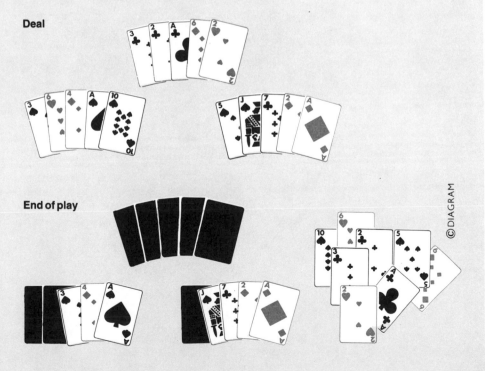

End of play

©DIAGRAM

Banker and broker

This simple game has very fast betting action. Also known as Dutch bank and blind hooker, it is played in a number of slightly different ways.

Equipment:
1) one standard deck of 52 cards;
2) betting chips (or cash).
Players: two or more.
Rank of cards is normal (ace high). Suits are not ranked.
Objective Players try to bet on a card of higher denomination than that bet on by the banker.
Choice of first banker is by high cut (see p 381).
Shuffle and cut are normal (see p 381).
Betting limits are as agreed.

Deal

Play

Basic form of play

1) The banker cuts a number of sections from the deck: one for himself and one for each of the other players.

2) The other players lay bets on their sections by placing chips (or cash) beside them.

3) The banker turns all the sections face up to show the bottom cards.

4) The banker collects the bets on sections showing a lower denomination card than his own. He pays 1 to 1 on sections showing a card of higher denomination.

Points of variation

1) Discarding the bottom card: either the banker removes and discards the bottom card from the deck before cutting; or he leaves an unused bottom section after cutting.

2) Timing of bets: bets are placed either before or after the sections are cut.

3) Number of sections cut:

either the banker cuts one section for each player and one for himself (up to a limit of seven), and each player may only bet on the section cut for him; or

the banker cuts three sections, two for the players and one for himself, and each player bets at will on either or both of the players' sections; or

the banker cuts as many sections as he likes, varying the number from deal to deal if he wishes, and the players bet as they please but leave one section for the banker.

4) When the banker's denomination is the same as that bet on by a player: either the bank wins, or the player's bet is returned.

5) Change of banker:

either the bank passes one player to the left after each deal or set number of deals; or

players cut for the bank after each deal or after a set number of deals; or

the bank is passed when a player bets on an ace – if two players (or player and banker) both have an ace, or if two players have bet on the same ace, the deck is cut and the bank goes to the player with the higher card.

Blackjack

Blackjack is the world's most widespread banking card game. It is also known as BJ, twenty-one, vingt-et-un, pontoon, and vanjohn. There are two main forms: that with a "changing bank" – the usual private game; and that with a "permanent bank" – the casino game. The two forms of the game have many features in common.

Players Games are played by a banker/dealer and from one to six or seven or more other players (private games can have as many as 14 other players).

Value of cards Standard playing cards are used.
a) An ace counts as 1 or 11, at the option of the holder.
b) A "face" card counts as 10.
c) All other cards count their numerical face value.
A joker, if used, is only an indicator card and does not enter play.

Objective Each player tries to get a higher point count in his hand than the dealer – but the value of his hand must not exceed 21. A hand whose point count exceeds 21 is immediately lost.

A two-card hand with a value of exactly 21 (a face card, or 10, and an ace) is called a "natural" or a "blackjack."

Betting With the exception of the dealer, each player bets at the beginning of each hand. Only bets against the dealer are allowed.

At the end of each hand, the dealer pays those with point counts higher than his own.

Onlookers may be allowed to bet on any player's hand, but not on the dealer's hand.

Basic sequence of play
1) Betting, and deal of two cards to each player.
2) Receipt of further cards on request by each player in turn – with the dealer last.
3) Settlement of bets.

BLACKJACK WITH A CHANGING BANK

Cards A standard deck of 52 cards (or sometimes two decks shuffled together), plus a joker that does not enter play.

Choice of first banker/dealer is by deal: usually the first ace, but in some versions the first black jack, decides (see p 381 for procedure).

Change of banker/dealer There are two alternative systems.
1) Each player has five deals as banker/dealer, after which the role passes to the next player to the left.
2) The deal passes whenever there is a hand in which a "natural" is dealt – ie when a player's first two cards total 21. The player with the natural has the option of becoming the new banker/dealer on the completion of that hand.

When two or more players hold naturals, the player nearest the dealer's left has the first option.

If all players with naturals refuse the option, the present banker/dealer continues – unless he also refuses, in which case the role is offered around the table clockwise, beginning with the player to the immediate left of the present banker/dealer. If all refuse, a new banker/dealer is chosen in the same way as the original one.

Card values

Examples of 21-point hands

©DIAGRAM

21-point hands

Auctioning the bank Private games are occasionally run so that the banker/dealer is always decided by auction.

In all private games, however, a player who no longer wants to be banker/dealer may, between hands, put the bank and deal up for auction.

However, if there are no bids he loses the bank and deal to the first player to his left (or, if that player refuses, the bank and deal are offered clockwise around the table until accepted or until a new dealer has to be chosen in the original way).

Shuffle and cut

1) The dealer shuffles the cards. (Any player has the right to shuffle at any time but the dealer has the right to shuffle last.)

2) Any other player cuts the cards. If several players want to cut, each of them must be allowed to do so.

3) The deck is placed, face down, on an upturned joker, which acts as an indicator card. (If no joker is available, the dealer "burns" a card – ie he takes the top card from the deck, shows it to all players and places it face up at the bottom of the deck. An ace may not be burned, and if an ace is turned up the deck must be reshuffled and cut again.)

Betting limits The dealer decides the minimum and maximum allowable bets, and can alter them at will between hands.

Bet and deal for the two forms of the private game The betting and dealing stage of the private game takes two main forms.

a) As in the casino blackjack game, the players place their bets before they have seen any of their own cards.

b) As in the pontoon game of the British Commonwealth, the players bet after looking at their own first card.

There is no standard way of distinguishing between these: American rules for private blackjack games may quote the pontoon form, while a few Americans use "pontoon" to mean standard blackjack. We have used the name "blackjack" for form (a), and "pontoon" for form (b).

Bet and deal: "blackjack"

1) Before any cards are dealt, each player but the dealer puts his bet in front of him in full view.

Dealer   Player 1

2) The dealer deals one card to each player but himself, face down, beginning with the player to his immediate left and going clockwise. He then deals one card to himself, face up.

3) A second card is then dealt to each player, including the dealer, face down.

4) If the dealer's face-up card is an ace or a card worth 10 points, the dealer looks at his face-down ("hole") card to see if he has a natural.

If he has, he immediately announces this and turns his cards face up. The other players then show their own cards. The dealer collects the bets of all players not having naturals; players with naturals usually have their bets returned, but in some versions of the game they also pay the dealer.

5) If the dealer's face-up card is not an ace or a 10 point, or if he finds that he does not have a natural, then the player to the dealer's left commences play.

©DIAGRAM

21-point hands

Bet and deal: "pontoon"

1) The dealer deals one card face down to each player, including himself, beginning with the player to his immediate left and going clockwise.

Each player, including the dealer, looks at his own card.

2) Each player, except the dealer, puts his bet in front of him in full view.

The dealer may call for all bets to be doubled. Any player refusing to double drops out of the hand and loses his original bet.

If the dealer has doubled, any other player may then redouble his own individual bet.

3) The dealer deals a second card, face up, to each player including himself.

4) The dealer then considers if he has a natural, as in the "blackjack" game. If he has a natural, he collects from each player twice the amount of that player's current bet – except that from any other player with a natural he collects only that player's bet.

5) If the dealer's face-up card is not an ace or a 10 point, or if he finds that he does not have a natural, then the player to the dealer's left commences play.

First player's hand The player to the dealer's left looks at his hand and commences play.

a) If he has 21 points, he shows his cards, claims a natural, and is paid by the dealer unless the dealer also has a natural.

b) If his card total is less than 21 points, he has the option of taking further cards.

If he feels that the points count he already holds is closer to 21 than the dealer is likely to achieve, then he can say "I stand," and he receives no further cards.

If he decides to attempt a total closer to 21, he can say "I draw" or "Hit me," and receives another card face up.

He can repeat this until he is satisfied with his hand, when he says "I stay." However, if his points count goes over 21 he must announce this immediately by saying "I bust."

If a player goes "bust," he turns his cards face up, the dealer collects his bet, and the player's cards are placed face up at the bottom of the deck. He is then out of the game until the next hand.

Subsequent player's hands Once a player has said "I stand," "I stay," or "I bust," play passes to the player to his left. This continues until all players have had the chance of drawing further cards.

Dealer's hand The dealer plays last.

If all players have bust, he simply discards his cards and begins the next hand.

Otherwise he turns his hidden card face up, and decides to stay or to "draw" (giving himself further cards, face up) until he is satisfied or he exceeds 21 (busts).

Once the dealer's hand is completed, all hands still in the game arc shown.

Doubling down is a procedure allowed in the "permanent bank" game and often incorporated in the "blackjack" form of the "changing bank" game.

In his turn a player may, after looking at his first two cards, decide to "double down" – ie with his original two cards face up, he doubles his original bet and receives one further card only, face down. He may not look at this card until the dealer turns it up after all other players and the dealer have completed their turns of play.

(Sometimes doubling down is allowed only when the first two cards total 10 or 11.)

Buying is a procedure sometimes played in the "pontoon" form of the "changing bank" game.

At his turn, a player may "buy" a card: instead of receiving a further card face up, he adds to his original bet and receives a further card face down. The amount of the additional bet must be at least the minimum, but not greater than the original bet.

Buying can be repeated for further cards if the player wishes; or he may "twist" – ie draw further cards face up in the normal way. However, once a player has twisted he is not allowed to buy.

Splitting pairs is a procedure allowed in the "permanent bank" game, and often incorporated in both the "blackjack" and "pontoon" forms of the "changing bank" game.

If a player's first two cards are a pair (eg two 6s or two kings), they may be "split" if the player wishes – ie they may be treated as the basis of two separate hands.

In his turn of play, the player with the pair turns it face up – one card to his right and one to his left. He places his original bet by one of the cards and an equal amount by the other.

The dealer then deals one card, face up, to the card to the player's right – after which the player plays this hand off in the normal way. When he has finished (stood, stayed, or bust), he receives another face-up card, dealt to the card to his left, and then plays off this hand.

If, on splitting and receiving a new card other than an ace, a player forms a further pair, he may split the pair again if he again puts out an amount equal to his original bet. Any further pairs may also be split.

If aces are split, one card may be drawn to each split ace.

A 21 point count made in two cards after splitting does not count as a natural – it is paid off at even money and the bank does not change hands.

Irregularities

a) If a player is missed on the first round of dealing, he must ask for a card from the top of the deck before the second round of dealing begins, or must stay out for that deal.

b) If a player receives two cards on the first round of dealing, he has the choice of: discarding either one, or playing both hands with his original bet on each.

c) If a player in the "pontoon" game receives his first card face up, he can either: bet, and receive the next card face down, or drop out of that hand.

d) If a player receives two cards on the second round of the dealing, he discards either one.

e) If a card appears face up in the deck, a player has the choice of accepting or refusing it.

f) If a player receives a card that he did not ask for, he may either keep or discard it.

g) If a player has stood on a total of over 21, he pays the dealer twice his original bet even if the dealer has bust.

(All discards are placed face up at the bottom of the deck. They may not be claimed by the next player in turn.)

Settlement If the dealer goes bust, he pays all players who have not bust.

If he does not bust, he collects the bets of all players with a lower total, and pays out to all players with a higher total who have not bust.

Where a player and the dealer have the same total, rules vary. Sometimes the player's bet is returned, but often (more commonly in the "pontoon" game) the dealer collects.

All winning bets are paid off by the dealer at even money, except that a player who has beaten the bank with a natural is paid off at two to one.

Continuing play As each bet is settled, the player's cards are given to the dealer and placed face up at the bottom of the deck.

Play of further hands then continues from the same deck, without a shuffle, until the face-up cards are reached. All face-up cards are then shuffled by the dealer, cut by another player, and a joker or burnt card is used as an indicator as before.

Bonus payments In the "pontoon" game, a player other than the dealer can win his bet with certain special hands. These hands are declared and paid off as soon as they have been achieved.

a) A hand with five or more cards totaling 21 or under: for a five-card hand, a player receives double his bet; for a six-card hand, a player receives four times his bet; for a seven-card hand, eight times his bet; and so on. The win stands even if the dealer achieves a total nearer to 21.

b) Triple 7s: for a 21 made with three 7s, a player receives three times his bet.

Bonus payments

a

b

c

c) 8, 7, 6: for a 21 made with an 8, 7, and 6, a player receives double his bet.

None of these is a special hand if held by the dealer. They are then judged only according to their points count: a banker's five-card hand is beaten by a player's hand with a higher point count, and a player's win on a natural stands against a banker's triple 7s or 8, 7, 6.

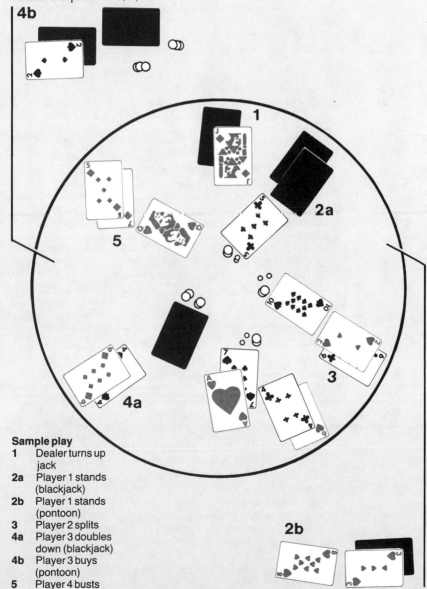

Sample play
1   Dealer turns up jack
2a   Player 1 stands (blackjack)
2b   Player 1 stands (pontoon)
3   Player 2 splits
4a   Player 3 doubles down (blackjack)
4b   Player 3 buys (pontoon)
5   Player 4 busts

©DIAGRAM

BLACKJACK WITH A PERMANENT BANK

Equipment:

a) a regulation blackjack table, with six or seven betting spaces on the layout;

b) a rack containing betting chips;

c) a card-dealing box ("shoe");

d) a discard receiver;

e) one, two, or four standard 52-card decks, shuffled together;

f) two blank or advertising cards to be used as indicator cards – one to cut the deck and one to mark the end of the shuffled cards.

Participants:

1) a permanent house dealer/banker;

2) one to six or seven active players.

There is also a casino observer/supervisor, who controls play and whose decision is final.

Shuffle and cut

1) Only the dealer shuffles. He may reshuffle at any time.

2) After he has shuffled, he offers the deck to a player to cut. (Casino regulations may require an "indicator card" cut, in which the dealer holds the deck and the player inserts a blank or advertising card to indicate the point where he wants the deck cut. The dealer then cuts the deck, with the indicator card going to the bottom.)

3) In many casinos, the dealer then inserts a second indicator card about 40 cards from the bottom of the deck to prevent the last cards of any shuffle coming into play.

4) If a shoe is being used, the dealer places the deck in it, face down.

5) The dealer then deals a few (usually three) cards from the top of the deck and places them to one side, out of play.

Betting limits The casino sets the minimum and maximum bet limits. (A casino will often agree to raise the maximum at a player's request.)

Bet and deal

1) Before any cards are dealt, each player except the dealer puts his bet on the layout in the betting space directly in front of him. If empty betting spaces are available, players are allowed in most casinos to bet on and receive more than one hand.

2) The dealer deals one card to each player, beginning with the player to his immediate left and going clockwise, and then deals one card to himself.

Then in the same way he deals a second card to each player and to himself. Whether cards are dealt face up or face down varies from casino to casino (see the section on dealing possibilities, p 576).

3) If the dealer's face-up card is a 10 point or an ace, he looks at his face-down card to see if he has a natural, exactly as in the "changing bank" game. If he has a natural, he

immediately collects the bets of all players who do not have naturals; players with naturals always have their bets returned.

(In some casinos, to prevent cheating by the collaboration of a player and a crooked dealer, the dealer is not allowed to look at, or sometimes even to deal, his own face-down card until all other players' hands are completed.)

4) If the dealer's face-up card is not a 10 point or an ace; or if he finds that he does not have a natural; or if he may not look at his face-down card: then the player to the dealer's left commences play.

© DIAGRAM

Dealing possibilities The usual arrangements are listed here, and shown in the diagrams.

a) Dealer and all players: first card received face down, second face up.

b) Dealer's first card face up, second face down; players' first and second cards face down.

c) Dealer's first card face up, second face down; players' first and second cards face up.

d) Dealer's first card face down, second face up; players' first and second cards face up.

e) Dealer's first card face up, second face down; players' first card face down, second face up.

Insurance bet If the dealer's face-up card is an ace, players are in many casinos allowed to place an insurance bet against being beaten by a dealer's natural.

Before the dealer looks at his face-down card, a player wishing for insurance puts out an amount equal to half his present bet. If the dealer has a natural, the player gets two to one on his insurance bet; otherwise the insurance bet is lost.

Play If a player is playing more than one hand, he must play out the hand farthest to his right before looking at his next hand or hands.

Play is as for the private game, with splitting and doubling down but no buying allowed.

Dealer's play In the "permanent bank" game, the dealer has no decisions to make:

a) if his count is, or reaches, 17 or more – he must stay;

b) if the count is 16 or less he must draw;

c) when he holds an ace he must accept a count of the ace as 11 and not draw if this gives him 17 or more without busting.

(As the dealer has no option in his play, it does not matter if he sees the players' hands. For this reason players' hands are dealt face up in some casinos.)

Settlement is as for the "changing bank" game, except that:

a) when a player and the dealer have the same total, the player's bet is always returned;

b) naturals are paid at odds of three to two, not two to one;

c) there are no bonus payments.

Irregularities are treated in the same way as in the "changing bank" game.

Dealing possibilities

$^{1}/_{2}$

$^{1}/_{2}$

$^{1}/_{2}$

Any value

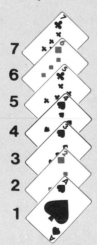

7

6

5

4

3

2

1

Ten and a half: values

$^{1}/_{2}$

$^{1}/_{2}$

$^{1}/_{2}$

VARIANTS OF BLACKJACK

There are a number of games whose basic differences from blackjack are the card values and the points count that the players are attempting to reach.

SEVEN AND A HALF

This is an Italian-American variant of blackjack. The rules are as for blackjack with the following exceptions.

Cards The 8s, 9s, and 10s are removed from a standard deck to give a deck of 40 cards. No indicator card is used.

Objective Players aim to get a total points count of $7^{1}/_{2}$: non-face cards count their face value, with aces 1 point; the king of diamonds can be given the value of any card the holder chooses;

other face cards each count $^{1}/_{2}$ point.

Play The player receiving the king of diamonds in a preliminary deal becomes the dealer for the first hand.

The dealer decides and alters betting limits at will. A player not wishing to bet on a round can say "Deal me out."

The deal is one card face down, after which a player stands or draws one or more cards face up.

$7^{1}/_{2}$ in two cards is announced and settled immediately. Unless the dealer also has $7^{1}/_{2}$ in two cards, it is paid double and wins the bank. (If two or more players have $7^{1}/_{2}$ in two cards, the bank goes to the player nearest the banker's left.)

Bust – 8 or more with any number of cards – is also settled immediately.

The dealer then plays, and pays surviving players with a higher total. He returns the bet of any player with the same total as himself.

The dealer shuffles the deck after every round.

TEN AND A HALF

Ten and a half or *"saton pong"* is the Dutch equivalent of seven and a half. The rules are as for seven and a half, with the following exceptions.

It is played with a standard 52-card deck.

Players aim for a total points count of $10^{1}/_{2}$. A count of $10^{1}/_{2}$ is announced immediately. $10^{1}/_{2}$ in two cards is paid double.

The dealer places discards at the bottom of the deck, face up. The deal changes by passing to the left when the whole deck has been used – though the current dealer is allowed to reshuffle used cards to complete a half finished hand.

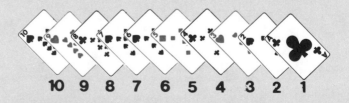

10   9   8   7   6   5   4   3   2   1

MACAO

Macao or "three naturals" is a variant of blackjack that was popular in the 1920s and 1930s.

It is played with a standard 52-card deck.

Players aim for a total points count of 9 in one or more cards.

Card values are:

zero for face cards and 10s;

the face value of all other cards (with aces counting 1).

The deal is one card, face down.

A player with a 9, 8, or 7 in one card announces it immediately. The dealer then shows his own card, and pays if the player's card is higher.

For a 9 in one card a winning player is paid three times his bet, for an 8 twice, and for a 7 one for one.

Players and dealer without a 7, 8, or 9 in one card, then draw one or more cards toward a total of 9.

The dealer then collects and pays out on remaining bets. A player who ties with the dealer has his bet returned.

Macao: values

K	0
Q	0
J	0
10	0
9	9
8	8
7	7
6	6
5	5
4	4
3	3
2	2
A	1

Race Results 8/7/32

LITTLE BUT	7 - 1
MONEYS DREAM	3 - ?
PINK HUME	5
LINK LOOK	
GONE	

FIFTEEN

Fifteen: values

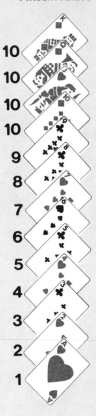

Fifteen, also called quince, cans, or ace low, is a blackjack variant for two players with one acting as dealer.

Players aim for a points count of 15. Face cards count 10; other cards their numerical face value (with ace as 1).

Dealer and non-dealer place equal amounts in a pool before the deal.

The deal is one card face down. The non-dealer stands, or draws one or more cards face up. He does not announce if he busts – he says only "I stay." The dealer then stands or draws. Both players then show their face-down cards. The player nearer 15 without busting wins. If both players tie or bust, bets are left in the pool for the next deal.

The loser of one hand deals for the next.

FARMER

This is an interesting variant of blackjack for two to eight players.

One player, the "farmer," is the equivalent of the banker/dealer in other games of the blackjack family, but in this game players also make an ante bet into a central pool or "farm."

The money in the farm is won only when a player has a points count of exactly 16; other settlements are made between player and farmer after each round.

Cards 45 cards are used: a standard 52-card deck with all the 8s and three of the 6s removed (the 6 of hearts is retained in the deck).

Objective Players aim for a total points count of 16: face cards count 10 points; other cards their face value (with ace as 1).

Farmer:
sample settlement

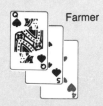

Farmer

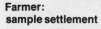

Player 3
loses

Player 2
wins the farm

Player 1
pays one unit

Choice of first farmer is as for the banker/dealer in blackjack, except that the deciding card is the 6 of hearts.

Ante bet Each player puts one unit into the farm.

Shuffle The farmer shuffles. Any other player has the right to shuffle, but the farmer has the right to shuffle last.

Cut The player to the farmer's right is offered the cut. If he does not wish to cut, any other player may do so. If no other player wishes to cut, the farmer must cut.

Deal The farmer deals one card face down to each player, including himself, beginning with the player to his left and going clockwise.

Play The player to the farmer's left begins. He looks at his card and then receives one further card from the farmer.

If his total now exceeds 16, he does not announce this but says "I stay" and receives no further cards. He does not show his hand.

If his card total is less than 16, he can either stay or receive further cards as he wishes.

When he is satisfied with his hand or when his total exceeds 16, he says "I stay," receives no further cards, and keeps his hand concealed.

Play then passes to the player to the first player's left, and play continues as described until all other players, including the farmer, have received at least one further card and had the chance to draw others.

Settlement At the end of the round, all hands are shown and settlement is as follows.

a) Each player who has a count of over 16 points must pay one unit to the farmer who dealt the hand. (The farmer does not have to pay anyone if his hand exceeds 16 points.)

b) A player holding 16 points wins the farm (the central pool) and becomes the next farmer. If more than one player holds a total of 16, the order of precedence when deciding the new farmer is:

the player with the 6 of hearts;
the player with the fewest cards;
the current farmer if he has 16 points;
the player nearest the farmer's left.

c) If no one holds a total of 16, the farm is not won. The player with the total nearest 16 then receives one unit from each player with a lower total (but not from players who have bust).

If two or more players have equal totals, they divide the units won from the other players. The same farmer then deals the next hand, and all players put a further ante into the farm.

Farmer: values

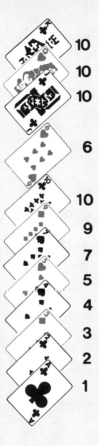

10
10
10
6
10
9
7
5
4
3
2
1

Blücher

This private banking game is named after a Prussian general who fought against Napoleon. Modified rules are given here.

Equipment:
1) one standard deck of 52 cards;
2) betting chips;
3) a betting layout with areas representing each denomination of card (it can be made up of cards from another deck, or may be drawn on paper).

Players: three or more.

Objective Players aim to bet on a denomination on the layout that is not matched during the hand.

A denomination is matched when the dealer, having called that denomination, turns up a card of that rank.

Choice of first banker is by high cut (see p 381).

Shuffle and cut are normal (see p 381).

Betting limits are agreed beforehand.

Betting Each player but the banker places as many bets on the layout as he wishes. Each bet must be placed on only one denomination.

Play The banker turns up cards one at a time from the top of the deck to form a face-up pile on the table. As he turns the first card up he says "Ace." He says "Deuce" for the second, "Three" for the third, and so on. For the eleventh, he says "Jack," for the twelfth, "Queen," and for the thirteeth, "King."

For each card, if the denomination of the exposed card matches the rank called, the bank collects any bets placed on that denomination on the layout.

For example, if the eighth card is an 8, the banker wins the bets on section 8; if the twelfth card is a queen, he wins the bets on the queen's section.

Each time the banker wins a bet on the layout, he is paid an additional equal amount by the player who made that bet.

When the banker has counted to king he begins again from ace, still turning up a card from the deck for each rank he calls.

The players may not add to, remove, or change their bets. The banker collects bets as before, if rank and card match.

Play continues in this way until the banker has counted from ace to king four times. All the deck has then been dealt.

Doubling This occurs if at any time the banker counts from ace to king without any of the 13 cards matching the rank called. The banker must then, with his own chips, double all players' bets that are then on the layout.

However, the bets stay on the layout and are still at risk. This doubling only takes place once in a single deal. If the banker counts from ace to king again without any cards matching, he does not add again to the players' bets.

If the banker wins a player's bet that has been doubled, he wins all the doubled bet plus an equal amount from the player.

Final settlement Any bets still on the layout at the end of the game are returned to the players who placed them.

Continuing play Bank and deal pass one player to the left. All the cards are collected for the next deal, and new bets are placed.

Brag

Brag was one of the ancestors of poker and still remains very popular in Britain. There are many forms and variants but basically the game is a form of three-card poker with no "draw."

Hands

Pryle

On a bike run

Run

Flush

Equipment:
a) one standard deck of 52 cards;
b) betting chips or cash.

Rank of hands A "hand" at brag contains only three cards. Originally only threes and pairs scored but today, through poker influences, all the following are generally recognized (with the highest listed first).
a) "Pryle": three cards of the same denomination.
b) "On a bike" run: three cards in sequence from the same suit.
c) Run: three cards in sequence.
d) Flush: three cards of the same suit.
e) Pair: two cards of the same denomination and one unmatched card.
f) "High card": three unmatched cards.

Rank of cards The cards rank in normal order, with ace high, except:
a) ace can rank low to make a 3, 2, ace run or on a bike run – which then counts as the highest hand of that rank, beating ace, king, queen.
b) for pryles only, a specified denomination varying with the game played (eg three 3s) is ranked above three aces.

Wild cards Today brag is usually played with no wild cards, or sometimes with 2s (deuces) wild.

However, the traditional wild cards for the game, listed in order of rank, are: ace of diamonds; jack of clubs; 9 of diamonds.

Hands of the same rank are valued according to the denomination of cards used – as in poker. For two special cases, see "rank of cards." Otherwise:
1) for pryles, on a bike runs, flushes, and high cards, the hand with the highest denomination card wins;
2) for pairs, the hand with the highest denomination pair wins or, if these match, the hand with the highest ranking odd card wins.

Rank of hands with wild cards A hand using wild cards is valued in the usual way (with the wild card valued according to the card it represents). However, a hand using wild cards loses to a hand that uses none.

Note that a pair using a wild card loses to the same pair in natural cards even if the wild card hand has the higher odd card.

Arrangements:
1) choice of first dealer is by low cut (see p 381).
2) shuffle and cut are normal (see p 381).

THREE-CARD BRAG
This is the basic form of the game.
Players: from three to 12.
The objective on each deal is to win the pool by holding the best ranking hand on a showdown or by having all the other players drop out of the betting.
Betting limits are agreed beforehand. Typical limits would be:
1) maximum one unit bet or raise;
2) one to five or one to ten units bet or raise.
Ante Sometimes rules specify that, before each deal, each player must contribute one unit to the pool.
Deal The dealer deals one card face down to each player, including himself, beginning with the player to his left going clockwise, and continuing until each player has three cards.
Play Players look at their hands and bet accordingly, beginning with the player to the dealer's left and going clockwise. Bets are placed in a central pool. Players may bet on any hand – bluffing is unrestricted.
There is only one betting interval. A player cannot "pass" and stay in the game – he must bet or drop out. If all the players but one drop out the remaining player wins the pool.
Otherwise betting continues until there is a showdown, when the player with the best hand wins. A showdown is not allowed until all players but two have dropped out.
Dealt cards are replaced at the bottom of the deck, face down. The cards are reshuffled for the next hand only if a pryle has just appeared on showdown.
Betting principles There are several alternatives:
a) "round the table";
b) "bet or raise";
c) poker betting.
Round the table betting Each time it is his turn to bet a player must bet one unit or drop out.
This continues even when there are only two players left, but then either player may in any of his turns pay a double amount to "see." Both players then show their cards without further betting.
Bet or raise In this system limits are agreed beforehand and affect only the opening bets and raises.
In the betting interval betting is as for the round the table system, but in any turn a player may choose to bet more than one unit.
All active players must then bet exactly the same amount each time their turn comes around – or must drop out or raise again. Raises are therefore not like the raises in poker. Instead of players just having to "call," they set a new minimum contribution to the pool per turn.

Pair

High card

Wild cards

Each player must contribute at least that full amount in subsequent turns – regardless of his previous contributions to the pool – or must drop out.

Each time the bet is raised only the increase is limited. The total bet of a player in a turn can therefore exceed the "limits."

As in the round the table system this can continue when only two players remain – until one of them pays double the amount at that time to see.

Poker betting is sometimes used (see poker, p 629). In this system the interval ends when bets are equalized.

However, unless modified, poker rules can leave more than two active players at showdown. This can be accepted, or the following rules may be observed:

a) when there are three or more active players, a player may not call if this equalizes all players' bets (he must raise or drop out);

b) if a player drops out and so equalizes the bets between the remaining three or more active players, the last player to raise must raise again.

"Blind" betting It is sometimes ruled that a player may bet without looking at his cards.

In this case, any player who has looked at his cards must in each turn pay double the blind bettor if he is to stay in.

When only two active players are left an "open" bettor cannot double his stakes to see a blind bettor. To remain in the game he must continue to bet until the blind bettor doubles his bet to see him.

When the last two active players are both blind bettors either of them can pay double to see the other.

Covering the kitty If a player runs out of money during a betting interval he places his hand face down on the pool.

Subsequent bets by other players are then placed in a side pool. Showdown is then between three players: between the last two active players for the side pool and between these two and the player who covered the kitty for the main pool.

Seven-card brag: pryles

7s beat aces

SEVEN-CARD BRAG

This version is for two to seven players.

Before each deal, players contribute equal amounts to a pool. Each player then receives seven cards, looks at them, discards one face down, and visibly splits the remainder into two unexposed three-card brag hands.

When all are ready, each player in turn exposes one hand, beginning with the player to the dealer's left.

Then each player in turn exposes his other hand, beginning with the player whose first hand was highest.

A player has complete discretion on how he splits his cards between the two hands, but he must expose the best hand first.

The rank of cards is as in three-card brag, except that the highest pryle is three 7s, followed by three aces. (Three 3s rank normally – below three 4s and above three 2s.)

If the same player has the highest hand both times, he wins the pool.

Alternatively, a player whose original seven cards contain four cards of the same denomination wins the pool if he declares this at once without discarding.

Otherwise the pool is not won, but players still contribute again before the next deal.

A deal is usually one card at a time, face down. It may however, be three cards to each player, followed by another three, and then by a single card.

In the latter case, dealt cards are usually not shuffled between hands but replaced face down at the bottom of the deck with no shuffle or cut.

NINE-CARD BRAG

This is similar to seven-card brag. A maximum of five can play, as nine cards are dealt to each player. The deal is usually in ones, but sometimes in threes.

Players divide their cards into three brag hands, exposing the highest hand first.

Any player with the highest hand in all three exposures wins the pool (or, under some rules, the pool is won by a player with two out of three highest hands).

Nine-card brag: pryles

Alternatively, as in seven-card brag, the pool is won immediately by a player with four cards of a kind.

The rank of hands is as in three-card brag, except that the highest pryle is three 9s, followed by three aces. (Three 3s rank normally – below three 4s and above three 2s.)

If no one wins the pool, players still contribute again before the next deal.

Sometimes a pool may not be won for many hours – by which time it can be very large.

9s beat aces

STOP THE BUS

This British students' game is a variant of three-card brag. All players start with an equal number of betting chips. An additional three-card hand – the dummy – is dealt face up onto the table.

In play, each player in turn may exchange one card in his hand for one from the dummy. The discarded cards go into the dummy face up.

This continues until one player does not wish to alter his hand. All players then show their cards, and the lowest hand pays a previously agreed amount into the pool (eg five units).

Further hands are played until only one player has any chips remaining. He then wins the whole pool.

Card craps

Cards used

This game was created to bypass laws banning dice craps. The "shooter" deals cards instead of throwing dice.

Equipment:
a) a special deck of 48 cards. It is made up of six denominations only – ace, 2, 3, 4, 5, and 6. In each denomination there are eight cards, two in each suit. For example there are eight 6s made up of two hearts, two spades, two diamonds, and two clubs;
b) betting chips or cash.

Players Any number can play from two upward. One person is dealer and is known as the "shooter."

Choice of first shooter is by any agreed method.

Shuffle See p 381.

Cut Any player may cut; but the player to the dealer's left has the right to cut last. If he does not wish to do so, the right to cut last passes clockwise.

Basic play The shooter deals two cards from the top of the deck face up onto the table. This constitutes a "throw." The value of the two cards added together gives the score for the throw in just the same way as the two dice in dice craps.

The first throw in a shooter's turn is called a "come-out" throw, as is the first throw after each time the cards win or lose.

On a come-out throw:
a) if the shooter throws a 7 or 11, he has thrown a "natural": the cards "pass" (ie win) immediately.
b) If the shooter throws a 2, 3, or 12, he has thrown "craps": the cards "miss out" or "crap out" (ie lose) immediately.
c) If the shooter throws a 4, 5, 6, 8, 9, or 10, he has thrown a "point": for the cards to win he must "make the point," ie throw the same number again before he throws a 7 – no other numbers matter.

If the shooter throws the same number again before he throws a 7, the cards pass (win).

If he throws a 7 before he throws the number again, the cards miss out or "seven out" (lose).

After a come-out throw the shooter shuffles the two cards back into the deck and he cuts the deck.

If the shooter then still has to make a point, he deals further throws but does not shuffle these back into the deck. This continues until he makes the point (wins) or sevens out (loses) – ie until a "decision" is reached. The entire deck is then shuffled together and cut.

If, on a point, the whole deck is used without a decision, the

shooter reshuffles and cuts the deck; he then continues, trying for the same point.

Change of shooter If the shooter sevens out he must give up the cards. He may also give up the cards if:

a) he has not made any throw in his turn; or

b) he has just thrown a decision.

The cards pass to the next player to the left.

Change of deck When two decks are available, any player may request a change of deck at any time. The change is made immediately before the next come-out throw.

Betting and odds Players arrange bets among themselves.

Center bet On each come-out throw, the shooter places the amount he wishes to bet in the center of the playing area. He announces the amount, saying "I'll shoot . . . .'

Any of the other players then "fade" (accept) whatever part of the total they wish, by placing that amount in the center alongside the shooter's bet.

Unless agreed at the beginning of the game, there is no set order or amount by which players fade center bets. Players simply place money in the center until all the shooter's bet has been faded, or until no one wishes to place any further amount. (However, it is sometimes agreed that any player who faced the entire center bet on the preceding come-out, and lost, can claim the right to fade the entire present bet.)

If the center bet is not entirely faded by the players, the shooter may either:

a) withdraw the part not faded; or

b) call off all bets, by saying "No bet."

Players may not fade more than the shooter's center bet; but if the players show eagerness to bet more, the shooter can decide to increase the amount of his bet.

Settlement of center bet If the cards miss out (lose), the players who faded the center bet each receive back their money together with the equivalent amount of the center bet. If the cards pass (win), all the money in the center is collected by the shooter.

The center bet is therefore an even money (1 to 1) bet. Since the probability of the cards passing is in fact 970 occasions in 1,980, the shooter has a 1.414% disadvantage on the center bet.

Other bets are known as side bets. Like the center bet, they must be arranged before the cards are dealt.

Note that the shooter himself may make any of the side bets he wishes, in addition to the center bet.

Hardway bet (or gag bet) This is a bet on whether the shooter will throw a certain number "the hard way" – ie as the sum of a double. Hardway bets can be placed on 4 (2+2), 6 (3+3), 8 (4+4), or 10 (5+5).

The right bettor loses if a 7 is thrown, or if the number bet on is thrown any other way before being thrown as a double.

Double hardway This is not a bet but a double payment made when the shooter throws a point number (4, 6, 8, or 10) with two cards that are pairs of the same suit, eg 8 with two 4s of hearts.

The payment is made by wrong bettors to those who have taken a normal "right bet" on the shooter making the point. This serves to equalize the right and wrong bettors' chances on even number points.

Off-number bet Two players agree to bet on any number they choose. The right bettor wins if the shooter throws the number before he throws a 7. Bettors may call off this bet before a "decision" is reached.

Proposition This refers to any other kind of side bet agreed upon – limited only by players' imaginations!

Such bets are always offered at odds designed to give the proposing player an advantage. There are two main categories:

1) bets on whether the specified number(s) will appear within a certain number of throws after the bet: "one-throw bets," "two-throw bets," "three-throw bets;" or

2) bets on whether the specified number(s) will appear before other specified number(s) or before a 7.

In each case, the specified number(s) bet on may be:

a) a certain number to be thrown in any way;

b) a certain number to be thrown in a specified way;

c) any one of a group of numbers (eg a group of specified numbers, odd numbers, numbers below 7, etc).

Right and wrong bets All these bets require agreement
between two players.
One is the "wrong" bettor: he "lays" odds that the cards will
not pass or will not make the number(s) bet on.
The other is the "right" bettor: he "takes" odds that the cards
will pass or will make the number(s) bet on.
The bet and odds may be proposed by either the right or the
wrong bettor; in practice, however, more experienced players
tend to be "wrong" bettors and propose odds that the less
experienced player will "take."
Flat bet This is a normal bet on whether a shooter's come-out
throw will pass, and is made as a side bet between two players
(of which one may be the shooter). Flat bets occur especially
if one player has faded the entire bet.
Point bet If the shooter throws a point on his come-out throw,
players may bet on whether he will "make the point." (The
center and flat bets still remain to be settled in the same way.)

Come bet This is a bet on whether the cards will pass – but treating the next throw after the bet as the bet's come-out throw (when in fact the shooter is throwing for a point).

If on this throw the shooter throws a 7, he sevens out on his point – but for the come bet the cards "come," because a 7 on a come-out throw is a natural.

Similarly, 11 is a natural for the come bet, but 2, 3, or 12 is craps – the cards "don't come." (But all of these leave the center bet undecided, because they are neither the point number nor a 7.)

If the shooter throws a point number on the come-out throw for the come bet, this number becomes the point for the come bet. The outcome then depends, in the usual way, on whether the point or a 7 appears first.

If the shooter makes the point on his center bet without making the come bet point, the players making the come bet can agree to withdraw the bet or to continue the number sequence into the shooter's next turn.

True odds Table 1 gives the true odds for various bets on or between single numbers, and provides the information from which the true odds for any bet between groups of numbers can be calculated. (A player should particularly avoid accepting 1 to 1 odds on 6 to 5 bets.)

Table 2 gives the true odds for hardway bets.

Table 1: True odds for bets on or between single numbers

	A	B	C
Number	Single throw	Before a 7	Comparative odds
12	35-1	6-1	12
11	17-1	3-1	2-1 **11**
10	11-1	2-1	3-1 3-2 **10**
9	8-1	3-2	4-1 2-1 4-3 **9**
8	31-5	6-5	5-1 5-2 5-3 5-4 **8**
7	5-1	—	6-1 3-1 2-1 3-2 6-5 **7**
6	31-5	6-5	5-1 5-2 5-3 5-4 1-1 5-6 **6**
5	8-1	3-2	4-1 2-1 4-3 1-1 4-5 2-3 4-5 **5**
4	11-1	2-1	3-1 3-2 1-1 3-4 3-5 1-2 3-5 3-4 **4**
3	17-1	3-1	2-1 1-1 2-3 1-2 2-5 1-3 2-5 1-2 2-3 **3**
2	35-1	6-1	1-1 1-2 1-3 1-4 1-5 1-6 1-5 1-4 1-3 1-2 **2**

Table 2: Hardway bets

Bet	Odds against hardway	Payment on double hardway
10	8-1	4-1
8	10-1	12-5
6	10-1	12-5
4	8-1	4-1

Notes on table 1

A) Odds against making a number on a single throw.

B) Odds against throwing the number before throwing a 7: for point and off-number bets.

C) Odds against making the higher number before the lower number (eg 12 before 4: 3-1). Reverse the odds to give odds against making the lower number before the higher (eg 4 before 12: 1-3).

To calculate the odds between any groups of numbers: add all ways of making the numbers in one group, and compare with the total of all ways of making the numbers in the other group.

True odds for other one-throw bets:

a) against any specified pair (eg 3+3): 35-1;

b) against any specified combination of two different numbers (eg 6+5): 17-1;

c) against any craps (2, 3, or 12): 8-1.

Card put-and-take

Taking its name from the game of put-and-take played with a
specially marked teetotum, this private banking card game has
some features in common with red dog

Equipment:
1) one standard deck of 52 cards;
2) betting chips.
Players: from two to eight.
Objective On the "take" deal each player aims to hold, and on
the "put" deal not to hold, cards of the same rank as those
turned up by the banker.
Choice of first banker/dealer is by high cut (see p 381).
Shuffle and cut are standard (see p 381).
Deal The banker deals five face-up cards to each player except
himself, dealing them one at a time in a clockwise direction.
Betting limits Payments are one to 16 chips. One chip's value is
agreed beforehand.
Play
1) Players look at their cards.
2) The put deal is made. The banker deals five face-up cards
one at a time onto the table.
After each card is dealt, any player holding a card of the same
rank must pay chips into a pool. The payment doubles with
each card: one chip for the first card turned up; two for the
second; four for the third; eight for the fourth; and 16 for the
fifth. A player with two or more cards of the same rank as the
banker's card must pay for each one.
The banker makes no payments.
3) The banker takes the five cards from the table and places
them face up at the bottom of the deck.
4) The take deal is made, for which the banker deals five more
cards as before. This time each player takes chips from the pool
for each of his cards of the same rank. The number of chips
taken increases exactly as in the put deal.
5) Any chips left in the pool after the five cards have been
played go to the banker. Any chips still owing are paid by the
banker from his own chips.
Change of banker/dealer After each hand the bank and deal
pass to the player to the banker's left.

Sample play

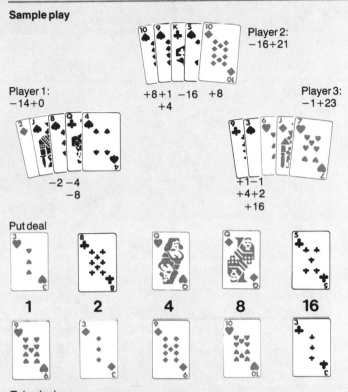

Player 2:
−16+21

Player 1:
−14+0

+8+1 −16 +8
     +4

Player 3:
−1+23

−2 −4
  −8

+1−1
+4+2
+16

Put deal

| 1 | 2 | 4 | 8 | 16 |

Take deal

VARIANTS

Ante payment Sometimes each player but the banker puts one chip into the pool before each hand.

Easy go has an additional payment and claim. Players pay – and take – one additional chip for each card that, besides being of the same rank as the card played by the banker, is also of the same colour.

Red and black has an additional payment and claim for any player with three or more cards of the same suit as the card played by the banker.

Players pay – and take – one chip for the first card the banker turns up, two for the second, three for the third, four for the fourth, and five for the fifth, in addition to regular payments.

Up and down the river has a different payment and claim system. Each player pays – and takes – according to the rank of the matching cards, not according to whether it is the first, second, third, fourth, or fifth card turned up.

Payment for an ace is one chip; for a jack, 11 chips; for a queen, 12 chips; and for a king, 13. Payments on other cards match their face value.

Chinese fan-tan

This simple game works on the same principle as the Chinese bean game of fan-tan. It was once an American gambling house game but disappeared because it gives no advantage to the banker.

Equipment:
1) one standard deck of 52 cards;
2) one joker to be used for the betting layout;
3) betting chips – preferably a different colour for each player.
Players The game is for two or more players.
Objective Players aim to guess how nearly the number of cards in a section cut from the deck will be divisible by four.
Choice of first banker is by high cut (see p 381).
Betting limits are agreed beforehand.
Bank Because each player may make more than one bet, the betting limits do not limit a bank's losses. A banker therefore places to one side, before his first hand as banker, any of his fund of chips he is not prepared to put at risk. The remainder constitutes the bank. Any winnings gained during a player's turn as banker must remain at risk in the bank until the role of banker passes to the next player.
The betting layout consists of the joker, turned face up in the center of the table. The card is placed so that one of its short sides is facing the banker.
Each of the joker's corners is allocated a number. As the banker looks at the card, the bottom left hand corner is 1, the top left hand corner 2, the top right hand corner 3, and the bottom right hand corner 4.
Bets at the corners of the joker are on one number only. Bets

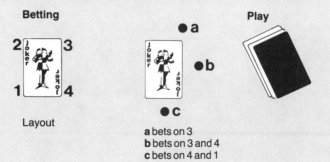

Layout

a bets on 3
b bets on 3 and 4
c bets on 4 and 1

along the side of the joker are on the numbers of the two adjacent corners. In the example illustrated, bet (**a**) is on 3, bet (**b**) on 3 and 4, and bet (**c**) on 4 and 1.

A player may place as many bets as he likes, provided each bet is within the betting limits. For each bet, he puts down the number of chips he wishes to put at risk.

More than one player may make the same bet. The banker does not bet.

Shuffle The player to the banker's left shuffles the deck thoroughly and gives it to the banker.

Play The banker cuts a section of at least one third of the cards from the deck, and then counts them out face down onto the table in groups of four.

If the section divides exactly into groups of four, 4 is the winning number.

If a number of cards is left over after counting out in fours, the number left over is the winning number.

In the example illustrated, the section comprised 15 cards – three groups of cards and three over.

Settlement of bets The banker first collects losing bets and then pays winning ones.

Bets on single numbers are paid at 3 to 1 – bet (**a**) in the example illustrated. Bets on two numbers are paid at evens – bet (**b**) in the example; bet (**c**) loses.

The banker first pays any winnings due to the player to his left and then those due to the other players in turn.

If the bank is emptied before all winnings have been paid, the winning bets that remain unpaid are simply returned to the bettors.

Change of banker Unless the bank has been emptied, bank and deal remain with one player for a set number of hands agreed beforehand. After this the banker receives all the chips then in the bank, and bank and deal pass one player to the left.

The bank and deal pass immediately if a bank is emptied.

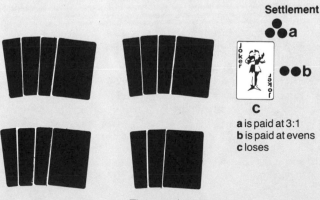

Settlement

a is paid at 3:1
b is paid at evens
c loses

Three cards over

Faro

Faro or farobank is a very old banking game. It was known as pharaon in the French court of Louis XIV. In the 1700s it was the most popular gambling house game in England. The following century it became equally popular in the United States, where it was often called "bucking the tiger."

Equipment
a) A table covered with green baize, bearing the faro layout. The complete spades suit is usually used for the layout.
b) A dealing box from which one card can be slid at a time.
c) A casekeeper. This is a frame like an abacus used to show which cards in the deck have been played.
d) A standard deck of cards.
e) Betting chips.
f) Faro "coppers" – round or hexagonal chips of either red or black – used for betting a denomination to lose.
g) Bet markers – small flat oblongs of ivory or plastic – used to make bets over the limit of a bettor's funds.
Players Up to ten can play. House officials are a dealer, a lookout who supervises betting, and a casekeeper official. The house always banks.
Objective Players try to predict whether the next card to appear, of the denomination bet on, will be a winning or a losing card.
Cards appear in play two at a time. The first in each pair is always the losing card, the second the winning card.
Shuffle, cut, and bet The dealer shuffles the cards, cuts them, and puts them in the dealing box face up. The exposed top card is called the "soda". It is ignored for betting.
Bets are now placed (see p 600).
First turn The dealer puts the soda card face up to one side to start the discard pile or "soda stack."
He then takes the next exposed card from the box and places it face up to the right of the box. This card is the losing card. The card now exposed in the box is the winning card.
Between turns Any bets on the two exposed denominations are settled. Other bets may be changed and new bets made. The casekeeper is altered to show the cards that have already appeared.
Continuing play Play continues through the deck. In each turn:
1) the dealer removes the last winning card from the box and places it face up on the discard pile;
2) a new losing card is taken from the box as in the first turn;
3) the new winning card is exposed at the top of the box.

Casekeeper

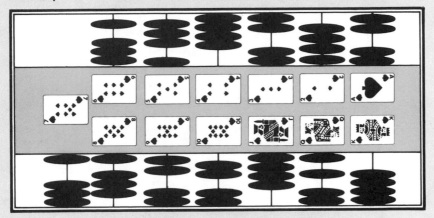

The casekeeper has pictures of the 13 denominations, with four large wood buttons on a spindle opposite each picture.

At the beginning of the deal all the buttons are positioned at the inner ends of the spindles.

As a card is taken from the box, one of the buttons on the relevant spindle is moved along toward the outer edge of the frame.

How far it is moved depends on whether it represents a winning or a losing card:

a) for a losing card it is moved until it touches the outer frame or an earlier button on the same spindle;

b) for a winning card a gap of about ½in is left between the button and the frame or between this and an earlier button.

When the fourth card of a denomination appears, whether it is a winning or a losing card, all four buttons are pushed together against the outer frame to show that betting on this denomination is at an end.

The last turn Three cards are left in the box for the last turn. The casekeeper shows which cards they are. The last card in the box is called the "hoc" or "hock" card.

For the last turn players may normally:

a) bet on any one of the cards to win or lose as usual;

b) "call the turn" – ie try to predict the precise order of all three cards (eg, queen first to lose, 6 second to win, ace last).

The turn is played in the usual way, except that when the winning card has been removed from the box the losing card is half slid out to confirm the denomination of the hoc card.

A player's bet is returned if the card that he bet to win or lose appears as the hoc card.

Continuing the game After the last turn all cards are gathered and shuffled for the next deal.

Betting There are three kinds of bet apart from bets on the last turn:

bets on a single denomination;,
bets on a set of denominations;
bets that take action in every turn.

Bets on a single denomination are settled when a card of that denomination appears. To make the same bet again a player places a new stake on the layout.

Bets on a set of denominations are bets on groups of different numbers that appear close together on the layout (see placing of bets diagram and explanation). They are settled as soon as any one of the denominations bet on appears.

To make the same bet again, a player places a new stake on the layout.

Bets that take action in every turn remain on the layout until removed by the player. There are two such bets: a "high card" bet and an "even or odd card" bet.

In a high card bet the player bets that the higher denomination card of each pair will win in each turn, or, if he has "coppered" the bet, that the higher card will lose. (For this bet ace ranks low.)

In an even or odd card bet the player bets that either the even card or the odd card will win in each turn. (For this bet ace, jack, and king count as odd, and queen as even.)

With these two bets the player wins or loses on every turn. Each time he loses he gives the dealer a number of chips equal to his stake. Each time he wins he receives an equal number. The actual stake remains on the table until the player stops making the bet.

Placing of bets

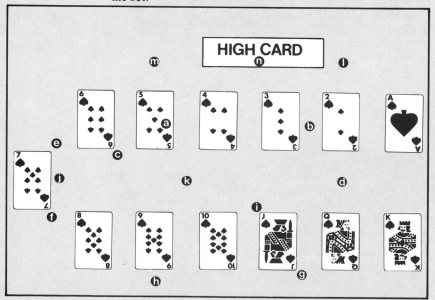

Explanation of placing of bets diagram:
a) bets a single denomination (5);
b) bets two denominations horizontally adjacent (2+3);
c) bets two denominations diagonally adjacent (6+9);
d) bets two denominations vertically adjacent (2+q);
e) bets 6+7;
f) bets 7+8;
g) bets two denominations horizontally adjacent and separated by one other denomination (j+k);
h) bets three denominations horizontally adjacent (8, 9, 10);
i) bets three denominations in a right angle (3, 10, j);
j) bets 6, 7, 8;
k) bets adjacent denominations in a square (4, 5, 9, 10);
l) bets the even denomination card in each turn (the chip position is between the 2 and the table edge);
m) bets the odd denomination card in each turn (the chip position is between the 5 and the table edge);
n) bets the higher denomination card in each turn.

Bets to win using one or several chips All bets may be made with one chip or several chips.

If several chips are used, they are stacked vertically except for bet (c). For that bet they are tilted or "heeled," by moving the bottom chip in to rest on the corner of one card and tilting the remainder toward the other card.

Bets to lose using one or several chips In general these bets are placed as for bets to win but are "coppered" – ie a faro copper is placed on top of the betting chip(s).

The only exception is where bet (c) is made with a single chip. In this case the copper is placed in the usual position not far from the tip of one of the cards, with the chip on top of it tilting toward the other card.

Betting one card to win and one to lose This bet can be placed on any two adjacent denominations or on bet (g).

If the bet is made with a single chip, a copper is placed on the edge or corner of the lose card and the chip is tilted toward the win card.

If the bet is made with several chips, one chip is placed on the edge or corner of the lose card and the remaining chips are tilted on it in the direction of the win card.

This bet is settled as soon as one of the denominations appears as a winning or losing card.

Last turn bet: "calling the turn" The stake is placed on the card bet to lose and angled toward the card bet to win.

a) When made with a single chip, a copper is placed on the card bet to lose on the edge nearest the card bet to win. The single chip is placed on it, tilted toward the card bet to win. Another copper is placed on top of the single chip.

b) When made with several chips, one chip is placed on the card bet to lose on the edge nearest the card bet to win. The remaining chips are tilted on the bottom chip so that they point toward the card bet to win.

When the third card lies between the winning and losing cards, the bet is tilted toward the outside of the layout. This shows that it avoids the middle card, ie the middle card is bet to be the hoc card.

Last turn bet: "cat hop" The stake is placed as for calling the turn.

Bet markers are used when a player wants to place on the layout at one time more bets than he has funds for.

For each marker placed on the layout the player must have staked an equal value in chips elsewhere on the layout.

If one of the player's bets loses, the dealer takes payment in chips. The player must then withdraw his marker bet unless the value of his chips on the layout still exceeds the value of the markers he has used.

If one of the player's bets wins, the player wins an equivalent amount in chips.

A **"split"** occurs in a turn when a single bet has covered both winning and losing cards.

a) A split on a single denomination occurs when two cards of the same denomination appear in a turn. The house takes half

of any bet on that denomination; the other half is returned to the bettor.

b) A split on a set of denominations occurs when two cards of a group bet on by a player appear in a single turn. The bet is returned to the bettor.

c) A split on bets that take action in every turn occurs when both cards in a turn are of the same denomination or are both odd or both even. The bet remains on the table and the bettor neither makes nor receives any payment.

Betting on "cases" When only one card of a denomination is left in the box, this is called "cases" – eg, "cases on the queen."

Most houses forbid a player to bet on cases until after he has bet on a denomination that could be split.

"Cat hop" bet On the last turn the casekeeper may show that the three cards left are not all of different denominations. "Calling the turn" is then replaced by the "cat hop" bet. It may be made on denominations or on colors.

a) If two of the three cards are of the same denomination, a player may make a cat hop on denominations, predicting the order of denominations as usual – eg, 10, 6, 10. (A player may still bet one denomination to win or lose as usual.)

b) If all three cards are of the same denomination, a player may make a cat hop on color, predicting the order of suit colors – eg, red, black, red.

Cat hop bets are placed in front of the dealer according to whatever temporary regulations he states.

Settlement A player who calls the turn successfully is paid at 4 to 1. A player who makes a successful cat hop bet is paid at 2 to 1. All other bets are paid at even money (1 to 1).

Hoggenheimer

A game of pure chance in which the settlement of bets depends on how soon the banker turns up a joker.

Equipment:
1) one standard deck of 52 cards from which the 2s, 3s, 4s, 5s, and 6s have been removed.
2) one joker (or any discarded card if a joker is not used);
3) betting chips.
Players The game is for two or more players.
Objective Players try to bet on a card (or cards) exposed before the joker is exposed.
Choice of first banker is by high cut (see p 381).
Shuffle and cut are normal (see p 381).
Dealing the layout The banker deals four rows of eight cards face down, and the 33rd card face down to one side. He takes care that no card's face is seen during the deal.
Betting limits are agreed beforehand.
Betting Each player except the banker places as many bets as he likes. The card bet on is shown by the bet's position on the layout. The top row represents spades, the next hearts, the next diamonds, and the bottom row clubs. The column farthest to the right represents 7s, the next 8s, and so on; the column farthest to the left represents aces.

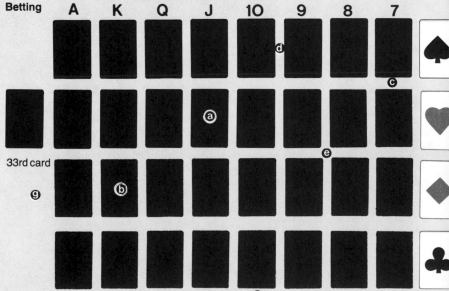

Examples of betting are shown in the illustration:

a) is a bet on the jack of hearts;

b) is on the king of diamonds;

c) is on two adjacent cards – the 7s of spades and hearts;

d) is on two adjacent cards – the 9 and 10 of spades;

e) is on four cards in a square – the 8s and 9s of hearts and diamonds;

f) is on a column of cards of a single denomination – all the 10s;

g) is on a row of cards of the same suit – all the diamonds.

Play The banker turns the 33rd card face up.

If it is a joker the deal ends and the banker collects all bets.

If it is any other card the banker places it face up in its correct position on the layout.

Any bet on that position is replaced on top of the card.

The face-down card that was in that position is removed, turned face up, and placed in its correct position in the layout.

Play continues in this way until the joker appears.

Settlement A player's bet wins if all the cards bet on are turned up before the joker. The banker collects all other bets.

In the example illustrated: bets (**a**), (**c**), and (**d**) win; bets (**b**), (**e**), (**f**), and (**g**) lose.

Bets on single cards are paid 1 to 1. Bets on two cards are paid 2 to 1. Bets on four cards in a square or column are paid 4 to 1. Bets on eight cards in a row are paid 8 to 1.

Continuing play The bank and deal pass one player to the left. All cards are collected for the next hand.

Play

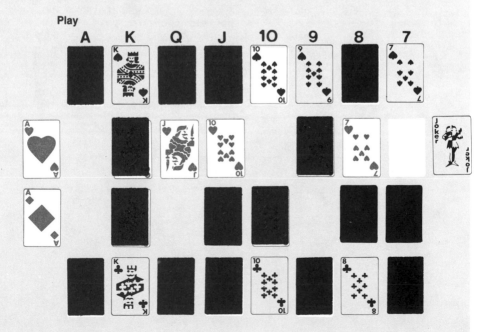

Horse race

An exciting game emulating the thrills of the racetrack. Bets are laid on cards that are moved like horses toward the finish line.

Equipment:
1) one standard deck of 52 cards;
2) betting chips.

Players The game is for three or more players.

Objective Players try to "win the race" by betting on the first suit to appear eight times in a deal.

Choice of first banker is by high cut (see p 381).

The "horses" The banker takes the four aces from the deck and lines them up in any order.

Shuffle and cut are standard (see p 381).

The "course" After the shuffle and cut, the banker deals seven face-up cards in a line at right angles to the horses. If five or more of the cards dealt are of the same suit, the banker takes them all up, reshuffles, and deals the course again.

Betting limits are decided by the banker for each race.

Betting The banker declares the odds on each horse (suit), taking into account the cards that were dealt to form the course. If one suit has appeared predominantly in the course, there will be fewer cards of that suit to appear in the race.

The table gives an example of the odds that a banker might

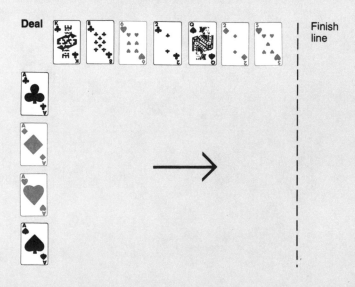

offer. He will choose odds that give him some degree of advantage; it is up to each player whether or not to place a bet at those odds.

The players then state their bets, placing their stakes in front of them. The banker makes a note of how much each player bets on each horse and what the odds are.

The "race" The banker deals the top card from the deck face up onto the table. The horse (ace) of the same suit as the dealt card is then moved up the course one space. The banker then deals another card face up on top of the first, and again moves the horse of the corresponding suit one space. This continues until one horse has passed the end of the course. This horse is the winner.

Settlement of bets The banker collects all bets placed on the losing horses. He pays at the quoted odds each bet on the winning horse.

Change of banker After each hand, the bank and deal pass one player to the left.

Betting odds

Number of cards of suit in course	Odds offered on suit
0	Evens
1	2-1
2	3-1
3	5-1
4	10-1
5 or more	Layout redealt

Play

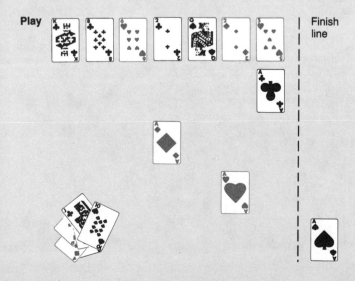

Finish line

Injun

This fast, amusing game is very simple to play. But it can see a lot of money change hands very rapidly, and offers opportunities for skillful judgment to anyone familiar with mathematical odds. Bets are placed in a central pool; there is no banker.

Equipment:
a) one standard deck of 52 cards;
b) betting chips or cash.
Players: from two to about 15.
Rank of cards The cards rank in normal order, with ace high. The suits are not ranked.
The objective is to bet on holding a higher ranking card than any other player.
Choice of first dealer is by deal: first ace to appear (see p 381).
Shuffle and cut are normal (see p 381).
Ante Before each deal, each player, including the dealer, puts an equal amount into the center of the table to form a pool.

Deal The dealer deals one card face down to each player
including himself, beginning with the player to his left and
going clockwise.

Play Players are not allowed to look at their own cards. Each
picks up his own card and puts it against his forehead.

He holds it there, face outward, so that all the other players in
the game can see the card.

Players should watch carefully at this stage of play to check that
no player glimpses his own card.

Betting begins with the player to the dealer's left, and goes
clockwise.

Each player bets according to his judgment of whether his own
card, which he cannot see, is likely to be higher in rank than all
the other players' cards – which he can see.

A player must bet to stay in the game. If he drops out at any
time, he places his card face down on the table in front of him.
All bets are placed in the pool.

Betting principles There are two alternatives:
a) poker betting;
b) brag betting.

Poker betting In this alternative each player in turn bets, calls,
raises, or drops out until the bets are equalized. When this
happens, betting ends and there is a showdown between all
active players.

Brag betting In this alternative, betting is as in the "round the
table" system in brag. Each player in each of his turns
contributes one unit to the pool, or drops out.

No one can raise and betting continues until all but two players
have dropped out. These last two active players then continue
to put bets of one unit each into the pool, until:
a) one of them drops out leaving the other player the winner; or
b) one of them pays two units to "see the other" and there is a
showdown between these two players.

Showdown On showdown all active players look at their own
cards. The player with the highest card wins the play and takes
the pool. Ties for highest card divide the pool.

"Covering the kitty" If a player runs out of money during
betting he places his card face down on the pool – allowing all
players to remind themselves of its rank before he does so.
Subsequent bets of other players are then placed in a side pool.
Showdown is then between three players: between the last two
active players for the side pool, and between these two and the
player who covered the kitty for the main pool.

Continuing play After the pool has been won the deal passes
one player to the left and all players ante for the next play.

© DIAGRAM

Kentucky derby

Also called pasteboard derby, this pool betting game has a varied race and simple betting.

Equipment:
1) one standard deck of 52 cards;
2) betting chips (or cash).
Players: three or more.
Objective Players try to bet on the winning "horse."
Choice of first dealer is by high cut (see p 381).
Shuffle and cut The four aces are removed from the deck. The rest of the deck is shuffled and cut as usual (see p 381).
The "course" After the shuffle and cut, the dealer forms the course by dealing seven face-down cards in line.
The "horses" The four aces are the horses – they can be given the names of favourites. These cards are lined up just below the first course card, in the order: hearts, diamonds, spades, clubs. To make judging easier, the two red aces are put to one side of the course and the two black aces to the other.
The player to the dealer's left lines up the aces and moves them during the race.
Ante Before the game, each player including the dealer puts an equal agreed amount into the pool.

Betting Each player decides which horse he will back. A player may bet only on one horse; more than one player may bet on the same horse.

A horse still runs even if no one bets on it.

It is best to write down the selections if there are several players. This is done by the player to the dealer's right. He also has charge of the pool and pays out the winnings at the end.

Starting the race The dealer deals the top card from the deck face up onto the table just behind the ace of hearts.

The player to the dealer's left moves the ace of hearts the appropriate number of spaces up the course, if any (see moves table, p 612).

The dealer then deals a card behind the ace of diamonds, and so on.

Running the race How far a horse moves depends on the card dealt. The dealer deals one card to each ace in turn, in the order: hearts, diamonds, spades, clubs, and then starts again. Further cards dealt to each ace are placed face up on top of the cards first dealt, forming four discard piles.

Finishing the race A horse finishes when it passes the last course card.

But the winner is only decided when all horses have had an equal number of turns. The winner is then the ace that has gone farthest over the finishing line.

If the second place horse is to be decided too, and only the winning horse has crossed the finishing line, then the winner's discard pile is turned face down, and play continues with the remaining aces.

Splitting "dead heats" Sometimes two aces have gone an equal distance over the finishing line on the same turn.
Each is then dealt a further card from the deck. This continues until, with an equal number of cards dealt, one horse has gone farther past the post than the other.

Settlement: winning horse only With fewer than six players, races are run for first place only. The pool is won by the player or players betting on the winning horse. If there are two or more successful bettors, the pool is split equally between them. If the pool does not divide equally, any chips over stay in the pool for the next race.

Settlement: winner and second place With six or more players, races may be run for first and second places. Bettors on the second place horse receive back their ante from the pool.
The remainder of the pool is won (and divided if necessary) by the player(s) who bet on the winning horse.

Preparing for the next race The deal passes to the player to the dealer's left. He collects all the cards (except the aces) and reshuffles them.
The player to the new dealer's left controls the horses, and the player to his right the bets.

The moves

	Card played	*Distance moved*
Ace moves forward	king	2 lengths
	queen	1 1/2 lengths
	jack	1 length
	7, 8, 9, or 10 same color as ace	1 length
	3, 4, 5, or 6 same color as ace	1/2 length
	Any card dealt of the same suit as ace adds 1/2 length	
Ace moves back	2 same color as ace	1/2 length back
	2 not same color as ace	1 length back
No move	2 dealt while ace still on starting line	

Sample play

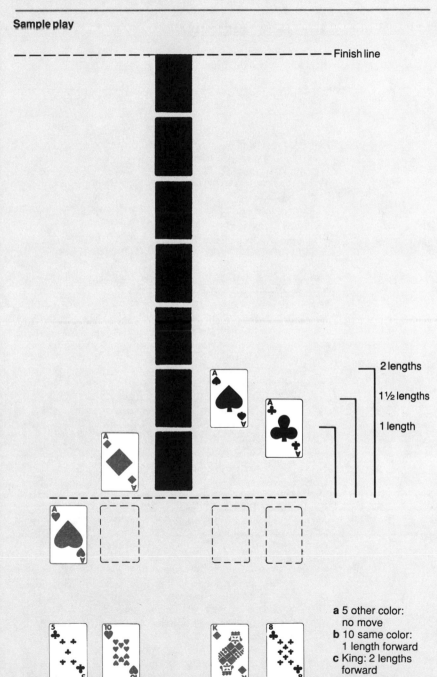

Finish line

2 lengths

1½ lengths

1 length

©DIAGRAM

a 5 other color:
no move
b 10 same color:
1 length forward
c King: 2 lengths
forward
d 8 same suit: 1½
lengths forward

a   b   c   d

Lansquenet

This private banking game is said to have been popular with German mercenaries in the 1600s. Its name derives from *Landsknecht,* the German word for mercenary. It is closely related to ziginette and skinball.

Equipment:
1) one standard deck of 52 cards;
2) betting chips.
Players: two or more.
Objective Players aim to bet on a card that has not been "matched" by the time the banker's card is matched.
A card is matched when a card of the same denomination is dealt from the deck.
Choice of first banker is by deal: first ace to appear. (See p 381.)
Shuffle and cut are normal (see p 381).
Dealing the layout Provided that none of the cards dealt for the layout matches, the procedure is as follows. The banker deals the top two cards from the deck (the "hand" cards) face up onto the table. He then deals one card face up to himself (the "banker's card"), followed by another one face up (the "players' card").
Matching cards in the layout The following procedure must be observed if matching cards are turned up for the layout.
1) If the card dealt for the second hand card matches the first, it is placed on top of it. A further card is then dealt as the second hand card. If necessary this process is repeated until the hand cards do not match.
2) If the card dealt as the banker's card matches one of the hand cards, it is placed on top of that card and a new banker's card dealt. This process is repeated if necessary until the banker's card is of a different denomination than the hand cards.
3) If the card dealt as the players' card matches one of the hand cards, the procedure is as for the banker's card. If the players' card is the same denomination as the banker's card, the deal is void and a new deal made.
Betting limits are decided by the banker for his hand's duration.
Betting Each player places his bet alongside the players' card. If all chips are of the same color, the bets may be placed at different corners of the card to distinguish them.
First turn The banker deals one card from the top of the deck face up onto the table.
If the dealt card does not match any card on the layout, it is placed face up next to the players' card. It is now a further players' card, on which players may place bets.
If the dealt card matches one of the hand cards, it is placed on

top of the matched card. This denomination is now out of play. The hand cards have no effect, except to remove two denominations from the betting.

If the dealt card matches the players' card, the banker wins the players' bets. There is then no further betting on the matched denominations for the rest of the deal.

The matched and matching cards are dead, but are left on the layout, on top of each other, as a reminder that this denomination is out of play. Any further cards of that denomination are placed on top of the matched cards.

If the dealt card matches the banker's card, the banker pays all bets at even money, ie each winning player receives his stake plus an equal amount from the bank. Play on this deal then ceases and the bank and deal pass one player to the left.

Continuing play If the banker's card is not matched immediately, play continues in the same way until it has been matched – when the banker pays all outstanding bets.

A card is dealt in each turn – and either matches a card on the layout or becomes a new players' card.

Each time one of the players' cards is matched, the banker collects the bets on that card.

Between turns, players may place new bets on the players' cards. But a bet that has once been placed may not be removed or transferred to another card.

Explanation of play diagram

a) The 8 was dealt first, and became a players' card.

b) The king was dealt, matching a hand card and having no effect on play.

c) The 6 was dealt. It matches the banker's card – so players win all bets and the deal ends.

Betting

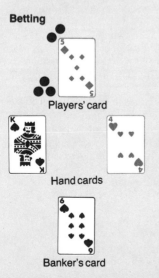

Players' card

Hand cards

Banker's card

Play

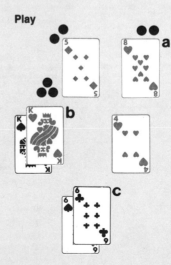

© DIAGRAM

Monte bank

Monte bank is the major banking card game of illegal gambling clubs. It is also called monte or Spanish monte.

CASINO VERSION

Cards: a standard deck with the 10s, 9s, and 8s removed.

Players From two to as many as can get around the gaming table. One of the players is banker.

There is also a non-playing house official called a "cutter." He assists the banker and collects a 25% cut from certain bets. When the bank passes, the amount collected by the cutter is divided equally between the house and the retiring banker.

The objective for a player is to bet on the layout card or cards that will first be matched in play.

Normally a card is "matched" when another card of the same denomination appears at the top of the deck.

Choice of first banker/dealer is by low cut.

Bank The banker places in front of him, in cash, the total amount he wishes to put at risk. The banker does not have to pay out an amount greater than this on any one hand. If the result of a hand presents a banker with losses exceeding the bank total, he pays off the highest bet first, then the next highest, until the bank is exhausted. Other bets are then void and are returned to the players.

Cards used

Betting limits The minimum bet is governed by house rules. The maximum bet is the amount of the bank. A player betting the maximum on a hand does not prevent other players betting because his bet may lose.

Shuffle and cut The dealer shuffles. Any other player may claim the right to shuffle before the cut but the dealer shuffles last. The dealer then places the cards in front of the player to his right. Any other player may claim the right to cut but the player to the dealer's right must cut last.

Dealing the layout Holding the deck face down, the banker deals two cards from the bottom. He places them face up on the table, slightly apart. These form the "top layout." He then deals two cards from the top of the deck and places them face up on the table just below the first two cards and slightly apart. These form the "bottom layout."

Pairs and triples If the two cards of the bottom layout are of the same denomination, the deal is void. The cards are collected and reshuffled.

The same applies if two cards, one in each layout, are of the same denomination.

If the two cards of the top layout are of the same denomination, the dealer places them one on top of the other and deals another card alongside.

If this card is also of the same denomination, it is placed with the others and a further card is dealt.

If this card is the fourth of the same denomination, the deal is void.

The cards are collected and reshuffled.

Sample layouts

Top layout

Bottom layout

Pair in top layout

Top layout

Bottom layout

Triple in top layout

Top layout

Bottom layout

©DIAGRAM

Betting involves predicting which of two cards or two groups of cards on the layout will be matched earliest.

Players back a certain card or cards to be matched before another specified card or cards. Normally a card is "matched" when another card of the same denomination appears at the top of the undealt portion of the deck.

Bets are placed in cash on the layout. The position of a bet shows the card(s) bet and the card(s) bet against. There are four types of bet:

1) circle bet;
2) crisscross bet;
3) doubler bet;
4) Monte carlo bet.

Circle bet The player bets that a specified card will be matched before any of the other three cards on the layout (**a**).

A successful circle bet is paid at 3 to 1.

Crisscross bet The player bets that a specified card will be matched before another one specified card on the layout (**b**).

A successful crisscross bet is paid at evens (1 to 1).

Doubler bet The player bets that one of the cards (unspecified) in the top layout will be matched before either one of the cards in the bottom layout (**c**), or vice versa.

Alternatively, he bets that one of the cards (unspecified) to the dealer's right will be matched before either one of the cards to the dealer's left (**d**), or vice versa.

A successful doubler bet is paid at evens (1 to 1).

Monte carlo bet This is a combination of the other three types of bet.

Types of bet

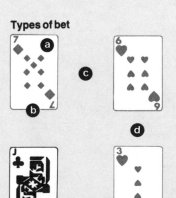

a Circle
b Crisscross
c Doubler (top before bottom)
d Doubler (right before left)

Matching with pairs and triples in the layout When cards of
the same denomination have been dealt to the top layout,
they are placed together (see sections on pairs and triples).
A pair or triple is matched as usual when a further card of the
same denomination appears from the undealt part of the
deck.

But other cards on the layout are not necessarily matched when
a card of their own denomination appears. To give all cards an
equal chance, the color of the cards appearing at the top of the
deck is taken into consideration.

Matching with pairs in the layout When a denomination in
the top layout has been paired, then another card on the layout
is matched only by a card which is of its own denomination
and of a different color.

Matching with triples in the layout When a denomination on
the layout has been tripled, another card on the layout is
matched only by a card which is of its own denomination and
of the same color.

Matching with pairs

Same color:
no match

Other color:
match

Matching with triples

Other color:
no match

Same color:
match

©DIAGRAM

Crisscross bets An unmatched pair or triple will be involved in some way in all bets on a layout, with the exception of those crisscross bets in which neither of the two cards bet is the pair (or triple).

Such crisscross bets are settled as soon as one of the two cards involved is matched in the normal way, ie by the appearance of any other card of its denomination.

For other purposes the card is not considered matched.

Play After bets have been placed the cutter says "That's all." The dealer then turns the deck face up, showing the bottom card only.

If the card matches any of the cards on the layout, all bets involved are settled and the matched card is removed from the layout.

If the card does not match any card on the layout, or if there are still other bets unsettled, the dealer removes the bottom card and places it to one side, exposing the next face-up card. This continues until all bets have been won or lost, each exposed card being added to the discard pile.

The deal is complete as soon as the last bet on the layout has been settled. (This will happen before all cards on the layout have been matched.) The dealer then gathers all cards and shuffles them for the next deal.

House cut and banker's cut When a player wins because the card he has backed is matched by the very first card exposed, the house takes a 25% cut from the player's winnings.

When the bank passes, the total collected is divided equally between the house and the retiring banker.

House cuts are collected by the cutter.

Change of banker A banker may hold the bank for as long as he wishes, or he may be limited to a set number of deals agreed by players beforehand. However, a banker may pass the bank at any time when there are no unsettled bets on the table. He indicates that he is passing the bank by saying "Aces."

If the bank becomes exhausted, the role of banker passes immediately.

The role of banker always passes to the next player to the left.

Variant Sometimes the dealer adds unmatched cards from the deck to the layout. Players may place further bets on them as in ziginette

**Sample betting
and play**

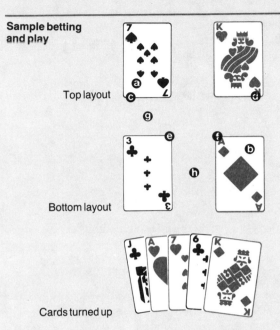

Top layout

Bottom layout

Cards turned up

Sample betting

a) bets 7 of spades;

b) bets ace of diamonds;

c) bets 7 of spades against 3 of clubs;

d) bets king of hearts against ace of diamonds;

e) bets 3 of clubs against king of hearts;

f) bets ace of diamonds against 7 of spades;

g) bets left layout;

h) bets bottom layout.

Sample play with pairs Cards turned up:

1) jack of clubs, no action;

2) ace of hearts, bet (**d**) loses (crisscross bet not involving pair); all other bets undecided;

3) 7 of hearts, bet (**a**) wins, paid 3–1; bets (**c**) and (**g**) win, paid evens; bets (**b**), (**f**), and (**h**) lose; bet (**e**) undecided;

4) 6 of clubs, no action;

5) king of diamonds, bet (**e**) loses.

MONTE BANK: PRIVATE

This is a simple version of the gambling club game
Cards are matched by suit not by denomination.

Equipment:

1) one standard deck of 52 cards with all 10s, 9s, and 8s
removed to leave a 40-card deck;

2) betting chips.

Players The game is for two or more players.

Objective Players bet that one of two cards on a "layout" (pair
of cards) will be matched.

A card is matched when the next card exposed from the deck is
of the same suit.

Choice of first banker/dealer is by low cut (see p 381).

Shuffle and cut are normal (see p 381).

Dealing the layouts Holding the deck face down, the banker
deals two cards from the bottom. He places them face up on the
table, slightly apart. These form the "top layout."

He then deals two cards from the top of the deck and places
them face up on the table, slightly below the first two cards.
These form the "bottom layout."

The deal is valid whatever suits appear – even if all four cards
are of the same suit.

Betting Each player except the banker may bet on the top or
the bottom layout or on both. A bet on a particular layout is
shown by placing the chips between that pair of cards.

Betting limits are agreed beforehand.

Play The banker turns the deck face up, exposing the bottom
card. This card is known as the "gate."

If the gate card's suit matches one (or both) of the cards in a
layout, the players win any bets on that layout.

If the gate card matches cards in both layouts, the players win
their bets on both layouts.

If no layout card is matched all bets are lost.

Settlement The banker collects all losing bets.

Winning bets are paid at 1 to 1, even if both cards in a layout
were matched.

Continuing play The banker collects together the layout cards,
and places them to one side to form a discard pile.

He then turns the deck face down, takes the next gate card
from the bottom of the deck and puts it on the discard pile.

He then deals the layout cards for the next hand. There is no
shuffle or cut.

Change of banker Bank and deal remain with one player for a
previously agreed number of hands (up to a maximum of six).
At least 10 cards of the deck should remain unplayed to prevent
players calculating which suits remain.

The bank and deal then pass one player to the left. All cards are
collected, and the deck shuffled and cut as before. If the bank is
emptied at any time bank and deal pass immediately.

Poker

Poker is played all over the world. It has been called the national card game of the United States, where it developed its present form. Poker ranks with blackjack among card games. Although the betting element is central to both games, they also allow for great skill; it is this that sets them apart from most pure gambling games.

Equipment
1) One standard deck of 52 cards (see also the section on arrangements p 268).
2) One or two jokers as "wild" cards if desired (see also the section on wild cards p 260).
3) Betting chips or cash.

Players: two to eight or more. Certain forms of poker can be played by up to 14 people. No alliances are allowed; a player may play only for himself.

Basic terms The usage of some poker terms is not standard. In the following text a "hand" means the cards, or the particular combination of cards, held by a player.

A single game, from one shuffle to the next, is here called a "play" (rather than a "hand").

Objective Each player tries to maximize his winnings.
On each play all bets are put into a common pool (the "pot").
One player wins the pool on a play if:
a) he holds a higher ranking hand than anyone still betting at the end (the "showdown"); or
b) all other players drop out of the betting before the showdown in the belief that they cannot win.

Rank of cards Cards rank in the normal order. Ace usually ranks high, except in the 5, 4, 3, 2, ace sequence; in a "high-low" game it may rank either high or low (see p281). Sometimes low-ranking cards (2s, 3s, and even 4s and 5s) are removed from the deck to speed up the game.
The suits are not ranked.

Poker hands In standard poker all hands must, for scoring (showdown) purposes, contain five cards, although fewer or more than this may be held at different stages of the game. The following hands are universally recognized. Each hand loses to the one listed before it, and defeats the one listed after it. This order derives from the mathematical probabilities involved.

Rank of hands

1

Straight flush

2

Four of a kind

3

Full house

1) Straight flush: five cards in sequence of the same suit. (A, k, q, j, 10 of the same suit is known as a "royal flush.")

2) Four of a kind or "fours": four cards of the same denomination, and one unmatched card.

3) Full house: three cards of one denomination, and two cards of another denomination.

4) Flush: five cards of the same suit, but not in sequence.

5) Straight: five cards in sequence, but not of the same suit.

6) Three of a kind or "threes": three cards of the same denomination, and two unmatched cards.

7) Two pairs: two cards of one denomination, two cards of another denomination, and one unmatched card.

8) One pair: two cards of the same denomination, and three unmatched cards.

9) High card: five unmatched cards.

Other hands are sometimes accepted locally (eg a "blaze" denotes any five court cards). Their inclusion and their ranking should be agreed before the game begins.

Hands of the same rank When poker hands are of the same rank, the winning hand is decided by the rank of the cards involved.

The following rules apply where no wild cards are used.

1) Straight flush: the highest ranking card in a sequence decides the best hand. Thus a royal flush is the highest when there are no wild cards. Note that the ace in a 5, 4, 3, 2, ace sequence ranks low, so this hand would be beaten by 6, 5, 4, 3, 2. The same rule applies to straights.

2) Four of a kind: the hand with the highest ranking matched cards wins.

3) Full house: the hand with the highest ranking "three of a kind" wins.

4) Flush: the hand with the highest ranking card wins. If the highest cards are the same denomination, the next highest are compared. This continues down to the lowest, until a difference is found.

5) Straight: as for straight flush.

6) Three of a kind: as for four of a kind.

7) Two pairs: the hand with the highest ranking pair wins. If the higher pairs in two hands are the same, the lower pairs are compared. If both pairs in two hands are the same, the hand with the best-ranking unmatched card wins.

8) One pair: the hand with the highest ranking pair wins. If the pairs in two hands are the same, the highest unmatched cards are compared. If these are the same, the next highest are compared. This continues down to the lowest, until a difference is found.

9) High card: as for flush.

4

Flush

5

Straight

6

Three of a kind

7

Two pairs

8

Pair

9

High card

©DIAGRAM

Wild cards

Hands tie if they contain exactly the same denominations: the suits are irrelevant. Hands that tie as highest in a showdown divide the pool between them. If the pool is not exactly divisible, the amount left over goes to the player who was "called" (ie the player who first made the highest bet).

Wild cards Sometimes players agree at the beginning of a game to designate certain cards "wild." A wild card is one that may represent a card of any denomination.

Any card or group of cards may be agreed on, but the following are popular choices:

the joker (or two jokers);

the "deuce" (2) of spades if no joker is available;

all the deuces;

all the deuces and "treys" (3s);

red 10s.

In some forms of the game, a card that occupies a particular position in the game may count as wild, for example each player's "hole" (concealed) card in some stud poker games.

Two alternative rules govern the use of a wild card. The holder may either:

a) use it to represent any card (denomination and suit) he does not hold; or

b) use it to represent any card even if he holds that card.

In either case, a wild card ranks the same as the card it represents.

If a joker is used as a wild card, it may be used either like any other wild card, or alternatively as a "bug." The bug may be used to represent only an ace or any card the player needs to complete a straight or a flush. Again, the use of the joker as the bug may or may not be limited to cards not held by the players.

Hands with wild cards Wild cards rank exactly the same as the cards they stand for, so when comparing hands of the same rank, ties are possible between same-denomination fours, full houses, and threes. With fours and threes, the rank of the other cards in the hands decides the winner where possible.

If hands with wild cards are of identical rank, the hand with no or fewer wild cards wins. If there are the same number of wild cards, the hands tie.

Where wild cards are used for any card (even one held by the player) two new hands are possible.

1) Five of a kind: five cards of the same denomination. This ranks as highest hand, above a straight flush.

Hands with wild cards

Five of a kind

Double ace high flush

2) Double ace high flush: flush including two aces. This ranks above flush and below full house.

Sometimes, a wild card may be used only to make five of a kind – but not to make double ace high flush. This must be decided before the start of play.

Prohibitions A player may not:

a) attempt to make a private agreement with any other player (eg divide the pool without a showdown);

b) waive his turn as dealer, unless physically unable to deal;

c) look at the discards (either before or after showdown), at undealt cards, at another player's hand, or at a hole card (in stud poker);

d) take chips or money from the pool during play, except as correct change for a verbally stated bet;

e) leave the table taking his cards with him (he should ask another player, preferably a non-active one, to play his hand for him – if he fails to do so and misses his turn, his hand is dead).

Bluffing is allowed (ie trying to mislead other players by statements, actions, or manner). Bluffing may include:

making announcements out of turn about one's hand or plan of play that are not true or are not subsequently kept to;

playing so as to make one's hand seem weaker than it is.

Sarcasm, heckling, and derision are allowed – help is not!

Betting intervals In a single play there will be at least one betting interval, and normally two or more.

These always follow receipt of cards by players, but the precise number and when they occur depend on the form of poker being played.

In each betting interval, a certain player will have the right to bet or not to bet first. (How he is chosen depends on the form of the game.)

Thereafter players bet or do not bet in clockwise rotation.

Principles of betting All bets on a play are placed together near the center of the table to form a pool. One player bets first ("opens the betting"). Thereafter, each player in turn must either "drop out," "stay in," or "raise."

In his turn, a player announces what he is doing before he places any chips in the pool.

For a first bet or a raise, he also announces the amount of the bet or raise.

A bet is not considered made until the bettor has removed his hand from the chips bet: until then it can be withdrawn.

a) Drop out (or "fold"): the player discards his hand and gives up his chance of winning the pool on this play.

A player may drop out at any time, even if he has previously bet on this play in an earlier interval or in this interval; but any chips he has already bet remain in the pool and go to the pool winner.

A player who has dropped out is no longer "active," and may not take further action in this play.

b) Stay in (or "call" or "see"): the player puts in just enough chips to make the total he has bet so far in this play exactly equal to the total bet by the player with the highest total bet.

c) Raise (or "up" or "go better"): the player puts in enough chips to stay in, plus an additional number. The additional amount is that by which he "raises the last bet."

Every other player in the game must then either stay in (by bringing his total bet up to the raised amount), drop out, or raise again ("reraise").

Checking is allowed in many games of poker. A player who checks at the beginning of a betting interval stays in the game for the moment without making a bet. If all active players check, the betting interval ends.

But if one player bets, the interval continues as usual: all other players (including those who have checked) must now stay in, drop out, or raise. To stay in, a player who has checked must equal the highest bet made so far.

If all players check on the first betting interval, the play is void and ends. The next player in turn deals the next round (see the section on the pattern of play, p 636).

A betting interval ends when either:

a) all players have checked;

b) only one player is still active (and therefore wins), all the others having dropped out; or

c) the bets of active players are equalized. This happens when all players still active have put equal amounts in the pool, and the turn has come round again to the last person to raise (or, if no one raised, to the person who opened the betting): he may not then raise again. As long as the bets are unequal any player may raise, but as soon as the bets are equal, no one may raise.

Passing may mean either:

a) to drop out; or

b) to check (where checking is allowed).

In games where checking is allowed, a player who says "Pass" is assumed to be checking, if checking is available to him. (A player shows that he is dropping out by discarding his hand.) Games in which no checking is allowed are referred to as "pass and out" (or "pass out" or "bet or drop").

© DIAGRAM

Sandbagging is poker slang for either:

a) checking to disguise a good hand – this is sometimes considered unethical, but is better accepted as a regular part of bluffing; or

b) constant raising and reraising by two players, forcing a third along with them if he wishes to stay in the play.

Raising to force out other players is an essential part of poker, but beyond a certain point it can spoil the game's character. Two optional rulings can keep it in check: limiting raises, and freezing raises.

A limit on raises is often agreed beforehand. Possible limits are:

a) three (or sometimes two) by one player in one betting interval;

b) a total of three by all players in one betting interval.

Freezing the raise is becoming accepted procedure. If there have been two or more raises (whether by one or several players) in a single betting interval, any player who has not raised in that interval may "freeze the raise."

In addition to betting sufficient to stay in, he bets a previously agreed amount, usually two to five times the normal maximum bet (see the section on betting limits, p 632).

Other active players must then drop out or stay in by equaling his bet.

The action only freezes the raise for that betting interval.

Side bets are sometimes made between players. For example, in a "high card bet" in stud poker, players bet on who will have the highest first upcard.

Example of a betting interval

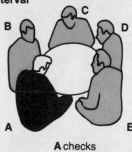

A checks

B opens for 1

C drops out

A stays in

B raises 1

D drops out

Bonuses It is sometimes agreed before play that, on showdown, a player holding a royal flush, straight flush, or four will receive a payment from each player, whether active or not. The amount agreed is usually three to five times the maximum bet.

Betting prohibitions A player may not:

a) bet for another player;

b) borrow money or chips from another player during a play;

c) take back a bet after it has been placed in the pool and the bettor's hand been removed. An inadequate bet must be added to, otherwise it is lost and the player's cards are dead.

Example of a betting interval

Player	Bet	Action	Total bet
A	0	checks	0
B	1	opens for 1	1
C	0	drops out	(0)
D	1	stays in	1
E	3	raises 2	3
A	3	stays in	3
B	3	raises 1	4
D	0	drops out	(1)
E	1	stays in	4
A	1	stays in	4

The betting interval ends. The only three players still active have bet equal amounts; B may not raise the betting again.

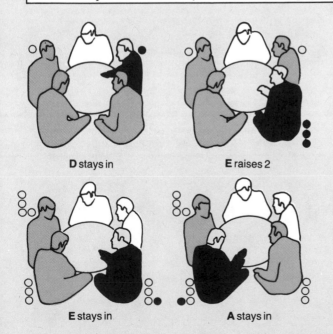

D stays in   E raises 2

E stays in   A stays in

Betting limits The system to be used must be decided upon before play. The betting limits are also the raise limits.

Note that a player forced to bet, for example, the maximum amount to stay in, may still in that turn raise by the maximum (or by any lesser amount).

Specified limits: fixed Minimum and maximum amounts are specified before play starts. Sometimes it is agreed that either:

a) any amount between the limits is acceptable as a bet or raise;

b) only specified amounts between the limits are acceptable as a bet or raise; or

c) no amount between the limits is acceptable as a bet or raise.

Specified limits: varying The minimum and maximum limits change during a play; for example, limits for the final betting interval are always twice the earlier limits.

Last bet limit The opening bet is governed by agreed limits. Thereafter, the maximum bet or raise is the amount put in the pool by the previous bettor's action.

Players must decide that either:

a) each betting interval recommences at the original limits; or

b) continuous growth is allowed over a single play.

Pot limit The opening bet is governed by agreed limits. Thereafter, the maximum bet or raise is the total amount in the pool at that time. To calculate this, a player wishing to raise may include in the pool total the sum needed for him to stay in. Agreement on an absolute maximum is still necessary.

Table stakes Before the session, each player puts any amount of money he wishes onto the table, or buys chips to that amount. (A minimum is agreed beforehand, and sometimes a maximum too.)

Any amount a player wins is added to his table amount. He may also, from his own pocket, increase his table amount – but not during a play, and only by at least the agreed minimum.

During a play, a player may not:

borrow from, or owe money to, the pool;

decrease his table amount or withdraw chips from it;

sell chips back to the banker until he withdraws from the game.

The maximum betting limit for a player is his table amount at the time (the minimum is the amount agreed beforehand).

If a player's table amount is used up in a play, he has the right to remain in for the main pool showdown. Any amounts bet by other players, above the amount he has bet, are put into a side pool.

No limit A player can bet or raise any amount. He may borrow during a play, if he can, but he may not put IOUs in the pool. To stay in, he must equal the highest bet.

In the old no limit games, a player had 24 hours to raise money for a bet. No limit games have now virtually disappeared.

Freeze-out This can be played with any limits system except table stakes.

Before the session, each player puts an equal number of chips on the table in front of him. Winnings are added to this amount, but no players may add new chips, lend chips, or remove chips from the game.

As soon as a player has lost all his chips, he drops out. The session continues until one player has won all the chips.

Jackpot This ruling can be played with any limits system. It applies if all other players drop out in a play, after one player has opened the betting. In the next play and before the deal, the others must each "ante" (put) into the pool an amount equal to the single bet made in the previous play.

The new maximum limit (for this play only) is the total amount now in the pool before play starts (providing that this is higher than the normal maximum).

The minimum is as usual.

Whangdoodle This ruling can be played with any limits system. After the appearance of any very good hand (eg full house or better), the usual or opening limits are doubled for the next play.

Sometimes the special limits hold for the next round of play, ie one deal by each player.

Example of table stakes

In the example shown: of three active players, player B has only 30 units left on the table.

a) Player A bet 40 units: 30 go into the main pool; 10 start a side pool.

b) Player B bets his 30 units, if he wants to stay in the main pool.

c) Player C bets 50 units: 30 go into the main pool, the rest into the side pool.

Betting between A and C then continues until their side pool bets have been equalized.

B makes no further bets, and there are no further payments into the main pool, on this or any further betting intervals in this play.

At the showdown, B wins the main pool if he has the best hand. The side pool can only be won by A or C.

Example of table stakes

a

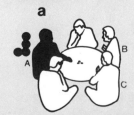

b

c

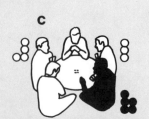

©DIAGRAM

Arrangements

Banker Poker is not a banking game. Bets are made as contributions to a pool. The "banker" simply supervises the supply of betting chips. He records how many have been issued to each player, including himself, and keeps the payments and the unissued stock to one side.

Players must not make exchanges or transactions among themselves. A player needing more chips must purchase them from the banker's stock, a player with surplus chips may sell them back into stock.

The banker is either the host or any player chosen by lot (eg high cut) or agreement.

The kitty is a fund for buying new cards or refreshments, set up by agreement before the game starts.

Usually, one betting unit is contributed to it from any pot in which there has been more than one raise or, alternatively, where the winner holds a hand of a specified rank or better. The banker arranges all this.

Any chips in the kitty at the end of the game are divided equally among those still playing. (A player who leaves before the end loses the right to any part of the kitty.)

Betting chips are almost always used rather than cash. Usually different colors represent different values, for example: white, one unit; red, five units; blue, 10 units; yellow, 25 units.

A game with seven or more players needs about 200 chips. The best value distribution depends on the maximum betting limit.

At the start of play, each player buys chips to the same total value, for example 50 units.

A player's stock of chips must always be kept in full view of other players, and not taken from the table except for cashing.

Two decks of cards with contrasting backs are usually used in club play. At the end of one play, one deck is collected and shuffled by the player who dealt last, while the other is dealt into play by the new dealer.

New deck(s) may be called for by any player at any time.

Seating at the start of a session is random, unless a player demands a reseating after the first dealer has been chosen but before play begins.

On reseating, the first dealer has first choice of seat. He then shuffles the deck, has it cut by the player to his right, and deals one card face up to each player in rotation, beginning with the player to his left.

The player with the lowest ranking card sits to the dealer's left, the player with the next lowest card to that player's left, and so on. Of two cards of the same denomination, that dealt first ranks higher.

The dealer then gathers the cards and has them shuffled and cut for play.

After play starts, or after a reseating, no one may demand a

reseating for at least an hour, provided no one joins or leaves the game.

If a player joins the game after it starts and someone questions the seat he takes, the dealer, between plays, deals a card to each existing player, and the new player takes his seat to the left of the player with the lowest card. This is done separately for each player joining.

If a player replaces another player, he must take the seat vacated, provided no one objects.

Two players may exchange seats just before any play, provided no one objects.

Time limit The time at which the game will end should be agreed before play starts, and be strictly observed.

Any players who then wish to continue can do so, but should set a new time limit.

Time limit for a decision by a player during play (eg how many cards to draw, how to bet) is five minutes. This is important in a high-limit game. If a player fails to act within this time, his hand is dead.

Rules to be agreed before the start of a game (and best written down) are:

a) the form of game to be played;
b) wild cards and their use;
c) any special hands and rulings;
d) the value of chips;
e) betting limits and checking;
f) limits on raises and/or payment for freezing a raise;
g) bonus payments and payments to the kitty.

Club and casino poker The management supplies table, chips, cards, dealer and/or inspector. It takes a cut – usually a direct charge on the winner of each pool, but sometimes an hourly charge for tables and officials.

Irregularities Because poker can be played for very high stakes, innumerable rules govern irregularities of play, both accidental and deliberate. It is impossible to treat all these here. The reader who wishes to play poker for high stakes should consult an advanced book on the subject.

Pattern of play

Rotation of play is clockwise. No player acts until the active player nearest to his right has acted.

Choice of first dealer is by deal: the first jack to appear.

Shuffle and cut See p 381.

The deal is clockwise to active players only, beginning with the active player nearest the dealer's left.

Play varies from one form of poker to another.

Showdown After the final betting interval, players still active expose their hands (in draw poker) or hole card(s) (in stud poker), beginning with the player being called, and in a clockwise direction.

Each player announces the rank of hand he is claiming. In any discrepancy the cards "speak for themselves" – this includes giving the hand a higher rating than claimed, except if there are wild cards (when the player's announcement cannot be improved on).

The hand of highest rank wins.

Tied hands divide the pool equally.

Change of dealer After each play, the deal passes one player to the left of the previous dealer.

Play rotates clockwise

Deal passes to left

Forms of poker

Closed and open poker are the two main forms.

1) Closed poker, usually played in the form of draw poker. Players receive their cards face down. After a betting interval, they discard the cards they do not want, and receive replacements from the deck.

A second betting interval is followed by a showdown if more than one player is still active.

2) Open poker, known as stud poker. This is a faster game than draw poker and allows for more skill. As there is no exchange of cards, the average rank of winning hands is lower than in draw poker.

Players receive some cards face down, some face up. Betting intervals interrupt the deal. After the deal, players cannot receive replacements, but (in versions where more than five cards per player are dealt) each chooses only five cards to form his final hand.

A final betting interval is followed by a showdown if more than one player is still active.

Choice of form The form to be played may be decided by the host or by club rules; but if a decision has to be made, two factors should be taken into account.

1) Number of players. The best games for a particular number of players are as follows:

four or under, stud poker;

five to eight, any form of poker;

nine or ten, five card stud;

more than ten, any variant with fewer than five cards per player – or split into two tables.

2) Relative experience. If some players are considerably more experienced than others, it is best to choose one of the less common variants in which the element of skill is lower.

Dealer's choice If it is agreed to play "dealer's choice," the dealer chooses the game to be played: a standard form, a known variant, or any new and easily explained variant he can devise.

He designates any wild cards. He may not, however, alter the betting limits, add cards to or remove them from the deck, or alter basic poker rules.

His choice of game holds by agreement, either:

a) for his deal only; or

b) for a complete round of dealing. The next dealer in turn then chooses for the next complete round.

Sometimes, a play or round of dealer's choice is played whenever a very good hand appears (eg full house or better).

STUD POKER: STANDARD GAME (FIVE-CARD)

Players Up to ten may play.

Ante Usually, a small compulsory bet is made by all players.

Opening deal One card is dealt face down to each player (the "hole" card), then one card face up. Each player examines his hand.

First betting interval The player with the highest ranking face-up card must open or drop. A wild card is considered higher than an ace. If two players hold equal-ranking cards, the player nearer the dealer's left opens.

After the opener, each player drops, stays in, bets, raises, or reraises in the normal way until betting is equalized.

Continuing play Further rounds of dealing one card face up to each player alternate with betting intervals, until the end of the fourth interval (when each player has one face-down and four face-up cards). On these deals, the dealer leaves the deck resting on the table and takes cards one at a time from the top. On the betting intervals, the player with the right to open is the one with the highest ranking completed hand in exposed cards – the dealer announces that player and also announces exposed hands, possible flushes and straights, and the last deal.

The showdown follows the fourth betting interval; all active players expose their hole cards.

Additional rules

1) If all the players check, the betting interval ends and the play continues.

2) If a player drops out, he turns all his cards face down and does not reveal his hole card.

3) If on any betting interval only one active player is left, he wins and the play ends. He need not show his hole card.

4) A "four flush" is often ruled a ranking hand in stud poker, ie four cards of the same suit plus one other. At showdown (and in deciding the start of a betting interval) it beats a pair but loses to two pairs.

Five-card stud: end of betting

Player 3 dropped out

STUD POKER: VARIANTS

Six-card stud This is like five-card stud, except that after the fourth betting interval each player receives a sixth card face down. This is followed by a fifth (final) betting interval.
At the showdown, each active player chooses five cards from his six to form his final hand.

Seven-card stud (or seven-toed Pete or down the river). This game is for two to eight players.
The opening deal is of three cards: two hole cards, then one face up. Betting intervals and rounds of dealing face-up cards then alternate as usual, until active players have seven cards (including the two hole cards).
After a final betting interval, each active player chooses five cards from his seven to form his showdown hand.

Seven-card stud: low hole card wild As above, but each player's lower ranking hole card is wild – as, for him, is any other card of that denomination. Sometimes players are allowed to choose either one of their hole cards (and its denomination) as wild.

Mexican stud is like five-card stud, except that all cards are dealt face down.
After the second and each subsequent dealing round, each player turns up any one of his face-down cards, leaving one chosen card as hole card.
Sometimes a player's final hole card is ruled wild, together with any other cards of that denomination that he holds.

Other five-card stud variants
1) Last card down: the last card is dealt face down, giving two hole cards.
2) Last card optionally down: a player may turn up his hole card before the last dealing round and receive his fifth card face down.

Low-hand stud The lowest hand wins the pool. The lowest exposed hand begins each betting interval. Other rules are as for the form of stud being played.

Seven-card stud: end of betting

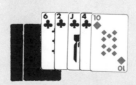

Player 3 dropped out

©DIAGRAM

DRAW POKER

The basic pattern of the game is as follows:

1) Ante: a small compulsory bet is made by all players.

2) Deal: five face-down cards are dealt to each player in the normal way. Players count their cards, then look at them.

3) First betting interval: the player to the dealer's left has the right to bet first; if he does not bet, the other players may bet in turn.

4) Draw: each active player in turn may discard one or more cards and receive from the dealer the same number, face down, from the undealt part of the deck. A player need not draw – he may "stand pat."

5) Second betting interval: the player who made the first bet in the first interval has the right to bet first. If he has dropped out, the first active player to his left may bet.

6) Showdown takes place if more than one active player is left at the end of the second betting interval.

DRAW POKER: STANDARD GAME

Players Up to ten may play. No more than six should play in high-betting games, since with more players it may be necessary to use discards to complete the draw.

Ante Either:

a) each player puts an equal agreed amount into the pool; or

b) only the dealer antes ("dealer's edge").

The ante amount is usually the same as the minimum bet.

First betting interval There are two forms:

1) "Jacks or better." A player may not open the betting unless he holds a pair of jacks or any better hand. (Before betting is opened, players may check.) After betting has opened, a player may bet on any hand, and must bet or drop out. At the end of the play, the opener must show the cards he opened on.

2) "Pass and out" (or "pass out" or "bet or drop"). A player may open the betting on any hand. Each player must bet or drop out; no one may check. In either case, the player to the dealer's left is the first to "speak."

Once the betting has opened, it proceeds in the normal way. If no one opens, all players ante again, and the next dealer deals for the next play.

Draw poker: sequence of play

Deal

Betting

The draw

The draw occurs if more than one player is still active after the first betting interval. The dealer offers the draw to each player in turn in normal rotation, beginning with the player to his left and ending with himself.

Each player in his turn either:

a) states the number of cards he requires and places that number from his hand face down on the table in full view – the dealer then gives him the same number from the undealt part of the deck; or

b) says "I stand pat," or knocks on the table, to indicate that he wishes to keep the hand that he has.

In his turn, the dealer also either states the number of cards he has drawn (exchanged), or indicates that he is "standing pat."

Normally it is ruled that a player may draw one, two, or three cards at his discretion.

With four or fewer players, four and five card draws are sometimes allowed.

A player may use the draw to bluff in any way he wishes about the value of his hand.

The dealer must answer truthfully how many cards he himself drew. No other question need be answered truthfully by anyone.

The bottom card of the deck is not used. If further cards are required, the bottom card and the cards discarded so far are shuffled together and cut to allow the draw to continue. The usual rules apply, but the player due to draw next cuts last. No other shuffling or cutting on the draw is allowed.

Sometimes, in "jacks or better," the opening bettor discards one of his "openers" (ie one of the cards that gave him the right to open). If he does so, he must state this, and the discarded opener is kept to one side to be inspected at the end of the play. It is not used if the discards are reshuffled.

Betting

Showdown

Second betting interval This follows the usual rules. All players may check, even if "pass and out" was enforced for the first interval. If all the players check, the interval ends. If all players except one drop out, that player wins without showing his hand (except for showing his openers in "jacks or better," if he opened the betting).

Showdown Each active player in turn must place all his five cards face up on the table, to be seen by all players (active or otherwise). At the same time he announces the value of his hand – he must do this even if he sees he is beaten.

If all players checked in the second betting interval, the opener shows his hand first; but if bets were placed in the second betting interval, the player who was called shows first. In either case, other active players then follow in normal rotation.

Dropping out In draw poker a player indicates that he is dropping out by placing his cards face down on the table when his turn in the betting interval arrives.

As long as a player wishes to remain in the game he must keep his cards in his hands, above table height, unless he is forced to put down the cards temporarily for some reason, in which case he must state this.

DRAW POKER: VARIANTS
"Jacks or better" variations
1) Progressive openers: if no one opens on a play, two queens or better are required to open on the next play. If again no one opens, two kings or better are required on the next play; then two aces or better; then back down to two kings or better, two queens or better, and two jacks or better.

Each time, players must ante again; and sometimes the limits are doubled. Once a player opens, the next play reverts to jacks or better (and limits go back to normal).

2) "Jack or bobtail" to open. This is like "jacks or better" but a player may also open on a "bobtail" (four cards of the same suit plus one other card) or a "bobtail straight" (four cards in sequence plus one other card – but the sequence may not be: a, k, q, j; or 4, 3, 2, a).

These hands have no showdown value.

Blind opening (or "blind tiger" or "blind and straddle"). In this variation, players bet "blind," ie before receiving their hands. Before the deal:

1) the dealer antes only one chip;
2) the player to his left bets one chip blind ("edge");
3) the next player raises him, betting two chips blind ("straddle"),

After the deal, the next player after the blind raiser has the first voluntary bet. He may call (two chips), drop out, or raise (three chips). The betting interval then proceeds as normal. The maximum raise before the draw is one chip. (Note that the dealer's ante does not count toward staying in, but the two players' blind bets do.)

In the second betting interval, the bet and raise limit is two chips. Betting begins with the first blind bettor or the (still active) player nearest his left. Players may check until a bet is made.

Sometimes, in the predeal betting, up to three voluntary blind bets – each doubling the last bet – are allowed after the blind raise. These bets count toward staying in the game in the first interval.

Shotgun Play is as in the standard game, except for an additional (first) betting interval during the deal, after each player has received three cards.

Any hand can open. There is no checking.

Stormy weather Each player receives four cards. Three face-down cards are dealt to the table, one each after the second, third, and fourth dealing rounds.

There is then a betting interval. A player may open on any hand. There is no checking.

In the draw, each player may change up to four cards. After the draw, the dealer turns up the table cards one at a time, with a betting interval as each one is turned up.

At the showdown, a player uses any one of the table cards as his fifth card. None of the table cards is wild.

Stormy weather: deal

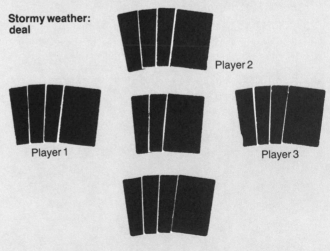

Player 2

Player 1

Player 3

Dealer

Lowball is often played during "jacks or better" sessions. When no one has openers for "jacks or better," lowball is played for that play only.

In lowball the lowest hand wins. Rules are as for the standard game, with the following exceptions.

1) Ante: the dealer and the player to his left (sometimes also the second player to his left) ante.

2) First betting interval: the player to the left of the last player to ante must open or drop out. No checking is allowed. The limit is the ante amount. Antes count toward staying in.

3) Draw: before the draw the dealer "burns" (exposes and then discards) the top deck card.

4) Second betting interval: this begins with the active player nearest the dealer's left. Checking is allowed, but a player who checks cannot later raise on that play.

Limits are agreed beforehand.

5) Showdown is won by the lowest hand.

Ace always counts low, and straights and flushes do not count. Therefore 1, 2, 3, 4, 5 (known as a "bicycle") counts as five low cards and is the lowest hand – regardless of suits.

The joker can be used for any card not in the player's hand.

Spit in the ocean There are many versions of this; some are given in the section on closed poker games, p 280.

1) Basic game: each player receives four cards. The next card is dealt face up to the center. The game proceeds as usual, but at showdown each active player must count this table card as the fifth card in his hand.

2) Pig in the poke: as above, but the face-up card and all the others of the same denomination are wild (or sometimes only cards of the same denomination as the face-up card, but not the face-up card itself).

Low ball: lowest hand

Spit in the ocean: deal

Player 2

Player 1

Player 3

Dealer

© DIAGRAM

CLOSED POKER GAMES

These are variants in which there is no draw.

Showdown straight poker (or cold hand poker) There is one betting interval before the deal. The deal is normal, but the cards are dealt face up and the best hand dealt wins.

Double barrel shotgun Each player receives five face-down cards. Beginning with the player to the dealer's left, all the players then expose any one of their cards.

Betting intervals then alternate with further rounds of exposing one card each. On the fifth and final round of exposure, the best hand wins.

Spit in the ocean variants

1) Crisscross (or X marks the spot): each player receives four cards. Five cards are then dealt face down to the center of the table in the shape of a cross.

Players examine their hands. The dealer then turns up any one of the table cards except the one at the center of the cross. A betting interval follows.

Exposure of the cards in the cross alternates with betting intervals until all but the central card of the cross have been exposed.

After the fourth betting interval the center card is exposed; showdown follows immediately.

The center card of the cross is wild, as are all other cards of the same denomination.

Each player mentally selects his final five-card hand from any cards in his hand and the table cards. (Sometimes, he is only allowed to choose table cards from any three that form a straight line in the cross.)

2) Cincinnati: five cards are dealt to each player, and the next five cards are dealt face down to the center of the table.

The game is the same as crisscross, but without the cross pattern. None of the table cards is wild; a player may use any of the table cards in his final hand.

3) Lame-brain Pete: this is played like Cincinnati, but the lowest-ranking table card is wild, as are all the other cards of that denomination.

Three-card poker Each player receives three face-down cards, and there is a betting interval after each round of cards is dealt Showdown follows immediately after the third interval.

The rank of hands (with the highest given first) is: threes; three-card straight flush; three-card flush; three-card straight; pair; high card.

Two-card poker (usually played with wild cards) comprises: a deal of two face-down cards to each player; a single betting interval; and a showdown.

Pairs and high cards are the only hands.

HIGH-LOW POKER

Almost any standard game or variant, draw or stud, can also be played as a high-low game. Especially popular is seven-card high-low stud.

At showdown, the highest and lowest hands split the pool.

Usually a player must declare, just before showdown, whether he is competing for highest hand, lowest hand, or both.

It is possible to declare for both in any game where a player has more than five cards from which to select his final hand, for he is then allowed to select two different hands.

Rank of cards is as usual.

If a player is competing for the lowest hand, ace ranks low;
if competing for the highest hand, ace is high or low, as he wishes;
if competing for highest and lowest hands, ace can be both high and low as he wishes.

Rank of hands is as usual. Hence the lowest possible hand, without wild cards, is 6, 4, 3, 2, a in different suits (5, 4, 3, 2, a would be a straight).

The usual rules for comparing hands apply – highest card first, then next highest, until a difference is found. Thus 9, 7, 6, 5, 4 ranks lower than 9, 8, 4, 3, 2.

Wild cards A wild card can only be given one denomination and suit at showdown.

If declaring for lowest hand, a wild card ranks the same as a low ace, without pairing any ace in the hand. Thus 4, 3, 2, a, wild card becomes the lowest possible hand.

Declaring follows the last betting interval. There are two methods.

a) Beginning with the player to the dealer's left, each active player in turn declares himself as competing for highest hand or lowest or both.

b) Each player takes one of his chips in his hand, without revealing its color. He takes a white one if declaring low, a red one if declaring high, or a blue one if declaring both.

High-low: lowest hand

When all the players have decided, they show their chips.

The highest hand and lowest hand divide the pool equally (if an exact division is impossible, the highest hand receives any odd chips).

A player can only win the part of the pool for which he has declared. If more than one player has declared the same way, the player with the best hand wins that part of the pool.

If all the players have declared the same way, the player with the best hand wins the whole pool.

If a player has declared for both high and low, he must at least tie each way at showdown, or his hand is dead and he receives nothing.

Polish red dog

Also known as stitch and Polish pachuk, this game was played by Polish immigrants to the United States.

Equipment:
1) one standard deck of 52 cards;
2) betting chips (or cash).
Players The game is for two to ten players.
Rank of cards is normal, with ace high. The suits are not ranked.
Objective Players aim to hold a card in the same suit but of a higher rank than the banker's card.
Choice of first banker is by deal: first ace to appear. (See p 381.)
Shuffle and cut are normal (see p 381).
Bank The banker places in the center of the table the amount he wishes to put at risk. A minimum is usually agreed before the game.
Deal The banker deals three face-down cards to each player except himself, dealing one card at a time.
Play Players bet without looking at their cards. Play begins with the player to the banker's left. He places his bet in front of him: this may be any amount up to half the total of the bank.
The banker then "burns" the top card of the deck, ie he turns it

Deal

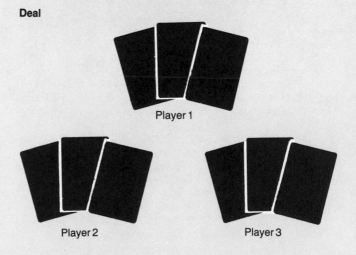

Player 1

Player 2   Player 3

face up, shows it to all players, and places it face up at the bottom of the deck. He then turns up the next card and this becomes the banker's card.

The first player then turns his own cards face up. If he holds a higher ranking card of the same suit as the banker's card, he wins; if not, he loses.

If he has won, he receives back his bet and twice that amount from the bank.

If he has lost, his bet is added to the bank.

His cards are then placed face up at the bottom of the deck. Bet and play then pass one player to the left. After the player has bet, the banker burns one card before exposing a new banker's card.

Change of banker If the bank is emptied at any time, the bank and deal immediately pass one player to the left and a new round is begun.

If the bank is not emptied at the end of a round, the same banker continues to deal.

If, at the end of any round, the bank has increased to three or more times the size it was when the present banker began, then the banker declares a "stitch" round. He deals one more round, and, at the end of this, collects anything left in the bank. Bank and deal then pass one player to the left.

A player must continue to act as banker until the bank is emptied or a stitch round has been completed.

Play

Player 1 wins

Banker's card
Player 2 loses

Player 3 wins

Red and black

This is a private banking game derived from the casino game of trente et quarante

Equipment:
1) two standard decks of 52 playing cards;
2) betting chips.
Players: two or more.
Objective Each player tries to forecast correctly whether he will hold more red or more black cards in his hand.
Choice of first banker is by high cut (see p 381).
Shuffle and cut are standard (see p 381) – with the two decks shuffled together to form a single deck.
Betting limits are agreed beforehand.
Betting Each player bets on red or black. He bets any amount within the limits. A player bets on black by placing his bet in front of him to his left; he bets on red by placing it in front of him to his right.

(Alternatively each player may be given two colored tokens: one red and one black. He places one of these beside his bet.)

Play The banker deals five cards, one at a time, face up, to the player to his left. He deals them directly in front of the player, so that it is clear whether the player's bet lies to the right or left. If the first four cards consist of two red and two black cards, the player may double his bet before he receives his fifth card. After the first player's bet is settled, the banker deals to the next player to the left. He continues dealing until all players but himself have received a hand.

Settlement of bets A player wins from the banker if he is dealt three or more cards of the color bet on. If he has three of that color, he wins the amount of his bet. If he has four, he doubles his bet. If he has five, he wins four times his bet.

A player loses to the banker if he is dealt three or more cards of the color not bet on. If he has three, he loses his bet. If he has four, he pays the banker twice his bet (his original bet and a further payment equal to it). If he has five cards, he pays four times his bet (his original bet plus a payment equal to three times his bet).

Change of banker After the banker has dealt a hand to all the other players, the bank and deal pass one player to the left.

Red dog

This fast betting game, also known as high card pool, is very popular among American news reporters. It needs little skill and is usually played for low stakes.

Equipment:
1) one standard deck of 52 cards;
2) betting chips (or cash).
Players: from two to ten.
Rank of cards is normal (ace high). Suits are not ranked.
Objective Players aim to hold a card in the same suit but of higher rank than a card dealt from the deck.
Choice of first dealer is by deal: first ace to appear. (See p 381.)
Shuffle and cut are normal (see p 381).
Ante Before each deal, each player, including the dealer, puts an equal amount (known as the "ante") into the pool.
Deal The dealer deals five face-down cards to each player including himself, beginning with the player to his left and going clockwise.
(Four cards each are dealt if players prefer or if more than eight are playing.)
Betting All players look at their cards. Play begins with the player to the dealer's left. He must bet if he wants to stay in the game. To bet he places his stake in front of him, near the pool. The minimum bet is equal to the ante. The maximum bet is equal to the total in the pool at the time. The dealer must keep note of all bets.
If a player does not wish to stay in the game, he must pay a forfeit equal to the minimum bet but may then place his hand face down on the table without showing it.

Deal

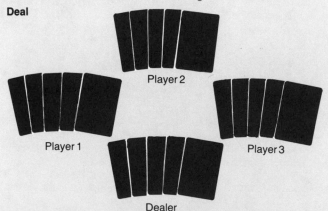

Player 2

Player 1

Player 3

Dealer

Play The dealer deals the top card from the deck face up onto the table in front of the bettor.

Play

If the player holds a card of higher rank in the same suit, he wins; if not, he loses. If he has won, he shows the winning card only (**a**), and receives back his bet and an equal amount from the pool. If he has lost, he shows all his hand (**b**), and his bet is added to the pool.

In either case, his hand is then placed face down in front of him.
Bet and play then pass one player to the left.
When all players including the dealer have had a turn of play, the deal passes to the next player to the left. Any money in the pool remains, but all players ante again before the next deal.

Empty pool If the pool is emptied during a round, all players ante again to allow the round to continue. They must still ante again before the next round begins.

Division of the pool Sometimes the pool becomes too large for the level of betting. It is best if a limit for the pool is agreed beforehand. If the pool passes that limit, it is divided among the players at the end of that round.

Irregularities
1) If a player receives no hand, or too many cards in his hand, he may not take part in the round. The dealer is not penalized.
2) If a player receives too few cards in his hand, he may bet if he wishes, or he may discard his hand without showing it and without betting or paying a forfeit. The dealer is not penalized.
3) If the top card of the deck is accidentally exposed, it is discarded.
4) Once a player has stated his bet, he cannot alter it. A bet paid into the pool in error cannot be returned. A bet received from the pool in error cannot be taken back once the top card for the next player has been dealt.

VARIANTS OF RED DOG
Burning card version The dealer "burns" a card from the top of the deck before each card that he exposes to settle a bet. That is, at each bettor's turn, the dealer discards the topmost card after turning it face up and showing it to all the players. The next card is then turned up to decide whether the bettor has won or lost.

Banking version Red dog can also be played as a banking game. The current dealer acts as banker. He does not deal to himself. Before the hand, the dealer places in front of him the money or chips he wishes to put at risk. This can be any amount he wishes. The players do not ante.
Each player in turn, excluding the banker, bets any amount he wishes up to the total then in the bank.
Any amount left in the bank at the end of the hand is returned to the banker. The bank and deal then pass one to the left.
If the bank is emptied before all players have had a turn, the hand ends and the bank and deal pass at once.

© DIAGRAM

SIX-SPOT RED DOG: POOL VERSION

In this version there is no banker; players ante into a pool.

Equipment:

1) one standard deck of 52 cards;

2) betting chips (or cash).

Players The game is for two to 15 players.

Rank of cards is normal (ace high).

Objective Players aim to hold a card in the same suit but of higher rank than the pool card.

Choice of first dealer is by deal: first ace to appear. (See p 381.)

Shuffle and cut are normal (see p 381).

Ante Before each deal, each player including the dealer puts an agreed equal amount into the pool.

Deal

Play

Deal The dealer deals three face-down cards to each player including himself, beginning with the player to his left and going clockwise.

The dealer then deals one card from the top of the deck face up to the center of the table. If it is a 6 or lower (6, 5, 4, 3, or 2) it becomes the pool card. If it is a 7 or higher, it is discarded and the next card from the top of the deck is dealt face up onto the table. This procedure is repeated until a 6 or lower card is dealt to become the pool card. If there is no such card left in the deck, the hand is redealt.

Betting All players including the dealer bet immediately without looking at their cards. The minimum bet is one chip (or a previously agreed sum of money); the maximum is the amount in the pool. More than one player may bet the maximum.

Play Players then turn their hands face up. If a player has a card of the same suit but ranking higher than the pool card, he has won. If not, he has lost.

Settlement of bets is supervised by the dealer. He first adds to the pool the bets of all players who have lost. Then he pays out to those players who have won, beginning with the player to his left and going clockwise. Winning bets are returned together with an equal amount from the pool.

If the pool is emptied before all winning players have been paid, the remaining players receive back only their bets.

If anything remains in the pool after all bets have been settled, this amount is carried over to the next round.

The deal then passes one player to the left, and all players ante again to begin the next round.

SIX-SPOT RED DOG: BANKING VERSION

In this version the dealer acts as banker; he does not bet.

Bank Before the hand, the banker places in front of him any amount he wishes to put at risk. The players do not ante.

Deal The banker deals to the players as usual but excludes himself. He then deals one card at a time to the table in the usual way, until a 6 or lower card is dealt. This is now referred to as the banker's card.

Betting begins with the player to the banker's left. He may bet ("cover") any amount up to the total of the bank. Subsequent players may only bet against any amount of the bank that has not yet been "covered." The total of bets against the bank cannot therefore exceed the amount in the bank.

If all the bank has been covered before all players have bet, the remaining players are not allowed to bet on that hand.

Any part of the bank that is not covered when all players have bet is not at risk in that hand.

Play and settlement of bets takes place in the usual way. When all bets have been settled, any amount left in the bank is returned to the banker. The bank and deal then pass one player to the left.

Skinball

Skinball is a very fast action game played in gaming houses in the American South and Midwest. It is very similar to ziginette and seems originally to have been a black American version of that game. It is also called skin or skinning.

Equipment:
a) one standard deck of 52 cards;
b) a card box that allows only one card to be removed at a time.
Players The game is played by three or more people. One person is banker.
There is also a house official who keeps a watch on proceedings, transfers dead cards to the discard pile, collects and pays bets for the banker, and takes the house's percentage cut. (The house never banks the game.)

The objective is for a player not to have his card matched before the banker's card has been matched. Also, if the player has made side bets, he aims not to have his card matched before the card of any player that he has bet against has been matched. A card is "matched" when another card of the same denomination is dealt from the card box.

Choice of first banker is by deal – the first ace to appear.

Shuffle and cut See p 381. After the cut, the banker places the deck face down in the card box.

Betting limits are decided by the banker and can be altered by him at will.

Opening play The banker slides the top card from the card box and deals it face up to the first player to his right.

The player may accept the card or may refuse it for any reason. If a player refuses a card he is out of the game until the next turn of play. The card that has been refused is offered to the next player to his right.

As soon as a player accepts this first card, the banker deals a second face-up card from the box to himself: this is the banker's card.

Opening bet The player who has accepted the card states his bet. This may be for any amount within the betting limits.

Even if the bet is within the limits, however, the banker need not accept it. He may reduce it to any amount he chooses. If the banker does this, the player must accept the decision; he cannot withdraw.

Whichever bet the banker accepts, he places the corresponding amount of money in the centre of the player's card.

The player then makes his bet by literally "covering" the banker's money with his own.

Next card in play The banker deals a third card from the box. If this card's denomination matches either the banker's or the player's card, then the bet involved is settled.

If the card matches the banker's card, the amount on the player's card is won by the player.

If the card matches the player's card, the amount on his card is won by the banker.

If the third card does not match either of the earlier cards, it is dealt to the next player in turn. He may accept or refuse it. If he refuses it, it is offered to the next player in turn. Once the card is accepted, a bet is placed against the banker in the usual way.

Bets between players When more than one player has a card, bets may be made between them.

A player bets that the other player's card will be matched before his own.

Either of the two players may suggest the bet; the other player must be in agreement for the bet to take place.

Money involved in bets between players is stacked to one side.

Matched cards Each time a card is matched, the houseman takes both cards and puts them in a discard pile. The other two cards of the same denomination still in the deck are not allowed to enter play. When one appears it is put directly into the discard pile and a further card is dealt.

Continuation of play As long as the banker's card is not matched, the deal and betting continue as above until each player has been offered a card.

The banker then continues to deal further cards (one at a time and face up) to the table. Any card that appears that does not match either a player's card, a discarded card, or the banker's card is called a "fresh" card.

If there is a player without a card – either because he refused an earlier card or because his card has been matched – he is offered the first fresh card to appear.

If there is more than one player without a card, the fresh card is offered first to the player without a card who is nearest the banker's right.

If he refuses it, it is offered to the next player to his right without a card.

Any fresh cards that appear when every player is holding a card are placed face up in the centre of the table. A player may

accept any one of them as soon as the card he holds has been matched.

Each time a player accepts a card, he makes a bet against the banker in the usual way. A player with a card will often have side bets against every other player, but he must bet against the banker first.

Banker's card matched Whenever the banker's card is matched, all the players betting against him at the time win the amounts on their cards.

If there are no unsettled side bets, the bank passes to the next player to the right. All cards are collected and shuffled for the next deal.

If there are unsettled side bets, the banker chooses either:
a) to continue to deal for the betting players only – he does not enter into any further bets himself and does not give out any fresh cards; or
b) to take the first fresh card dealt from the deck as his new banker's card.

Any player's cards that are matched while the banker has no card become dead without the players losing their bets.

After the banker has a new card, players without cards may take fresh cards as they appear, and place new bets. Although players with outstanding side bets may make new bets against the banker, they are not obliged to do so.

When the bank is exhausted, the bank must pass.

House percentage The house takes either:
a) 25% of the last winning bet of each deal; or
b) 2% from each bet won by a player against the banker, plus 2% of the banker's winnings, if any, at the end of his deal.

Slippery Sam

This is a private banking game related to red dog. It is popular in parts of America's Midwest.

Equipment:
1) one standard deck of 52 cards;
2) betting chips or cash.
Players: ideally six to eight but two or more can play.
Rank of cards is normal (ace high). Suits are not ranked.
Objective Players aim to hold a card in the same suit but of a higher rank than the banker's card.

Deal

Player 1   Player 2   Player 3

Banker

Play

Player 1 wins   Player 2 loses

Banker's new card   Player 3 wins

Choice of first banker is by high cut (see p 381).

Shuffle and cut are normal (see p 381).

Bank The banker places in the center of the table the amount he wishes to put at risk. This is any amount above an agreed minimum.

Deal The banker deals three cards to each player, dealing them one at a time and face down. He then deals one card face up to himself.

Play Players bet without looking at their hands. Play begins with the player to the banker's left. He may agree or refuse to bet against the exposed banker's card.

1) If he agrees, he bets any amount he chooses, above an agreed minimum, up to the total amount in the bank.

He then looks at his cards. If he holds a card in the same suit but of higher rank than the banker's card, he wins; if not, he loses.

2) Alternatively, he refuses to bet against the exposed banker's card. In this case he says "Deal me another card." For this privilege he must pay into the bank an amount equal to one fifth of the bank (or, under alternative rules, he pays a previously agreed amount).

The exposed banker's card is then discarded and another card dealt from the top of the deck face up onto the table.

This becomes the new banker's card. The player either bets against this card in the usual way, or pays again for a new banker's card to be dealt.

A player may reject the banker's card up to three times on a single hand, paying the same amount each time.

After the third rejection, the player may either bet in the usual way against the banker's card now exposed, or he may pass his turn without betting.

3) If the player has bet and won, he shows his winning card only. His bet is returned plus an equal amount from the bank. If he has bet and lost, he shows all his hand and his bet is added to the bank.

Whether he has won or lost, his hand is then added face down to a discard pile.

4) Bet and play then pass one player to the left, and continue in the same way. Each player's turn begins with the banker's card on which the last player bet or passed: a new banker's card is dealt only when paid for.

When all players except the banker have had a turn, the banker collects whatever amount is now in the bank. Bank and deal then pass one player to the left.

If the bank is emptied ("bust") before each player has had a turn, the bank and deal pass immediately.

Stuss

Stuss is a simplified form of faro with a larger percentage in the gambling house's favor.
~~favour.~~

Equipment:
a) a table with the stuss layout, usually made up of the entire spades suit.
b) a dealing box allowing one card to be removed at a time, but with a recess ("pocket") at the bottom of the box that prevents the last four cards of the deck appearing in play;
c) a standard 52-card deck;
d) betting chips of various colors.
Players Up to ten can play. House officials are a dealer and a lookout who supervises betting.
The objective is for a player to bet on a denomination that subsequently appears as a winning card before it appears as a losing card.
Cards appear in play two at a time. The first in each pair is always the losing card, the second is the winning card.
Shuffle, cut, and bet The house dealer shuffles the cards, cuts the deck, and puts it face down in the box.
Bets are then placed on the layout.
Betting A player may place as many bets as he wishes, but each bet is on one denomination only. A bet is always for a denomination to win – ie that the next card of that denomination to appear will be the second (winning) card in a turn.
A turn
1) The dealer removes the top card from the box and places it face up to the right.
2) Any bets on the denomination of this (losing) card are collected by the house.
3) The dealer removes the next card from the box and places it face up to the left.
4) Any bets on the denomination of this card are won by the bettors. Their bet is returned together with an equal payment by the house.
Between turns Other bets may be changed and new bets placed.
Continuing play Play continues in this way through the deck. The two cards in play in each turn are added to those played previously, to form a winning and a losing pile.
Eventually no more cards can be dealt. There will then have been 24 two-card turns, and four cards will still remain in the pocket of the box.

Pocket cards The dealer opens the box and shows the four remaining cards. If any bets have been placed on their denominations, they are all won by the house.

Splits If two cards of the same denomination appear on a turn (a "split"), any bets on that denomination are won by the house.

Second bets are bets on a denomination of which one card has already been dealt; usually they are bet on in the normal way. Some casinos, however, do not allow second bets. In this case, the last four cards are not "pocketed" but appear for play and for betting in the normal way.

Variants

1) In a very simple form of stuss, the cards are dealt from the hand.

2) Stuss is sometimes played as a private banking game; the role of banker is taken by the player willing to put up the largest bank.

©DIAGRAM

Thirty-five

Thirty-five is a modern version of the Italian game of trentacinque. Bets are placed in a central pool; there is no banker.

Equipment:
1) one standard deck of 52 cards;
2) betting chips (or cash).
Players The game is for two to five players.

Deal

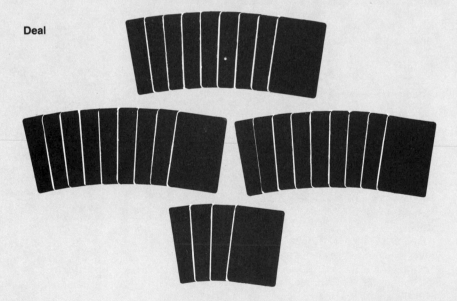

End of play

Making 35 – in hearts

Rank of cards Face cards count 10 points; others count their numerical face value.

Objective Each player aims to hold a total of 35 points or more in one suit.

Choice of first dealer is by high cut (see p 381).

Shuffle and deal are normal (see p 381).

Ante Before each hand, each player including the dealer places an agreed equal amount in the center of the table to constitute the pool.

Deal

1) The dealer deals one card face down to each player including himself and then one card face down to the center of the table. He continues in this way until each hand, including the hand on the table, contains four cards. He then deals no further cards to the center of the table, but continues dealing to each player, including himself, until each has a further five cards. Thus the hand at the center of the table contains four cards and the other hands nine cards each.

2) The remaining cards of the deck are placed to one side and do not enter subsequent play.

3) The players then examine their cards. A player who holds cards in any one suit to the value of 35 or over announces this and takes the pool. If two or more players have 35 or more, the pool is divided between them.

4) If no player claims the pool, bidding begins.

Bidding for the "buy" Betting takes the form of bidding for the table hand – the "buy."

Bidding begins with the player to the dealer's left. His opening bid may be any amount up to the total in the pool. (If he does not wish to bid, he throws in his cards.)

Thereafter, each player may raise the bid or throw in his cards until only one player is left prepared to bid. He then takes the table hand and adds it to the nine cards he already holds.

Settlement involves only the pool and the player who has taken the table hand. If the player now holds cards to the value of 35 or over in any one suit, he declares this, shows his cards, and takes an amount from the pool equal to his bid. If his bid exceeded the amount of the pool, he takes all the pool but has no further claim.

If the player does not hold cards in one suit to the value of 35 or more, he pays into the pool an amount equal to his bid.

Division of the pool Sometimes the pool becomes too large for the level of betting. It is best if a limit for the pool is agreed beforehand. If the pool passes that limit, it is divided among the players.

Change of dealer The deal passes one player to the left after each hand.

Card values

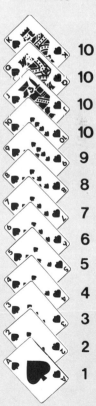

K	10
Q	10
J	10
10	10
9	9
8	8
7	7
6	6
5	5
4	4
3	3
2	2
A	1

©DIAGRAM

Thirty-one

The name thirty-one comes from the number of points awarded to the highest scoring hand (ace, queen, 10 of the same suit) in this pool betting game. An alternative name is Schnautz.

Equipment:
1) one standard deck of 52 cards;
2) betting chips (or cash).
Players: from three to 15.
Value of cards Aces count 11, face cards 10, and all other cards their numerical face value.
Rank of cards is normal, ace high. Thus although face cards all count 10, king beats queen, and queen beats jack.
Objective Players aim to obtain the highest points count from three cards of the same suit or rank.
Choice of first dealer is by low cut (see p 381).
Shuffle and cut are normal (see p 381).
Ante Before each hand, each player including the dealer puts an agreed equal amount into a pool.
Deal The dealer deals one card face down to each player including himself, beginning with the player to his left and going clockwise; and then one card face up to the center. This continues until all players and the table hand (the "widow") each have three cards.
Play Each player examines his cards and announces immediately if he holds:
a) three cards of one suit – with a points total of 31 ("31 points");
b) any three cards of the same rank ("three cards");
c) three cards of one suit – with a points total that he feels is high enough to win ("x points").
If a player announces immediately, all players show their hands and the highest point count wins.
If no player announces immediately, the player to the dealer's left must exchange one of his cards with any face-up card on the table. (Sometimes it is agreed that two or even three cards may be exchanged in one turn.) He is not allowed to pass.
The next player then does the same. Cards that have been put out by a player may subsequently be picked up.
Play continues around the table in this way until one player has 31 points or is satisfied with his cards.
If a player has 31 points he must announce it immediately, and all exchanging ends. All players then show their hands.
If a player is satisfied with his hand he knocks on the table instead of exchanging a card in his next turn. In this case, hands are not shown until each of the other players in turn has had the

Card values

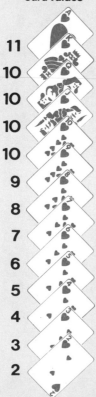

11
10
10
10
10
9
8
7
6
5
4
3
2

option of exchanging one more card.

The pool is won by the player who shows the best hand.

The deal then passes to the next player to the left.

Scoring of hands A hand with three cards of the same rank scores 30½; all others score their points count.

Where two or more players have hands scoring the same number of points, the hand containing the higher ranking card wins. For example: ace, king, queen beats ace, queen, jack. (Note that a score of 25 or 26 points often wins.)

"Widow"

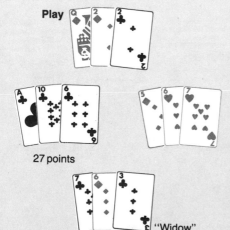

27 points

"Widow"

Trente et quarante

Trente et quarante is one of the most popular games in French and Italian casinos, although it is rarely found elsewhere. It originated in seventeenth-century Europe and is also known as rouge et noir.

Equipment:
a) regulation table with trente et quarante double layout;
b) six standard 52-card decks shuffled together to form a single deck of 312 cards;
c) an indicator card for cutting the deck.

Players Any number of people can play up to the limit that the table will accommodate.

Five croupiers operate the game: four control the bank and one acts as dealer ("tailleur"). A supervisor sits on a stand overlooking the table.

Value of cards Court cards count 10. All other cards count their face value, with aces counting one.

The objective is to bet which of two rows of cards will give a total points count nearer 31.

Shuffle and cut At the start of a round of play the dealing croupier spreads all six decks on the table. (If it is not the first round of play, the cards must first be taken from the discard receiver and sorted until they are all face down.)

All croupiers and players each take a group of cards and shuffle them. The croupier then gathers all the cards and gives them a further shuffle. He offers one player the whole deck to cut. The player inserts the indicator card at the point at which he wants the cards cut. The dealer cuts the deck at this point and the indicator card and all cards above it go to the bottom of the deck.

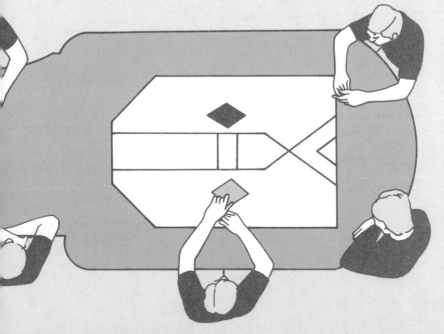

Betting All bets are placed against the bank. Before the play, players bet in one or both of the following ways, placing their bets on the layout.

a) Players bet which row will win, either black (N for "noir" on the layout) or red (R for "rouge").

b) Players bet whether the suit color of the very first card dealt will or will not match the color of the winning row. If they want to bet that it will match, they bet on C for "couleur" on the layout. If they want to bet that it will not match, they bet on I for "inverse."

Play The players place their bets (see the section on betting). The dealing croupier then takes about 50 cards from the top of the deck and deals one card face up onto the table.

He then deals further cards face up, placing them alternately to the right and left of the first card. After each card he announces the total number of points now contained in the row. When the total equals or passes 31 points he stops dealing. This first row is called the "black" row whatever the suit color of the cards it contains.

The dealing croupier in exactly the same way then deals a second row below the first. This is the "red" row. He again stops dealing when the total equals or passes 31 points.

The row with the points total nearer to 31 is the winning row. The winning total will always be in the range 31 to 39 inclusive – ie between 30 and 40. It is from this that the game takes its name.

Settlement of bets After the deal the dealing croupier announces the result.

Traditionally he calls the results for red and color only, ie "Rouge gagne" (red wins) or "Rouge perd" (red loses), and "Couleur gagne" (color wins) or "Couleur perd" (color loses).

The croupiers collect all losing bets. All winning bets are paid off at even money (1 to 1). If both rows tie at more than 31 (a "refait"), all bets are returned.

If both rows tie at 31 ("refait de trente et un") the bank takes half of all bets and returns the remainder, or, rather than lose half his bet, a player may decide to leave his bet in "prison" (P on the layout) for the next deal. If his original bet is successful in this next deal, his bet is returned but earns no money. If it is unsuccessful he now loses all his bet. (Sometimes with a bet in prison the player may choose whether to maintain his original bet or transfer it to its opposite.)

Insurance bet Before a hand is dealt, a player can indicate that he wishes to insure against a tie at 31. The charge for this is 5% of his wager.

**Sample betting
and play**

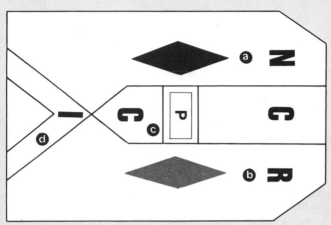

a bets black row to win
b bets red row to win
c bets first card will match winning row
d bets first card will not match winning row

Black row

33 points

Red row

37 points

The black row is nearer to 31, and so wins
a wins
b loses
c wins
d loses

Yablon

This game is also called in between and ace-deuce. It is most commonly played as a pool game.

Equipment:
1) one standard deck of 52 cards;
2) betting chips (or cash).
Players: from two to eight.
Rank of cards is normal, ace high. Suits have no significance.
Objective Each player hopes to draw a card ranking between his first two cards.
Choice of first dealer is by deal: first ace to appear. (See p 381.)
Shuffle and cut are normal (see p 381).
Ante Before each deal each player including the dealer puts an equal agreed amount into the pool.
Deal The dealer deals two face-down cards one at a time to each player including himself.
Play begins with the player to the dealer's left.
1) He examines his cards and decides whether to bet.
2) If he does not wish to bet he says "No bet," and returns his cards to the dealer to be placed on a discard pile. Play then passes to the left.
If the first player does wish to bet, he places his bet in front of him near the pool. The minimum bet is the same amount as a player's ante; the maximum is the total then in the pool.
3) The dealer deals him the top card from the deck, face up. This is called the player's draw card.
4) The player turns his two original cards face up.
5) If his draw card ranks between his original two cards, the player wins. For example, if he has a 5 and a 9 he must draw a 6, 7, or 8 to win; if he has a 2 and an ace he can draw any card except a 2 or an ace to win. Note that if a player holds two identical cards (eg two 6s) or two consecutive cards (eg 10 and jack), he cannot win and will not bet.
6) If the player has won, he retains his bet and takes from the pool a similar sum. If he has lost, his bet goes to the pool.
7) Each player including the dealer has a turn of play, with turns passing to the left.
Continuing play After each player has had a turn, the deal passes to the player to the dealer's left. He collects all the cards, shuffles them, and has them cut for the next hand.
Any money left in the pool remains for the next hand, but players also ante again.
Division of pool If the pool passes a limit agreed beforehand it is immediately divided among the players.

Deal

Play

Player wins

Consecutive cards: no bet

Player loses

BANKING VERSION

Yablon can also be played as a banking game. The dealer acts
as banker and does not deal himself a hand.

Before the hand, the dealer places in front of him the money or
chips he wishes to put at risk. This can be any amount he
wishes. The players do not ante.

Each player in turn bets any amount he wishes, up to the
amount then in the bank. The dealer does not have a turn.

Any amount left in the bank at the end of the hand is returned
to the banker. The bank and deal then pass one player to the
left.

If the bank is emptied before all the players have had a turn, the
hand ends and the bank and deal pass at once.

©DIAGRAM

Ziginette

Ziginette is the Italians' favorite way of seeing money change hands at cards. The rules given here are those played in American gaming houses.

Equipment:
1) one standard 52-card deck from which all the 8s, 9s, and 10s have been removed, leaving 40 cards;
2) a metal card box that allows only one card to be removed at a time.

Players Two or more people can play. One person is banker. There are also two house officials. One, the "cutter," collects and pays bets for the banker and takes the house's percentage cut. (The house never banks the game.) The other, the "lookout," keeps a watch on proceedings and transfers dead cards to the discard pile.

The objective is for a player to bet on a table card that is not matched by the time the banker's card has been matched. A card is "matched" when another card of the same denomination becomes visible at the top of the card box.

Choice of first bank is by deal – the first ace to appear. The cutter carries out the deal after he has shuffled the cards and had them cut by any player.

Shuffle and cut See p 381.

Any player other than the banker cuts the cards. The banker places the deck face up in the card box.

Deal The banker deals two cards from the box face up onto the table. The next card in the box is now visible: this is the banker's card.

If all three cards are of different denominations, players may now bet; if they are not, special rules govern further procedure (see the section on "playette," p 677).

Opening bet Any player other than the banker may place a bet on one or both of the table cards.

Betting limits The banker decides the minimum and maximum allowable bets and can alter them at will between stages of play.

Opening play The banker takes the banker's card from the box and places it so that one end rests beneath the card box but most of it is visible. It stays in this position for the rest of the deal.

This action exposes the next card in the box. If this card matches any card on the table (including the banker's card), any bets involved are settled. But if it does not match any card on the table, there is no further action in this turn, unless any player wishes to place a further bet.

Cards used

Opening play

Banker's card matches

Table card matches

©DIAGRAM

Settlement of bets If at any time a card exposed in the box matches the banker's card, the banker loses all unsettled bets, ie he pays all outstanding bets by players on all table cards. Settlement is at even money – a winning player gets back his stake plus an equal amount from the bank. Play on this deal then ceases and the bank and deck pass one player to the right. If a card exposed in the box matches a table card on which bets have been placed, these bets are won by the banker and he continues to operate the bank.

The house cutter pays out the banker's losses and collects his winnings for him. He takes a 10% house cut from each bet won by the bank.

Next turn of play If the banker's card has not been matched, then any settlement of bets and placing of new bets ends the turn of play.

The exposed card is then taken from the card box.

1) If the exposed card has matched a table card, then the exposed card and the table card it matched are now dead (even if the table card had no bets placed on it).

The cutter takes both cards and places them to one side out of play. They are dead for the remainder of the deal, as are the other two cards of the same denomination still in the card box. If cards appearing in the box are the same denomination as cards already matched, they are removed and added to the discard pile. The discard pile is kept fanned out so that the denominations of dead cards can be seen.

2) If the exposed card has not matched a table card, then it is placed face up on the table alongside the other table cards. It is now available for players to bet on in the usual way at the end of a turn of play, provided it is not immediately matched by the new exposed card in the box. If it is immediately matched, both it and the matching card are transferred to the discard pile in the usual way and the other cards of the same denomination are also dead.

Summary of continuation play After the opening play, turns are as follows.

1) The top card is removed from the card box. If, on the previous turn, this card matched a table card, both are placed on the discard pile. If the top card was the same denomination as a card already matched, the top card is added to the discard pile. If the top card matched neither a table card nor a dead card, it is added to the table cards.

2) If the card now exposed in the box matches a table card, any bets involved are settled. If it matches the banker's card, the banker collects all bets and the deal ends.

3) If the banker's card has not been matched, players can bet on any card now on the table. This includes any card just added to the table, providing that this card has not been immediately matched by the new card exposed in the box.

Playette This is the term used when two cards of the same denomination appear in the opening deal. It is usually ruled "no deal." The cards are removed from the box and reshuffled. Sometimes the rule is that the duplicate cards are "doubled up."

Doubling up – opening deal If two table cards match, they are placed together, and the top card from the box is dealt to fill the empty table position.

If a table card and the box card match, the box card is added to the table card's position. In either case, the next card in the box becomes the banker's card.

Doubling up – settlement of bets When any two cards have been doubled up, whatever the denomination, no bets are settled until three cards of that denomination have appeared. For example, the bank does not win the bet on the 6s until a further 6 has been exposed;

the bank does not win the bet on the queen of hearts until two further queens have been exposed;

the bank does not lose until two further 10s have been exposed.

Tripling If all three cards of the opening deal are of the same denomination, then (providing "doubling up" is allowed) they are all placed together on one of the table hand positions.

No decision is reached on any bet, or on the bank, until four cards of a denomination have been exposed.

Change of banker A banker may pass the bank at any time when there are no unsettled bets on the table.

When the banker's card is matched he must pass the bank.

All cards are collected, shuffled, and cut before the new game begins.

Doubling up

©DIAGRAM

Section 5
Solitaire card games

Procedure and terms

Patience and solitaire are general names for any card game for one player. The exact origin of such games is obscure, but they have probably existed for centuries and several hundred different games exist today. Although the outcome of many of these games depends mainly on the luck of the shuffle, others involve real skill and judgment. In addition to games for one player, this section also includes two games for two players: Russian bank and spite and malice, which share many of the features of games devised for one.

Cards Some games are played with a standard 52-card deck, others with two decks shuffled together.
Yet others are played with a "stripped" deck, from which certain cards have been discarded prior to play.
Special cards, smaller than ordinary playing cards, may be used; these are especially useful when playing in a confined space.
Certain games allow for the inclusion of a joker.
Ace, unless otherwise specified, ranks low.
Objective The object of many games is to build up sequences of cards in their suits onto base cards known as "foundations."
A second group of games involves the pairing up of certain cards.
Other games have a quite different objective, such as rebuilding the deck into a single pile, or discarding all the cards in the deck.
If a game is successful, ie if the game's objective is exactly achieved, it is said to "come out" or to "go through."
If a game is "blocked," this means that the cards are such that the game cannot possibly be won.
Layout At the start of most games, cards are laid out in a prescribed formation that varies from game to game. This formation or "tableau," together with any other cards dealt out at the beginning of play, forms the "layout."
Foundation cards are the first cards of certain piles onto which sequences of cards are built (the objective of many games).
In some games they form part of the layout and are set out at the beginning of the game. More often, they are not included in the layout, but are put out as they come into play.
They are usually cards of a specified rank – often aces. With rare exceptions (such as in King Albert) a card cannot be removed once it has been placed on a foundation.

Spaces (sometimes called vacancies) are gaps in the layout into which cards may legitimately be played, or places from which cards have been removed and which may or may not be reoccupied, depending on the rules of the game.

Reserve In some games the layout includes one or more cards that may be brought into play as appropriate. This "reserve" of cards may not, however, be built onto – unlike the cards in the tableau.

The stock comprises those cards that remain after the layout has been dealt.

The stock is invariably kept face down, and may be brought into play in different ways according to the rules for particular games.

Waste pile or heap Cards from the stock that cannot immediately be played onto the layout are sometimes placed face up in one or more waste piles, to be brought back into the game as appropriate.

The discard pile is made up of any cards that have been set aside during the course of play and that are not brought back into the game.

The objective of some games is to discard all or most of the deck.

Available cards Any card that can, in accordance with the rules, be played onto the tableau, foundations, or spaces is termed "available."

Sometimes the removal of a card "releases" the card next to it,

Building

a

b

c

for example when the top card of a waste pile is removed and makes the next card in the pile available for play.

Exposed cards A card is usually only available for play if it is fully exposed, ie if no other card covers it either wholly or partially.

Building is the term used for placing a card onto the tableau, foundations, or a space in its correct sequence. This may be done numerically, by suit, or by color.

a) Cards may be "built down" numerically (eg a 7 is built onto an 8, a 6 onto the 7, etc).

b) Cards may be "built up" numerically (eg a 3 is built onto a 2, a 4 onto the 3, etc).

c) Sometimes the numerical sequence may be continuous or "round the corner" (eg 3,2,a,k,q), or in twos (eg 7,9,j,k,2,4, etc).

d) A card may only be built onto another card of the same suit (eg all hearts). Or, in other games, a card may only be built onto a card of a suit other than its own.

e) A card may only be built onto a card of the same color (eg all red cards).

f) A card may only be built onto a card of the other color (eg red, black, red, black).

d

e

f

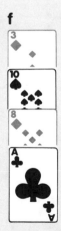

©DIAGRAM

Accordion

Accordion, also called Tower of Babel, idle year, or Methuselah, is one of the most difficult single-deck games to get out. It is unusual in that there is no formal layout at the start of the game: the cards are merely dealt in a single row.

Cards One standard 52-card deck is used.
Objective The player aims to rebuild the deck into a single pile.
Play The cards are dealt out face up in a row, as many at a time as space allows.

Any card may be moved onto the card immediately to the left, or onto the third card to the left, provided it is of the same suit or has the same rank.

A pile of two or more cards, identified by its top card, can be similarly moved.

If a card matches both its neighbour and the card three to the left, the player may choose either move, taking into account the various possibilities.

©DIAGRAM

Beleaguered castle

Beleaguered castle is also known by the names of sham battle and laying siege.

Cards One standard deck of 52 cards is used.
Layout Set out the four aces in a column as foundation cards. Then deal out the rest of the deck face up to form wings of six overlapping cards to the left and right of each ace; it is usual to deal columns of four cards alternately to the left and to the right of the aces.
The objective is to build up each suit in ascending numerical order, from ace through king, on its correct foundation card.
Play Only the fully exposed cards at the ends of the rows in each wing are available for play (one card only being moved at a time). Available cards can either be moved onto one of the foundations, building suits numerically upward, or be transferred to the end of another wing, building numerically downward with no regard to suit. Spaces, created by the removal of an entire row, may be filled by transferring any exposed card.

Layout

Foundations

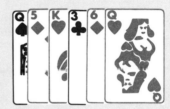

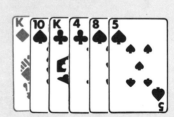

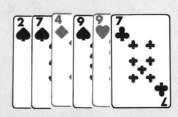

©DIAGRAM

Bisley

Kings as well as aces come into play as foundation cards in this single deck game.

Cards A standard 52-card deck is used.

Layout Set out the four aces at the beginning of the top row of the tableau. Deal nine cards to the right of the aces; then deal the rest of the deck to complete a layout of four rows of 13 cards each. In the course of play, as they become available, the four kings are put out in a row above their aces (king of hearts above ace of hearts, etc).

Layout

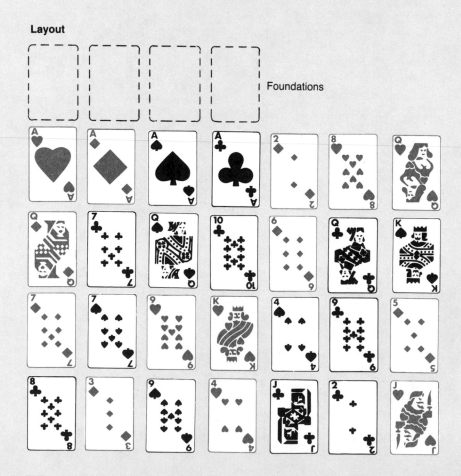

Foundations

Objective The aces and kings are foundation cards, and the aim
is to complete entire suits, by building up in suit sequence on
the aces and building down in suit sequence on the kings.
When the two sequences meet they are put together (it does not
matter at which point they meet).

Play The bottom card of each column of the tableau is available
for play, either onto a foundation or onto the bottom card of
another column.
Building onto the bottom cards of the columns is in ascending
or descending suit sequence as the player wishes, and he may at
any time reverse the order.
Spaces created in the tableau are not filled.
It is evidently important to free the kings as soon as possible,
and to use every opportunity of building onto the foundations.

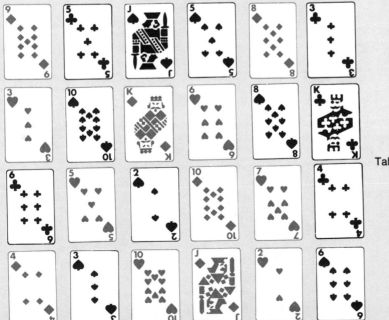

Tableau

Braid

Braid, or plait, is a straightforward game that gets its name from its particularly attractive layout.

Cards Two standard 52-card decks are used.

Layout Twenty cards are dealt face up in the form of a braid: the cards are laid out diagonally, and alternately pointing to right and left – each card partially covering the card beneath it (as illustrated).

Columns of six face-up cards are dealt to either side of the braid; the braid and the columns together form the reserve. The next (33rd) card is placed to the right of the reserve. It determines the rank of the other seven foundations, which are set out as they become available to make two rows of four cards.

Objective The player tries to build ascending "round the corner" suit sequences on the eight foundations (ace following king and preceding 2).

Play The bottom (fully exposed) card of the braid and all the cards in the two columns are available for play onto the foundations.

The stock is dealt one card at a time, and if the card is unplayable it is placed on a waste heap.

Any number of redeals is permitted, until the game either becomes blocked or goes through.

A space in the columns must be filled as soon as it occurs. If the top or bottom card of a column has been removed, the vacancy may be filled by the available card of the braid, or from the top of the waste heap (which is always available). If the vacancy is anywhere else in the column, it may only be filled from the stock.

Layout

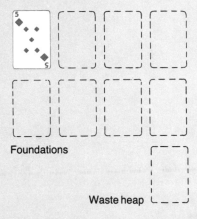

Foundations

Waste heap

Reserve   Reserve

Bristol

In this game, eight fans and three waste heaps provide the cards to be transferred onto four foundations.

Layout

Foundations

Tableau

Waste heaps

Cards One standard deck is used.
Layout Deal 24 cards, face up, in eight fans each of three cards. Any kings that turn up in the deal are placed at the bottom of their respective fans.
Next to this tableau, deal three more cards face up in a row to form the start of the waste heaps or reserve.
Objective The foundation cards are the aces, which are set out in a row above the tableau as they occur in play. The aim is to build four ascending sequences, ace through king, regardless of suit or color.

Play The top cards of the fans and the three waste heaps are available for play, but only one card may be moved at a time – either to a foundation or in descending sequence, regardless of suit or color, onto the exposed card of another fan.

The stock is dealt three cards at a time, one card to each of the three waste heaps.

Spaces in the waste heaps are filled only in the deal. Spaces in the tableau (caused by the removal of an entire fan) remain unfilled. Only one deal is permitted.

©DIAGRAM

Calculation

Calculation is an aptly named game, for it involves a considerable amount of thinking ahead. (It is sometimes called broken intervals.)

Cards One standard 52-card deck is used.
Layout Set out in a row any ace, 2, 3, and 4 as the foundation cards.
The objective is to build up the rest of the deck on these base cards regardless of suit or colour, but strictly in accordance with the following order:
On the ace: 2, 3, 4, 5, 6, 7, 8, 9, 10, j, q, k.
On the 2: 4, 6, 8, 10, q, a, 3, 5, 7, 9, j, k.
On the 3: 6, 9, q, 2, 5, 8, j, a, 4, 7, 10, k.
On the 4: 8, q, 3, 7, j, 2, 6, 10, a, 5, 9, k.
Play Cards are turned up one at a time and either built onto the appropriate base card or placed on one of four waste heaps immediately beside these.
Only the top card on each waste heap is available and cards cannot be moved from one waste heap to another.
Any space in the waste heaps is filled with the top card of the stock.
Much of the skill of the game lies in playing the cards to the various heaps in such a way that they are later readily available for transfer to the foundations.
For example, it is best to keep kings in one waste heap or, if they come out early, at the bottom of waste heaps. Cards of the same rank should be dispersed among the waste heaps rather than concentrated in any single heap.
Whenever possible, cards should be played to the waste heaps in the reverse order to their build-up on the foundations.

Layout

Foundations   Waste heaps

Order or building

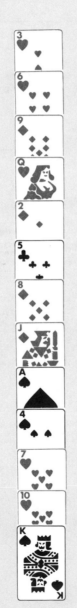

Canfield

Named for the nineteenth-century American gambler and art collector Richard A. Canfield, this game is one of the most popular single-deck games. It is sometimes known as demon in the United Kingdom. (Another game sometimes known as Canfield in the United Kingdom is described here as Klondike.)

Cards One stardard 52-card deck is used.

Layout Deal out a reserve pile of 13 cards face down, then turn the pile over to expose one card. Deal four more face-up cards to the right of the reserve to form the tableau.

Above the first card of the tableau place the next card face up; this is the first of the four foundation cards and its rank determines the other three cards (which are laid out as they come into play).

Should one of the tableau cards have the same rank as the foundation, move it up into position and deal another card into the space left in the tableau.

The object of the game is to build up the four suits on the foundation cards.

The cards rank continuously, ie if the foundation cards are kings, the next cards in the sequences must be aces.

Play The stock is turned over three cards at a time, only the exposed card of each three being in play (although cards below it can be played as they become available).

If there are only one or two cards at the end of the stock, they are dealt singly.

Cards are built up by suit on the foundations, and in descending alternate-color sequence regardless of suit on the columns of the tableau.

Provided the correct color and numerical sequences are maintained, an entire column of the tableau can be transferred to another column.

Spaces in the tableau are filled immediately from the reserve. If the reserve is exhausted, the player may fill the space from the top of the waste heap, but he need not do so immediately.

Redeal The stock may be redealt, without shuffling, as many times as necessary until the game either blocks or is won.

Layout

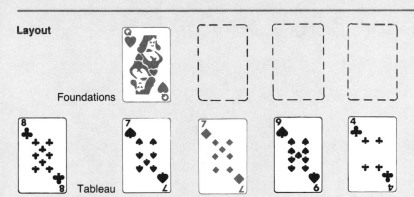

Foundations

Reserve   Tableau

Play

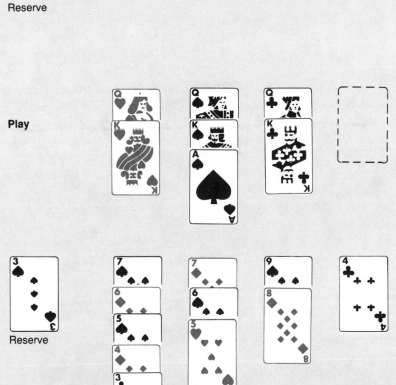

Reserve

Waste heap

©DIAGRAM

Clock

Although the chances of winning this game are slight, it is fun to play and very fast-moving. The name clock comes from the layout, which takes the form of a clock dial. Other names by which this game is known are sun dial, travelers, hidden cards, and four of a kind.

Layout

Cards One standard 52-card deck is used.

Layout The deck is dealt face down into 13 piles of four cards each. The cards may be dealt singly or in fours. The piles are arranged to represent a clock dial, one pile corresponding to each hour. The thirteenth pile is placed in the centre.

Objective By rearranging the cards, the player hopes to end up with thirteen piles of like-numbered cards in their correct "time" position: the four aces at one o'clock, the four 2s at two o'clock, and so on around the dial.

The jacks represent 11 o'clock and the queens 12 o'clock. The four kings make up the thirteenth, central pile.

Play The player takes the card at the top of the central pile and places it face up at the bottom of the pile of the same number or "time." For example, if the card is a 7, it is put face up underneath the seven o'clock pile.

The player then takes the top card of the seven o'clock pile and puts it under its matching pile.

In this way the player works his way from pile to pile, always removing the top card of the pile under which he has just put its matching card.

If the player turns a card that happens to be on its correct pile (eg a 3 is turned up from the three o'clock pile), it is still placed at the bottom of the pile in the usual way, and the next face-down card is taken from the top of the pile.

The outcome depends on the order in which the kings are turned up. If the fourth king is turned up before all the other cards are face up, then the game is blocked.

This means in effect that the game can only be won if the last card to be turned up is the fourth king. As the chance of this happening is very small, the king may be exchanged for any one face-down card in the layout. Only one exchange is allowed, and if the fourth king is again turned up before the other cards are in the correct piles, then the game is lost.

Crazy quilt

Crazy quilt is an unusual and interesting solitaire that gets its name from its layout of interwoven cards. It is also known as Indian carpet or Japanese rug.

Cards Two standard 52-card decks are used.

Layout Take an ace and a king of each suit and set them out face up in a row. These are the eight foundations.

Above them, deal out a reserve or "quilt" of eight rows of eight face-up cards each, laying the cards vertically and horizontally in turn.

Any card in the quilt that has one or both of its narrow sides free is available for play. For example, at the start of play the four projecting cards at each side of the quilt are available.

Objective The aim is to build ascending suit sequences on the aces, and descending suit sequences on the kings.

Play Study the reserve to see if any available cards can be built onto the foundations. The removal of a reserve card releases one or more other reserve cards for play.

Spaces in the reserve remain unfilled.

Then turn up the stock one card at a time, putting the card in a waste heap if it cannot be played to a foundation. (The top card of the waste heap is always available.)

In order to release a useful card in the quilt, an available card may be played from the quilt to the top of the waste heap in either ascending or descending suit sequence.

The stock may be redealt once.

Layout

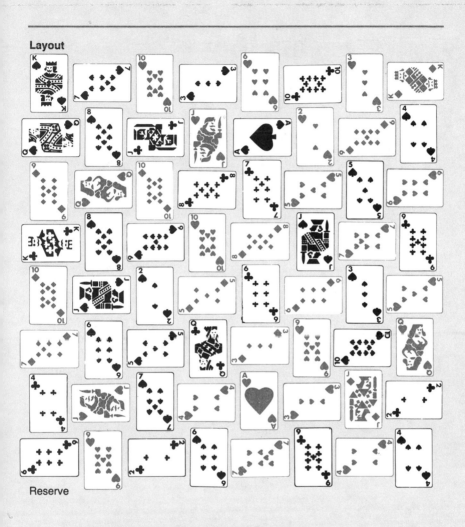

Reserve

Foundations

Waste heap

©DIAGRAM

Eight away

Also called eight off, this game has a tableau of eight columns, none of which must ever contain more than eight cards.

Cards One standard deck is needed.

Layout Deal 48 cards face up in eight columns of six cards each. The cards in each column should overlap so that all are visible. Deal the remaining four cards face up in a row below the tableau to form the start of the reserve.

Objective The player's aim is to free the aces (which are moved as they become available to form a row above the tableau), and to build on them suit sequences, ace through king.

Play The exposed cards in the tableau (those at the bottoms of the eight columns) and all the reserve cards are available for play.

They can be moved to the foundations, built in descending suit sequence on other exposed cards, or moved to the reserve – which, however, must never contain more than eight cards. Only one card may be moved at a time. Any space that occurs in the tableau can be filled only by an available king.

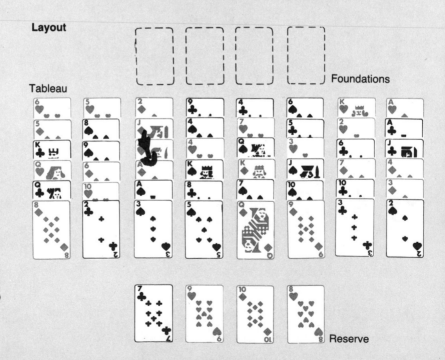

Layout

Foundations

Tableau

Reserve

Florentine

Features of this game are a tableau in the form of a five-card cross, and four foundations of which the bases are determined by the sixth card to be dealt.

Cards One standard deck is used.
Layout Deal five cards face up to form a cross. Deal a sixth card face up at the top left-hand corner. The rank of this card denotes the foundations; the other three cards of that rank being placed at the other corners as they come into play.

Layout

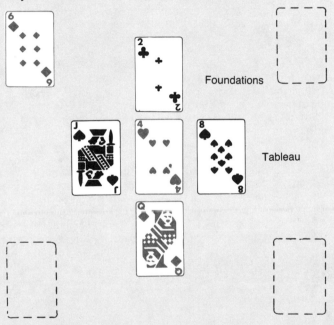

Foundations

Tableau

The objective is to build up ascending suit sequences on the four foundation cards.
Aces follow kings.
Play Cards from the stock are dealt one at a time. They can be played on the foundations if eligible, or packed in downward sequences regardless of suit on the four outer cards of the cross. The centre card of the cross is at all times kept clear.
If one of the outer cards is transferred to a foundation card or packed on another outer card, the vacancy thus created is filled by a card from the waste heap, or by the centre card of the cross (which is then replaced by a card from the waste heap).
The waste heap can be turned over and replayed once without shuffling.

Flower garden

In this game cards from fans, called flower beds, and cards from the hand, or bouquet, are built onto foundation cards. The flower beds are collectively called the flower garden.

Cards One standard deck is needed.
Layout Deal out 36 cards into six fans to form the flower garden. The remaining cards form the bouquet, and may be held in the hand or spread out on the table.
The objective is to free the aces, which are set out below the garden as they become available, and to build onto them suit sequences in ascending order, ace through king.
Play The exposed cards of each bed and all the bouquet cards are available for play. They may be played onto a foundation, or added to a bed in downward numerical sequence, regardless of suit.
A sequence may be transferred from one bed to another, provided that the correct numerical order is preserved.
If a space is created by the removal of an entire bed, it may be filled by any available card, or by a sequence from another bed.

Layout

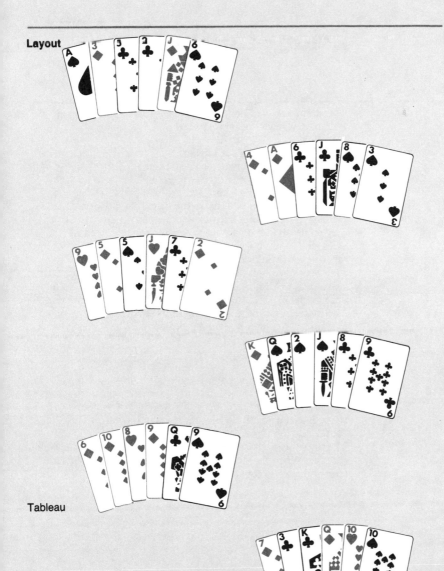

Tableau

Foundations

© DIAGRAM

Friday the thirteenth

This game requires the player to establish and build upon 13 foundations, each based on a card of a different rank.

Cards One standard deck is used.

Layout Set out in a row from left to right any jack, queen, king, and ace – regardless of suit. Leave enough space to the right of them for a further nine cards to be added to the row.

The objective is to establish a total of 13 foundation cards – the jack, queen, king, and ace and then any 2 through 10 as they come up in play – onto which the remaining cards (the stock) are built up four to a pile in ascending numerical order, regardless of suit or color.

Play Work through the stock, turning one card at a time face upward and building it onto one of the foundations (eg a queen onto the jack), or putting it out as the next foundation card. The foundations must be set out in their correct order: for example, a 3 cannot be laid out before the 2 has been established.

If a card cannot be played immediately, it is put face up on a waste heap.

Where there is a choice, it is usually better to establish a new base card rather than to build onto an existing pile. For example, if the first card turned up were a 2, it would be wiser to use it as the next base card rather than building it onto the ace.

The waste heap Any exposed card on the waste heap is available for play. When the stock is exhausted, the waste heap is turned over and may be replayed once without shuffling.

Layout

Foundations

Frog

This two deck game is also called toad in the hole. There are eight foundations based on aces, and five waste heaps.

Layout

Reserve   Foundations

Waste heaps

Cards Two standard decks are used.

Layout Deal a reserve pile of 13 cards face up. If any of these cards are aces, set them out to the right of the reserve as foundations.

If no aces are turned up, take one ace of any suit from the stock to begin the foundation row.

The other aces are added to the row as they turn up in play, to give a complete row of eight foundations.

The objective is to build on the aces, ascending sequences from ace to king, regardless of suit or color.

Play Cards are turned up from the stock one at a time and played either onto the foundations or onto any one of five waste heaps.

The waste heaps are set out below the foundations, and cards may be added to them in any order the player chooses.

The top card of the reserve and the top cards of the waste heaps are available at all times for playing onto the foundations.

If a space occurs in the waste heaps it is filled from the stock; if the reserve is exhausted it is not replaced.

It is sound strategy to keep one waste heap for high-value cards such as kings and queens, and – if at all possible – to add cards to the waste heaps in descending numerical order so as to avoid burying low-ranking cards.

King Albert

This game is named for King Albert 1 of the Belgians, who during World War 1 led his country's army against the Germans. Cards from the tableau and from the "Belgian Reserve" are built onto four foundation cards.

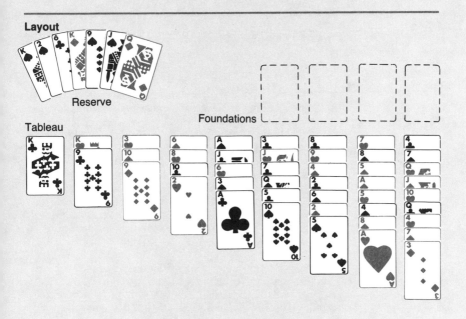

Cards One standard deck is used.

Layout Forty-five cards are dealt face up in rows from left to right, to form a tableau of nine columns.

The first column has one card, the second column two, and so on – the last column comprising nine cards.

The cards in each column should overlap so that all are visible. The remaining seven cards, known as the "Belgian Reserve," may either be held in the hand or fanned out next to the tableau.

The objective is to free the four aces (the foundations), which are placed above the tableau as they come into play.

Cards are built onto them in ascending suit sequence, from ace through king.

Play All cards in the reserve are available, as are the exposed cards of the tableau.

Only one card may be moved at a time, either onto a foundation pile or in descending, alternate-color sequence on the columns of the tableau.

If an entire column becomes vacant, the space may be filled by any available card.

If the player wishes, he may transfer cards from the foundations to the tableau, provided that they fit into the correct numerical and color sequence.

Klondike

Klondike probably owes its great popularity to its combination of judgment, luck, attractive layout, and fast-moving tempo – all ingredients of a good patience game. (In the United Kingdom this game is sometimes called Canfield.)

Cards One standard 52-card deck is used.
Layout Deal a row of seven cards, with only the first card face up. Add another row of six cards, with the first card face up on the second card of the first row, and the others face down. Deal five more rows in the same way, each row having one card fewer than the row beneath it and having only its first card face up.
Objective The four aces are the foundation cards, and they are set out above the tableau as they become available. The object is to build up the four suits on their respective aces in correct ascending order.

Layout

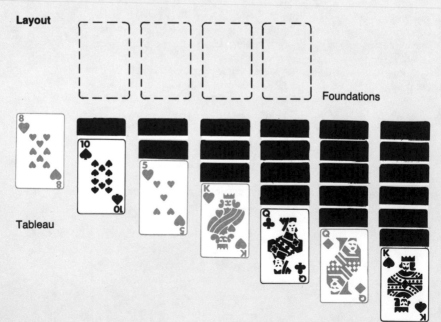

Foundations

Tableau

©DIAGRAM

Play The hand is played one card at a time and once only.
Cards that are not immediately playable are put face up in a
waste heap, the top card of which is always available.

Cards are built up in their correct suits on the foundations, or
added to the columns of the tableau in descending, alternate-
color order (regardless of suit).

The top (fully exposed) card of each tableau column is always
available for play onto a foundation or another column.

By removing an exposed card the face-down card beneath it is
turned up and becomes available.

Sequences in the tableau may be transferred from one column
to another, but only as a complete unit.

Spaces created in the tableau can only be filled by kings. These
may be taken (together with any cards built onto them) either
from the stock or from anywhere in the tableau.

La belle Lucie

This game has an attractive layout in which cards are arranged initially in fans of three cards each. Cards are then moved from fan to fan to free cards to be built onto four foundation piles.

Cards One standard deck is used.
Layout The deck is dealt out into 17 fans of three cards each and one single card.
Objective The aces are the foundation cards, and they are set out in a row above the tableau as they come into play. Cards are built onto the foundations in ascending suit sequence, from ace through king.
Play The top card of each fan and the single card are available for play. One card at a time may be moved onto a foundation, or built onto another fan in downward suit sequence.
Cards may always safely be built onto the foundations, but any building down on the fans should be carefully considered, as any cards to the left of the built-down cards will consequently be immobilized.
Any spaces caused by the removal of a fan are left unfilled.

Redealing Two redeals are permitted. When no further play is possible, all cards other than those on the foundation piles are gathered up, thoroughly shuffled, and redealt into fans of three cards (any one or two remaining cards forming a separate fan). After the second redeal, the player may pick out and play one card from any fan of his choice.

Layout

Foundations

Tableau

Leapfrog

Moving cards leapfrog fashion about the tableau makes for an unusual and interesting game.

Cards One standard deck is required.
Layout Deal out 20 cards face up into four rows of five cards each.
The objective is to deal out all the remaining cards onto the table, and to end with as many spaces as possible in the layout.
Play Moves in leapfrog are very like the "taking" moves in a game of draughts.
A card in the layout may be "leapfrogged" over an adjoining card (either horizontally, vertically, or diagonally), provided that the card onto which it lands is of the same suit or rank.
A card so played now becomes the top and identifying card of a pile, and in any subsequent leapfrogging the whole pile is moved.
A move is not limited to a single leapfrog: a succession of leapfrogs is sometimes possible.
Any card leapfrogged by another card is removed to a waste heap.
Empty spaces are filled by cards dealt from the hand whenever the player wishes. (It is better to fill the gaps as soon as they occur, in order to provide a wider choice of moves.)

Layout

Maze

Although maze is not one of the better known patience games, it is particularly satisfying and requires time and ingenuity to succeed.

Cards One standard 52-card deck is used.

Layout The entire deck is dealt face up into two rows of eight cards and four rows of nine cards.

The four kings are then discarded, leaving a total of six spaces.

Objective By rearranging the cards one at a time, the player aims to get the four suits into their correct ascending sequence, ace through queen – one suit following the next. (The order of the suits is immaterial.)

The cards must run from left to right and from the end of one row to the beginning of the next. During play the top row is counted as following on from the bottom row.

In the final sequence, the first card must be an ace and the last card a queen.

For example, in a successful game the order might be: ace of hearts through queen of hearts, ace of spades through queen of spades, ace of clubs through queen of clubs, ace of diamonds through queen of diamonds.

Play A card may be moved into any of the six spaces provided it is in the same suit as the card to the left or the right side of the space and that it is either:

lower than the card to the right of the space, or

higher than the card to the left of the space.

(For example, a 2 of diamonds may be moved into a space that either has an ace of diamonds to its left or a 3 of diamonds to its right.)

Whenever there is a space to the right of a queen, it may be filled with any of the four aces (even if there is no matching 2 on the right of the space).

Layout

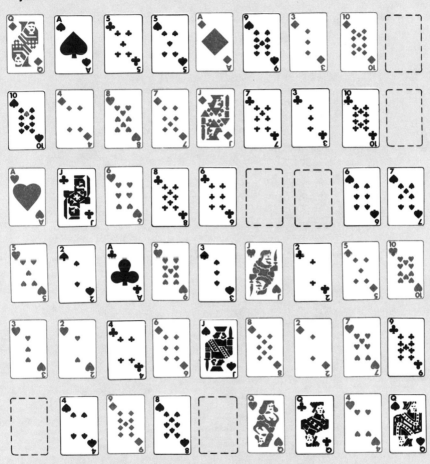

Miss Milligan

In this two-deck game, cards are dealt eight at a time onto the tableau for transference onto eight foundations based on aces.

Cards Two standard decks are required.
Objective With the eight aces as the foundations, the player aims to build up the cards into ascending suit sequences.
Play Deal out eight cards face up in a row. If any of these is an ace, set it out above the row as a foundation. Also move any cards that can be built up on the ace in correct suit sequence, or arranged in descending alternate-colour sequence on other cards in the row.

Now deal out another row of eight cards, overlapping cards already in position or filling in any spaces as appropriate.
Once again, study the layout to see which cards may be built onto the foundations or transferred to other columns. (Several cards may be transferred together, provided they are in correct sequence.)
If at this stage a space occurs, it may only be filled by a king (plus any cards built onto it).
Continue in this way until the entire stock has been dealt – always completing all possible moves before dealing out the next batch of cards.

Start of play

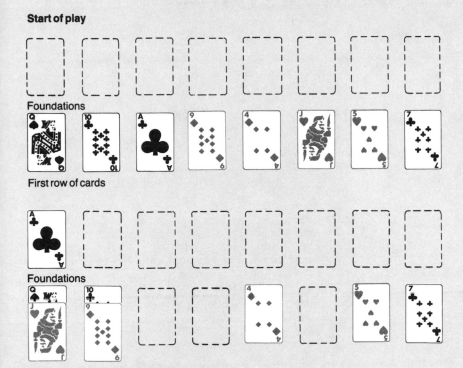

Foundations

First row of cards

Foundations

Cards moved into appropriate columns

Weaving When no cards remain in the stock, the player may lift up any one available card or build from the tableau, and set it aside as a reserve.

Each of these reserve cards is available, and the player tries to rebuild them onto the tableau or foundations.

If he fails in rebuilding the reserve, the game is lost. If he succeeds, however, he may repeat the "weaving" process until the game goes through or is blocked.

©DIAGRAM

Monte Carlo

Monte Carlo, also called weddings or double and quits, is a straightforward pairing game.

Cards One standard deck of 52 cards is used.

Layout Twenty cards are dealt out into four rows of five cards each. (Some players may prefer to deal out 25 cards in five rows of five cards each.)

Objective At the end of a successful game the player will have dealt out the entire deck and paired up all the cards, leaving an empty layout.

Play Any two cards of the same rank that touch each other top to bottom, side to side, or corner to corner, are discarded.

The spaces thus made are filled by closing up the remaining cards of the layout from right to left, moving up cards from row to row as necessary, but preserving their order as originally laid out.

Extra cards are added from the stock to complete the layout, and the process is repeated until further pairing is impossible, or until the game goes through.

Layout

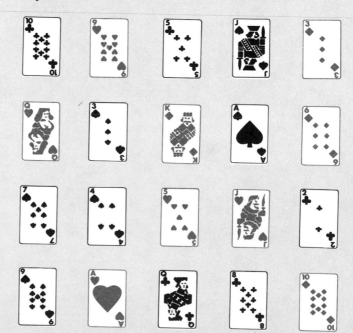

Napoleon at St Helena

Although Napoleon was recorded as having played patience while in exile on St Helena, it is most unlikely that he invented or even played the many games attributed to him today. The game described here is among the most interesting of this group. Its other names are forty thieves and big forty.

Cards Two standard 52-card decks are used.
Layout Deal out forty cards into four overlapping rows of ten cards each. The bottom card in each column is available for play.
The objective is to build up suit sequences through to the kings on the eight aces, which are set out in a row above the tableau as they come into play.
Play The stock is turned over one card at a time and is either played onto the foundations, or built onto the tableau in downward suit sequence. If unplayable, cards are placed on a waste heap, of which the top card is always available.
Available tableau cards may similarly be played one at a time onto the foundations or onto another column of the tableau.
Spaces If an entire column of the tableau is cleared away, the resulting space may be filled by any one available card from elsewhere in the tableau or from the top of the waste heap. The player should choose this card carefully, as it may give him the opportunity of releasing useful cards.

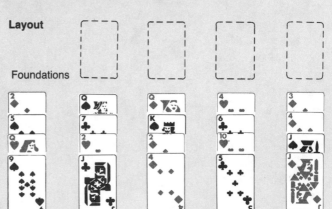

Layout

Foundations

Tableau

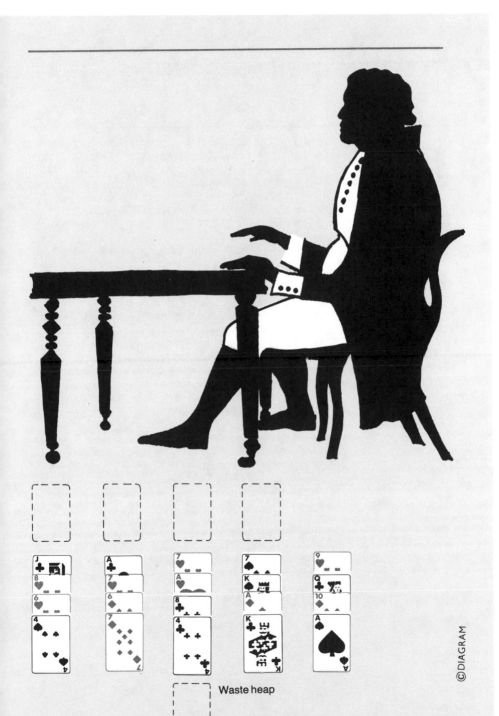

Waste heap

©DIAGRAM

Poker solitaire

Poker solitaire is a very challenging game that needs a mixture of luck, judgment, and practice to score well. It is a useful game for familiarizing the beginner with the scoring combinations used in regular poker.

Cards One standard deck of 52 cards is used.
Layout The tableau for poker solitaire comprises five rows of five face-up cards each.
Play The cards are dealt out one by one from a thoroughly shuffled deck. Each card may be placed anywhere within the limits of the tableau.
Once in position a card may not be moved; its placing on the tableau is therefore of great importance.
Objective Each row and each column of the tableau is the equivalent of a poker hand (ie there is a total of 10 hands). The player tries to place the cards of each "hand" to give the highest possible scoring poker combinations.
Scoring Two different scoring systems – British and American – are given in the table. A score of about 50 (British) or 150 (American) is considered good, and a score of about 60 (British) or 200 (American) excellent.
Ace can rank either high or low, but may not form part of a "round the corner" sequence (ie king, ace, 2 is not allowed).
Alternative rules
1) In order to improve his chance of a good score, the player may include a joker in the deal.
He can either:
a) substitute the joker for one of the 25 cards before dealing them; or
b) play all 25 cards in the usual way, exchanging the joker for any one card of his choice before totalling the score.
2) Another simplification of the game involves dealing out all 25 cards at the start of play in random order, and then rearranging them at will to form the best possible hands.
3) If the player wishes to make the game more taxing, he may only place a card onto the tableau if it touches a previously played card either horizontally, vertically, or diagonally (rather than placing it anywhere within the confines of the tableau).

Sample play

One pair	Flush	One pair	Flush	Straight	
					Full house
					Three of a kind
					Straight
					Four of a kind
					No score

© DIAGRAM

Scoring table

Combination	British	American	Definition
Royal flush	30	100	A, k, q, j, 10 of one suit
Straight flush	30	75	Sequence of five cards in one suit
Four of a kind	16	50	Four cards of the same rank with one odd card
Full house	10	25	Three cards of one rank and two of another
Flush	5	20	Any five cards of the same suit
Straight	12	15	Five cards in sequence regardless of suit
Three of a kind	6	10	Three cards of the same rank with two odd cards
Two pairs	3	5	Two pairs with one odd card
One pair	1	2	One pair with three odd cards

Puss in the corner

This game has one of the most straightforward layouts of all single deck games.

Cards One standard deck is used.
Layout The four aces are placed face up in a square, and then during the course of play four waste heaps are established at its corners.

Layout

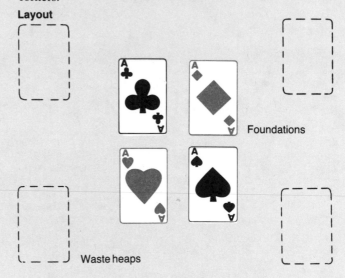

Foundations

Waste heaps

The object of the game is to build up ascending sequences, ace through king, according to color but irrespective of suit.
Play Cards are played from the stock one at a time, either onto the aces (the foundation cards) or – if ineligible – onto one of the four waste heaps.
The top cards of the waste heaps are always available for play. The player can choose onto which of the four waste heaps he wishes to put a card.
It is wise to reserve one heap for face cards, and if possible to avoid burying low-value cards under higher ones.
Redeal When the stock is exhausted, the cards in the waste heaps are collected in any order and redealt once without shuffling.

Pyramid

In its opening stages this game of pairing cards appears
deceptively easy, and the player may think he is well on the way
to winning. He will need a lot of lucky card combinations,
however, for the game to go through!

Cards One standard deck of 52 cards is used.
Layout Twenty-eight cards are dealt face up in seven rows to
form a pyramid.
Each card is overlapped by two other cards in the row below,
except for the cards in the bottom row, which are fully exposed.
Only the fully exposed cards are available for play (ie at the
start of the game the seven cards in the bottom row).
When two cards are discarded during the course of play, the
card they were overlapping becomes exposed and available for
play.
The objective is to pair off the entire deck.
Play Any two available cards that together total 13 (regardless
of color or suit) are paired off and placed in a waste heap.
The kings are worth 13 and may be discarded singly.
Queens are worth 12, jacks 11, and aces one.
For example, a 10 can be paired with a 3, a jack with a 2, or a 4
with a 9.
Cards in the stock are turned up one by one onto a waste heap,
of which the top card is always available.
A pair may be made up of:
two tableau cards;
one tableau card and one card from the stock; or
two stock cards (the top card from the waste pile plus the next
stock card turned up).
Redeal When the stock has been dealt once and no further
pairing is possible, the waste pile may be redealt without
shuffling.
Some players permit two redeals; others prefer not to allow any
redeal.

Layout

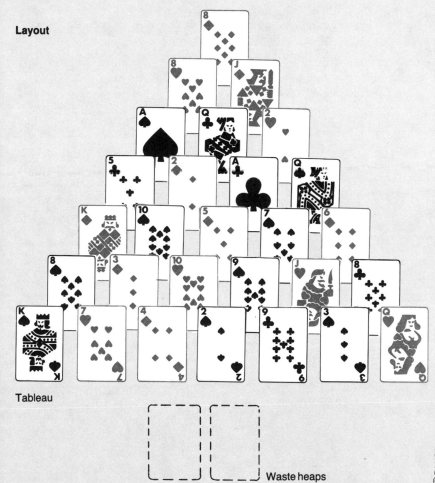

Tableau

Waste heaps

©DIAGRAM

Royal cotillion

Named for an eighteenth-century French court dance for four couples, this two deck game uses for its foundations four aces coupled with four 2s.

Cards Two standard decks are needed.
Layout Set out face up in two columns an ace and a 2 of each suit.
To the left of the ace column, deal 12 cards face up in three rows of four cards each.
To the right of the 2 column, deal 16 cards face up in four rows of four cards each.
(Some players prefer to establish the two central columns by putting out the aces and 2s as they come into play.)

Layout

The objective is to build suit sequences in the following order:
on the aces, 3, 5, 7, 9, j, k, 2, 4, 6, 8, 10, q;
on the 2s, 4, 6, 8, 10, q, a, 3, 5, 7, 9, j, k.

Play Only the bottom card of each column in the left wing of cards is available for play onto a foundation card, and the space made by such a move is not filled.

All the cards in the right wing are available, however, and spaces that occur must be filled immediately, with the top card of either the waste heap or the stock.

The stock is played one card at a time. Any card that cannot be built on a foundation or is not required for filling a space, is put on the waste heap, of which the top card is always available. There is no redeal.

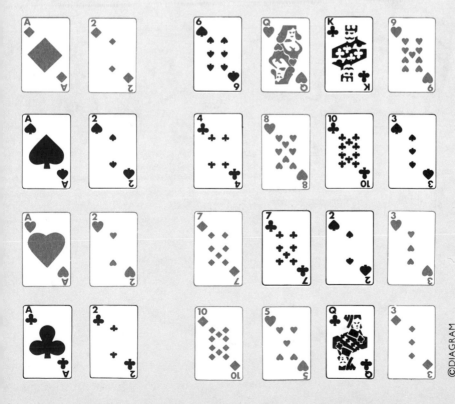

Russian bank

Also known as crapette, this patience game for two players requires a great deal of concentration. Moves are made according to a strict procedure which, if broken, may result in the player forfeiting his turn.

Cards Two standard decks are used. Each player should have his own deck with a distinctive back in order to avoid confusion. Cards rank: k (high), q,j,10,9,8,7,6,5,4,3,2,a (low).
The objective A player's objective is to build all or as many as possible of the cards in his deck onto the foundations, the tableau, or his opponent's reserve or discard piles.

Preliminaries Each player draws a card from one of the decks: the player drawing the lower card will play first. Players then shuffle and cut their opponent's deck.

Layout To establish his reserve, each player counts out 12 cards from his deck and places them face down in a pile to his right. Both players then deal out a column of four face-up cards above their reserve: these eight cards form the tableau and are for common use.

The remaining cards in each deck are placed face down in a pile in front of each player and form his stock.

Foundations The eight aces are the foundations. They are laid out between the two columns of the tableau as they come into play. Cards are built onto the foundations in ascending suit sequence.

Building cards onto the foundations is also called building to the "center." Once a card has been built onto a foundation, it may not be removed.

Layout

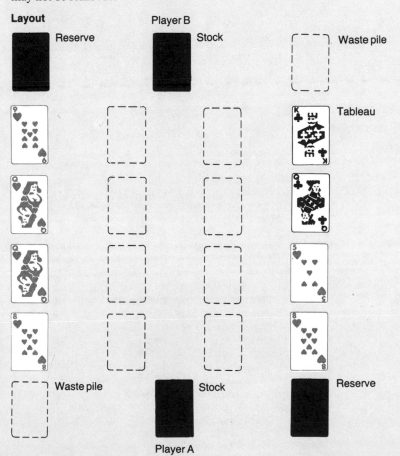

Play The player who drew the lower card plays first; thereafter players take alternate turns.

Cards must be moved according to a set procedure, as follows.

1) Both players must start their opening turns by playing any available tableau cards to the center. They must then turn up the top card of their reserve and – if possible – play that to the center. If it cannot be played to the center, it may be played elsewhere on the layout.

2) In subsequent turns, players may turn over the top card of their reserve prior to making a play.

3) Building onto the foundations always takes precedence over building elsewhere on the layout. Also, if there is a choice of cards for building onto the center, cards from the reserve must always be used before cards from the tableau or stock.

4) If no more cards can be built onto the foundations, the player may build onto the tableau in descending alternate-color sequence. He may use the top card from another tableau pile, the reserve, or the stock – there is no order of precedence. (Players should take every opportunity of rearranging tableau cards, so as to free blocked cards for play to the center.)

Cards in the tableau piles should be built in overlapping rows, so that all the cards are visible.

5) A space in the tableau may be filled by the top card of another tableau pile, the reserve, or, once the reserve is exhausted, from the stock. (Spaces need not be filled as soon as they occur.)

6) If no cards can be built to the center and the top reserve card cannot be built onto the tableau, the player may turn up the top card in his stock. If this card can be played directly to the center or the tableau, the next card in the stock may be turned up, and so on until an unplayable stock card is turned up. As soon as this happens, the player must move the unplayable card face up onto a waste pile to his left. His turn then ends.

7) Cards in the waste pile cannot be played. If the player's stock is exhausted, he may, however, take the waste pile and turn it face down and unshuffled to form a new stock.

Loading Once all available cards have been played to the centre, the player has the option of "loading" cards onto his opponent's reserve or waste piles in up or down suit sequence. The player may use cards from the tableau, or from his own reserve and stock.

Should the opponent's top reserve card be face down, the player may ask him at any time to turn it face up.

If an opponent has used up his reserve or waste pile (ie toward the end of the game) a player cannot off-load cards onto the resultant spaces.

Stops If a player thinks that his opponent has made an error in procedure, he may call "Stop," and play must immediately be halted.

If the error is proved, the wrongly moved card is returned to its former position and the offending player forfeits the rest of that turn.

Should an error not be noticed until after further moves have been made, the offender is allowed to continue without penalty.

Result The game is won by the first person who succeeds in discarding his entire deck, ie all the cards in his reserve, stock, and waste pile.

He scores 30 points for winning, plus two points for each card left in his opponent's reserve and one point for each card left in his opponent's stock and waste pile.

If neither player succeeds in winning outright, the game is considered a draw.

Alternatively, players can evaluate their remaining cards to decide who wins. Each player counts two points for each card in his reserve and one point for each card in his stock and waste pile: the player with fewer points then scores the difference between his points total and that of his opponent.

Scorpion

The unwary player may be caught out by the scorpion's "sting" at the tail end of the game – since delay in exposing the hidden cards may prevent the game going through!

Cards One standard deck of 52 cards is used.

Layout Deal three rows of seven cards each – the first four cards in each row face down and the remainder face up.

Below these deal four more rows of seven cards each, all face up. This makes a total of 49 cards in the tableau, and the three cards left over are put face down as the reserve.

Objective The four kings are the foundations onto which the cards are built in descending suit sequence (king through ace). The kings are not removed to separate foundation piles, but are built onto within the tableau.

Play Cards are built on the exposed cards of the layout (ie the bottom card of each column) in correct descending order and suit.

If, as in the example illustrated, the 6 of hearts is exposed, the 5 of hearts may be moved onto it. It may be taken from anywhere within the layout, but all the cards laid on top of it must also be moved.

Nothing may be built onto an ace.

Face-down cards As each face-down card is reached (by the removal of the card or cards on top of it) it is turned face up. The sooner the hidden cards are uncovered, the better the player's chances of getting the game through. It is therefore advisable to plan moves that will clear the face-down cards as rapidly as possible.

Spaces and reserve If an entire column is cleared away the space may be filled by a king (and any cards laid on top of it).

A space need not be filled as soon as it occurs.

When no further moves are possible, the three reserve cards are turned up and added to the layout, one to the foot of each of the three left-hand columns.

Not all spaces need to be filled before using the reserve cards. It often helps to see the reserve before filling a space, and this may be done provided that all other moves have been exhausted.

Layout

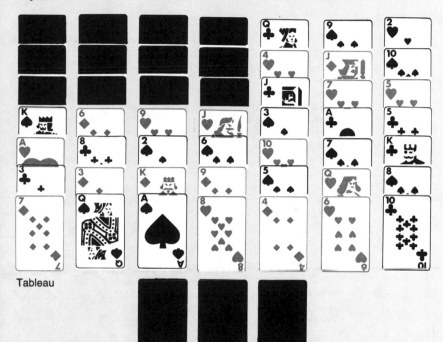

Tableau

Reserve

Play

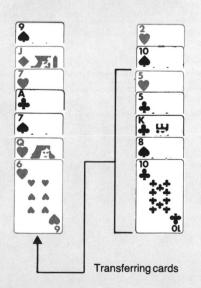

Transferring cards

Spider

There are numerous versions of spider, the one described here is reputed to have been the favorite solitaire of President Franklin D. Roosevelt.

Cards Two standard 52-card decks are used.

Layout Deal out a tableau of four overlapping rows, each row having ten cards. Deal the first three rows face down and the fourth row face up.

Objective Cards are built onto the eight kings in descending suit sequence. Instead of setting out the kings in separate piles as they come into play, they are built onto within the tableau. Only when a sequence is complete (ie king through ace in any one suit) is it discarded from the tableau.

If the solitaire comes out, all eight completed sequences will have been discarded.

Play The face-up cards in the bottom row are all available, and may be built on any other available card in descending numerical sequence, irrespective of suit or color.

When a card is moved to another column, the player must also transfer all the cards built onto it.

Nothing may be built onto an ace, which ranks low and can only follow a two.

When a face-down card is reached, it is turned face up and becomes available for play.

A space in the tableau may be filled by any available card or build.

Stock When there are no more moves to be made in the tableau and all the spaces have been filled, ten cards are dealt face up from the stock – one to the bottom of each column.

Play continues in the same way, a fresh batch of ten cards being dealt from the stock each time all possible moves in the tableau have been completed.

(The last deal will be of only four cards, one to be dealt to the bottom of the first four columns.)

Layout

Spite and malice

Like Russian bank, this is a solitaire game for two players. The players' objective is to be first to get rid of all the cards from their own "payoff pile"; to achieve this end, cards are built in sequence onto stacks at the center and sides of the table. table.

Cards Two standard decks and four jokers are used. The decks should be distinctively backed. Ace ranks low; jokers are wild.

Layout

Payoff pile

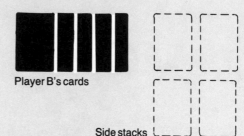

Player B's cards   Side stacks

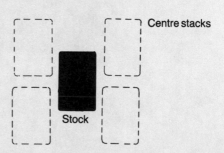

Centre stacks

Stock

Side stacks

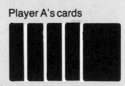

Player A's cards

Payoff pile

The objective A player aims to get rid of all the cards on his payoff pile.

Preliminaries One of the decks is shuffled – without its jokers – and divided into two separate "payoff" piles of 26 cards, one for each player. The top card of each pile is turned face up and the player with the highest card will play first.

If by chance the two cards have the same value, the procedure is repeated.

The player with the lower card shuffles the second deck, including the four jokers. He then gives himself and his opponent five cards, dealing them one at a time and face down. The remaining cards form the stock and are placed face down in a pile in the middle of the table.

Play The player who had the higher card has the opening turn; thereafter play is alternate.

1) Aces must be played to the center of the table as soon as they become available; they are the base cards of "center stacks" (equivalent to foundation piles).

Available 2s must be built on the aces whenever possible. Cards are built on the center stacks in ascending sequence regardless of suit; a card from the payoff pile, the hand, or a side stack (see paragraph 3) may be used.

Whenever a center stack has been built up through to the king, it is shuffled together with the stock at the next break in play.

2) The top card of the payoff pile may be played only to the center stacks. Whenever this happens, the player may turn up the next card in the ``spayoff pile, and so on, until an unplayable card is turned up.

3) Each player may build up to four "side stacks" using only cards from his hand. A side stack may be started with a card of any value, and is built on regardless of suit either in descending sequence or with a card of the same value (eg 7 on a 7). Only one build onto a side stack may be made in any one turn.

4) Jokers may take the place of any card except an ace.

End of turn A player may make any number of legal plays to the center stacks, but his turn ends as soon as he plays a card from his hand to a side stack.

A player may also finish his turn by saying "End" if he cannot, or wishes not to, make further moves.

Stock At the start of their second and subsequent turns, players take as many cards from the stock as they need to replenish their hand (ie anything up to five cards).

Result The winner is the first player to have exhausted his payoff pile. Should neither player be able to make any further moves but still have cards left in his payoff pile, the game is considered drawn.

Windmill

This is a two deck game in which cards are laid out to represent the four sails of a windmill. An alternative name for the game is propeller – in which case the arms of the cross in the layout represent propeller blades.

Cards Two standard decks are used.
Layout Place any king face up at the centre of the playing area. Then deal out a reserve (called the "sails") of eight face-up cards: two above the king, two below it, and two to either side.
The objective is to build:
a) a descending sequence of 52 cards on the central king, regardless of suit or color and with kings following aces;
b) ascending sequences, ace through king and regardless of suit and color, on the first four aces that come up in play.
Play Cards are turned up from the stock one at a time and if unplayable are put on a waste heap. The stock is only dealt once.
The first four aces to appear are put as foundation cards in the four angles of the sails.
Cards are played to the foundations from either the stock, the sails, or from the top of the waste heap (which is always available for play).
The top card of any ace foundation may be transferred to the central king foundation (building on the central pile is of prime importance if the game is to go through).
Spaces A space in the layout must be filled by the top card of either the stock or the waste heap, but it need not be filled as soon as it occurs.
This means that a space can be "saved" for a useful card – and by using his judgment in the way he fills spaces, the player can greatly increase his chances of winning.
Alternative rule Some players prefer the central foundation card to be an ace and the other four foundations to be kings. Should he choose this alternative, the player must build an ascending sequence on the central ace and descending sequences on the four kings.

Layout

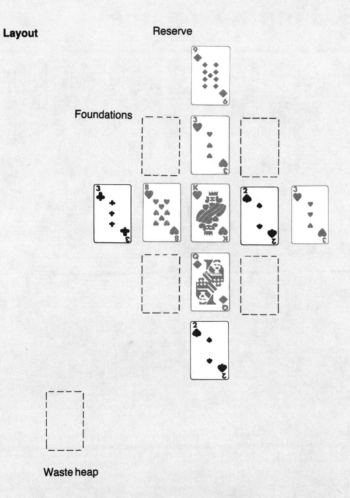

Reserve

Foundations

Waste heap

Section 6
Finding a game

What type of game?

In this section of the book, games are grouped in cross-referenced alphabetical lists according to type. For easy reference our five main groups – board games, dice and tile games, party games and races, target games, and word and picture games – have been further subdivided to indicate characteristics of play or the type of equipment needed. (Remember when wondering what to play that equipment for games can often be improvised.)

BOARD GAMES
Race games

Acey deucey 29
Alleyway 16
Ashte kashte 18
Backgammon 20
Dutch backgammon 28
Game of goose 156
Gioul 29
Horseshoe 174
Hyena chase 176
Ludo 184
Nyout 214
Pachisi 216
Plakato 29
Snakes and ladders 334

Strategic games

Canadian checkers 44
Checkers 34
Checkers fox and geese 46
Checkers go-moku 46
Chess 48
Chinese checkers 64
Chinese rebels 68
Conquest 76
Continental checkers 42
Diagonal checkers 40
Draughts 34
Fighting serpents 146
Fox and geese 154
German checkers 42
Giveaway checkers 38
Go 158
Go-moku 166
Halma 168
Halma solitaire 170
Hasami shogi 167

Hex 172
Italian checkers 40
Lasca 180
Losing checkers 38
Mancala games 200
Nine men's morris 210
Owari 200
Queen's guard 298
Reversi 302
Ringo 308
Russian checkers 42
Salta 312
Shogi 316
Six men's morris 213
Solitaire board games 336
Spanish checkers 40
Three men's morris 213
Tournament checkers 38
Turkish checkers 44

DICE AND TILE GAMES
Dice games (family)
Baseball 92
Basketball 93
Beetle 90
Centennial 91
Cheerio 94
Chicago 88
Double Cameroon 97
Drop dead 88
Everest 91
Fifty 86
General 96
Going to Boston 89
Hearts 90
Multiplication 89
Pig 89
Round the clock 86
Shut the box 87

Dice games (gambling)
Aces 108
Bidou 110
Buck dice 106
Craps 114
Crown and anchor 103
English hazard 109
Help your neighbor 105
Hooligan 106
Indian dice 100
Liar dice 102
Montevideo 113
Par 104
Poker dice 98
Ship, captain, mate, and crew 108
Thirty-six 105
Twenty-one 104

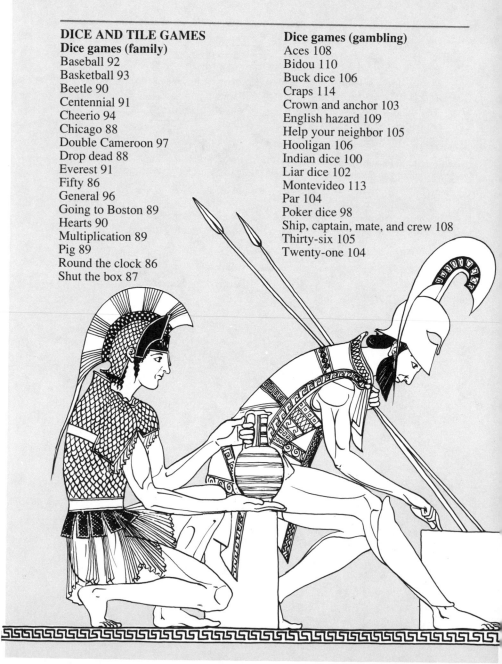

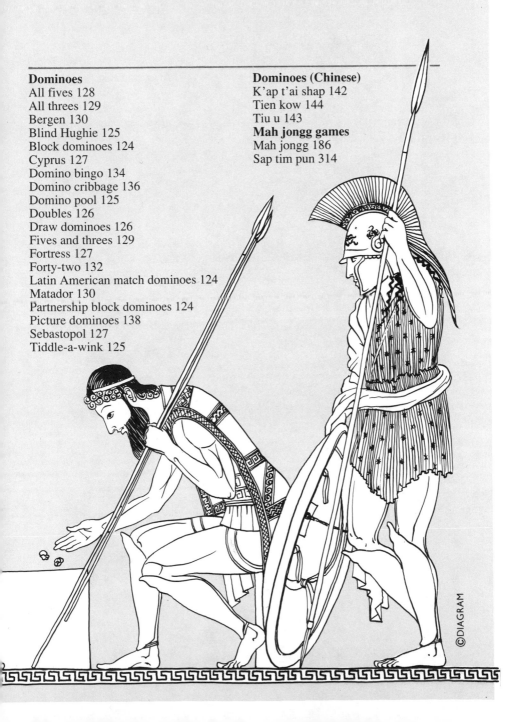

Dominoes
All fives 128
All threes 129
Bergen 130
Blind Hughie 125
Block dominoes 124
Cyprus 127
Domino bingo 134
Domino cribbage 136
Domino pool 125
Doubles 126
Draw dominoes 126
Fives and threes 129
Fortress 127
Forty-two 132
Latin American match dominoes 124
Matador 130
Partnership block dominoes 124
Picture dominoes 138
Sebastopol 127
Tiddle-a-wink 125

Dominoes (Chinese)
K'ap t'ai shap 142
Tien kow 144
Tiu u 143
Mah jongg games
Mah jongg 186
Sap tim pun 314

©DIAGRAM

PARTY GAMES
Games (blindfold)
Blind judgment 221
Blind man's buff 220
Blind man's sort out 224
Blind man's stick 221
Blind man's treasure hunt 221
Blind postman 222
Blindfold obstacle walk 224
Elephant's tail 223
Jailer 222
Murals 223
Murder in the dark 225
Nelson's eye 225
Pin the tail on the donkey 223
Squeak-piggy-squeak 221
Sweet tooth 224
Ten step buff 220
Thieves 222

Games (contests)
Apple on a string 228
Apple paring 228
Arm wrestling 233
Balloon flights 227
Candy wrapper 228
Card and bucket 229
Cock fighting contest 232
Grandmother's footsteps 230
Happy travelers 229
Hoppit 227
Limbo 230
Printers' errors 229
Rumors 232
Singing high jump 227
Static electricity 227
Stork fighting contest 232
Triangular tug-of-war 233
Two-minute walk 231
Games (goal-scoring)
Astride ball 237
Avenue goals 234
Balloon volleyball 236
Blow volleyball 236
Hockey rag time 237
Overhead goals 234

Games (musical)
Gods and goddesses 240
High steppers 239
Musical blackout 238
Musical bumps 238
Musical chairs 238
Musical hotch potch 239
Musical islands 240
Musical magic carpet 240
Musical rings 240
Musical statues 241
Ownership musical chairs 238

Games (observation)
Bean hunt 246
Butterfly hunt 246
Card hunt 247
Color hunt 247
Cut-out pairs 243
Detective treasure hunt 248
Easter egg hunt 247
Hidden objects 248
Hide and seek 249
Hot and cold thimble 246
Hunt the ring 244
Hunt the slipper 244
Hunt the thimble 246
Jigsaw hunt 247
Memory game 242
Mismatches 243
Mothers and babies 243
Present hunt 247
Sardines 249
Singing hunt the thimble 246
Sit down hunt the thimble 246
Storekeepers 248
Up Jenkins! 245
Wrong! 243

Games (parcel)
Forfeits parcel 250
Hot parcel 252
Lucky chocolate game 252
Mystery parcel 252
Pass the parcel 250
Games (trickery)
Do this, do that! 257
In the ditch 257
Laughing handkerchief 255
My little bird 255
Simon says 256
Yes-no beans 255

PARTY RACES

Back-to-back race 260
Balloon hop 272
Balloon pass 272
Bottle fishing 259
Burst the bag 269
Crocodile race 267
Double pass 270
Dumb artists 263
Egg cups 273
Emptying socks 271
Fishermen 259
Flying fish 268
Fruit colours 271
Hat and scarf 270
Hurry waiter! 273
Ladders 266
My mother's cake 266
Mystery numbers 265
Necklace race 262

Newspaper walk 258
Nose in the matchbox 269
Number parade 264
Palms 274
Passing the orange 275
Patches 262
Pick and cup 274
Piggy back race 261
Rabbit race 259
Simple numbers 265
Straws and beans 274
Sugar and spoons 275
Surprise sentences 269
Switchback 270
Three-legged race 261
Tortoise race 259
Tunnel ball 272
Word parade 265
Yarn tangles 267

TARGET GAMES
Ball games
Blow football 32
Containers 30
Cup and ball 30
Holey board game 33
In the bowl 30
Jam jars 30
Through the tunnel 33
Darts
Around the clock 81
Closing 81
Darts baseball 85
Darts cricket 85
Darts soccer 85
Darts shove ha'penny 85
Fifty-one 84
Fives 84
Halve it 84
Killer 82
Scram 81
Shanghai 81
Standard tournament darts 80
Coin throwing games
Brother Jonathan 70
Catch 72
Coin archboard 72
Cover it 70
Crack loo 71
Heads or tails 73
Hitting the mummy 70
Hole in one 72
Pennies on the plate 72
Penny roll 72
Roll a goal 72
Spinning a coin 73
Tossing a coin 73
Wall Jonathan 71

Fivestones/Jacks
Backward ones, two, threes, fours 153
Building a tower 153
Bushels 150
Claws 150
Demolishing a tower 153
Fivestones (basic throws) 149
Horse in the stable 152
Jacks 178
Ones, twos, threes, fours 148
Over the jump 150
Over the line 150
Pecks 150
Snake in the grass 153
Threading the needle 151
Toad in the hole 152
Towers 153
Under the arch 151

Marbles
Archboard 208
Bounce eye 206
Capture 203
Die shot 206
Dobblers 209
Fortifications 204
Hundreds 207
Increase pound 204
One step 209
Picking plums 209
Ring taw 204
Spangy 206
Spanners 203
Three holes 207
Wall marbles 203

Other target games
Conkers 74
Conquerors 75
Hoopla 304
Pick-up sticks 344
Ring the bull 306
Ringboard 304
Ringolette 307
Shove soccer 328
Shove ha'penny 330
Shovelboard 332
Soldiers 75
Spellicans 344
Squails 346
Tiddlywinks 348

WORD AND PICTURE GAMES
Pencil and paper games
Acrostics 277
Aggression 296
Anagrams 280
Battleships 292
Boxes 288
Buried treasure 294
Categories 278
Consequences 282
Crosswords 276
Crystals 290
Fill ins 280
Geography race 281
Guggenheim 279
Hangman 284
Keyword 276
Noughts and crosses 286
Noughts and crosses, three-dimensional 286
Picture consequences 282
Pictures 284
Sprouts 289
Squiggles 295
Synonyms 280
Telegrams 281
Tick-tack-toe 286
Tick-tack-toe, three-dimensional 286
Transformation 280

Word games (acting)
Category charades 353
Charades 352
Dumb crambo 357
In the manner of the word 357
Proverb charades 353
Spoken charades 353
The game 354

Word games (guessing)

Animal, vegetable, or mineral 359
Botticelli 363
Coffeepot 360
I-spy 358
Join the club 360
Man and object 359
Mora 365
Proverbs 361
Scissors, paper, stone 364
Shoot 366
Spoof 366
Teakettle 360
What is my thought like? 362
Who am I? 362

Word games (vocabulary)

A was an apple pie 372
Association chain 374
Associations 374
Backward spelling bee 368
Buzz 375
Buzz-fizz 375
City of Boston 373
Fizz 375
Ghosts 370
Grab on behind 371
Greedy spelling bee 368
I love my love 372
I went on a trip 373
Initial answers 371
Initial letters 371
Number associations 374
One minute please 373
Right or wrong spelling bee 369
Spelling bee 368
Taboo 375
Traveler's alphabet 372

© DIAGRAM

How many players?

These lists show at a glance which games are suitable for one, two, three, or four players. Lists of games for groups of varying size follow on p. 764.

GAMES FOR ONE PLAYER
Also remember that most target games (see p. 758) and some word and picture games (p. 760) can be enjoyed by individuals seeking to improve on their previous best score.
Board games (strategic)
Halma solitaire 170
Solitaire board games 336
Target games
Cup and ball 30
Fivestones 148
Jacks 178

GAMES FOR TWO PLAYERS
Also see games for two or more players (p. 764).
Board games (race)
Ashte kashte 18
Backgammon 20
Backgammon variants 28
Ludo 184
Pachisi 216
Board games (strategic)
Checkers 34
Checkers variants 38
Chess 48
Chinese checkers 64
Chinese rebels 68
Conquest 76
Draughts 34
Draughts variants 38
Fighting serpents 146
Fox and geese 154
Go 158
Go variants 166
Halma 168
Hex 172
Lasca 180
Mancala games 200

Nine men's morris 210
Queen's guard 298
Reversi 302
Ringo 308
Salta 312
Shogi 316
Six men's morris 213
Three men's morris 213
Dice games
Baseball 92
Bidou, two-hand 110
Target games
Conkers 74
Conquerors 75
Marbles:
  Capture 203
  Hundreds 207
  Spanners 203
Soldiers 75
Tile games
Dominoes:
  All fives 128
  All threes 129
  Bergen 130
  Domino bingo 134
  Domino cribbage 136
  Fives and threes 129
Dominoes (Chinese):
  Tiu u 143
Word and picture games
Pencil and paper games:
  Battleships 292
  Boxes 288
  Buried treasure 294
  Noughts and crosses 286
  Sprouts 289
  Squiggles 295
  Tick-tack-toe 286
Word games:
  Mora 365
  Scissors, paper, stone 364
  Shoot 366

GAMES FOR THREE PLAYERS
Also see games for two or more players (p. 764) and for other groups (p. 765).
Board games (race)
Ashte kashte 18
Ludo 184
Pachisi 216
Dice games
Round the clock 86
Tile games
Dominoes:
  All fives 128
  All threes 129
  Bergen 130
  Fives and threes 129
Dominoes (Chinese):
  Tiu u 143
Mah jongg 186

GAMES FOR FOUR PLAYERS
Also see games for two or more players (p. 764) and for other groups (p. 765).
Board games (race)
Ashte kashte 18
Ludo 184
Pachisi 216
Dice games
Round the clock 86
Tile games
Dominoes:
  All fives 128
  Bergen 130
  Block (partnership) 124
  Cyprus 127
  Fortress 127
  Forty-two 132
  Latin American match 124
  Sebastopol 127
Dominoes (Chinese):
  Tien kow 144
Mah jongg 186

**GAMES FOR TWO OR
MORE PLAYERS**
*Note that many of these games
become impracticable for groups of
more than seven or eight players.*
Board games (race)
Alleyway 16
Game of goose 156
Horseshoe 174
Hyena chase 176
Nyout 214
Snakes and ladders 334
Dice games
Aces 108
Basketball 93
Beetle 90
Buck dice 106
Centennial 91
Cheerio 94
Chicago 88
Craps 114
Crown and anchor 103
Double Cameroon 97
Drop dead 88
English hazard 109
Fifty-one 86
General 96
Hearts 90
Help your neighbor 105
Hooligan 106
Indian dice 100
Par 104
Pig 89
Poker dice 98
Ship, captain, mate, and crew 108
Shut the box 86
Thirty-six 105
Twenty-one 104

Target games
Ball games 30
Coin throwing games 70
Darts 78
Marbles:
 Bounce eye 206
 Die shot 206
 Fortifications 204
 Increase pound 204
 Ring taw 204
Pick-up sticks 344
Ring target games 304
Shove soccer 328
Shove ha'penny 330
Shovelboard 332
Spellicans 344
Squails 346
Tiddlywinks 348

Tile games
Dominoes:
  Blind Hughie 125
  Block dominoes 124
  Domino pool 125
  Doubles 126
  Draw dominoes 126
  Matador 130
  Picture dominoes 138
Dominoes (Chinese):
  K'ap t'ai shap 142
Mah jongg tiles:
  Sap tim pun 314
Word and picture games
Pencil and paper games:
  Acrostics 277
  Aggression 296
  Anagrams 280
  Categories 278
  Consequences 282
  Crosswords 276
  Crystals 290
  Guggenheim 279
  Hangman 284
  Keyword 276
  Picture consequences 282
  Telegrams 281
  Transformation 280
Word games (guessing):
  I-spy 358
  Spoof 366

OTHER GAMES FOR GROUPS
All these games need a minimum of three players and many can be played by quite large groups.
Dice games
Bidou, multihand 112
Going to Boston 89
Liar dice 102
Montevideo 113
Multiplication 89
Party games
Blindfold games 220
Contests 226
Goal scoring games 234
Musical games 238
Observation games 242
Parcel games 250
Trickery games 254
Party races
Individuals 258
Pairs 260
Teams 264
Tile games
Dominoes:
  Sebastopol 127
  Tiddle-a-wink 125
Word and picture games
Pencil and paper games:
  Fill-ins 280
  Geography race 281
  Pictures 284
  Synonyms 280
Word games (acting) 352
Word games (guessing) 358
Word games (vocabulary) 368

How many for cards?

This section of the book shows at a glance which games are suitable for different numbers of players. It begins with lists of games for specific numbers and ends with games for groups of two or more (p. 772) and three or more (p. 774) players.

GAMES FOR ONE PLAYER
With the exception of two double solitaire games (Russian bank, and Spite and malice), all the games in Section 5 of this book are for one player.

GAMES FOR TWO PLAYERS

Also see games for two or more players (p. 772).

General games

All fives 384
Auction pinochle 459
Auction piquet 467
Bezique 388
California Jack 479
Casino 414
Cribbage 418
Draw casino 417
Ecarté 422
Euchre, two-handed 425
Five hundred, two-handed 427
Forty-five 428
Gin rummy 476
Hearts, two-handed 438
Imperial 440
Kalabriasz 442

Pinochle 456
Piquet 462
Royal casino 417
Rubicon bezique 390
Russian bank 736
Rummy 474
Seven up 478
Spade casino 417
Spite and malice 744

Children's games

Persian pasha 544
Spit 540
Stealing bundles 542
War 544

Gambling games

Brag, nine-card 587
Fifteen 580
Thirty-five 664

©DIAGRAM

GAMES FOR THREE PLAYERS

*Also see games for two or
more (p. 772) and three or
more (p. 774) players.*

General games
All fives 384
Auction pinochle 459
Bezique, three-handed 390

Calabrasella 408
California jack 479
Casino 414
Cribbage, three-handed 421
Draw casino 417
Euchre, three-handed 425
Five hundred 426
Kalabriasz, three-handed 445
Knaves 446

Preference 472
Royal casino 417
Rummy 474
Seven up 478
Skat 480
Solo, three-handed 487
Spade casino 417

Children's games
Animal noises 520
Menagerie 520
War, for three players 545

Gambling games
Brag, nine-card 587
Thirty-five 664

©DIAGRAM

GAMES FOR FOUR PLAYERS
Also see games for two or more (p. 772) and three or more (p. 774) players.

General games
Auction bridge 406
Auction forty-five 431
Auction pinochle 459
Bezique, four-handed 393
Boston 394
California jack 479
Call-ace euchre 425
Canasta 410
Casino 414
Contract bridge 396
Cribbage, four-handed 421
Draw casino 417
Duplicate contract bridge 404
Euchre, four-handed 424
Five hundred, four-handed 427
Forty-five 428
Gin rummy, partnership 476
Grand 432
Kalabriasz, partnership 445
Polignac 446
Railroad euchre 425
Royal casino 417
Rummy 474
Seven up, four-handed 479
Skat 480

Solo whist 486
Spade casino 417
Vint 490
Whist 492

Children's games
Animal noises 520
Menagerie 520
My ship sails 522
Rolling stone 530
Stealing bundles 542

Gambling games
Brag, nine-card 587
Thirty-five 664

GAMES FOR FIVE PLAYERS

*Also see games for two or
more (p. 772) and three or
more (p. 774) players*

General games
Call-ace euchre 425
Polignac 446

Children's games
My ship sails 522
Rolling stone 530

GAMES FOR SIX PLAYERS

*Also see games for two or
more (p. 772) and three or
more (p. 774) players.*

General games
Auction forty-five 431
Call-ace euchre 425
Forty-five 428
Gin rummy, partnership 476
Polignac 446
Rummy 474
Skat 480

Children's games
My ship sails 522
Rolling stone 530

Gambling games
Brag, nine-card 587
Thirty-five 664

©DIAGRAM

GAMES FOR TWO OR MORE PLAYERS

Note that many of these games become impracticable for groups of more than seven or eight players.
Also see games for three or more players (p. 774).

General games

Auction pitch 386
Auction pitch, with joker 387
Nap, seven-card 453
Napoleon 452
Purchase nap 453
Spoil five 488

Children's games

Beggar my neighbour 500
Card dominoes 502
Concentration 506
Crazy eights 513
Give away 510
Go boom 512
Go fish 514
Knockout whist 516
Menagerie 520
Racing demon 528
Scoring go boom 512
Sequence 532
Slapjack 534
Snap 536

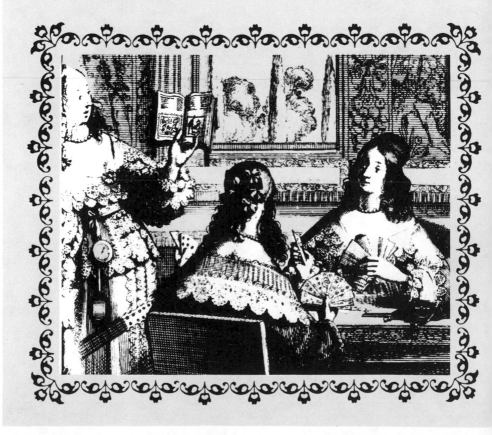

Gambling games
Ace-deuce-jack 550
Banker and broker 564
Baccarat/Chemin de fer 552
Blackjack 566
Brag, nine-card 587
Brag, seven-card 586
Card craps 588
Card put-and-take 594
Chinese fan-tan 596
Farmer 580
Faro 598
Hoggenheimer 604
Injun 608
Lansquenet 614

Macao 579
Monte bank 616
Poker 624
Polish red dog 648
Red and black 650
Red dog 652
Seven and a half 578
Six-spot red dog 654
Slippery sam 660
Stop the bus 587
Stuss 662
Ten and a half 578
Trente et quarante 668
Yablon 672
Ziginette 674

© DIAGRAM

GAMES FOR THREE OR MORE PLAYERS

Note that many of these games become inpracticable for groups of more than seven or eight players.

General games

Black lady hearts 437
Black Maria 439
Domino hearts 438
Greek hearts 437
Hearts 436
Heartsette 438
Irish loo 449
Joker hearts 438
Loo 448
Michigan 450
Oh hell 454
Pope Joan 468
Spot hearts 436

Children's games
Cheat 504
Donkey 508
Jig 538
Le vieux garçon 525
Linger longer 518
Old maid 524
Pig 509
Play or pay 526
Snip-snap-snorem 538
Up and down cheat 505

Gambling card games
Bango 562
Blücher 582
Brag, seven-card 586
Brag, three-card 585
Horse race 606
Kentucky derby 610
Skinball 656
Thirty-one 666

©DIAGRAM

Card game variations and alternative names

VARIATIONS

The following games are included in this book as sub-sections or variations of a game with a different name (here given in brackets).

Animal noises (Menagerie) 520
Black lady (Hearts) 437
Black Maria (Hearts) 439
Blind and straddle (Poker) 643
Blind opening (Poker) 643
Blind tiger (Poker) 643
California jack (Seven up) 479
Call-ace (Euchre) 425
Chemin de fer (Baccarat) 552
Cincinnati (Poker) 646
Crazy eights (Go boom) 513
Criss cross (Poker) 646
Down the river (Poker) 639
Easy go (Card put-and-take) 595
Farmer (Blackjack) 580
Fifteen (Blackjack) 580
Gin (Rummy) 476
Heartsette (Hearts) 438
Jacks or better (Poker) 643
Jig (Snip-snap-snorem) 538
Lame-brain Pete (Poker) 646
Le vieux garçon (Old maid) 525
Lowball (Poker) 645
Macao (Blackjack) 579
Mexican stud (Poker) 639
Persian pasha (War) 545

ALTERNATIVE NAMES

The following games appear in this book under an alternative name (given here in brackets).

Ace-deuce (Yablon) 672
Ace low (Fifteen) 580
All fours (Seven up) 478
Animals (Menagerie) 520
Belote (Kalabriasz) 442
Big forty (Napoleon at St. Helena) 726
BJ (Blackjack) 566
Blackout (Oh hell) 454
Blind hooker (Banker and broker) 564
Boodle (Michigan) 450
Broken intervals (Calculation) 694
California loo (California jack) 479
Cans (Fifteen) 580
Chicago (Michigan) 450
Chinese bezique (Six-deck bezique) 391
Chip hearts (Spot hearts) 436
Clab (Kalabriasz) 442
Clobber (Kalabriasz) 442
Crapette (Russian bank) 736
Cutthroat euchre (Three-handed euchre) 425
Demon (Canfield) 696
Double and quits (Monte Carlo) 724
Draw seven (California jack) 479
Dutch bank (Banker and broker) 564
Eight off (Eight away) 702
Enflay (Rolling stone) 530
Fan-tan (Card dominoes) 502
Fan-tan (Chinese fan-tan) 596
Farobank (Faro) 598
Forty thieves (Napoleon at St. Helena) 726
Four of a kind (Clock) 698
Hidden cards (Clock) 698
High-card pool (Red dog) 652
High-low-jack (Seven up) 478
I doubt it (Cheat) 504
Idle year (Accordion) 684
In between (Yablon) 672
Indian carpet (Crazy quilt) 700
Japanese rug (Crazy quilt) 700
Klaberjass (Kalabriasz) 442
Lanterloo (Loo) 448
Laying siege (Beleaguered castle) 686
Memory (Concentration) 506

Pig (Donkey) 509
Pig in the poke (Poker) 645
Polignac (Knaves) 446
Railroad (Euchre) 425
Rubicon (Bezique) 390
Seven and a half (Blackjack) 578
Seven-toed Pete (Poker) 639
Shotgun (Poker) 643
Six spot (Red dog) 654
Spit in the ocean (Poker) 645
Stop the bus (Brag) 587
Stormy weather (Poker) 644
Ten and a half (Blackjack) 578
Up-and-down river (Card put-and-
    take) 595

Methuselah (Accordion) 684
Monte (Monte bank) 616
Nap (Napoleon) 452
Newmarket (Michigan) 450
Old man's bundle (Stealing bundles)
    542
Old sledge (Seven up) 478
Parliament (Card dominoes) 502
Pass the lady (Old maid) 524
Pasteboard derby (Kentucky derby)
    610
Pelmanism (Concentration) 506
Penuchle (Pinochle) 456
Pisha pasha (Persian pasha) 545
Plait (Braid) 690
Polish pachuk (Polish red dog) 648
Pontoon (Blackjack) 566
Propeller (Windmill) 746
Put-and-take (Card put-and-take)
    594
Quince (Fifteen) 580
Rauber skat (Skat) 480
Rouge et noir (Trente et quarante)
    668
Round the corner (Play or pay) 526
Saratoga (Michigan) 450
Saton pong (Ten and a half) 578

Schnautz (Thirty-one) 666
Schwellen (Rolling stone) 530
Setback (Auction pitch) 386
Sevens (Card dominoes) 502
Sham battle (Beleaguered castle) 686
Skin (Skinball) 656
Skinning (Skinball) 656
Slippery Anne (Black Maria) 439
Spanish monte (Monte bank) 616
Stitch (Polish red dog) 648
Sun dial (Clock) 698
Three naturals (Macao) 579
Toad in the hole (Frog) 710
Tower of Babel (Accordion) 684
Travelers (Clock) 698
Twenty-one (Blackjack) 566
Vanjohn (Blackjack) 566
Vingt-et-un (Blackjack) 566
Weddings (Monte Carlo) 724

Index

A

A was an apple pie 372
Accordion 684
Ace-deuce (see Yablon) 672
Ace-deuce-jack 550
Ace-low (see Fifteen) 580
Aces 108
Acey deucey 29
Acrostics 277
Acting word games 352
Aggression 296
All fives (card game) 384
All fives (domino game) 128
All fours (see Seven up) 478
All threes 129
Alleyway 16
Alpha and omega (see Grab on behind) 371
Anagrams 280
Animal noises 520
Animal, vegetable, or mineral 359
Animals (see Menagerie) 520
Apostles, The 341
Apple on a string 228
Apple paring 228
Archboard 208
Arm wrestling 233
Around the clock 81
Ashte kashte 18
Association chain 374
Associations 374
Astride ball 237
Auction bridge 406
Auction forty-five 430
Auction pinochle 459
Auction piquet 467
Auction pitch 386
Auction pitch, with joker 387
Avenue goals 234

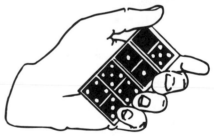

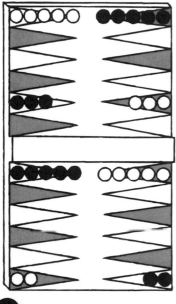

B

Baccarat 552
Baccarat banque 558
Baccarat-chemin de fer 552
Back-to-back race 260
Backgammon 20
Backward ones, two, threes, fours 153
Backward spelling bee 368
Ball games 30
Balloon flights 227
Balloon hop 272
Balloon pass 272
Balloon volleyball 236
Bango 562
Banker and broker 564
Battleships 292
Bean hunt 246
Beetle 90
Beggar my neighbour 500
Beleaguered castle 686
Belote (see Kalabriasz) 442
Bergen 130
Bezique 388
Bezique, eight-deck 392
Bezique, four-handed 393
Bezique, rubicon 390
Bezique, six-deck 391
Bezique, three-handed 390
Bezique, two-handed 388
Bidou 110
Bidou, multihand 112
Big forty (see Napoleon at St.
  Helena) 726
Birds fly (see My little bird) 255
Bisley 688
BJ (see Blackjack) 566
Black lady hearts 437
Black Maria 439
Blackjack 566

**Blackout –
Buried treasure**

Blackout (see Oh hell) 454
Blind and straddle 643
Blind hooker (see Banker and broker) 564
Blind Hughie 125
Blind judgment 221
Blind man's buff 220
Blind man's sort out 224
Blind man's stick 221
Blind man's treasure hunt 221
Blind opening 643
Blind postman 222
Blind tiger 643
Blindfold games 220
Blindfold obstacle walk 224
Block dominoes 124
Blow football 32
Blow volleyball 236
Blücher 582
Boodle (see Michigan) 450
Boston 394
Botticelli 363
Bottle fishing 259
Bounce eye 206
Boxes 288
Brag 584
Brag, nine-card 587
Brag, seven-card 586
Brag, three-card 585
Braid 690
Bridge, auction 406
Bridge, contract 396
Bridge, duplicate contract 404
Bridge board (see Archboard) 208
Bristol 692
Broken intervals (see Calculation) 694
Brother Jonathan 70
Buck dice 106
Building a tower 153
Buried treasure 294

Burst the bag 269
Bushels 150
Butterfly hunt 246
Buzz 375
Buzz-fizz 375

C

Calabrasella 408
Calculation 694
California jack 479
California loo (see California jack)
  479
Call-ace euchre 425
Canadian checkers 44
Canasta 410
Candy wrapper 228
Canfield (also see Klondike) 696
Cans (see Fifteen) 580
Capture 203
Card and bucket 229
Card craps 588
Card dominoes 502
Card hunt 247
Card put-and-take 594
Casino 414
Casino, draw 417
Casino, royal 417
Casino, spade 417
Catch 72
Categories 278
Category charades 353
Centennial 91
Charades 352
Cheat 504
Cheat, up and down 505
Checkers 34
Checkers fox and geese 46
Checkers go-moku 46
Cheerio 94

**Chemin de fer –
Craps**

Chemin de fer 552
Chess 48
Chicago (card game: see Michigan)
  450
Chicago (dice game) 88
Chinese bezique 391
Chinese checkers 64
Chinese dominoes 140
Chinese fan-tan 596
Chinese rebels 68
Chinese whispers (see Rumors) 232
Chip hearts 436
Cincinnati 646
City of Boston 373
Clab (see Kalabriasz) 442
Claws 150
Clobber (see Kalabriasz) 442
Clock 698
Closing 81
Cock fighting contest 232
Coffeepot 360
Coin archboard 72
Coin throwing games 70
Collecting tens (see K'ap t'ai shap)
  142
Color hunt 247
Concentration 506
Conkers 74
Conquerors 75
Conquest 76
Consequences 282
Containers 30
Contests 226
Continental checkers 42
Contract bridge 396
Corsair, The 340
Cover it 70
Crack loo 71
Crapette (see Russian bank) 736
Craps 114

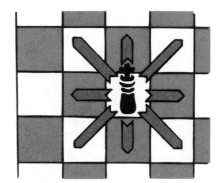

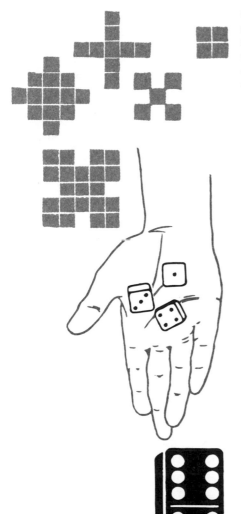

Crazy eights 513
Crazy quilt 700
Cribbage 418
Cribbage, five-card 421
Cribbage, four-handed 421
Cribbage, seven-card 421
Cribbage, six-card 419
Cribbage, three-handed 421
Criss cross poker 646
Crocodile race 267
Cross, The 339
Crosswords 276
Crown and anchor 103
Crystals 290
Cup and ball 30
Cut-out pairs 243
Cutthroat euchre 425
Cyprus 127

D

Darts 78
Darts baseball 85
Darts cricket 85
Darts soccer 85
Darts shove ha'penny 85
Demolishing a tower 153
Demon (see Canfield) 696
Detective treasure hunt 248
Diagonal checkers 40
Dice 86
Dice baseball 92
Dice basketball 93
Die marble (see Die shot) 206
Die shot 206
Do this, do that! 257
Dobblers 209
Domino bingo 134
Domino cribbage 136
Domino hearts 438

Domino pool 125
Domino rounce (see Forty-two) 132
Dominoes 120
Donkey 508
Double and quits (see Monte Carlo) 724
Double Cameroon 97
Double pass 270
Doubles 126
Down the river (see Seven-card stud) 639
Draughts 34
Draw casino 417
Draw dominoes 126
Draw poker 640
Draw poker, variants 643
Draw seven (see California jack) 479
Drop dead 88
Dumb artists 263
Dumb crambo 357
Duplicate contract bridge 404
Dutch backgammon 28
Dutch bank (see Banker and broker) 564

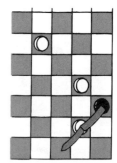

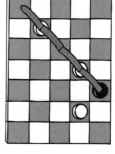

E

Easter egg hunt 247
Easy snap 537
Ecarté 422
Egg cups 273
Eight away 702
Eight off (see Eight away) 702
Elephant's tail 223
Emptying socks 271
Enflay (see Rolling stone) 530
English hazard 109
Euchre 424
Euchre, call-ace 425
Euchre, cutthroat (see Euchre, three-handed) 425

Euchre, four-handed 424
Euchre, railroad 425
Euchre, three-handed 425
Euchre, two-handed 425
Everest 91

F

Family dice games 86
Fan-tan (see Card dominoes) 502
Fan-tan (see Chinese fan-tan) 596
Farmer 580
Faro 598
Farobank (see Faro) 598
Fifteen 580
Fifty 86
Fifty-one (see Fives) 84
Fighting serpents 146
Fill ins 280
Fingers (see Mora) 365
Fishermen 259
Fishing (see Tiu u) 143
Five hundred 426
Five hundred, four-handed 427
Five hundred, three-handed 426
Five hundred, two-handed 427
Fives 84
Fives and threes 129
Fives up (see All fives) 128
Fivestones 148
Fizz 375
Florentine 704
Flower garden 706
Flying fish 268
Flying high (see My little bird) 255
Forfeit tiddlywinks 349
Forfeits parcel 250
Fortifications 204
Fortress 127
Forty-five 428

**Forty-five, auction –
Guggenheim**

Forty-five, auction 430
Forty thieves (see Napoleon at St. Helena) 726
Forty-two 132
Four of a kind (see Clock) 698
Fox and geese 154
Friday the thirteenth 708
Frog 710
Fruit colors 271

G

Game of goose 156
Game, The 354
General 96
Geography race 281
German checkers 42
Ghosts 370
Gin rummy 476
Gioul 29
Give away 510
Giveaway checkers 38
Go 158
Go-bang (see Go-moku) 166
Go boom 512
Go boom, scoring 512
Go fish 514
Goal scoring games 234
Gods and goddesses 240
Going to Boston 89
Go-moku 166
Grab on behind 371
Grand 432
Grandmother's footsteps 230
Greedy spelling bee 368
Greek hearts 437
Guessing games 358
Guessing proverbs (see Proverbs) 361
Guggenheim 279

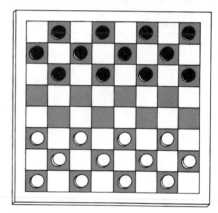

DIA_BA_
ONCLEHSTUB

DIA_RAM
ONCLEHSTUBP

DIA_RAM
ONCLEHSTUBPF

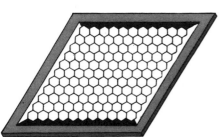

H

Halma 168
Halma solitaire 170
Halve it 84
Hangman 284
Happy travelers 229
Hasami shogi 167
Hat and scarf 270
Heads or tails 73
Hearts (card game) 436
Hearts (dice game) 90
Hearts, black lady 437
Hearts, domino 438
Hearts, Greek 437
Hearts, joker 438
Hearts, spot 436
Hearts, two-handed 438
Hearts due (see Hearts: dice game) 90
Heartsette 438
Help your neighbor 105
Hex 172
Hic, haec, hoc (see Scissors, paper,
    stone) 364
Hidden cards (see Clock) 698
Hidden objects 248
Hidden proverbs (see Proverbs) 361
Hidden words (see Keyword) 276
Hide and seek 249
High-card pool (see Red dog) 652
High-low-jack (see Seven up) 478
High-low poker 647
High steppers 239
Hit and span (see Spanners) 203
Hitting the mummy 70
Hockey rag time 237
Hoggenheimer 604
Hole in one 72
Holey board game 33
Hooligan 106

**Hoopla –
Jackstraws**

Hoopla 304
Hoppit 227
Horse in the stable 152
Horse race 606
Horseshoe 174
Hot and cold thimble 246
Hot parcel 252
Hundreds 207
Hunt the ring 244
Hunt the slipper 244
Hunt the thimble 246
Hurry waiter! 273
Hyena chase 176

I

I doubt it (see Cheat) 504
I love my love 372
I went on a trip 373
Idle year (see Accordion) 684
Imperial 440
In between (see Yablon) 672
In the bowl 30
In the ditch 257
In the manner of the word 357
Increase pound 204
Indian carpet (see Crazy quilt) 700
Indian dice 100
Initial answers 371
Initial letters 371
Injun 608
Irish loo 449
I-spy 358
Italian checkers 40

J

Jacks 178
Jacks or better 643
Jackstraws (see Pick-up sticks) 344

Jailer 222
Jam jars 30
Japanese rug (see Crazy quilt) 700
Jerkstraws (see Pick-up sticks) 344
Jig 538
Jigsaw hunt 247
Join the club 360
Joker hearts 438
Juggling sticks (see Pick-up sticks) 344
Jumbled words (see Anagrams) 280

K

Kalabriasz 442
Kalabriasz, partnership 445
Kalabriasz, three-handed 445
K'ap t'ai shap 142
Kentucky derby 610
Keyword 276
Killer 82
King Albert 712
Kippers (see Flying fish) 268
Klaberjass (see Kalabriasz) 442
Klondike 714
Knaves 446
Knockout whist 516

L

La belle Lucie 716
Ladders 266
Lame-brain Pete 646
Lansquenet 614
Lanterloo (see Loo) 448
Lasca 180
Last and first (see Grab on behind) 371
Latin American match dominoes 124
Laughing handkerchief 255

Laying siege (see Beleaguered castle)
   686
Le vieux garçon 525
Leapfrog 718
Letter E, The 341
Liar dice 102
Limbo 230
Linger longer 518
Loo 448
Loo, five-card 449
Loo, Irish 449
Loo, three-card 448
Losing checkers 38
Lowball poker 645
Low-hand stud 639
Lucky chocolate game 252
Ludo 184

M

Macao 579
Mah jongg 186
Maltese cross (see Doubles) 126
Man and object 359
Mancala games 200
Marbles 202
Martinetti (see Centennial) 91
Matador 130
Maze 720
Memory (see Concentration) 506
Memory game 242
Menagerie 520
Merels (see Nine men's morris) 210
Methuselah (see Accordion) 684
Mexican stud poker 639
Michigan 450
Mill (see Nine men's morris) 210
Mismatches 242
Miss Milligan 722
Monte (see Monte bank) 616

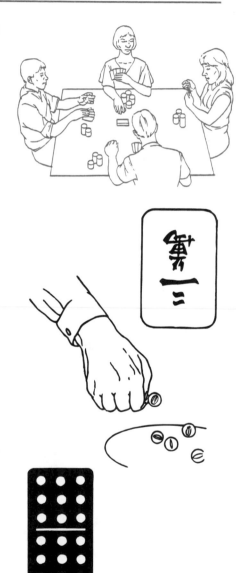

Monte bank 616
Monte bank, casino 616
Monte bank, private 622
Monte Carlo 724
Montevideo 113
Mora 365
Morelles (see Nine men's morris) 210
Mothers and babies 243
Muggins (see All fives) 128
Multihand bidou 112
Multiplication 89
Murals 223
Murder in the dark 255
Musical blackout 238
Musical bumps 238
Musical chairs 238
Musical games 238
Musical hotch potch 239
Musical islands 240
Musical magic carpet 240
Musical rings 240
Musical statues 241
My little bird 255
My mother's cake 266
My ship sails 522
Mystery numbers 265
Mystery parcel 252

N

Nap (see Napoleon) 452
Nap, purchase 453
Nap, seven-card 453
Napoleon 452
Napoleon at St. Helena 326
Necklace race 262
Nelson's eye 225
Never say it (see Taboo) 375
Newmarket (card game: see
    Michigan) 450

Newmarket –
Partnership block dominoes

Newmarket (dice game: see Going to
    Boston) 89
Newspaper walk 258
Nine men's morris 210
Nose in the matchbox 269
Noughts and crosses 286
Noughts and crosses, three-
    dimensional 286
Number associations 374
Number parade 264
Nyout 214

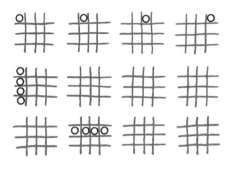

O

Observation games 242
Octagon, The 340
O'Grady says (see Simon says) 256
Oh hell 454
Ohio (see Centennial) 91
Old maid 524
Old man's bundle (see Stealing
    bundles) 542
Old sledge (see Seven up) 478
One minute please 373
One step 209
Ones, twos, threes, fours 148
Over the jump 150
Over the line 150
Overhead goals 234
Owari 200
Ownership musical chairs 238

P

Pachisi 216
Palms 274
Par 104
Parcel games 250
Parliament (see Card dominoes) 502
Partnership block dominoes 124

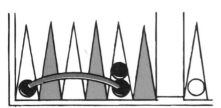

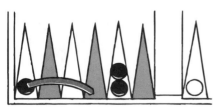

Pass the lady (see Old maid) 524
Pass the parcel 250
Passing the orange 275
Pasteboard derby (see Kentucky derby) 610
Patches 262
Pattern forming solitaires 341
Pecks 150
Pelmanism (see Concentration) 506
Pencil and paper games 276
Pennies on the plate 72
Penny roll 72
Penuchle (see Pinochle) 456
Persian pasha 545
Pick and cup 274
Pick-a-stick (see Pick-up sticks) 344
Picking plums 209
Pick-up sticks 344
Picture consequences 282
Picture dominoes 138
Pictures 284
Pig (card game) 509
Pig (dice game) 89
Pig in the poke 645
Piggy back race 261
Pin the tail on the donkey 223
Pinochle 456
Pinochle, auction 459
Piquet 462
Piquet au cent 466
Piquet, auction 467
Pisha pasha (see Persian pasha) 545
Plait (see Braid) 690
Plakato 29
Play or pay 526
Poker 624
Poker, closed games 646
Poker, draw 640
Poker, draw variants 643
Poker, high-low 647

Poker, stud 638
Poker, stud variants 639
Poker dice 98
Poker solitaire 728
Polignac 446
Polish checkers (see Continental checkers) 42
Polish pachuk (see Polish red dog) 648
Polish red dog 648
Pontoon (see Blackjack) 566
Pope Joan 468
Preference 472
Present hunt 247
Printers' errors 229
Propeller (see Windmill) 746
Proverb charades 353
Proverbs 361
Purchase nap 453
Puss in the corner 730
Put-and-take (see Card put-and-take) 594
Pyramid 732

Q

Queen's guard 298
Quince (see Fifteen) 580

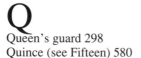

R

Rabbit race 259
Races 258
Racing demon 528
Railroad euchre 425
Rauber skat (see Skat) 480
Red and black 650
Red dog 652
Red dog, Polish 648
Red dog, six-spot 654

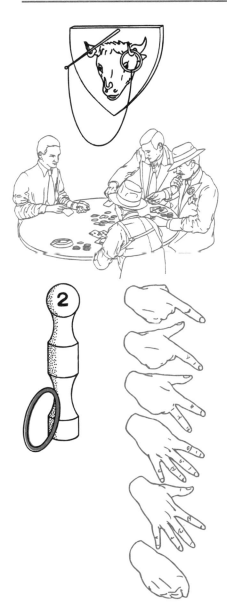

Reversi 302
Right or wrong spelling bee 369
Ring target games 304
Ring taw 204
Ring the bull 306
Ringboard (see Hoopla) 304
Ringo 308
Ringolette 307
Roll a goal 72
Rolling stone 530
Rotation (see Chicago) 88
Rouge et noir (see Trente et quarante)
    668
Round the clock 86
Round the corner (see Play or pay)
    526
Royal casino 417
Royal cotillion 734
Rubicon bezique 390
Rummy 474
Rummy, gin 476
Rumors 232
Russian bank 736
Russian checkers 42

S

Salta 312
Sap tim pun 314
Saratoga (see Michigan) 450
Sardines 249
Saton pong (see Ten and a half) 578
Schnautz (see Thirty-one) 666
Schwellen (see Rolling stone) 530
Scissors, paper, stone 364
Scoring go boom 512
Scorpion 740
Scram 81
Sebastopol 127
Sequence 532

Setback (see Auction pitch) 386
Seven and a half 578
Seven-card stud (poker) 639
Seven-toed Pete (see Seven-card stud) 639
Seven up 478
Seven up, four-handed 479
Sevens (see Card dominoes) 502
Sham battle (see Beleaguered castle) 686
Shanghai 81
Ship, captain, mate, and crew 108
Shogi 316
Shoot 366
Shotgun 643
Shove soccer 328
Shove ha'penny 330
Shovelboard 332
Shut the box 87
Simon says 256
Simple numbers 265
Singing high jump 227
Singing hunt the thimble 246
Sit down hunt the thimble 246
Six men's morris 213
Six-spot red dog 654
Skat 480
Skin (see Skinball) 656
Skinball 656
Skinning (see Skinball) 656
Slapjack 534
Slippery Anne (see Black Maria) 439
Slippery Sam 660
Snake in the grass 153
Snakes and ladders 334
Snap 536
Snap, easy 537
Snap, speed 537
Snip-snap-snorem 538
Soldiers 75

Solitaire board games 336
Solo (see Solo whist) 486
Solo, three-handed 487
Solo whist 486
Spade casino 417
Spangy 206
Spanish checkers 40
Spanish monte (see Monte bank) 616
Spanners 203
Speed snap 537
Spellicans 344
Spelling bee 368
Spider 742
Spillikins (see Spellicans) 344
Spinning a coin 73
Spit 540
Spit in the ocean 645
Spite and malice 744
Spoil five (card game) 488
Spoil five (board game: see Go-moku)
    166
Spoken charades 353
Spoof 366
Spot hearts 436
Sprouts 289
Squails 346
Squeak-piggy-squeak 221
Squiggles 295
Static electricity 227
Stealing bundles 542
Stitch (see Polish red dog) 648
Stop the bus 587
Storekeepers 248
Stork fighting contest 232
Stormy weather 644
Straws and beans 274
Stud poker 638
Stuss 662
Sugar and spoons 275
Sun dial (see Clock) 698

Surprise sentences –
Tiddlywinks golf

Surprise sentences 269
Sweet tooth 224
Switchback 270
Synonyms 280

T

Table bowls (see Squails) 346
Table shovelboard (see Shovelboard)
    332
Taboo 375
Teakettle 360
Telegrams 281
Ten and a half (card game) 578
Ten and a half (tile game: see Sap tim
    pun) 314
Ten step buff 220
The apostles 341
The corsair 340
The cross 339
The letter E 341
The game 354
The octagon 340
The world 341
Thieves 222
Thirty-five 664
Thirty-one 666
Thirty-six 105
Threading the needle 151
Three holes 207
Three men's morris 213
Three naturals (see Macao) 579
Three-legged race 261
Threes up (see All threes) 129
Through the tunnel 33
Tick-tack-toe 286
Tick-tack-toe, three-dimensional 286
Tiddle-a-wink 125
Tiddlywinks 348
Tiddlywinks golf 350

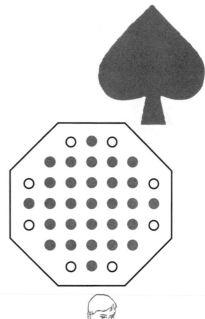

Tiddlywinks target games 350
Tiddlywinks tennis 350
Tien kow 144
Tiu u 143
Toad in the hole (card game: see
    Frog) 710
Toad in the hole (played with stones)
    152
Tortoise race 259
Tossing a coin 73
Tournament checkers 38
Tournament darts 80
Tower of Babel (see Accordion) 684
Towers 153
Transformation 280
Traveler's alphabet 372
Travelers (see Clock) 698
Trente et quarante 668
Triangular tug-of-war 233
Trickery games 254
Tunnel ball 272
Turkish checkers 44
Twenty-one (card game: see
    Blackjack) 566
Twenty-one (dice game) 104
Twenty questions (see Animal,
    vegetable, or mineral) 359
Two-minute walk 231

U

Under the arch 151
Up and down cheat 505
Up and down river 595
Up Jenkins! 245

Vanjohn –
Ziginette

V

Vanjohn (see Blackjack) 566
Vingt-et-un (see Blackjack) 566
Vint 490

W

Wall Jonathan 71
Wall marbles 203
War 544
War, for three players 545
Weddings (see Monte Carlo) 724
Wei-ch'i (see Go) 158
What is my thought like? 362
Whist 492
Whist, knockout 516
Whist, solo 486
Who am I? 362
Windmill 746
Word games 352
Word parade 265
World, The 341
Wrong! 243

Y

Yablon 672
Yankee grab (see Going to Boston) 89
Yarn tangles 267
Yes-no beans 255

Z

Ziginette 674